# Springer Studies in Law & Geoeconomics

Volume 1

The series 'Springer Studies in Law & Geoeconomics' is devoted to analyzing the role of law in conditioning the use of geoeconomic power and the role of geoeconomic power in conditioning the formation, enforcement, and systematic variation of laws and (public and private) norms. The series specializes in the application to these problems of insights developed across scientific disciplines, not only law and IR, but also geography (economic and political), economic sociology, economic anthropology, comparative politics, epistemology, history, economics and game theory, probability theory, negotiation theory, cognitive science, and social psychology. The range of disciplinary approaches dealt with by the series is virtually unlimited, in line with its commitment to transcending disciplinary boundaries.

The series welcomes contributions from distinguished legal scholars working in international, comparative, or domestic law, empirical legal studies, or different "law and . . ." areas, as well as IR scholars, political economists, and political scientists with an interdisciplinary focus. The series also strives to offer a forum for contributions to legal theory by scholars working in disciplines outside of law. For thematic issues, particular issues are commissioned and a call for papers is distributed. The series also publishes open issues that provide publication possibilities for uncommissioned manuscripts intended to stimulate submissions by talented master students and Ph.D. candidates.

The series publishes contributions following a substantive review by the editors and rigorous double-blind peer-review by external experts as appropriate. The series editors have published extensively in the field of law and geoeconomics. They are supported by an international board of advisory editors consisting of established scholars of the highest reputation.

Jens Hillebrand Pohl • Joanna Warchol •
Thomas Papadopoulos • Janosch Wiesenthal
Editors

# Weaponising Investments

Volume I

Springer

*Editors*
Jens Hillebrand Pohl
Finnish Institute of International Affairs
Helsinki, Finland

Joanna Warchol
European Parliament
Strasbourg, France

Thomas Papadopoulos
Department of Law
University of Cyprus
Nicosia, Cyprus

Janosch Wiesenthal
University of Passau
Passau, Germany

ISSN 2948-1899 ISSN 2948-1902 (electronic)
Springer Studies in Law & Geoeconomics
ISBN 978-3-031-41477-0 ISBN 978-3-031-41475-6 (eBook)
https://doi.org/10.1007/978-3-031-41475-6

This work was supported by Universiteit Maastricht


This Springer imprint is published by the registered company Springer Nature Switzerland AG
The registered company address is: Gewerbestrasse 11, 6330 Cham, Switzerland

Paper in this product is recyclable.

*Dedicated to Steffen Hindelang*

# Introducing Springer Studies in Law & Geoeconomics: A Manifesto

This is a moment of unprecedented global economic interdependence. But it is also a moment of unprecedented global legalization. And yet both the international economic order and the international economic legal order that underpins it are in crisis. Economic interdependencies are being instrumentalized for power political purposes. This instrumentalization is putting pressure on the laws and institutions governing the international economic system. Key actors in world politics are simultaneously employing and redefining international economic law in the process.

Power politics is reemerging between states that have become deeply enmeshed economically and who increasingly view economic interdependence as a potential security vulnerability. In response to newly perceived vulnerabilities, governments are increasingly turning to policies that integrate economic and security rationales as part of a process of economic re-regulation. This development holds major ramifications for international trade and investment flows.

These policies are intensifying at the expense of global cooperation, coordination, and existing legal frameworks, with governments progressively embracing and expanding policy instruments and legal avenues that had come to be considered exceptional during the post-1989 era of "hyper-globalization." This includes investment screening, economic sanctions, export controls, industrial policy, and security exceptions in trade and investment agreements.

Private enterprises and other non-state actors are catching up with and increasingly contesting or adapting to this new reality. They are seeking ways to protect themselves against new types of geopolitical risk and beginning to discover their strategic value to their host states, whether to build resilience or exert influence.

As the world economy heads deeper into uncharted territory, the term "geoeconomics" has become increasingly popular in international relations (IR) scholarship to describe the growing application of power politics by economic means and the rapidly evolving transformation in the logic underpinning global economic relations. At the same time, diverse strands of literature in the social sciences have emerged and engaged with the shifting policy locus for balancing economic liberalization and national security. These strands are linked by recurring and conceptually overlapping terminology, including "economic statecraft," "weaponized interdependence," "weaponized trade," "economic diplomacy," "economic security," "economic warfare," or, simply put, "geoeconomics."

Law is central to international ordering and stability of governance and is a means to operate and contest established power and economic relations. Law structures the political and economic orders in world politics and may equally serve as a hedge against abuses of power or an instrument of such abuse. At the same time, power and wealth condition domestic and international legal orders.

How should scholars and practitioners – judges, lawyers, legislators, government officials, diplomats – respond to this emerging reality? We see the contours of a new path emerging that addresses the nexus between economics, law, and politics in international relations. Its goal is to develop a holistic academic analysis of the most pressing and understudied phenomena in an international economic order undergoing systemic change. We call this new interdisciplinary movement "law and geoeconomics."

Law and geoeconomics represents a reorientation from conversations about power and wealth as organizing principles of separate domains – "politics" and "economy," mediated by "law" – toward an integrated conversation about competing politico-economic interests. Scholars adopting this perspective seek to make sense of behaviors that "instrumentalize" the means of one domain for purposes of achieving ends in another. This includes economic means to achieve political ends and political means to achieve economic ends. Likewise, included are situations where law is instrumentalized for economic or political ends, while recognizing that law rarely is an end pursued for its own benefit.

The recognition that law shapes and mediates the relations between politics and the economy is hardly new. It is a cornerstone of legal realism and critical legal approaches alike and remains as relevant now as when first proposed. It is also well-recognized in political science scholarship on legal institutionalism and the legal-economic nexus.

While the intersection of law and economics has been studied for decades, political economists have turned increasing attention to the study of phenomena at the intersection of law, politics, and the economy over the last few years. This "law and political economy" approach takes an interdisciplinary perspective, which views markets as fields of social power that are not spontaneous but created and reproduced in the meeting of legal norms, political action, and economic activity. Through regulating economic relationships, the politico-legal order constitutes and reconstitutes the power relations that comprise society. This, in turn, is driven by sociological processes, including the formation of class, sectoral and geopolitical interests, as well as ideological convictions, which harness political and legal authority.

To date, the growing IR literature on "geoeconomics," "economic statecraft," and its many variants has primarily concentrated on the role of economic interdependence in conditioning the ability of states to use economic relationships as bargaining leverage when exercising power in world politics. The role that international and domestic laws and regulations play in shaping the use of (geo) economic power has received considerably less attention. Likewise, IR scholars have paid limited attention to the distinction between legal and non-legal instruments and the role of institutions in conditioning the ability of states to pursue their preferred geoeconomic strategies.

As the study of geoeconomics is coming of age and is emerging from a proto-theoretic approach to a practice-based phenomenon in its early stages of being theorized, interest in the intersection between law and geoeconomics has escalated, creating a substantial academic and professional audience for new IR works in the field.

More recently, geoeconomics has begun to receive considerable attention in legal scholarship, although without any clear consensus on what the term means and what the implications of geoeconomics are. This is partly a result of insufficient engagement with the disciplines from which the concept of geoeconomics originates, notably international political economy and international security studies. The burgeoning interest in geoeconomics in legal scholarship has concentrated on international economic law, specifically international trade law and international investment law. Scholarship in these fields has thus far been largely influenced by positivist, global constitutionalist, and global administrative approaches that regard the law as more or less strictly separated from politics and the economy.

Aside from emerging scholarship on investment screening, the geoeconomic aspect of public law, private law, and comparative economic law, among others, remains uncharted territory, leaving out such important topics as the geoeconomics of domestic competition laws, tax laws, intellectual property laws, data protection legislation, financial regulation, and dispute resolution in the economic domain. The topic of "geo-regulation" – the use of technical standards, process and production methods, and the range of internal regulations for goods and services as a means of geoeconomic competition – remains in its infancy and deserves further attention. Perhaps most notably, legal theory has not properly engaged with geoeconomics. Therefore, while the world is turning attention to geoeconomics, legal scholarship must play catch-up.

The law and geoeconomics movement we are calling for brings together scholars and practitioners across the relevant disciplines who share an interest in a common set of questions. To what extent and in what ways is the pursuit of power displacing the pursuit of profit in shaping global economic relations? What are the respective roles of states and non-state actors in carrying out these pursuits? How does this phenomenon challenge existing international economic law regimes? How do states – alone or in groups – and non-state actors use laws and regulations, legal arguments or narratives, the judicial apparatus and the legal system, other legal constructs, or other institutions to exert influence using economic means? How do states' efforts to exert influence using economic means shape the interpretation and application of laws and regulations, the use of legal arguments or narratives, the operation of the judicial apparatus and the legal system, or the use of other legal constructs or institutions? What are the means to pursue geoeconomic aims, how does existing law impact their use, and how does their use shape the evolution of existing legal regimes? To what extent and in what ways does the legal-(geo)economic nexus vary across spatial and temporal dimensions?

The Springer Studies in Law and Geoeconomics (SSLG) seeks to contribute to engaging the questions in the preceding paragraphs. SSLG is devoted to analyzing (a) the role of law in conditioning the use of geoeconomic power and (b) the role of geoeconomic policy in the formation, enforcement, and systematic variation of laws and norms regulating international economic relations. The series specializes in interdisciplinary analysis of such problems, drawing on insights developed across social scientific disciplines, with a strong focus on international relations, international political economy, international security studies, comparative law, and legal theory. We expect scholars across fields such as political science, economic sociology, political and economic geography, international business, and economic history to also be well placed to make meaningful contributions.

SSLG welcomes and provides a platform for scholars from diverse disciplines, including political science, law, international relations, economics, history, geography, and sociology, to engage in rigorous scholarly inquiry at the intersection of these fields on the broad relationship between law and geoeconomics in world politics. SSLG seeks to be at the forefront of scholarly inquiry in this rapidly evolving area, promoting cutting-edge research that advances theoretical understanding, informs policy debates, and fosters interdisciplinary dialogue and exchange.

Alongside developing intellectual leadership in the field of law and geoeconomics, a further important role of the series is to engage with relevant policy debates and contribute to policy advice and agenda-setting. Accordingly, SSLG will, in addition to book reviews, publish reviews of policy briefs. In carrying out our editorial mission, we will endeavor to the best of our abilities to balance any tendency toward "publication-friendly rigor" with a sound dose of critical awareness, common sense, and receptiveness to different methodological approaches. SSLG will also support conferences, workshops, education, and outreach, and stay committed to maintaining open and inclusive debate across disciplinary boundaries and between academia and practice.

Our journey begins here.

# Foreword: The Dissemination of Investment Screening Mechanisms – The Vocabulary for a New Logic Driving Global Economic Relations[1]

The recent dissemination of investment screening mechanisms was arguably the first evidence that the liberal tenets underpinning International Economic Law faced a challenge at their core by a geoeconomic logic. This logic, in turn, points to more active state intervention in managing global economic relations, which contrasts with the post-Cold War years of economic interdependence led by market players.

The most consequential signal that economic regulation was gradually inspired by a different logic was the adoption in 2018, with bipartisan support, of new legislation reinforcing the US regimes for investment screening (FIRRMA)[2] and export controls (ECRA).[3] At the time, most analysts seemed too overshadowed by the erratic and unusual governing style of the Trump administration to identify in those pieces of legislation the expressions of a new approach to economic regulation. Most legal commentaries of that period focused on the blatant illegalities of measures such as the imposition of steel tariffs under the guise of national security and missed the broader trend that was effectively redefining the national security exception – and which was epitomized by the adoption of the new investment screening and export controls regimes in the USA.[4]

The enactment of the EU's first ever investment screening mechanism,[5] a year after the passing of the US legislation, provided additional evidence that a trend was unfolding which had little to do with the vagaries of the then US administration. Unlike the USA, though, the EU initiative found political support on the need to

[1]The views and opinions in this Article are the sole responsibility of the author and do not necessarily reflect the positions of the government of Brazil.

[2]Foreign Investment Risk Review Modernization Act (FIRRMA), 50 U.S.C. § 4565 (2018).

[3]Export Control Reform Act, 50 U.S.C. § 4811(3) (2018).

[4]Henrique Choer Moraes, 'The turn to managed interdependence: a glimpse into the future of international economic law?', *EJIL Talk!*, August 14, 2018.

[5]Regulation (EU) 2019/452 of the European Parliament and of the Council of 19 March 2019 establishing a framework for the screening of foreign direct investments into the Union, *OJ L 791*, *21.3.2019, p. 1–14.*

preserve reciprocity in market access, even if security was also raised among the justifications for the new EU framework. One of the triggers to what became the EU regulation on investment screening was a request by the economy ministers of France, Germany, and Italy to the European Commission expressing concerns "about the lack of reciprocity and about a possible sell-out of European expertise, which we are currently unable to combat with effective instruments."[6]

What started as individual – however transformational – domestic measures in the USA and the EU have ushered in a new regulatory context, heavy with geoeconomic elements. In 2023, the OECD reports that, while "security implications of foreign investment were a low or no priority for most economies until about a decade ago," "[t]he number of economies that [now] operate mechanisms to manage security implications of foreign investment is growing steadily, a trend that is unlikely to slow or stop in the medium term."[7] Just as in the USA, in a growing number of countries the adoption of investment screening mechanisms was followed by a panoply of additional tools aimed at doing what was anathema in the preceding decades: to manage the level of exposure of national economies to economic interdependence. States' geoeconomic action translates into a number of offensive and defensive measures and policies aimed at attaining the goal of strengthening the national economy vis-à-vis other economies. This entails both fostering national capabilities – e.g., technological expertise – and the protection of assets considered strategic from being acquired by foreign actors – in this latter case, investment screening mechanisms are a key example.

The dissemination of investment screening mechanisms offers a couple of insights to understand key elements of the geoeconomic order that has since taken hold.

First, the rise of a geoeconomic logic behind economic regulation is directly associated with the *consolidation of strategic competition* particularly between the USA and China. Specially in the years following its accession to the WTO, China was perceived predominantly as an economic competitor, to which developed economies could respond by resorting to existing trade rules. Yet, as China's political, military, and economic global heft increased, economic competition gave way to strategic and security rivalry, with the 2017 U.S. National Security Strategy labeling China "a revisionist power"[8] and the EU considering China "a systemic rival promoting alternative models of governance."[9] While it may have been accelerated by the advent of Covid-19, the shift toward a new logic driving economic regulation precedes the pandemic.

---

[6]Reuters, "France, Germany, Italy urge rethink of foreign investment in EU," February 15, 2017, https://www.reuters.com/article/uk-eu-trade-franceidUKKBN15T1ND.

[7]OECD, *Investment policy developments in 61 economies between 16 October 2021 and 15 March 2023*, April 2023, p. 7 and 9, available at https://www.oecd.org/daf/inv/investment-policy/Investment-policy-monitoring-April-2023.pdf.

[8]Donald J. Trump, *National Security Strategy of the United States of America* 25 (2017).

[9]*Joint Communication to the European Parliament, the European Council and the Council: EU-China – A Strategic Outlook*, at 1, JOIN (2019) 5 final (Mar. 12, 2019).

Second, the shift to a geoeconomic logic is *not explained solely by security concerns*. It is also about seeking goals that fall short of security objectives, while being strategic nevertheless. The emergence of a geoeconomic logic suggests that governments become more wary of where production is located. A geoeconomic world is one where states actively seek to keep within their jurisdiction the capabilities (e.g., manufacturing capacities to produce from semiconductors to vaccines) or assets (e.g., raw materials, food, and data) needed for strategic industries or for the provision of strategic goods. In legalese, this is a world not only populated by invocations of national security exceptions, but also filled with subsidies that fuel industrial policies.

Third, geoeconomics does not equate to the "weaponization" of interdependence. Geoeconomic measures have a predominantly inward-looking approach in the sense that they focus on securing access to capabilities and assets a state considers strategic or that have a security relevance. In contrast, measures of economic statecraft meant to "weaponize" asymmetries emerging from economic interdependence display an outward-looking characteristic: states adopt this latter type of measures with the purpose of influencing the behavior of others.[10] Thus, states implement investment screening mechanisms with the purpose of retaining within their jurisdiction the control of certain capabilities, such as relevant technologies (a geoeconomic goal). They do not immediately seek to influence the behavior of other states with such mechanisms (which would amount to a goal of economic statecraft or of a "weaponization" of such mechanisms).

As this new scenario changes the logic of global economic regulation, it also introduces vocabulary that was virtually foreign to international economic relations until recently. Accordingly, a growing number of governments embark on surveys aimed at providing a better grasp on how dependent they are on trade with foreign partners;[11] many governments enlist "resilience" as an economic priority; and some governments, in particular developed economies, chart a path of emphasizing economic relations with "allies" and "friends."[12]

The emergence of a geoeconomic logic points to a global economy with more active governmental interference, guided by the occasional fracturing of global markets along discriminatory lines –distinguishing partners which are reliable from those that are not so considered. It is not so much a context of de-globalization, but of re-globalization. In such an environment, non-discrimination regimes such as those enshrined in the WTO agreements as well as in many international investment agreements are likely to be put under considerable strain.

---

[10]David A. Baldwin, *Economic Statecraft*, 1985, p. 40.

[11]White House, Building Resilient Supply Chains, Revitalizing American Manufacturing, and Fostering Broad-Based Growth – 100-Day Reviews Under Executive Order 14017 June 2021 – A report by the White House 8 (2021); *Commission Staff Working Document: EU Strategic Dependencies and Capacities: Second Stage of In-Depth Reviews*, SWD (2022) 41 final (Feb. 22, 2022).

[12]Christopher Condon, Heejin Kim, and Sam Kim, Yellen Touts "Friend-Shoring" as Global Supply Chain Fix, Bloomberg, July 18, 2022.

Judged against the recent past, there is no denying the emerging geoeconomic context poses a formidable challenge to the level of rule of law attained in the past decades. But possible solutions to mitigate this challenge will only emerge from a clear-eyed appraisal of the transformations taking place.

Katholieke Universiteit Leuven, Leuven, Belgium

Ministry of Foreign Affairs, Brasilia, Brazil

Henrique Choer Moraes

# Preface

The neoliberal transformation that took place in the 1990s and continued into the current century has in recent years ceded ground to a "geoeconomic transformation." Governments increasingly use economic policy to (unilaterally) defend their national security and other non-economic interests and pursue relative gains. Neomercantilism, e.g., the strategic build-up of foreign exchange reserves generated by trade surpluses, is an example of a policy aiming for relative, rather than absolute gains; instead of choosing to maximize global growth (absolute gain), the policy focuses on increasing the economic power of one state relative to its partners and rivals.

This shift toward "geoeconomic" competition challenges traditional liberal accounts of globalization that highlight mutual gains from cooperation; states that can exercise control over critical hubs in global economic networks can strategically manipulate economic flows of goods, money, and information to their advantage.[13] Geoeconomic competition has manifested itself in trade policy and sanctions but also in the area of international investments, most obviously through the rise of sovereign-driven investments (SDI), i.e., investments by sovereign wealth funds and state-owned enterprises, and "strategic" investments that are otherwise enjoying state support from its country of origin.

Despite the centrality of SDI in the geoeconomic transformation, the rise in SDI has been and remains in general an under-researched topic. The present volume seeks to take the lead in laying an analytical foundation and providing a framework for the emerging research field of foreign investment control. There is thus far little systematic empirical evidence on whether the renewed interest in foreign investment

[13] Farrell H, Newman AL (2019) Weaponized interdependence: how global economic networks shape state coercion. Int Secur 44(1):42–79; Gertz G, Evers MM (2020) Geoeconomic competition: will state capitalism win? Wash Q 43(2):117–136; Meunier S, Nicolaidis K (2019) The geopoliticization of European trade and investment policy. J Common Mark Stud 57:103–113; Roberts A, Choer Moraes H, Ferguson V (2019) Toward a geoeconomic order in international trade and investment. J Int Econ Law 22(4):655–676.

control at the policy level adds up to a coherent strategy that is reflected in relevant and observable outcomes.

*Weaponising Investments* collects in two volumes a selection of pioneering research papers for the purpose of facilitating the development of a common analytical foundation and framework for the emerging interdisciplinary research field of investment control. The papers published herein present different perspectives on how decision-makers go about the tasks of assessing risks and threats to national security that may be posed by FDI and then balancing those risks and threats against the economic interests of the parties concerned and society at large. Preliminary drafts of some of the papers were presented at Uppsala University, Faculty of Law, on 1–6 June 2022 at the CELIS Forum on Investment Screening organized by Prof. Dr. Steffen Hindelang and Jens Hillebrand Pohl.

The present book is the first of the two volumes that make up *Weaponising Investments*. In twelve chapters, it addresses questions that emphasize the political context and emergence of SDI as a geoeconomic problem. The opening chapter surveys the changes underway across the West and beyond in the understanding of foreign investments as vehicles of national security risk. *Sarah Bauerle Danzman* and *Gabriella Couloubaritsis* provide a descriptive overview of how countries conceptualize investment security risk and set out to explain why countries systematically vary in their risk approaches. They discuss changing dynamics around critical technologies and the implications of countries' security concepts for economic outcomes.

*Victoria Barbary, Adam D. Dixon,* and *Patrick J. Schena* turn their attention to sovereign wealth funds. Since their emergence in the early 2000s, globally focused state-owned investors quickly became a concern for politicians in the United States and in Europe. Concerns rooted in the liberal belief that global capital markets are the reserve primarily of private actors led Western governments to worry about possible financial and economic malfeasance and market distortion if capital allocation decisions are made on non-commercial (political) grounds. *Alexandr Svetlicinii* explores the treatment of state-owned enterprises (SOEs) in EU investment screening. Although the alleged security risks linked to SOE-led investments in the EU shaped the drafting and adoption of the EU FDI Screening Regulation, the key issues related to the definition of SOEs, determination of the foreign state's control/influence over foreign investors, and specific security risks stemming from foreign SOE-led investments have remained largely undefined. *Naoise McDonagh* broadens the focus to the implications of investment screening at the systemic level. Using the EU as a case study, he examines the crucial variables that both trigger investment screening and serve as the key criterion for screening, namely the concepts of "security" and "public order." However, these concepts have no clear definition, raising concerns that they may be abused for protectionist purposes. Identifying China as the real threat justifying the introduction of the EU investment screening regime, he identifies unique threats arising from the country's rule-by-law socialist system of governance, where traditional public–private distinctions are heavily blurred, if not obliterated.

With the scene thus set, the next three papers discuss the concept of security from different perspectives. *Alejandra Torres Camprubí* provides an historical exposé of the concept of security from the 1920s through the emergence of international security studies after the Second World War and beyond to the era of globalization. Considering how the notion of security has progressively developed and fundamentally changed during this period, she identifies the emergence of multiple layers of cumulative knowledge about the notion of security. The inherently ambiguous nature has been maintained because of disciplinary and political resistance to reaching a common understanding and shared methodological tools to apprehend this notion. *Francesca Ghiretti* continues by focusing on "economic security" and discusses how that concept in the EU has been influenced by Chinese sovereign investment practices in recent years. She asks how economic actors and stakeholders have transformed Chinese FDI from a purely economic matter into a security issue. She argues that security considerations related to traditional security were not the only reasons driving the process, but that economic considerations too played a central role in the securitization process. *John Lash* situates economic security and FDI within the broader tenets of a fully integrated cyber, economic, and information state of adversarial capabilities within an emergent threat landscape. This landscape is shaped by multidimensional strategic interactions that are not constrained by the traditional boundary conditions of national security or free trade. The complex concepts of power and influence within the broad scope of globalization and national security require an evaluation that adequately addresses the threat environment where investments, which create direct and indirect power over other nations, are weaponized.

The following three papers provide in-depth perspectives on the shifting attitude toward FDI and investment security risks. *Jonas Hallberg* and *Patrik Tingvall* propose that in a future Swedish investment screening mechanism, the investment screening authority will have to consult with the authority responsible for FDI promotion. They identify a gap in the literature in the sense that the broad mass of economic analysis of FDI focuses on the effects of production-oriented activities, while much of the security discourse also embraces ownership such as infrastructure and hospitals. To minimize uncertainty and the potential FDI-dampening effects of an investment screening regulation, the range of affected sectors should be narrowly defined, accompanied by a swift and transparent review process that provides predictability to the transaction parties. Inward FDI in general and high-tech investments can benefit innovation, stimulate investment, promote skill upgrading, improve resource allocation, sharpen competition, create high-wage jobs, and increase economic growth. *Thijs De Cuyper* examines the EU's shift away from principal openness to foreign capital and asks whether the EU and its member states are capable of effectively addressing the concerns and challenges that come with this new environment, particularly the lack of reciprocity. He identifies a function creep and seeks whether it is desirable to alter the standards that are used to shape investment relations with the third countries in line with geoeconomics desires.

*Peter Muchlinski* looks at the United Kingdom and the major reorientation in its international economic policy away from an "open door" to inward FDI. He explores the reasons behind this shift from a historical perspective since the Second World War until today's growing concern over the role of inward investment, especially Chinese investment, for reasons of national security.

The last two chapters broaden the discourse away from security to non-security related geoeconomics, namely the concern about foreign state-subsidized investments. *Phil Baumann* takes aim at the competitive advantages of SOEs that can distort the market in cross-border mergers and acquisitions and consequently lead to economic inefficiencies and welfare losses. The new EU Regulation on Foreign Subsidies distorting the Internal Market, which aims to fill this regulatory gap, is an example of a type of investment screening that is not (primarily) driven by security concerns. By introducing a kind of merger control regime for transactions facilitated by foreign subsidies, the new regulation allows the European Commission to investigate mergers and acquisitions undertaken by companies that benefit from foreign subsidies. To increase coherence and to reduce unpredictability and uncertainty regarding its new regulatory tools, the EU should aim to include general principles on subsidies and prohibitions of specific subsidies in its international investment agreements.

Continuing on the same theme, the last paper in this volume, by *Robert Basedow, Sophie Meunier,* and *Christilla Roederer-Rynning*, asks why the EU Foreign Subsidies Regulation was proposed when it was and what political-economy forces shaped its institutional design. Using process tracing, expert interviews, media research, and secondary literature, the authors trace the history of this policy project from its inception to today. They find that framing foreign subsidies as a competition issue insulated the policy from accusations of disguised protectionism and ensured political support across the EU.

| | |
|---|---|
| Helsinki, Finland | Jens Hillebrand Pohl |
| Strasbourg, France | Joanna Warchol |
| Nicosia, Cyprus | Thomas Papadopoulos |
| Passau, Germany | Janosch Wiesenthal |

# Contents

# About the Contributors

**Victoria Barbary** is the Director of Strategy and Communications at the International Forum of Sovereign Wealth Funds (IFSWF), a global network of sovereign wealth funds with members from nearly 50 countries. In her role, Victoria works with IFSWF members to curate a programme of online and offline knowledge-sharing and networking activities related to all aspects of their operations, from governance to investment strategies. Victoria has worked in the sovereign wealth fund world for over a decade and has become a noted author and commentator on SWFs. In 2012, she founded the Sovereign Wealth Center, an online provider of data and analysis about SWFs, now part of Institutional Investor's Sovereign Investor Institute. Before joining IFSWF, Victoria was Director of Investec Asset Management's Investment Institute, which was responsible for the firm's thought leadership. She started her career as the senior analyst in the Office of the Chairman at the Monitor Group, a strategy consultancy now part of Deloitte. Victoria earned a PhD in History from Pembroke College, University of Cambridge. She also has a BA (Hons) and MA with distinction in History from the University of Durham.

**Robert Basedow** is an Associate Professor for International Political Economy at the European Institute of the London School of Economics and Political Science. He studies international trade and investment policy and judicial politics notably in the realm of international economic and commercial law. Before joining the LSE, he was a civil servant at the Organization for Economic Cooperation and Development in Paris and a Max Weber post-doctoral fellow at the European University Institute in Florence.

**Sarah Bauerle Danzman** , PhD, is an Associate Professor of International Studies at Indiana University Bloomington, faculty director of the Tobias Center for Innovation in International Development, a non-resident senior fellow at the Atlantic Council, and a Council on Foreign Relations Term Member. In 2019–2020, she was Council on Foreign Relations International Affairs Fellow, working in the U.S. Department of State as a Policy Advisor in the Office of Investment Affairs. Prof.

Bauerle Danzman specializes in the political economy of international investment and finance. Her research explores how domestic and multinational firms influence and adapt to investment regulation, the nexus of national security and investment, and how rules governing capital shape global networks of ownership, production, and economic growth. She is the author of Merging Interests: When Domestic Firms Shape FDI Policy (Cambridge University Press, 2019) and many articles published in outlets including Foreign Affairs, International Studies Quarterly, Perspective on Politics, Review of International Organizations, Review of International Political Economy, and Business and Politics.

**Phil Baumann** studied law and economics at the University of St. Gallen. After his admission to the bar in the Canton of Zurich, Phil Baumann worked for several years at a major Swiss law firm in the Banking & Finance department. In 2017, he obtained a Master of Laws (LL.M.) in International Economic Law at the Chinese University of Hong Kong. After his return to Switzerland, Phil Baumann received his doctorate from the University of Lucerne with a dissertation focusing on competitive neutrality and state-owned enterprises. In July 2020, Phil Baumann joined the chair of Prof. Dr. Bernhard Rütsche at the University of Lucerne as a senior research assistant and post-doctoral lecturer in the areas of administrative law and public economic law. His research focuses on the regulations of universal services, competitive neutrality, and investment controls.

**Henrique Choer Moraes** is a diplomat with the Brazilian Ministry of Foreign Affairs since 2004 and a PhD candidate at Katholieke Universiteit Leuven. Throughout his diplomatic career he has been part of trade negotiations at the global and regional levels and has been involved with foreign policy planning as well. His academic research has focused on legal aspects of global economic governance, in particular the influence of geoeconomics on the evolution of the international economic law.

**Gabriella Couloubaritsis** is an undergraduate at Indiana University Bloomington studying Entrepreneurship and Corporate Innovation from the Kelley School of Business with a minor in Law and Public Policy. Since starting her research assistant position in October 2021, she has helped Professor Bauerle Danzman develop the first comprehensive dataset on foreign investment screening laws in all 38 OECD countries since 2007. Gabriella's internship experiences include Boston Consulting Group, the U.S. Securities and Exchange Commission, and the Federal Deposit Insurance Corporation. Gabriella also serves as President of the 114th Indiana Memorial Union Board, the largest programming group on campus and governing body of the student union building.

**Thijs De Cuyper** is a PhD candidate and teaching assistant at the University of Leuven, Belgium. He graduated at the same university in 2019. Afterwards, he pursued an LLM degree at the Humboldt University in Berlin. Thijs was a visiting researcher at the University of Cambridge (Lauterpacht Centre) from April to August

2023. Thijs' current research focuses on the division of competences between the European Union and its member states in the area of foreign economic policy.

**Adam D. Dixon** holds the Adam Smith Chair in Sustainable Capitalism at Edinburgh Business School, Heriot-Watt University. He is responsible for developing and leading academic research on sustainable capitalism at Panmure House, the last and final home of moral philosopher and economist Adam Smith, focusing inter alia on the role of the global finance industry, the role of the state, and the role of corporations. Trained as an economic geographer and political economist in the United States, Spain, France, and the United Kingdom, Adam brings an interdisciplinary perspective to this work. Previously, Adam worked at the University of Bristol and Maastricht University in the Netherlands, where he led a large European Research Council project on sovereign wealth funds. He holds a D.Phil. in economic geography from the University of Oxford, a Diplôme (Master) de l'Institut d'Etudes Politiques de Paris, and a BA in international affairs and Spanish literature from The George Washington University in Washington, DC.

**Francesca Ghiretti** , PhD, is analyst at the Mercator Institute for China Studies (MERICS) where her work focuses on economic security, EU-China relations, and the Belt and Road Initiative. Some of her most recent publications analyse the development of economic security policies and agenda in China, the US, the EU, the UK, Australia, Japan, and South Korea as well as how China approaches sanctions. Before joining MERICS, she worked as a Research Fellow Asia at the Istituto Affari Internazionali (IAI) in Rome leading a project on the Belt and Road Initiative in Italy. She co-edited the book *The Belt and Road Initiative in Italy*. Previously, Francesca worked as a geopolitical analyst for CQS, a London-based hedge fund and as assistant to Jaap de Hoop Scheffer, former Secretary General of NATO. Francesca received her PhD from King's College London as Leverhulme fellow at the Centre for Grand Strategy and her PhD thesis received the outstanding thesis award.

**Jonas Hallberg** is a legal adviser as well as policy adviser at Swedish National Board of Trade. He works primarily with international investment law and the intersection between investment law and EU law. He works closely with the Swedish Ministry for Foreign Affairs in all matters concerning international investment treaties as well as the negotiations of the investment screening regulation. On a regular basis, he represents Sweden at the OECD, UNCTAD, UNCITRAL as well as the council group TPCSI. He has, for example, written papers relating to the CETA-agreement between the EU and Canada, and the Most-Favoured Nation Clause in the Swedish bilateral investment treaties. During the year 2018, he published an article about the effects of the CJEU ruling *Achmea* and is currently conducting research on retroactivity in EU and investment arbitration law. Before working at the Board, he worked at the Upper Administrative Court of Appeal, at the Ministry of Justice and Ministry for Foreign Affairs.

**John Lash**, PhD, is a geo-economic and national security strategist focusing on global capital markets. His research on evaluating national security, trade policy, and economics is grounded in a mosaic grand strategy at the convergence of collaboration, competition, and pure-conflict game theory. Dr. Lash has advised on national security strategy, integration, and enforcement for M&A assignments totalling over USD 100 billion in transaction value, and he is on the Board of Directors of two U.S. companies with Chinese ownership under CFIUS jurisdiction. His work focuses on compliance strategy, mergers and acquisitions, and performance transformation across a variety of high tech and advanced-industrial subsectors, including semiconductors, telecommunications, and renewable energy. He earned his PhD from Robert Morris University, with his dissertation entitled: The Feasibility of Game Theory Approaches: An Investigative Study of Threats to U.S. National Security from Foreign Investment. Dr. Lash is an Assistant Professor of Management in the Accounting, Business, and Economics Department at Juniata College. He is an adjunct lecturer at the Cox School of Business at Southern Methodist University where he teaches Global Business Strategy, and at the University of Texas at El Paso where he teaches courses on national security, intelligence, and cybersecurity.

**Naoise McDonagh**, PhD is a Senior Lecturer in the School of Business and Law, Edith Cowan University (ECU) in Perth, Australia. His research focuses on how geopolitical tensions in an era of high economic integration are transforming the world economy, including reorganization of global supply chains for national security reasons and new export control and investment screening regimes. Prior to entering academia, Dr McDonagh served 2 years in the Irish Defence Forces (2002–2004) and worked in the private sector for over half a decade. He is a former President of the Australian Institute of International Affairs, South Australia (2021–2022). Dr McDonagh regularly publishes his research in international journals and leading policy forums and contributes to domestic and international media coverage of his research interests.

**Sophie Meunier** is Senior Research Scholar at the Princeton School of Public and International Affairs, Princeton University. She is Director of the Program in Contemporary European Politics and Society (from July 2022) and Co-Director of the EU Program at Princeton. She is the author of Trading Voices: The European Union in International Commercial Negotiations (Princeton University Press, 2005) and The French Challenge: Adapting to Globalization (Brookings Institution Press, 2001), winner of the 2002 France-Ameriques book award. She is also co-editor of several books on Europe and globalization, most recently Developments in French Politics 6 (Palgrave MacMillan 2020) and Speaking with a Single Voice: The EU as an Effective Actor in Global Governance? (Routledge, 2015). Meunier is Chair of the European Union Studies Association (2023–2024). Her current work deals with the politics of investment screening mechanisms and the political challenges posed by Chinese direct investment in the European Union, including as part of the PRISM project.

**Peter Muchlinski** is Emeritus Professor of International Commercial Law at the School of Law, the School of Oriental and African Studies, University of London. He is the author of *Multinational Enterprises and the Law* (Oxford University Press, 3rd ed, 2021) and *Advanced Introduction to Business and Human Rights* (Cheltenham, Edward Elgar, 2022). He specializes in the regulation of multinational enterprises, international investment law, and business and human rights. He has worked as a legal consultant for UNCTAD and is a door tenant at Brick Court Chambers, London. He is a member of the Editorial Board of the Business and Human Rights Journal.

**Thomas Papadopoulos** is an Assistant Professor of Business Law at the Department of Law of the University of Cyprus. He received his DPhil in Law from the Faculty of Law, University of Oxford, UK (2010). He received a degree of Magister Juris-MJur (2006) and a degree of MPhil in Law (2007) from the Faculty of Law, University of Oxford, UK. He also received his LLB with Distinction (ranked 1st) from the Department of Law, Aristotle University of Thessaloniki, Greece (2005). Previously, he was a visiting researcher at Harvard Law School, USA (2009–2010). He is also a Visiting Professor at University of Trento and at International Hellenic University, a Teaching Fellow at Open University of Cyprus and an Attorney at law (Greece). Additionally, he was a Visiting Researcher at King's College London and at Max Planck Institute Luxembourg. Moreover, he is a member of the editorial board of European Company Law (ECL) Journal published by Kluwer. He is a country reporter-legal expert for Cyprus at the European Model Company Act (EMCA) Group, the Common European Law on Investment Screening (CELIS) Institute, the Covid-19 Litigation Project of the University of Trento, Italy and research projects of the European Trade Union Institute (ETUI). He is also a member of the academic board of European Banking Institute (EBI). He was awarded the "Cyprus Research Award-Young Researcher (2014)" of the Research Promotion Foundation of the Republic of Cyprus (category of "Social Sciences & Humanities"). His articles were published in many top international law journals. He is also the author of the following monograph published by Kluwer: *EU Law and the Harmonization of Takeovers in the Internal Market, 2010, Kluwer*. Moreover, he is the editor of the following book published by Springer: *Cross-Border Mergers – EU Perspectives and National Experiences, 2019, Springer*. In February 2023, his 1280-page book on *Cyprus Company Law* was published in Greek by Nomiki Vivliothiki publications.

**Jens Hillebrand Pohl** is a legal scholar, geographer, and political scientist writing and lecturing at the intersection of law and geoeconomics. An experienced attorney having practiced before U.S. federal and state courts in New York and for EU institutions, Jens researches the (geo)politicization of the legal order. His PhD in law at Maastricht University concerns judicial deference to executive power in national security cases and his second PhD in political science at Tampere University analyses "lawfare" and the (mis)use of the legal system as an instrument of geostrategic power. Jens is an adjunct professor (docent) at Maastricht University and the United Nations University, a doctoral fellow of the Institute for Globalization and International Regulation (IGIR), a doctoral research scientist at Tampere University, and an Associate Fellow at the Royal Geographical Society. He is the founding series editor of Springer Studies in Law & Geoeconomics, an advisory editor of the Yearbook of Socio-Economic Constitutions, and a former article editor of the Harvard International Law Journal. He has held visiting appointments at the Max Planck Institute for Procedural Law, T.M.C. Asser Institute, and the World Trade Institute. He holds an LL.M. from Harvard Law School and an MSc in Economics and Business from the Stockholm School of Economics.

**Christilla Roederer-Rynning** is a professor in comparative European politics at the Department of Political Science and Public Management, University of Southern Denmark.

**Patrick J. Schena** , PhD is BLR Professor of Practice in Economics, and Director of the Finance Minor Program, at Tufts, University. He also holds an appoint as Adjunct Professor of International Business at The Fletcher School at Tufts, where he teaches finance and investments. Since 2009, he has served as Co-Head of SovereigNet, The Fletcher Network for Sovereign Wealth and Global Capital. In addition, he is an Associate-in-Research at the Fairbank Center for Chinese Studies at Harvard University. He has 30 years of industry experience in finance, investments, operations, and technology management with a disciplinary focus in asset management. His professional work has included finance and consultancy positions at Fortune 500 companies, as well as co-founding and serving in executive roles in several start-up businesses servicing the global asset management industry. Patrick Schena holds a PhD from the Fletcher School with a disciplinary concentration in international finance and capital markets, an MA in Law and Diplomacy from the Fletcher School, and MA and BA degrees from Boston College.

**Alexandr Svetlicinii** is Associate Professor of Global Legal Studies at the University of Macau, where he also serves as Programme Coordinator of the Master of International Business Law in English Language. He holds PhD in Law from the European University Institute and LL.M in International Business Law from the Central European University. Svetlicinii has written extensively in the fields of competition law and international economic law with his works published in Common Market Law Review, European Law Review, Journal of Antitrust Enforcement, World Competition Law and Economics Review, Journal of European Competition Law & Practice, Journal of World Trade, Journal of International Trade Law and Policy, Asian Journal of WTO & International Health Law and Policy, Journal of International Arbitration, etc. In addition to his academic work, Svetlicinii served as Co-Director of the Academic Society for Competition Law, South-East Europe chapter, and the Non-Governmental Advisor to the International Competition Network (working group Mergers). He has recently published the monograph *Chinese State Owned Enterprises and EU Merger Control* (Routledge, 2021).

**Patrik Tingvall** is a Professor in economics, specialized in international economics and micro econometrics. Tingvall holds since 2018 a position as Chief Economist at the National Board of Trade Sweden. Before taking up his current position, he held a position as Professor in economics at Södertörn University and Director of the graduate studies program. Tingvall holds a PhD in economics from the Stockholm School of Economics 2001. In the past, he was a Researcher at the European Institute of Japanese Studies at the Stockholm School of Economics, Affiliated Researcher at Copenhagen Business School, Head of Research at the Ratio Institute, start-up member of the Stockholm China Economic Research Institute (SCERI) at the Stockholm School of Economics, and Affiliated Researcher at Centre of Excellence for Science and Innovation Studies (CESIS) at the Royal Institute of Technology (KTH). Tingvall has also worked for Growth Analysis Sweden, a governmental agency specialized in industrial policy and evaluation of industrial policy incentives.

**Alejandra Torres Camprubí** is an international dispute resolution attorney in Foley Hoag's International Litigation and Arbitration Department. Based in the firm's Paris office, Alejandra is admitted to practice in the Madrid Bar as well as the Paris Bar as an EU lawyer. She focuses her practice on public international law and international investment arbitration. Alejandra represents sovereign States and State-owned entities in arbitration proceedings administered by the International Center for the Settlement of Investment Disputes and the Permanent Court of Arbitration (in matters relating to the energy and aeronautical industries), as well as in inter-State cases before the International Court of Justice and the International Tribunal for the Law of the Sea (in border disputes and cases involving violations of international humanitarian law and human rights law). From a research perspective, her areas of expertise include international environmental law, with a particular focus on climate change law and policy, and the interaction of this field with the international law of the sea and the law on statehood. She acted as legal counsel in the United Nations climate change negotiations and has recently been a post-doctoral research fellow at the Fridtjof Nansen Institute in Oslo, as part of an international and interdisciplinary project on the legal consequences of the Anthropocene for International Law. She has published in matters relating to loss of statehood due to sea-level rise, climate change and international security, and fairness in the international regime on climate change and has lectured on these topics in several universities and international organizations. She is also an active member of the ILA Committee on International Law and Sea-Level Rise.

**Joanna Warchol** is a legal and political adviser at the Committee on International Trade (INTA) at the European Parliament since 2010. She has been responsible for legislative acts on investment protections, the EU–WTO or OECD relations, better law making as well as proceedings on the conclusion of international free trade agreements aligning to the post-Lisbon decision-making procedures. In 2018, she was a member of the EPs Inter-Institutional negotiation in the team of EP Rapporteur, Franc Proust during trialogue negotiations on the *Proposal for a regulation* *establishing a framework for screening of foreign direct investment into the EU* (Screening of the FDI into the EU). Prior to working in INTA, she was working as a coordinating adviser between the German and Polish Delegation within the EPP Group starting from the German Presidency of the EU in 2007 with Prof. H-G. Poettering until the Polish Presidency working together with Prof. Jerzy Buzek, the first Polish President of the EP. Before joining the Parliament, she has obtained PhD in European Commercial Law at the University of Heidelberg in Germany. She was guest speaker among others: at the German University of Heidelberg, Hamburg and Bonn, in Italy at the Bocconi University in Milan, in Ferrara and in Bologna, in Austria at Vienna University of Economics and Business, as well as at University Louvain-la-Neuve in Belgium, University of Luxembourg and in Poland at Jagiellonian University in Krakow. She was as well senior fellow in frame of the DFG, Deutsche Forschungsgemeinschaft at the Ruperto Carola Heidelberg University and in Max Planck Institute for Comparative Public Law and International Law in Heidelberg.

**Janosch Wiesenthal** is a PhD candidate at the University of Passau currently working on a thesis which focuses on Foreign Investment Screening. He holds a PhD-scholarship from one of the German organizations promoting talent (*Begabtenförderungswerke*). Janosch is also Deputy Assistant Director of the CELIS Institute, an independent nonprofit, nonpartisan research enterprise dedicated to promoting better regulation of foreign investment in light of security and public order concerns. He co-founded the CELIS Early-Career Scholars' and Practitioners' Network on the Law and Practice of Economic Warfare (CELIS NOW). Formerly, Janosch worked as a research assistant to Prof. Dr. Steffen Hindelang at Uppsala University in Sweden. He completed his law studies at Humboldt-Universität zu Berlin by passing the first state examination (*Erstes Staatsexamen*). He also studied at the Université Paris II Panthéon-Assas, where he specialized in international law and obtained both the *Licence en droit* and the *Maîtrise en droit*.

# Balancing Risks: Investment Screening Mechanisms, Essential Security Definitions, and Standards of Evidence

**Sarah Bauerle Danzman and Gabriella Couloubaritsis**

## Contents



**Abstract** As governments reach more toward essential security exceptions to govern their economic regulatory environment, definitions of national security and related concepts become increasingly consequential. Most OECD countries now have investment screening mechanisms (ISMs) to review inward investment for potential security concerns, but there remains substantial variation in how essential security is delineated and the standards of evidence required to mitigate or block a transaction. This article advances the literature in four ways. First, it provides a descriptive overview of how countries' ISMs conceptualize investment security, creating a typology of country risk profiles. Second, it develops an explanation for why countries systematically vary in their approach to security risks. Third, it uses the case of Germany to discuss how dynamics around critical technologies are pushing some countries to decrease their standards of evidence requirements. Finally, it discusses the implications of countries' security concepts for economic outcomes.

S. Bauerle Danzman (✉)
Indiana University, Department of International Studies, Bloomington, IN, USA
e-mail: sbauerle@indiana.edu

G. Couloubaritsis
Indiana University, Kelley School of Business, Bloomington, IN, USA
e-mail: gcouloub@iu.edu



J. Hillebrand Pohl et al. (eds.), *Weaponising Investments*,
Springer Studies in Law & Geoeconomics (2023) 1: 1–16,
https://doi.org/10.1007/17280_2023_20, Published online: 22 August 2023

# 1 Introduction

In recent years, many advanced economies have developed new or strengthened existing investment screening mechanisms (ISMs). In contrast to economic benefit-oriented screening regimes that were prevalent in the mid-twentieth century, the new generation of ISMs is focused on reviewing inward investment for potential concerns related to essential security. However, governments differ in the language they use to construct their screening concepts. This, in turn, influences the standards by which transactions are evaluated, approved, or prohibited.

This chapter contributes to the understanding of ISMs, their politics, and their effects by providing descriptive and comparative data on blocking language and by developing a typology of this language that helps categorize countries by their conception of what rationales are appropriate, and according to what evidence, to block an inward investment. This conceptual and empirical exercise is important because it helps scholars make sense of how countries develop parameters over what kinds of risks constitute essential security consequences and how much risk economies should tolerate before acting. The self-judging nature of essential security exceptions gives governments wide latitude to act expansively if they so choose—at least with respect to their international legal obligations. Therefore, understanding not only the legal language of blocking but also the political and policy motivations behind developing blocking rationale can provide scholars with a path toward better explaining how and why countries develop their understandings of security risks in a global environment where clear distinctions between security and economic issues have rapidly deteriorated.

We develop these concepts with reference to the PRISM dataset, which maps the characteristics of ISMs—including blocking language—across OECD countries from 2007 to the current day.[1] We supplement a largely static mapping of blocking language into type with a more detailed case of the German blocking language, which underwent a subtle but significant change in 2020. This exercise helps to illustrate how many countries have attempted to keep blocking language relatively constrained across two dimensions—standards of breadth and standards of evidence. However, growing concerns over the proliferation of an expanding set of dual-use technologies have made the maintenance of narrow blocking concepts challenging. As countries increasingly see a national security imperative in denying advanced technology capabilities to adversaries, they face increasing pressure to both expand the breadth of essential security concepts and lower the standards of evidence necessary to act. These forces could substantially impede cross-border investment in technology companies unless the 'techno democracies' collaborate to standardize relatively narrow definitions of critical technology and proactively work to ensure foreign investments from 'likeminded' countries will continue to be viewed as low risk and growth-promoting.

[1] Bauerle Danzman and Meunier (2023).

## 2 Essential Security Concepts and Investment Screening Mechanisms

Appeals to essential security fit squarely into broader international trade law that allows governments to deviate from treaty commitments when adherence to such promises would interfere with countries' security interests.[2] Article XXI of the General Agreement on Tariffs and Trade (GATT) states, 'Nothing in this Agreement should be construed. .. (b) to prevent any contracting party from taking any action which it considers necessary for the protection of its essential security interests'.[3] The Multilateral Agreement on Investment, if passed, would have included a similar clause.[4] Many bilateral investment treaties and preferential trade agreements have similar carve outs.[5] Appeals to essential security concerns in ISMs can be interpreted as applying consistent standards to how inward investment is reviewed. This ensures that ISMs do not violate countries' treaty obligations. Constraining investment review to essential security concerns also allows governments to credibly claim that these investment control mechanisms are compatible with a broadly liberal investment regulatory regime and with OECD guidelines regarding the appropriate use of national security exceptions in investment policy.[6]

While essential security interests can be thought of as an umbrella term, countries vary a good deal with respect to the 'blocking language' they adopt. Blocking language refers to the legal standard used to justify prohibiting or mitigating an investment through an ISM. Some of the differences among countries relate to their legal traditions. For instance, EU member states are more likely to appeal to concepts of public order and public security, while common law countries tend to favor national security or national interest rationales. In the EU, interpretations of public order, *ordre public*, and public security have developed through jurisprudence in both domestic courts and the European Court of Justice (ECJ). A legal studies approach to the evolution and differentiation among these concepts is beyond the scope of this chapter, as we are not legal scholars.

However, the shifting use and meanings of these terms can also shed light on the political choices reflected in ISM design and implementation. What counts as national security, public order, and public security in the context of investment review is not always straightforward. These terms, to varying degrees, are usually not defined in law. The purposeful vagueness of these terms allows the interpretation of security concerns to shift over time as governmental priorities and interpretations of security risks change.

[2] Pinchus-Paulsen (2020).

[3] General Agreement on Tariffs and Trade art. XXI(b), Oct. 30, 1947, 61 Stat. A-11, 55 U.N.T.S. 194.

[4] OECD (2007), p. 96.

[5] OECD (2009), p. 6.

[6] OECD (2009).

**Table 1** Standards of breadth (low to high) across 27 OECD ISMs

| National Defense or Narrow Security | National Security, Public Order | Broader National Security | Broader National Interest |
|---|---|---|---|
| Estonia | Austria | Canada | Australia |
| Finland | Czech Republic | Germany | France |
| Spain | Denmark | Italy | Hungary |
| | Ireland | Poland | Japan |
| | Latvia | Portugal | New Zealand |
| | Lithuania | Slovak Republic | South Korea |
| | Mexico | United Kingdom | |
| | Netherlands | United States | |
| | Norway | | |
| | Slovenia | | |

The blocking language governments implement, therefore, set the outer bounds of what actions a state can take against an investment it deems problematic. Importantly, governments may choose to interfere less than their blocking language allows. This chapter focuses on the legal authorities the government has to intervene, not the extent of their use. For instance, the typology developed below characterizes Italy as reserving substantial powers for its government to intervene. In practice, Italy has not blocked a substantial number of transactions. Its rather expansive blocking language, however, could support more government action against inward investments if it so chooses.

Blocking language varies systematically over two dimensions: *standards of breadth* and *standards of evidence*. *Standards of breadth* refers to the capacity of the blocking rationale. Countries that provide their ISM with the authority to intervene in transactions that present unqualified national security, public order, or security threats retain a great deal of flexibility over how, precisely, to interpret what amounts to such a threat. Still others, such as Japan, reserve a right to intervene if a transaction would adversely affect 'the smooth management of the economy'. This is a more expansive blocking rationale because it makes explicit the government's authority to intervene for macroeconomic policy purposes. In contrast, some countries have adopted blocking language that circumscribes action to more narrowly defined concerns. For instance, Finland's mechanism can intervene when a transaction jeopardizes 'the organization of national defense, the control and safeguarding of territorial integrity, border control, border security, or security of supply'. This blocking language effectively reduces action to a clearly defined subset of national security concerns. Table 1 provides standards of breadth categories for OECD countries with ISMs.[7]

*Standards of evidence* refer to how certain a government must be that a transaction would impede security before it can act. In other words, what is the risk

[7] All data on OECD ISMs and their characteristics come from Bauerle Danzman and Meunier (2023).

threshold that must be crossed before a government can prohibit a transaction? The OECD's *Guidelines for Recipient Country Investment Policies relating to National Security* emphasizes the importance of specifying standards of evidence to facilitate a rigorous, fact-based, and transparent risk assessment of reviewed transactions.[8] Identifying a potential security risk to a transaction is usually not enough to block the transaction. Instead, ISMs develop assessments of the *vulnerabilities* to state interests that the target business exposes, the *threat* that the acquirer would exploit these vulnerabilities, and the *consequence* to (national) security that would arise if the transaction was finalized. This consequence is a function of vulnerabilities, threats, and some assessment of the likelihood that the 'threat actor' would successfully exploit these vulnerabilities. While most governments talk about assessments of harm through the language of *risk*, the likely consequences of most transactions are highly *uncertain*.[9] That is, it is difficult to assign a probability of negative consequences to transactions because they each reflect unique circumstances involving different actors and different vulnerabilities.

ISMs differ in terms of how strict the standards of evidence they require to block a transaction. At one extreme, governments have the authority to block covered transactions that *threaten* the state along the standards of breadth to which the mechanism adheres. This is a standards of evidence concept that provides the state with great latitude because it does not qualify the threat standard. A threat, at any degree of probability, could justify a government action in this framework. For instance, Australia's Treasurer, through the Foreign Investment Review Board, can intervene in a transaction if it is found to be 'contrary to the national interest'.[10] There is no legal circumscription of a risk threshold that must be met to act on a threat. Such blocking language could allow for quite attenuated risk scenarios in which a security-relevant consequence is *possible* due to the transaction but not *probable*.

At the other extreme, some countries employ much higher risk thresholds. For instance, Austria's ISM only allows government action against a transaction when it creates 'actual, serious danger to the public order and security of Austrian society'.[11] *Actual, serious danger* creates a standard of evidence where governments must demonstrate a high likelihood that the threat identified will actualize. That means that attenuated risk scenarios will likely not be tolerated by the investment review authorities because the ISM requires clear evidence not only of a threat and a vulnerability but also documented evidence that indicates a high probability that the threat actor will act to exploit the target's vulnerability.

Intermediate categories have threat thresholds that fall short of the immediacy of an 'actual, serious danger' threshold but are more exacting than a general appeal to threats to the state. For instance, many countries place their risk threshold at 'likely

[8] OECD (2009) Annex Part 3.

[9] This discussion draws on a Knightian conception of risk and uncertainty. Knight (1921).

[10] Government of Australia (2020), p. 52.

[11] Government of Austria (2020), section 3.

**Table 2** Standards of Evidence (Low to High) Across 27 OECD ISMs

| National Security Considerations | Capable of Creating a Threat | Likely To Affect or Significant Risk | Actual Threat or Danger |
|---|---|---|---|
| Australia | Canada | Denmark | Austria |
| Estonia | Czech Republic | Germany | Finland |
| Mexico (never been used) | France | Ireland | Hungary |
| New Zealand | Italy | Japan | Latvia |
| | Netherlands | Lithuania | Portugal |
| | | Norway | South Korea |
| | | Poland | Slovak Republic |
| | | Spain | Slovenia |
| | | United Kingdom | |
| | | United States | |

to effect' or 'significant risk'. These concepts allow for some uncertainty of outcome but demand a rather high bar of evidence that a transaction is likely to create negative national security consequences. The United States, Poland, and Germany all have standards of evidence language that fall into this category. Finally, some countries set their risk thresholds at transactions that have the 'potential' to or 'capability' of generating a threat. For instance, the Czech Republic's threshold for action is 'capable of compromising security and public order'.[12] Table 2 provides standards of evidence categories for OECD countries with ISMs.

## 3 Explaining Different Approaches to Risk, Standards of Breadth, and Standards of Evidence

What might explain the variation across countries with respect to their blocking languages' standards of breadth and evidence? Fundamentally, the standards set for intervention reflect countries' risk profiles. Do political leaders see foreign investment as having a high potential for threatening the state? Or do they worry more about the potential for a strong ISM to repel benign investment? Governments' risk profiles will depend on the structure of their economy—and therefore the relative political power of different interest groups—as well as the source of their external threats. Because economic structure and beliefs over the sources of external threats change over time, governments' risk profiles can also adapt to new circumstances.

Taking the two dimensions of blocking language described in Sect. 2, we can develop ideal types based on combinations of these two characteristics. While Tables 1 and 2 demonstrate intermediate categories for both standards of breadth and standards of evidence, simplifying each dimension to low/high categories helps

[12] Government of Czechia (2021).

**Table 3** Categorizing Country Approaches to Blocking Language

| | Evidence | | |
|---|---|---|---|
| Breadth | | Low | High |
| | Low | Targeted Intervener | FDI Booster |
| | High | Economic Securitizer | Tech Leader |

crystalize the key differences between types. Table 3 develops the resulting four ideal type categories.

First, *Targeted Interveners* have narrow concepts of what constitutes a threat while requiring minimal standards of evidence to justify intervention into these narrow categories. Countries that fit into this category may have particular vulnerabilities associated with their energy sectors or concerns about undue influence from rivalrous neighbors. For instance, prior to its recently passed broad ISM, the Netherlands confined national security review to oil, gas, and electricity. Estonia screens real estate investments, mostly to prevent Russian-linked persons from buying property on Estonia's land and islands closely proximate to Russia.[13] Other countries could become *targeted interveners* to address the security of supply, especially after COVID-related supply chain disruptions revealed problematic dependencies in many critical capabilities. Additionally, growing concerns about the unique risks posed by entities with foreign government control or influence (FGCI) may lead to regimes that approach presumptions of denial for FGCI transactions in certain industries. Over time, we could see a growth in targeted intervention, even as a subset of broader screening regimes that usually require higher levels of evidence before intervening.

*FDI booster* countries have both narrow concepts of threats and high standards of evidence for intervention. Most countries that have only erected ISMs recently fit into this category, especially EU member states that felt pressure from the Commission to develop a mechanism after the implementation of its framework for screening FDI in October 2020.[14] These countries have traditionally been more skeptical of investment screening and more concerned about the potential for ISMs to negatively affect benign, growth-promoting investment in their economies. However, the rise of non-traditional sources of FDI from non-market economies and prominent examples of Chinese investments that seemed to strip technology from home markets[15] have made these countries more willing to erect narrowly scoped ISMs with high bars for action. Additionally, *FDI booster* countries in the EU may view developing narrow ISMs as a way to prevent more stringent EU regulation over investment security in the future. Examples of FDI boosters include Austria, Denmark, and Ireland.

[13] Estonian Act on Restrictions on Acquisition of Immovables (2012).

[14] EU Regulation 2019/452.

[15] Midea's acquisition of Kuka Robotics is an often-used example of such a transaction, although others would counter that other potential European buyers such as Siemens were ultimately not interested in the transaction for financial reasons. See Freshfields (n.d.) for legal counsel's overview of the transaction.

The relationship between national security and economic security concerns has become increasingly blurred with the elevation of the People's Republic of China (PRC) to the level of strategic competitor with Europe and the United States. The PRC's economic model, which makes clean distinctions between state-owned and private entities difficult to maintain, adds to these concerns. The PRC's policy of military-civil fusion and its focus on obtaining indigenous technology autonomy through acquiring foreign entities also generates consternation in many capitols. Furthermore, many governments are concerned about unfair subsidization of these PRC-linked companies and how industry consolidation could create security of supply issues and underinvestment in research and development in host countries.

There are two ways that countries have dealt with these concerns while developing blocking language. First, some countries, mainly those with more history of state management of development priorities, have blocking language with broad notions of threats and low barriers to intervention. These *economic securitizer* types, such as France, are willing to interpret national security quite broadly and in ways that mix economic competitiveness concerns. Australia is another example of this type, as it allows action for national interest purposes, which could be interpreted quite broadly, and has more permissive language regarding the evidence needed to act.

Other countries are less comfortable with combining national security and economic competitiveness considerations for the purposes of investment screening. At the same time, they have advanced technology that may be more clearly targeted by threat actors for strategic acquisition. Concerns about advanced technology acquisition inherently broaden review breadth. Many of these critical technologies—a term that itself is hard to define—are dual-use in nature. That is, they have both legitimate commercial purposes and more problematic military, policing, and intelligence uses. For instance, five nanometer (nm) semiconductor chips can be used in the latest cell phone or in a precision-guided missile. Top of the line NAND memory chips (otherwise known as flash chips) can be used both in personal computing devises and in Artificial Intelligence (AI) applications that facilitate wide-scale surveillance and repression.

Accordingly, countries with advanced technology sectors have an increasingly challenging task of determining what kinds of foreign investments in dual-use technologies are sufficiently commercial in nature and which create unacceptable security risks. These risks stem either from the proliferation of technology that can be used for military purposes or from reducing domestic technological capabilities and superiority over military rivals. *Technology leaders* are countries that might otherwise be *FDI Boosters* but have felt pressure to broaden the scope of investment review to amorphous sets of critical technologies.

*Technology leaders* attempt to balance this expansion by retaining high standards of evidence requirements. However, as the case of Germany illustrates below, it is not clear if this category can be long lasting. Risks that emanate from critical infrastructure are relatively easily addressed in a high standards of evidence environment. Even if the government establishes a foreign acquirer's malintent after the transaction is finalized, the risks associated with critical infrastructure ownership dissipate substantially as soon as a threat actor is required to divest from the asset. In

**Table 4** Comparison of Breadth and Evidence Across 27 OECD ISMs

| Targeted Interveners (Low, Low) | FDI Boosters (Low, High) | Economic Securitizers (High, Low) | Tech Leaders (High, High) |
|---|---|---|---|
| Czech Republic | Denmark | Australia | Germany |
| Estonia | Ireland | Canada | Hungary |
| Mexico | Latvia | France | Japan |
| Netherlands | Lithuania | New Zealand | Poland |
| | Norway | Italy | Portugal |
| | Slovenia | | Slovak Republic |
| | Spain | | South Korea |
| | Austria | | UK |
| | Finland | | US |

contrast, national security risks associated with advanced technology lend themselves to prevention strategies rather than response strategies. Once an adversary gains access to a critical technology, it can replicate the technology even after a required divestment. A great deal of the national security consequence happens *at the moment* of transfer. The toothpaste is out of the tube, so to speak. The temporal dynamics of technology risks mean that governments will face pressure to decrease standards of evidence over time to *prevent* critical technology transfers rather than merely *respond* to them.

## 4 Germany's Change in Blocking Language

The above exercise (see Table 4) provides a sense of how we might categorize countries' approaches to blocking standards at a single moment in time. However, changes in standards for review and action also reveal important underlying concerns. In this section, we provide a brief overview of Germany's decision to change its review language. The German case helps illustrate why governments may face pressure to relax the standards of evidence they require for review to allow for more preventive action. It also speaks to the role of the EU in shaping attitudes toward risk.

In June 2020, the German Bundestag adopted a revision of the Foreign Trade and Payments Act to align the country's ISM with the EU FDI Screening Regulation.[16] While the EU regulation on investment screening does not require member states to adopt the strictest version of reviewing language within Article 4 of the FDI Screening Regulation, Germany did.[17] In doing so, Germany's investment review

[16] German Bundestag's Draft of a First Law To Amend the Foreign Trade Law and Other Laws, 19/18700, https://dserver.bundestag.de/btd/19/187/1918700.pdf.

[17] Regulation (EU) 2019/452 of the European Parliament and of the Council of 19 March 2019 establishing a framework for the screening of foreign direct investments into the Union, PE/72/2018/REV/1 *OJ L 79I, 21.3.2019, p. 1–14*, https://eur-lex.europa.eu/eli/reg/2019/452/oj.

language changed from 'immediate danger to security or public order of Germany' to 'likely to affect security or public order of Germany, any other EU member, or projects and programs of EU interest'. The new standard lowered the degree of risk the government needed to find in order to justify an investment prohibition from an actual and severe threat to an anticipated, probable impairment.

The explanatory text that accompanied the amendment articulated a view that Germany's screening body needed dynamic language to reflect the broadened understanding of an investment review. The German government justified this change as necessary to harmonize its blocking language with EU standards, which is an important illustration of the ways in which the EU's investment screening work program has helped shape the conversation about balancing risk and openness in the context of investment. The amendment's explanatory text specified that an investment review can 'go beyond (national) security, public utilities, and critical infrastructure'.[18] Individual cases related to critical technologies can represent 'an impairment of the community that is subject to a ban, without there necessarily having to be a pronounced connection to the above-mentioned basic interests of the community'.[19] The European Court of Justice itself conceded that 'the concept of public order or security must be interpreted dynamically, adapted to developments over time'.[20]

Before the amendment, Germany's best course of preventing sales of critical technology companies to foreign entities was using the state-owned, national shareholding instrument Kreditanstalt für Wiederaufbau (KfW) to purchase stakes in German firms to avoid potential acquisitions. In June 2020, the Bundesministerium für Wirtschaft und Energie (BMWi) announced that the KfW would acquire 23% of CureVac, a biopharmaceutical company that develops vaccines for infectious diseases such as COVID-19 and drugs to treat cancer and rare diseases, to avoid its potential acquisition by any foreign investor.[21] However, sometimes 'golden shares' arrangements were not possible, such as in the high-profile case of Chinese investor Midea's 2016 acquisition of robotics company Kuka.[22]

Arguably, the lowered degree of risk and broadened definition of an investment review have allowed the German government to block deals that may have previously not been captured by the 'actual threat' standard. In April 2022, the Bundesministerium für Wirtschaft und Klimaschutz (BMWK, renamed from BMWi in 2021) retroactively blocked the acquisition of German medical products

---

[18] German Bundestag's Draft of a First Law To Amend the Foreign Trade Law and Other Laws, 19/18700, Number 4 of Part B Special Part On Article 1 (Amendment to the Foreign Trade Act), pg. 18 https://dserver.bundestag.de/btd/19/187/1918700.pdf.

[19] Ibid.

[20] Ibid.

[21] Heinrich, Kuhn, and Wienke. "Foreign Direct Investment Reviews 2021: Germany." *White & Case,* 2021 https://www.whitecase.com/insight-our-thinking/foreign-direct-investment-reviews-2021-germany.

[22] Freshfields (n.d.) Midea-Kuka: A Blueprint for Chinese Outbound Investment. https://www.freshfields.com/en-gb/what-we-do/case-studies/midea-kuka-case-study/.

manufacturer Heyer Medical AG by the Chinese Aeonmed Group, which had taken place 2 years prior during the restructuring of Heyer Medical AG in late March 2020.[23] A veto proposal sent to the German cabinet acknowledged the potential for foreign political influence, saying that Aeonmed seems to receive 'support measures by the Chinese state', and Heyer's 'protected assets' would face 'serious danger' in the event of a full takeover.[24] The economic conditions surrounding the COVID-19 pandemic also heightened the priority of the healthcare sector and supply chain security more generally. Regarding the prohibition, the BMWK representative shared that 'During the COVID-19 pandemic, it became apparent that Germany needs to maintain its own manufacturing and production capacities to be able to supply itself with ventilators independently of non-European manufacturers.'[25]

In other words, an expansion of German understanding of what should be considered a national security threat has generated pressures to lower risk thresholds and standards of evidence. As governments continue to develop deeper concerns over the security risks associated with critical technologies and critical supply chains, we may see more governments adopting less strict evidentiary standards for action. In the particular context of the EU, the desire to stave off reviews of intra-EU investments may also lead governments to converge around this lower standard of evidence to demonstrate to members that national-level screening is robust enough to prevent problematic investments from entering the common market.

## 5 Conclusion and Implications

This chapter has provided a comparative assessment of blocking language in the investment screening regimes of OECD countries. We do so to further explore how concepts of essential security differ in subtle but important ways across country contexts. While some of this variation has to do with legal families and jurisprudence, our contribution highlights the political choices that governments face. The structure of the economy, problematic borders, histories of subjugation by expansionary neighbors, and state-business relationships all influence the types of assets and activities governments view as essential security interests and the degree to which their standards of evidence requirements allow for speculative risk scenarios.

[23] "Orrick Advises China's AEONMED Group on Acquisition of German Medical Device Manufacturer Heyer Medical AG." April 2020. *Orrick*. https://www.orrick.com/en/News/2020/04/Orrick-Advises-AEONMED-Group-on-Acquisition-of-German-Medical-Device-Manufacturer-Heyer-Medical.

[24] "Federal Government Stops Chinese Takeover of Ventilator Manufacturer." *Frankfurter Allgemeine*. April 2022. https://www.faz.net/aktuell/wirtschaft/bund-stoppt-chinesische-uebernahme-von-beatmungsgeraete-hersteller-17989193.html.

[25] Mayer-Kuckuk. "Three Years Later: Germany Prevents Acquisition of Heyer Medical." *China. Table*. April 2022. https://table.media/China/en/professional-briefing/heyer-medical-takeover-failed-borgward-scrap-metal/.

We develop four ideal types of blocking language positions and assess countries' current positionality to these types. This exercise can help uncover which ISMs are likely to be more willing to intervene in a larger number of transactions (*Economic Securitizers*), which ISMs will erect especially narrow but high walls around a small set of domestic vulnerabilities (*Targeted Interveners*), and which ISMs will likely have the least impact on investment flows (*FDI Boosters*).

Our fourth category—*Technology Leaders*—provides conceptual clarity along two dimensions. First, it helps explain much of the dynamism among these categories in recent years. As the importance of dual-use items increases in the information and technology economy, states that specialize in advanced technologies increasingly must contend with messy questions around the line between national security and economic competitiveness. While countries with strong histories of statism have responded by embracing economic security rationales, those closest to the *Technology Leaders* ideal type have somewhat reluctantly expanded the breadth of review without substantially relaxing their standards of evidence for action.

Second, *Technology Leaders* will likely face challenges retaining these high standards of evidence. The nature of essential security risks associated with critical technologies requires preventive rather than responsive action to threats. An aphorism commonly used to describe this problem is that requiring too much evidence of malintent before blocking a transaction with critical technology is akin to closing the barn door after the horse has bolted. In other words, critical technology-related reviews may increasingly belong to the category of low probability, high consequence transactions. For this reason, and as the German case illustrates, governments will likely face increased pressures to lower evidentiary standards for action, at least around investments in advanced technology sectors. The degree to which these pressures lead to a substantial curtailing of cross-border investment in technology companies will depend on how broadly or narrowly critical technology is defined and whether the 'techno democracy' states will continue to see foreign investments from 'likeminded' countries to be growth-promoting and benign.

## Appendix: Blocking Language

Australia

Key phrase: Australia's ability to protect its strategic and security interests.

Source: 2022 FIRB Foreign Investment Policy Description https://firb.gov.au/general-guidance/australias-foreign-investment-policy

Austria

Key phrase: An actual and sufficiently serious threat to public policy and public security.

Source: Investment Measure Relating to National Security Notification of Adopting the Austrian Foreign

Trade Act of 2011, DAF/INV/RD(2013)3, page 5

Canada

Key phrase: That could be injurious to national security.

Source: Investment Canada Act as of November 2022, https://laws-lois.justice.gc.ca/eng/acts/I-21.8/

Czech Republic

Key phrase: Capable of threatening the security of the Czech Republic or internal or public order.

Source: The Foreign Investments Screening Act 2021, https://www.mpo.cz/assets/en/foreign-trade/investment-screening/legislation/2022/11/Act-on-FDI-Screening_unofficial-translation_1.pdf

Denmark

Key phrase: May pose a threat to national security or public order.

Source: Act on screening of certain foreign direct investments, etc., in Denmark (the Investment Screening Act), ACT no. 842 of 10/05/2021, https://trade.ec.europa.eu/doclib/docs/2021/july/tradoc_159712.6.pdf

Estonia

Key phrase: National defense reasons.

Source: Estonian Act on Restrictions on Acquisition of Immovables (2012) https://www.riigiteataja.ee/en/eli/523102017002/consolide

Finland

Key phrase: Potential conflicts with a key national interest (which means securing national defense or safeguarding public order and security in accordance with Articles 52 and 65 of the Treaty on the Functioning of the European Union, should the fundamental interests of society be under actual and adequately serious threat)

Source: Act on the Monitoring of Foreign Corporate Acquisitions in Finland (172/2012), https://tem.fi/documents/1410877/2132272/Act+on+the+Monitoring+of+Foreign+Corporate+Acquisitions+in+Finland/60021eda-c318-4e6c-b12e-eb15f02f46d2/Act+on+the+Monitoring+of+Foreign+Corporate+Acquisitions+in+Finland.pdf

France

Key phrase: Likely to jeopardize public order, public safety, or national defense interests

Source: French Ministry of Economy and Finance, Guidelines, 8 September 2022, https://www.tresor.economie.gouv.fr/Articles/2022/09/08/publication-des-lignes-directrices-relatives-au-controle-des-investissements-etrangers-en-france#:~:text=La%20publication%20de%20lignes%20directrices,'attractivit%C3%A9%20de%20la%20France%20%C2%BB.

Germany

Key phrase: Likely to affect security or public order of Germany, any other EU member, or projects and programs of EU interest

Source: Draft of a First Law To Amend the Foreign Trade Law and Other Laws, German Bundestag, 19/18700 https://dserver.bundestag.de/btd/19/187/1918700.pdf

Hungary

Key phrase: Violates the security interests of Hungary

Source: LVII of 2018 Law On The Control Of Foreign Investments That Harm The Security Interests Of Hungary, https://njt.hu/jogszabaly/2018-57-00-00

Ireland

Key phrase: Affects or would be likely to affect the security or public order of the State

Source: Screening of Third Country Transactions Bill 2022, https://data.oireachtas.ie/ie/oireachtas/bill/2022/77/eng/initiated/b7722d.pdf

Italy

Key phrase: Poses a serious threat or would be capable of compromising defense and national security interests

Source: Decree-law Converted With Amendments By Law 11 May 2012, N. 56 (In Official Gazette 14/05/2012, N. 111). (Last Update To The Deed Published On 08/05/2022) https://www.normattiva.it/atto/caricaDettaglioAtto?atto.dataPubblicazioneGazzetta=2012-03-15&atto.codiceRedazionale=012G0040&tipoDettaglio=originario&qId=&tabID=0.9861907600069377&title=Atto%20originario&bloccoAggiornamentoBreadCrumb=true

Japan

Key phrase: May impair national security, disturb public order, or adversely affect the smooth management of the economy

Source: Cabinet Order Concerning Inward Direct Investment, etc. (Cabinet Order No. 261 of 1980, Revised by Cabinet Order No. 37 of 2022) https://elaws.e-gov.go.jp/document?lawid=355CO0000000261

Latvia

Key phrase: Threatens interests of national security

Source: Regulation No. 606, https://investmentpolicy.unctad.org/investment-laws/laws/242/latvia-regulations-to-the-national-security-law

Lithuania

Key phrase: May pose a real threat to national security interests

Source: Investment Policy Related To National Security Notification By Lithuania, https://one.oecd.org/document/DAF/INV/RD(2018)6/en/pdf

Mexico

*As of 2022, the national security test has never been used before.

Key Phrase: Reasons for national security

Sources: Foreign Investment Law, https://investmentpolicy.unctad.org/investment-laws/laws/136/foreign-investment-law

Netherlands

Key phrase: Is possible to lead a risk to national security

Source: Law of 18 May 2022, https://www.eerstekamer.nl/behandeling/20220419/gewijzigd_voorstel_van_wet_3/document3/f=/vlsai3pa5fjk_opgemaakt.pdf

New Zealand

Key phrase: Is contrary to New Zealand's national interest

Source: 2021 Foreign Investment Policy and National Interest Guidance, https://www.treasury.govt.nz/sites/default/files/2021-06/for-invest-pol-nat-interest-guidance-jun21.pdf

Norway

Key phrase: May entail a not insignificant threat to national security interests

Source: Norway ISM, https://one.oecd.org/document/DAF/INV/RD(2020)2/en/pdf

Poland

Key phrase: May threaten safety, order and public health

Source: The Act Of 19 June 2020 On Subsidies On Interest On Bank Loans Granted To Entrepreneurs Affected By COVID-19 And On The Simplified Procedure For The Approval Of Arrangements In Connection With COVID-19, https://trade.ec.europa.eu/doclib/docs/2020/september/tradoc_158930.pdf

Portugal

Key phrase: Real and sufficiently serious manner to national security and defense or the country's supply of services deemed to be fundamental for the national interest.

Source: Portugal ISM, https://one.oecd.org/document/DAF/INV/RD(2019)7/en/pdf

South Korea

Key phrase: Interferes with maintenance of national safety and public order, harms public health or environmental preservation, is significantly contrary to public morals, or is in violation of the laws of the Republic of Korea

Source: Foreign Investment Promotion Act, https://www.law.go.kr/LSW/lsInfoP.do?efYd=20200401&lsiSeq=213079&ancYd=20191231&nwJoYnInfo=Y&ancYnChk=0&ancNo=16859&chrClsCd=010202&efGubun=Y#0000

Slovak Republic

Key Phrase: Disrupts the public order or national security of the Slovak Republic or another Member State of the European Union or the interests of the European Union.

Source: Critical Infrastructure Act, https://trade.ec.europa.eu/doclib/docs/2021/march/tradoc_159517.pdf

Slovenia

Key Phrase: Poses a threat to security or public policy of the Republic of Slovenia

Source: Act Determining The Intervention Measures To Mitigate And Remedy The Consequences Of The COVID-19 Epidemic, https://trade.ec.europa.eu/doclib/docs/2020/october/tradoc_158966.6.2020.pdf

Spain

Key phrase: There is a serious risk that the foreign investor will carry out criminal or illegal activities affecting public security, public order, or public health in Spain

Source: Spanish ISM, as of Royal Decree 12/2021 of 24 June 2021, https://www.uria.com/documentos/circulares/1463/documento/12597/UM-note.pdf?id=12597&forceDownload=true

United Kingdom

Key Phrase: May give rise to national security risks

Source: National Security and Investment: Market Guidance Notes July 2022,

https://www.gov.uk/government/publications/national-security-and-investment-nsi-act-market-guidance-notes/national-security-and-investment-market-guidance-notes-july-2022

United States

Key phrase: Threatens to impair national security

Source: Notes on The Committee on Foreign Investment in the United States (CFIUS), https://sgp.fas.org/crs/natsec/RL33388.pdf

## References


Bauerle Danzman S, Meunier S (2023) Mapping the characteristics of foreign investment screening mechanisms: the new PRISM dataset. Int Stud Q 67(2). https://doi.org/10.1093/isq/sqad026

Estonian Act on Restrictions on Acquisition of Immovables (2012). https://www.riigiteataja.ee/en/eli/523102017002/consolide

Freshfields (n.d.) Midea-Kuka: A Blueprint for Chinese Outbound Investment. https://www.freshfields.com/en-gb/what-we-do/case-studies/midea-kuka-case-study/

German Bundestag's Draft of a First Law To Amend the Foreign Trade Law and Other Laws, 19/18700., https://dserver.bundestag.de/btd/19/187/1918700.pdf

Government of Australia (2020) Foreign Investment Review Board: Guidance 2, Key Concepts. https://firb.gov.au/guidance-notes

Government of Austria (2020) Investment Control Act. https://trade.ec.europa.eu/doclib/docs/2020/september/tradoc_158955.pdf

Government of Czechia (2021) Act No. 34/2021 Coll. on Screening of Foreign Investments. https://www.mpo.cz/assets/cz/zahranicni-obchod/proverovani-zahranicnich-investic/2021/4/sb0017-2021-_1_.pdf

Heinrich K, Wienke TM (2021) Foreign Direct Investment Reviews 2021: Germany. White & Case. https://www.whitecase.com/insight-our-thinking/foreign-direct-investment-reviews-2021-germany

Knight FH (1921) Risk, uncertainty, and profit. Hart, Schaffner & Marx; Houghton Mifflin Company, Boston, MA

Mayer-Kuckuk (2022) Three years later: Germany Prevents Acquisition of Heyer Medical. China. Table. April. https://table.media/china/en/professional-briefing/heyer-medical-takeover-failed-borgward-scrap-metal/

OECD (2007) International Investment Perspectives 2007: Freedom of investment in a changing world. Paris

OECD (2009) Guidelines for Recipient Country Investment Policies Relating to National Security. Paris

Orrick (2020) Orrick Advises China's AEONMED Group on Acquisition of German Medical Device Manufacturer Heyer Medical AG. April. https://www.orrick.com/en/News/2020/04/Orrick-Advises-AEONMED-Group-on-Acquisition-of-German-Medical-Device-Manufacturer-Heyer-Medical

Pinchus-Paulsen M (2020) Trade multilateralism and U.S. national security: the making of the GATT security exceptions. Mich J Int Law 41:109

Wittenbrink F (2022) Federal Government Stops Chinese Takeover of Ventilator Manufacturer. Franffurter Allgemeine. April. https://www.faz.net/aktuell/wirtschaft/bund-stoppt-chinesische-uebernahme-von-beatmungsgeraete-hersteller-17989193.html

# The Evolving Landscape of Sovereign Wealth Funds in a Changing World Economy: How Resilient Are the Santiago Principles?

**Victoria Barbary, Adam D. Dixon, and Patrick J. Schena**

## Contents



**Abstract** The emergence of sovereign wealth funds in the early 2000s as a growing pool of large, globally focused state-owned investors quickly became a concern for politicians in the United States and in Europe who were fearful of possible financial and economic malfeasance by these institutions. Underlying these concerns were normative foundations that presumed liberal global capital markets to be the reserve primarily of private actors. The presence of state actors also raised questions about possible market distortion if capital allocation decisions are made on non-commercial (political) grounds. Such concerns led to the creation of 24 Generally Accepted Principles and Practices for sovereign wealth funds, commonly referred to as the Santiago Principles, as a means of increasing the transparency of sovereign wealth funds and ultimately legitimizing their presence in global capital markets. Since then, the transparency of sovereign wealth funds in aggregate has

The views and opinions expressed in this paper are entirely those of the authors. In this respect, they do not directly or indirectly represent the opinions, policies, and commercial interests of the organizations in which the authors are involved or have been involved.

V. Barbary
International Forum of Sovereign Wealth Funds Secretariat, London, UK

A. D. Dixon (✉)
Edinburgh Business School, Heriot-Watt University, Edinburgh, UK
e-mail: a.dixon@hw.ac.uk

P. J. Schena
Tufts University, Fletcher School of Law and Diplomacy, Medford, MA, USA



J. Hillebrand Pohl et al. (eds.), *Weaponising Investments*,
Springer Studies in Law & Geoeconomics (2023) 1: 17–36,
https://doi.org/10.1007/17280_2023_1, Published online: 7 July 2023

increased, and much of the fervent concerns about sovereign wealth funds as 'barbarians at the gate' have subsided. However, this does not mean that concerns from investment-receiving countries have disappeared. Sovereign wealth funds are still state capital, and scrutiny thereof in general has increased. At the same time, the number of sovereign wealth funds has increased, as have the number of funds focused on strategic investments. This article discusses the changing landscape of sovereign wealth funds and the challenges this poses for the Santiago Principles as the global governance regime for sovereign wealth funds.

## 1 Introduction

When the attention of global markets was first drawn to sovereign wealth funds in the early 2000s, they were few and most were relatively conservative investors. Since the establishment of the Kuwait Investment Board in 1953, oil-rich states in the Middle East have recycled their wealth in global debt markets. However, as oil prices increased and national balance sheets grew, declining yields on low-risk government bonds challenged them to seek higher returns by investing in higher-risk, less liquid assets offshore. Expanding foreign exchange reserves in export-oriented economies in East Asia posed a similar dilemma. With few foreseeable liabilities, these governments could afford to diversify their surpluses and take on more risk with the promise of more return. In response, countries such as South Korea and China established sovereign investment institutions, joining the likes of Singapore and Malaysia, which had done so long before the term "sovereign wealth fund" entered the vernacular (Rozanov 2005). In short, global markets were infused with an expanding pool of capital from institutions owned and controlled by states. This contemporary history has been well documented by Balding (2012), Dixon (2017), Dixon et al. (2022), and Rietveld and Toledano (2017), among others.

The emergence of this expanding cohort of large, globally focused state-owned investors quickly became a concern for politicians in the United States and in Europe who were fearful of possible financial and economic malfeasance by these institutions (Cohen 2009; Reed 2009). This triggered concerns among government owners of sovereign wealth funds that perceptions of politically motivated activities would reflect poorly on all funds, souring their reputations and leading to higher cross-border investment barriers. Underlying these concerns were normative foundations that presumed liberal global capital markets to be the preserve primarily of private actors (Bahgat 2008). States may own large quantities of other states' debt but owning—and possibly controlling—the equity of commercial assets in other states raised geopolitical questions about the legitimacy of state activity in global commerce (Monk 2009; Clark and Dixon 2017; Thatcher and Vlandas 2022). There were also concerns that sovereign wealth funds would make capital allocation decisions on non-commercial grounds and that this would distort financial markets (Beck and Fidora 2008; Gilson and Milhaupt 2007; Rose 2013; Knill et al. 2012). To differing degrees and material effects, states possess resources and have capacities—territorial control, sovereign rights, military assets—which private actors cannot mobilize. Furthermore, states also have pressures and interests that emanate from their representative populations (Dixon and Monk 2012). This is not to imply that sovereign wealth funds are tools of geopolitics and economic nationalism but rather to acknowledge that they remain state-owned investment companies that manage state assets (Dixon et al. 2022).

In 2008, with the global financial crisis fully engaged, the International Monetary Fund (IMF) with the support of the US Treasury convened a working group of 26 countries with sovereign wealth funds to devise a set of principles to improve their disclosure and to frame their governance (Norton 2010). In certain respects, and somewhat ironically, the relevance of this initiative was accentuated by the nearly $90 billion of sovereign wealth fund investment into the global banking sector in 2007 and 2008, providing much needed capital support. The 24 Generally, Accepted Principles and Practices (GAPP) that emerged, now referred to simply as the Santiago Principles, sought to establish their signatory institutions (i.e., sovereign wealth funds) as stable and reliable actors who invest globally on criteria of economic and financial risk and return (Das et al. 2010). Similarly, they sought to demonstrate the commitment of sovereign wealth funds, as well-governed financial institutions, to fully comply with applicable disclosure and regulatory requirements of the markets in which they invest.

The centrality in the Santiago Principles of sound institutional governance and market-based investment criteria was intended to assure host governments that sovereign wealth funds would not be used to advance the (geo)political ambitions of the sponsoring state (Truman 2010). The Santiago Principles established that sovereign wealth funds should conform to the practices and behaviors of professional institutional investors, with decisions made without political bias or interference. This prompted some commentators to infer that an exemplar sovereign wealth fund, with a broadly diversified global portfolio modelled after professional investment institutions, such as pension funds or endowments, was implicit in this new governance regime (see, e.g., Clark et al. 2013). Once the Santiago Principles were agreed upon and promulgated, a permanent member organization, the International Forum of Sovereign Wealth Funds (IFSWF), was formed to operationalize and promote their implementation. Sovereign wealth funds' endorsement of the Santiago Principles and the formation of the IFSWF would, over time, encourage greater transparency.

In the intervening years, the sovereign wealth fund landscape has changed considerably. The number of sovereign wealth funds, as counted by the IFSWF, has almost doubled from 41 in 2008 when the Santiago Principles were written to approximately 85 currently.[1] Half are members of the IFSWF, but the membership covers most of the total assets under management and all the large sovereign funds save for Norway's GPFG and Singapore's Temasek (Singapore's GIC is a member).

[1] See footnote 3 below.

The composition of the IFSWF has also changed. Increasingly, sovereign wealth funds are being established with a strategic investment mandate tied to national development objectives, including industrial policy and core infrastructure construction. With meagre fiscal surpluses, the sponsors of this type of fund tend to have smaller balance sheets, leaving many strategic funds to seek complementary sources of funding. Thus, there is evidence that government sponsors are expanding the scope of traditional sovereign wealth fund policy objectives. Moreover, as global investment institutions, sovereign funds are increasingly drawn into the global dialogue on climate change, despite the underlying interests and objectives of owner-sponsors,[2] further complicating investment decision-making at the fund level.

Over the past decade, the concept of what a sovereign wealth fund is and what its mandate should be, has diverged from the type of diversified global portfolio investor implied in the Santiago Principles. Expanded investment mandates, an increasing focus on strategic domestic investment, or new initiatives focused on climate change and sustainability are not without (geo)political implications, whether real or perceived. This is particularly apposite in a global economy characterized by intensifying geoeconomic competition between major powers (Wigell et al. 2019; Babic et al. 2022), widening the adoption of protectionist measures, and increasing the caution of state capital (see also, Kurlantzick 2016; Gertz and Evers 2020; Alami and Dixon 2020a, b; Bauerle Danzman 2021).

Our aim in this article is to show how the landscape of sovereign wealth funds in the global political economy has evolved and the challenges this poses for the global governance regime for sovereign wealth funds, specifically the role of the Santiago Principles and the IFSWF. In the following two sections, we reflect on the inception of the Santiago Principles and the IFSWF, assessing their effectiveness in fostering enhanced sovereign wealth fund transparency. We then examine the governance order of sovereign wealth funds in light of the extension of their mandates, specifically those related to strategic national development and sustainable finance. We conclude by reflecting on the resilience of the Santiago Principles as the cornerstone of a voluntary global governance regime for sovereign wealth fund investment. Our analysis is based on external reporting, publicly available research, and analysis from the IFSWF, and our personal engagement over many years with the extended global sovereign wealth fund community.[3]

---

[2]For example, following the 2015 United Nations Climate Change Conference in Paris, French President Emanuel Macron championed the founding of the One Planet Sovereign Wealth Fund Group in 2017, to develop a sustainable finance framework to help accelerate the transition to a low greenhouse gas emissions economy. See www.oneplanetswfs.org.

[3]The authors of this article have each been involved in research on and engagement with sovereign wealth funds for more than 15 years. As such, we draw on significant firsthand knowledge and repeated interactions with the field developed over time, whereby our method can be distinguished as a form of 'close dialogue' (see Clark 1998). One of us, Victoria Barbary, has worked as Director Communications and Strategy for the IFSWF since 2016. She writes in a personal capacity. Any views expressed here do not represent the IFSWF nor any of its member institutions.

## 2 On the Road to Santiago

The new voluntary governance regime for sovereign wealth funds in the form of the Santiago Principles had four key drivers: (1) an effort by the International Monetary Fund to have a better accounting of country assets that were not included in official foreign exchange reserve statistics; (2) an accelerated uptick in the creation of new sovereign wealth funds driven by rising commodity prices and managed foreign exchange rate regimes; (3) an effort to quell protectionist impulses in investment receiving countries; (4) China's massive foreign exchange accumulation and generally the country's growing place in the global economy.[4] While this last point is specific to China and echoes the previous drivers, it nevertheless highlights China's rapid foreign exchange accumulation as motivating the process.

In the early 2000s, two separate trends drove the growth of national foreign exchange reserves. Rapid global economic growth, largely driven by China, increased the demand for hydrocarbons and minerals, resulting in price rises and thus significant hard currency inflows from royalties for producing countries (Jepson 2020). Concurrently, East Asian economies were also accumulating significant foreign exchange reserves due to their export-oriented economies and managed exchange-rate regimes. This accumulation was also an explicit effort by these governments to create a lender-of-last-resort buffer in the event of a balance of payments crisis (Griffith-Jones and Ocampo 2011). The 1997 Asian financial crisis left many of the region's countries exposed and in need of external support; accumulating reserves provided a form of insurance that such support and the accompanying conditionalities (i.e., economic reforms), would be unnecessary in a future crisis. Seeking better returns, countries established new sovereign wealth funds or expanded the remit of existing ones, shifting official foreign currency reserves from central banks to new bespoke institutions. The number of new sovereign wealth funds and the shift in the asset allocation of existing funds posed a technical problem for the IMF in its monitoring of balance of payments data and the potential effects of new asset allocation strategies on global capital market stability. In 2005, the IMF began to work to improve the accuracy and transparency of the balance of payments data to facilitate the regular surveillance of macroeconomic stability across member countries.

With this technical work going on in the background at the IMF, the political realm of the United States and Europe was becoming more concerned with the growth of reserves and the establishment of new sovereign wealth funds, particularly by countries such as Russia and China—the former as a historically significant security rival and latter a fast-growing global economic competitor (and growing security rival in the Pacific). Although sovereign wealth funds had not made any

[4] The narrative in this section is based in part on a booklet produced for the tenth anniversary of the Santiago Principles by International Forum of Sovereign Wealth Funds, for which Pat Schena and Victoria Barbary were key editors and contributors. The booklet is available at: https://www.ifswf.org/publication/origin-santiago-principles-experiences-past-guidance-future.

large strategic investment deals at the time, they got caught up in an emerging backlash to cross-border investment via state-owned enterprises in assets deemed sensitive to national security (Kirshner 2009).

In 2005, state-owned China National Offshore Oil Corporation (CNOOC) made an unsolicited $18.5 billion all-cash bid for US-based oil company Unocal, a significant premium to the cash and stock offer of $17.8 billion made and already agreed to by US-based Chevron. The deal would have required approval from the Committee on Foreign Investment in the United States (CFIUS), but before this happened, members of the US House of Representatives inserted language into an energy bill that would have delayed the transaction. CNOOC subsequently withdrew its bid. In 2006, state-owned Dubai Ports World's purchase of UK-based P&O, which had contracts to operate six major US seaport facilities, set off further alarm in the US Congress, even though the United Arab Emirates has good relations with the United States (Rose 2008). With growing foreign exchange reserves, mostly held in US dollars, coupled with moves to reallocate to different asset classes, particularly high-end real estate, labelling sovereign wealth funds as a possible threat to national security and capital market stability was not difficult.

Wanting to keep global capital markets open and the United States as a welcoming investment destination, the US Treasury set about formulating a set of principles for sovereign wealth funds and for investment-receiving countries in 2007 (Kimmitt 2008). To do so, the US Treasury solicited the help of Singapore's Government Investment Corporation (now GIC) and the Abu Dhabi Investment Authority (ADIA). Both sovereign wealth funds had become increasingly aware of the changing geopolitical mood around state-owned investment and were concerned that recipient countries would start erecting more barriers. A set of best-practice principles would hopefully allay receiving countries' fears, inasmuch as they were real or potential. The nine principles published in March 2008 consisted of five principles specific to sovereign wealth funds, namely, that they should have an exclusively commercial focus, embrace transparency, and compete fairly with the private sector, and four principles for investment-receiving countries, namely, that they should treat sovereign wealth funds no differently than other similar institutional investors and that any restrictions erected be proportional to genuine national security concerns (Treasury 2008). These principles would eventually serve as a basis for the wider-ranging Santiago Principles.

In parallel to the work with GIC and ADIA, the US Treasury was also in dialogue with the IMF, the World Bank, and the OECD. The OECD hastened its work on host country investment regimes, whereas the IMF, which had already been working to enhance transparency and accuracy of reserves, put together the International Working Group (IWG) of sovereign wealth funds to begin drafting a set of principles and practices at the 2008 Spring Meetings of the IMF and World Bank in Washington, DC. The 26-country IWG subsequently met in Singapore and in Santiago, Chile. The deadline for agreeing the GAPP was tight, with the aim of presenting them at the IMF/World Bank Annual Meeting in October 2008.

Coming to an agreement across a diverse range of sovereign wealth funds was difficult. While the IWG members were all either commodity or reserve-based funds generally focused on diversified portfolio investment, the specific national legal bases for each fund made agreeing to strict principles impossible, particularly regarding disclosure. Transparency and disclosure rules for funds reflected national standards and practices (Mehrpouya 2015). In the case of Western countries, sovereign wealth fund regulations regarding disclosure reflected comparable regimes for other institutional investors, such as public-employee pension funds. For sovereign wealth funds in the Middle East, by contrast, reporting was far less developed, where there were no requirements for external disclosure about portfolio composition and governance. Where information was publicly available, it was rarely geared toward an international audience or translated from Arabic into English. Consequently, rather than adopting a prescriptive rule-based regime, there was early agreement that the Santiago Principles were to be voluntary and sufficiently general to allow for domestic regulatory diversity. This does not mean, however, that the Santiago Principles are necessarily accommodative of all domestic regulatory diversity. There are minimum standards regarding the transparency of foundational legal and governance arrangements.

The resulting framework, the Santiago Principles, took the form of 24 voluntary principles divided into three sections: (1) legal framework, objectives, and coordination with macro-economic policies; (2) institutional framework and structure; and (3) investment and risk management. The first five principles focus on the legal foundations of the fund under domestic law, with a focus placed on defining the policy rationale and purpose of the fund and that the investments of the fund be aligned to this policy purpose and the macroeconomic basis underpinning this policy purpose, including disclosure of withdrawal rules. If seemingly basic, disclosure of the fundamental policy purpose of a sovereign fund is significant for framing and underwriting the scrutiny of the design and operation of the sovereign fund as a market-driven financial institution and its investment horizons and its risk tolerance. In short, alignment with a clearly defined policy purpose is an important element that limits potential political influence on investment decision-making. Hence, GAPP 1 to 5 delineate how the sovereign fund is integrated into the state apparatus, which is necessary for understanding and defining the fund's independence at the operational level in the GAPP thereafter.

GAPP 6 to 17 delineate principles underpinning how the fund should be governed as a financial institution, focusing on the roles, responsibilities, and accountability standards of the board and the management, how the fund engages with third-party asset managers, and compliance with laws and regulations in the countries in which the fund invests. GAPP 17 is the most explicit in terms of the intended effects of disclosure, where relevant financial information should be publicly disclosed to demonstrate the sovereign fund's 'economic and financial orientation, to contribute to stability in international financial markets and enhance trust in recipient countries'. The following GAPP—18 to 23—are more technical in nature, focusing on investment policy and risk management. GAPP 19 is significant for emphasizing that investment decisions should 'aim to maximize risk-adjusted financial returns in a manner consistent with [the sovereign fund's] investment policy, based on economic and financial grounds'. Again, emphasizing adherence to investing following norms typical of institutional investors in global markets. This principle was and is important for addressing the fundamental link of the sovereign wealth fund with its sponsoring state. In other words, accepting that the link between a sovereign wealth fund and the larger state apparatus is never fully broken, higher degrees of closeness are of limited concern if the fund is invested exclusively for financial gain and not for other (political) purposes.

Notwithstanding the emphasis on maximizing risk-adjusted returns, the framers of the Santiago Principles were not naïve regarding the additional criteria that may and are used to inform investment decision-making, as is common in institutional investment management. Sub-principle 19.1 acknowledges this, emphasizing that 'if investment decisions are subject to *other than* [original emphasis] economic and financial considerations, these should be clearly set out in the investment policy and be publicly disclosed'. What this sub-principle does, for example, is to allow additional criteria, such as environmental, social, governance (ESG) criteria or consideration for job creation, to inform investment decision-making. This does not mean that economic and financial considerations are, or made to be, less irrelevant. It does, however, open the door for criteria that allow the investment function of the sovereign wealth fund to focus on concerns other than maximizing risk-adjusted returns as an investment institution. In other words, it permits consideration of factors (e.g., environmental sustainability) that are of systemic significance, whose impacts are not readily identifiable in risk-return measures, particularly in the short term. We return to the potential issues, focusing on non-financial concerns, later particularly in the case of explicit strategic national objectives. Nonetheless, key to our point: The framers of the Santiago Principals recognized and emphasized the primacy of disclosure and clarity of purpose.

For the IFSWF, the last GAPP has become an important part of its ongoing work in promoting compliance with the Santiago Principles and hence encouraging greater transparency among sovereign wealth funds. GAPP 24 calls for 'a process of regular review and implementation of the GAPP should be engaged in by or on behalf of the SWF'. As we discuss in the next section, GAPP 24 has underpinned triennial self-assessments performed by IFSWF members since 2016.

## 3 Impacts of the Santiago Principles and the IFSWF

If the Santiago Principles were founded to assuage the concerns and potentially diverging interests of recipient countries and sovereign wealth funds (including their sponsoring governments), in short to neutralize their link with the sponsoring state, critics have argued that the Santiago Principles fall short of this fundamental purpose (Bismuth 2017). The Santiago Principles offer a non-binding, voluntary framework where disclosure and standards of investment governance are articulated and encouraged but nothing is mandated. Rather, the focus is on embedding a sovereign fund in domestic law, adhering to the laws and regulations in markets where the sovereign fund invests, and clarifying the relationship between the sovereign wealth fund, the third-party asset managers it engages, and the state.

While this interpretation has merit, the form and function of the Santiago Principles is also to promote an idealized form of institutional investment management. While it is possible to see the emergence of sovereign wealth funds as a significant institutional innovation, they can also be viewed as a variant of existing institutions. As articulated by Clark et al. (2013, p. xiii), sovereign wealth funds are to some extent a variation on 'funded supplementary pension schemes that are responsible for the long-term welfare of nominated beneficiaries and whose investment strategies are reliant upon financial markets and the global financial services industry.' Hence, if the emphasis of the Santiago Principles is placed on articulating the relationship between the sovereign wealth fund as an asset owner, its state sponsor, and the wider institutional investment community, it reflects the comparability of sovereign wealth funds with other large asset owners (e.g., public-employee pension funds). This suggests that it is better to mitigate the normative and material concerns posed by sovereign wealth funds as state entities by the diffusion of norms related to the design and practice of existing institutional investment organizations.

Seen through a legal lens, the Santiago Principles reflect a growing body of transnational 'soft law' (Norton 2010; Djelic and Quack 2010). Rather than strict, binding legal frameworks, soft law is expressed through standards, rankings, and monitoring frameworks, which exist outside of state and international regulatory enforcement. Compliance with standards, inclusion in rankings, and implementing monitoring frameworks, in effect, bestows membership in a club: soft law works through socialization and normative pressures in place of direct coercion and threats of legal sanctions. For sovereign wealth funds, adherence to the Santiago Principles and membership in the IFSWF provides a seal of approval that the fund (and by extension the government owner) is committed to transparency and disclosure in keeping with the norms of institutional investment management. Membership also holds the fund accountable to its peers for good practice, as bad practice reflects across sovereign wealth funds as a group. For example, the collapse of Malaysia's 1MDB in a shroud of scandal looms large across Asia, generally fostering negative perceptions of sovereign wealth funds in the region.

Given the voluntary nature of the Santiago Principles, however, and the lack of recourse to a higher legal authority that adjudicates their interpretation and implementation, the Santiago Principles are open to broad interpretation. Likewise, the IFSWF, which is a member-driven organization, is not designed, nor is it geared toward acting as an arbiter. Notwithstanding, the IFSWF has the power to eject members if they fail to implement the Santiago Principles. Moreover, new membership applications are reviewed by the IFSWF Secretariat and its Board of five sovereign wealth funds before membership is conferred. Demonstrating adherence and commitment to the Santiago Principles is a key requirement for new full members.

There have been several independent initiatives to index the transparency of sovereign wealth funds since before and after the publication of the Santiago Principles. These include the Geoconomica Santiago Compliance Index, which has not been updated since 2014, the Linaberg-Maudell Transparency Index, which is produced by the for-profit Sovereign Wealth Fund Institute, and the SWF Scoreboard developed by former US Treasury official Edwin Truman, while based at the Washington-based think tank Peterson Institute of International Economics. Truman's SWF Scoreboard was first published in 2007 and has been updated every few years since, with the most recent iteration in 2021. Based on Truman's Scoreboard, there is evidence that sovereign funds have shown improvement in the aggregate levels of transparency since 2007. Reflecting on the Santiago Principles at the 2018 Annual Meeting of the IFSWF in Marrakesh, Morocco, Truman concluded that they have made 'substantial contributions to the transparency and accountability' of many sovereign wealth funds and that membership in the IFSWF fosters peer pressure among members to improve their compliance (Truman 2018). Operationalizing GAPP 24 has become important in this regard.

In 2014, the IFSWF established a self-assessment procedure while including a self-assessment requirement for new members. The first self-assessments were completed in 2016 and published in early 2017. A subsequent round of self-assessments was undertaken in 2019, published in 2020, and another round of self-assessments is being undertaken in 2022. Given the voluntary nature of the Santiago Principles and the non-coercive comportment of the IFSWF, the self-assessments are not mandatory, but all full IFSWF members now undertake and publish their self-assessments.

The quality, consistency, and depth of the self-assessments improved with each cycle. With the 2017 cycle, the quality of the submissions was variable, with some funds providing detailed explanations for how they implement and comply with the Santiago Principles, including their provision of supporting documentation. Other submissions, by contrast, provided little detail and hence were of limited use in discerning compliance and understanding of the Santiago Principles. A narrow interpretation of these circumstances would seem to give credence to claims that some sovereign wealth funds are opaque and not committed to disclosure. Rather, the IFSWF attributed these findings to issues of organizational learning and development and, following the publication of the 2017 self-assessments, in consultation with member funds established a set of guidelines to support the preparation of the self-assessments. The guidelines were designed based on the commentaries and discussion in Part II of the Santiago Principles with the goal of improving the consistency and comparability of the self-assessments while focusing fostering within the IFSWF and guiding aspiring members through this required component of the IFSWF membership application process.

By the 2019 cycle, all member funds of the IFSWF were participating in the self-assessment process. With clearer guidelines in hand, the resulting self-assessments demonstrated more consistency and depth of engagement. With improved disclosure, the degree of transparency also improved. As with the 2017 self-assessments, Patrick Schena conducted an independent review of the 2019 self-assessments for the IFSWF (Schena et al. 2020; Schena 2017a). This review indeed found that many self-assessments were demonstrably improved from previous cycles. However, the entire body of self-assessments continued to reflect gaps in uniformity, partly as a function of the heterogeneity of the member funds and the application-cum interpretation of the Santiago Principles based on domestic law and context. On balance, the self-assessments are generally effective in outlining the policy goals and purpose of the sovereign wealth fund and its relationship with its sponsoring state, as well as the formal governance architecture of the fund as a financial institution. Some funds provide an in-depth account, whereas others are more circumspect in the volume and detail of information they provide. As with many institutional investors generally, we acknowledge that there is a thin line between disclosure and greater transparency, on the one hand, and commercial or competitive sensitivity on the other (for further discussion on sovereign wealth fund transparency, see Dixon 2014). Nonetheless, self-assessment reporting can and should be enhanced further, particularly with respect to investment policy, operational practices, investment performance reporting, and risk management.

In sum, while there is continued variation in the degree of disclosure and transparency among sovereign wealth funds, advances in transparency are evident and consistent with initiatives by the IFSWF to institutionalize self-assessment reporting through GAPP 24. Thus, the wider adoption of the Santiago Principles as a result of expanded IFSWF membership is in line with the motivations of the founding stakeholders and has contributed to their aims. However, the world—and financial markets—are not static. As noted, the Santiago Principles were formulated in a particular world-historical moment with the ideal sovereign wealth fund conceived as a broadly diversified institutional investor. The global political economy has since evolved, as has the landscape of sovereign wealth funds.

## 4 Prioritizing National Development

A decade ago, in the last paragraph of one of the earlier monographs on sovereign wealth funds, Clark et al. (2013, p. 154) opined:

> We foresee an eventuality whereby SWFs [sovereign wealth funds], cognizant of the fact that Western markets no longer offer a reliable investment risk premium, will evolve into different institutions in the coming decades. In effect, we envisage SWFs transforming themselves into long-term investors whose holdings are selected based on their strategic interests (of the fund <u>and</u> the nation) rather than the principles underpinning modern portfolio theory. If so, the future of SWFs will be more like that feared by their critics in the West than the ideal form argued to be consistent with a symbiotic relationship with the West. The costs of this transformation will be felt by global financial markets as liquidity ebbs away and SWFs make their own ways in the world of economic development rather than market arbitrage and speculation.

While sovereign wealth funds are still firmly rooted in global (Western) financial markets, this earlier speculation on the future of sovereign wealth funds has some truth. Indeed, many sovereign wealth funds established in the last decade or so have mandates focused on national economic development priorities, often emulating other strategic-focused sovereign wealth funds, namely, Singapore's Temasek

Holdings, Malaysia's Khazana Nasional Berhad, and Abu Dhabi's Mubadala Investment Company (Schena and Gouett 2022; Schena et al. 2018; Halland et al. 2016; Dixon 2022; Braunstein 2019). Examples include the Ireland Strategic Investment Fund, BpiFrance, Kazakhstan's Samruk-Kazyna, Rwanda's Agaciro Development Fund, Italy's CDP Equity, Senegal's *Fonds souverain d'investissements stratégiques*, Morocco's Ithmar Capital, The Sovereign Fund of Egypt, the Russia Direct Investment Fund, and the Türkiye Wealth Fund. These funds, occasionally referred to as strategic investment funds or sovereign development funds, employ a range of operational and investment strategies that are meant to be market generating and market conforming. In contrast to development banks where concessional terms (i.e., below-market rate financing) are normal, strategic investment funds follow market-based investment norms and risk-return metrics. The aim is not to replace traditional development finance mechanisms and institutions but rather to complement and enhance private capital investment (including capital from other foreign sovereign wealth funds).

The investment strategies of these funds typically fall into four categories (Gelb et al. 2017; Bruce-Clark and Monk 2017; Schena 2017b). First, they focus on investing in new sectors and infrastructure connectivity to catalyze industrial development and economic diversification. Second, a number of these funds are also structured as holding companies for other state assets and state-owned enterprises, for which they focus on improving corporate governance and operational/commercial performance. This generally entails monitoring and advising investee firms at the board level, as well as supporting corporate financing activities. Third, and related to the latter, some strategic investment funds contribute to local capital market development through the complete or partial privatization of state assets, hence creating investment opportunities for local and foreign investors. Finally, as many of these funds are comparatively small, they are focused on attracting foreign investors as co-investment partners. Here, such funds act as investment conduits for foreign investors to navigate the domestic market and political-economic context. In effect, these sovereign wealth funds are focused specifically on facilitating structural economic change and domestic market development.

Strategic investment funds, as a sub-class of sovereign wealth funds, are focused on domestic development, bringing them near the political realm. Because the investment function of these funds is intended to advance discrete development objectives, their mandates frequently target a so-called "double bottom line", which sets them apart from conventional asset allocators. Of course, in the broadest possible sense, all sovereign wealth funds are necessarily tools of national economic policy, whether development, fiscal, or monetary (Dixon and Monk 2017). In making this point, we do not imply that the investment function of sovereign funds necessarily is politicized with politicians dictating or even influencing investment decisions (but we also do not exclude the possibility as such). Rather, we aim to highlight the importance of the effective governance of a sovereign wealth fund, its relationship with its state sponsor, and its degree of political remoteness. In the case specifically of strategic investment funds, the strength of a fund's governance structure is essential to its ability to mobilize foreign and private capital in support of its investment objectives. As evidence, we point to the mandates of most newly inducted memberships of the IFSWF.

Sovereign wealth funds that are capitalized by natural resource rents can serve as critical components of an integrated natural resource revenue management framework that supports macro-economic management of the national economy. Natural resource revenues can be very volatile, making them an unstable source of income for national governments from one year to the next. Placing natural resource revenues in a sovereign wealth fund can provide stability to government spending and investment conducted via conventional fiscal channels. A sovereign wealth fund can also mitigate the effects of absorptive capacity constraints (i.e., the ability of the economy to absorb natural resource revenues efficiently and effectively, particularly during periods when world commodity prices are high). It can furthermore serve as a buffer from the 'Dutch disease', a condition under which non-resource sectors of the economy are made less competitive due to the adverse effects of local currency appreciation (Alsweilem and Rietveld 2018; Deléchat et al. 2017).

Whereas commodity-based sovereign wealth funds exist to manage natural resource revenues in support of macro-economic stability,[5] the policy goals of other funds are designed to serve long-term savings objectives contributing to inter-generational equity. In both cases, their investment policies contrast with those of strategic investment funds. However, the relevance of effective governance for these funds is no less important. Sovereign wealth funds with so-called stabilization and savings mandates are generally diversified portfolio investors that invest globally in major bond and equity markets, with variation in portfolio construction explained largely by a fund's risk tolerance and associated investment horizon. Norway's Government Pension Fund—Global (GPFG) is a good example, owning 1.3 percent of all publicly traded equities globally.[6] The GPFG has a long-term investment horizon, which reflects its mandate as an intergenerational savings fund designed to share the financial benefits of Norway's oil and gas assets with future generations.

Following trends among large asset owners such as pension funds and endowments, sovereign wealth funds have steadily embraced alternative asset classes such private equity and infrastructure in search of higher risk-adjusted returns (Capapé 2021; IFSWF 2016). Alternative assets are generally considered to be less correlated with traditional assets, such as traded equities and bonds, and, consistent with portfolio theory's rational investor assumption, enhance diversification benefits and thus maximize portfolio returns for a given level of risk. However, since the global financial crisis in 2008, this rationality assumption has yielded ground to those who view externalities created in the global economy—for example, with

[5]It is important to acknowledge also that there are broader political economy outcomes, such as supporting extant political regimes.

[6]This is based on figures reported by the manager of the GPFG, Norges Bank Investment Management. See https://www.nbim.no/. Last accessed 21 November 2022.

respect to low-wage earners or the environment (see, e.g., Nölke 2020)—as long-term systemic risks that cannot be perpetually ignored.

This explosion of interest in ESG or sustainable investing can be explained as identifying long-term risk factors—such as climate change—and factoring their impacts into asset valuations and portfolio investment decisions. Many sovereign wealth funds have accepted this reality and embraced sustainability as a fundamental component of their investment strategy. In fact, in a survey of 81 sovereign wealth funds conducted jointly by the IFSWF and OPSWF (2021), 71 percent of funds had adopted an ESG approach (see text below for discussion and definition of OPSWF). This represents a massive increase compared to results from the same survey in 2020, in which only 24 percent of funds indicated the adoption of sustainability practices.

An economic case for ESG is made by proponents, but what constitutes sound 'environmental', 'social', and 'governance' policies and investment practices is contested. Models of corporate governance, for example, continue to vary across countries, reflecting diverse national histories and politics (Roe 2006; Clark and Wójcik 2007). While corporate governance regimes cluster around versions of the Anglo-American shareholder-centered model preferred by institutional investors, differences persist in the degree to which stakeholders are actively involved in the governance process (such as the representation of workers on German corporate boards). Often referred to as "stakeholder capitalism", inclusive governance models are preferred by those who want corporations and financial institutions, including asset owners, to be more socially engaged (McCarthy 2019).

A similar point can be made about the 'E' in ESG. For some, achieving environmental sustainability, particularly regarding climate change, requires a radical removal of the entire global economy, including requisite patterns of consumption and production (Feola 2020). For others, divesting stranded assets is seen as a necessary end (Caldecott 2018). However, where to draw the line? In the European Union, a debate rages over whether nuclear energy and natural gas should be included in classification benchmarks for ESG investing.[7] Some argue that such forms of energy are a necessary part of the transition away from fossil fuels, whereas others seek inclusion of only renewable energy sources. Does this imply that ESG integration at the fund level should only permit investments in the latter and not the former?

Among the cohort of large globally diversified asset owners who invest long term, many sovereign wealth funds have sizable exposures to environmental, social, and governance risks that will manifest over decades. As such issues continue to foster political discourse, they will inevitably draw sovereign funds into discussions, even "calls-to-action", to invest—or divest—their capital or to exercise their shareholder rights *strategically* in global markets. In 2017, for example, French President

[7] See, for example, Zachmann, G. (2022) 'Europe's sustainable taxonomy is a sideshow', *Bruegel Blog*, 22 February, available at: https://www.bruegel.org/blog-post/europes-sustainable-taxonomy-sideshow.

Emmanuel Macron initiated the One Planet Sovereign Wealth Fund (OPSWF) network to encourage sovereign funds to contribute to advancing the Paris Climate Accords. Five of the six founding members are sovereign funds of major petroleum-producing countries. The sixth founding member is the New Zealand Superannuation Fund. Does such engagement inevitably draw sovereign funds closer to a political "third rail"?

The appropriateness of basing investment decisions on factors other than strictly the objective to maximize financial performance is ultimately a matter of fiduciary responsibility, i.e., a governance matter between a manager and asset owner defined by its mandate. Traditionally, this has been viewed narrowly through the lens of market risks with any deviation potentially open to challenges—including legal challenges—of a breach of fiduciary duty. Increasingly, the United Nations Environment Programme Finance Initiative and the Principles for Responsible Investment (2020), among others, have progressed the global dialogue on fiduciary duty based on the materiality of risks to long-term financial performance, particularly those related to ESG. This is consistent with the stated objective of the OPSWF: To integrate climate change issues into investment management practices to improve long-run returns by promoting knowledge sharing, identifying climate-related investment risks and opportunities, and enhancing investment decision frameworks with sensitivity to climate transition issues.

In the period since its establishment, the OPSWF has expanded with its membership more than doubling among funds from both oil-producing and oil-importing countries. Does this expansion walk a fine line between financial performance and sovereign funds advancing strategic objectives, including those related to economic, social, and governance interests? If the aim of establishing a global governance regime for sovereign wealth funds more than a decade ago was to demonstrate and encourage sovereign investment made on strictly commercial terms, then in some respects, GAPP 19 of the Santiago Principles might be seen as a legacy of a narrow interpretation of fiduciary duty. In actuality, the drafting of GAPP 19 in 2008 was extensible and quite forward-looking with respect to considerations other than the purely "economic and financial", including in particularly ESG, as the drafting notes of the Santiago Principles make clear.

Arguably, aligning investment policies with national development goals or global initiatives on environmental, social, and governance policy and practices draws sovereign wealth funds closer to the political sphere, both domestically and internationally. Of course, policy—or policy making—is not devoid of politics. Ultimately, however, the objective of a sovereign fund's investment policy is a matter of governance, i.e., its obligation to invest on behalf of and in the direction of its owner. GAPP 19 anticipates objectives beyond narrowly financial return, obliging only that the reasons and factors that drive them be publicly disclosed.

## 5 Conclusion: How Resilient Are the Santiago Principles?

The Santiago Principles, while not a set of strict enforceable rules, are nonetheless reflective of liberal internationalism, where capital mobility and the expansion of trade are key drivers of greater international integration. Underwriting the Santiago Principles is, as such, a commitment to keeping markets open to foreign capital, including state capital. The mechanism for achieving this is not a set of prescriptions for receiving countries but rather the diffusion of norms promoting clarity in the form and function of sovereign wealth funds and the governance of sovereign wealth funds as financial institutions. Put simply, the Santiago Principles call for sponsoring governments to define and explain the purpose of the sovereign wealth fund (i.e., its policy function) and how and by whom investment decisions are made (i.e., the investment function). The Santiago Principles do not prescribe what investments can be made but are unambiguous that investments should maximize risk-adjusted returns consistent with the fund's—and so its owner's—investment policy. Deviations from investment following this principle are permitted, where additional non-financial considerations can be included in investment decision-making. However, such deviations must be publicly disclosed in an investment policy statement. Thus, the expansion of fund mandates as reflected in the growth of discrete strategic investment funds or the growing uptake of ESG investing by sovereign wealth funds is afforded in the Santiago Principles.

Notwithstanding, sovereign funds and their sponsors must acknowledge that the liberal international order in which the Santiago Principles were introduced is changing. Global rivalries, and now the broader and more operationally focused use of economic and financial sanctions, are leading to increasing constraints on trade, while both soft and hard barriers to foreign capital flows are expanding (Babić and Dixon 2022; Meunier and Nicolaidis 2019). This poses a discrete problem for the Santiago Principles inasmuch as their adoption by sovereign wealth funds rests on a presumed quid pro quo that demonstrable governance would ensure that receiving country investment regimes would remain open.

Commitment to the Santiago Principles among the world's sovereign wealth funds has not waned even as the pace of new merger control and foreign investment review regimes in advanced economies continues to increase. While many of these discretely target state-owned (or state-aligned) enterprises—, i.e., commercial operating entities—increased scrutiny of foreign direct investment by recipient countries itself increases the costs of direct investment and can dissuade sovereign wealth funds from even pursuing investments in certain markets. Investment screening ultimately increases transaction costs. The risk of review and possible rejection adds additional complexity to investment decision-making and risk management. Given the expansion of investment screening regimes, the premium on disclosure and transparency is arguably even greater than it was when the Santiago Principles were originally devised. Receiving country perceptions of the motivation and remoteness of sovereign funds' investment decisions from political interference are critical to managing the impacts of investment screening. This reinforces the need for strong institutional governance, including disclosure and transparency. Moreover, given the increasing propensity for sovereign funds to partner and to co-invest, concerns about the opacity of some sovereign investment partners will potentially create frictions for other investors. Thus, rather than diverse investment consortia lowering barriers—and costs—to investment, perceived weak governance by investors may increase the costs and risks for all.

Emulation effects have been a tacit motivator of new funds seeking IFSWF membership and adopting the Santiago Principles. The institutionalization of self-assessment reviews as key and regular tasks of IFSWF members is foundational to continuous reflection on the implementation of the Santiago Principles and thus greater disclosure and transparency by sovereign funds. Since their introduction, the Santiago Principles have persisted in their original form despite the continuous evolution of the sovereign wealth fund landscape. Shifts in owner objectives have informed changes—even innovations—in fund mandates and investment policies and practices even beyond those related to developmental, environmental, social, or governance themes. To be certain, sovereign funds are diverse and at varying stages of maturity with governance practices that vary widely. Notwithstanding, strong governance remains essential to the capacity of these investors to carry out their mandates, both domestically and internationally. We posit that the Santiago Principles have remained resilient in the face of evolutionary pressures driven by shifting global demographic, economic, and financial forces. As the global political economy continues to evolve, new pressures will test this resiliency. The continued relevance of the Santiago Principles will attest to their original purpose: Strong institutional governance is essential to overcoming barriers to global capital flows and to maintaining the stability of global financial markets.

**Acknowledgements** This work was supported by the European Research Council (ERC) under the European Union's Horizon 2020 research and innovation programme (Grant agreement No. 758430).

## References

Alami I, Dixon AD (2020a) State capitalism(s) redux? Theories, tensions, controversies. Compet Change 24(1):70–94. https://doi.org/10.1177/1024529419881949

Alami I, Dixon AD (2020b) The strange geographies of the 'new' state capitalism. Polit Geogr 82: 102237. https://www.sciencedirect.com/science/article/pii/S0962629819302987

Alsweilem K, Rietveld M (2018) Sovereign wealth funds in resource economies: institutional and fiscal foundations. Columbia University Press, New York

Babić M, Dixon AD (2022) Is the China effect real? Ideational change and the political contestation of Chinese state-led investment in Europe. Chin J Int Polit 15(2):111–139. https://doi.org/10.1093/cjip/poac009

Babic M, Dixon AD, Liu I (eds) (2022) The political economy of geoeconomics: Europe in a changing world. Palgrave Macmillan, New York; London

Bahgat G (2008) Sovereign wealth funds: dangers and opportunities. Int Aff 84(6):1189–1204. http://www.jstor.org/stable/25144988

Balding C (2012) Sovereign wealth funds: the new intersection of money and politics. Oxford University Press, New York
Bauerle Danzman S (2021) Investment screening in the shadow of weaponized interdependence. In: Drezner DW, Farrell H, Newman A (eds) The uses and abuses of weaponized interdependence. Brookings Institution Press, Washington DC, pp 257–272
Beck R, Fidora M (2008) The impact of sovereign wealth funds on global financial markets. Intereconomics 43(6):349–358. https://doi.org/10.1007/s10272-008-0268-5
Bismuth R (2017) The "Santiago Principles" for sovereign wealth funds: the shortcomings and the futility of self-regulation. Eur Bus Law Rev 28(1):69–88
Braunstein J (2019) Capital choices: sectoral politics and the variation of sovereign wealth. University of Michigan Press, Ann Arbor
Bruce-Clark P, Monk A (2017) Sovereign development funds: the governance and management of strategic investment institutions. In: Cumming DJ, Filatotchev I, Reinecke J, Wood G (eds) The Oxford handbook of sovereign wealth funds. Oxford University Press, Oxford
Caldecott B (ed) (2018) Stranded assets and the environment: risk, resilience and opportunity. Routledge, Taylor & Francis Group, London; New York
Capapé J (ed) (2021) Sovereign wealth funds 2020: fighting the pandemic, embracing change. IE Center for the Governance of Change, Madrid
Clark GL (1998) Stylized facts and close dialogue: methodology in economic geography. Ann Assoc Am Geogr 88(1):73–87
Clark GL, Dixon AD (2017) Sovereign wealth funds and the global political economy of trust and legitimacy. In: Cumming DJ, Wood G, Filatotchev I, Reinecke J (eds) The Oxford handbook of sovereign wealth funds. Oxford University Press, Oxford, pp 145–158
Clark GL, Wójcik D (2007) The geography of finance: corporate governance in the global marketplace. Oxford University Press, Oxford
Clark GL, Dixon AD, Monk AHB (2013) Sovereign wealth funds: legitimacy, governance, and global power. Princeton University Press, Princeton and Oxford
Cohen BJ (2009) Sovereign wealth funds and national security: the Great Tradeoff. Int Aff 85(4): 713–731. https://doi.org/10.1111/j.1468-2346.2009.00824.x
Das US, Mazarei A, Hoorn H v d, International Monetary F (2010) Economics of sovereign wealth funds: issues for policymakers. International Monetary Fund, Washington, D.C.
Deléchat C, Villafuerte M, Yang S (2017) Sovereign wealth funds in the context of macro-fiscal frameworks for resource-rich developing countries. In: Rietveld M, Toledano P (eds) The new frontiers of sovereign investment. Columbia University Press, New York, pp 150–167
Dixon AD (2014) Enhancing the transparency dialogue in the "Santiago Principles" for sovereign wealth funds. Seattle Univ Law Rev 37(2):581–595
Dixon AD (2017) The state as institutional investor: unpacking the geographical political economy of sovereign wealth funds. In: Martin R, Pollard J (eds) Handbook of the geographies of money and finance. Edward Elgar, Cheltenham, pp 279–297
Dixon AD (2022) The strategic logics of state investment funds in Asia: beyond financialisation. J Contemp Asia 52(1):127–151. https://doi.org/10.1080/00472336.2020.1841267
Dixon AD, Monk AHB (2012) Rethinking the sovereign in sovereign wealth funds. Trans Inst Br Geogr 37(1):104–117
Dixon AD, Monk AHB (2017) A simple typology of sovereign development funds. In: Rietveld M, Toledano P (eds) The new frontiers of sovereign investment. Columbia University Press, New York, pp 83–100
Dixon AD, Schena PJ, Capapé J (2022) Sovereign wealth funds: between the state and markets. Agenda, Newcastle
Djelic ML, Quack S (2010) Transnational communities: shaping global economic governance. Cambridge University Press, Cambridge
Feola G (2020) Capitalism in sustainability transitions research: time for a critical turn? Environ Innov Soc Transit 35:241–250. https://doi.org/10.1016/j.eist.2019.02.005

Gelb A, Tordo A, Halland H (2017) Domestic investment practices of sovereign wealth funds: empirical evidence to inform policy debates. In: Rietveld M, Toledano P (eds) The new frontiers of sovereign investment. Columbia University Press, New York, pp 124–149
Gertz G, Evers MM (2020) Geoeconomic competition: will state capitalism win? Wash Q 43(2): 117–136. https://doi.org/10.1080/0163660X.2020.1770962
Gilson RJ, Milhaupt CJ (2007) Sovereign wealth funds and corporate governance: a minimalist response to the new mercantilism. Stan Law Rev 60:1345
Griffith-Jones S, Ocampo JA (2011) The rationale for sovereign wealth funds: a developing country perspective. In: Bolton P, Samama F, Stiglitz J (eds) Sovereign wealth funds and long-term investing. Columbia University Press, New York, pp 60–66
Halland H, Noël M, Tordo S, Kloper-Owens J (2016) Strategic investment funds: opportunities and challenges. World Bank Policy Research Working Paper, (7851). https://documents1.worldbank.org/curated/en/235311475681523659/pdf/WPS7851.pdf
IFSWF (2016) New challenges, private markets: sovereign wealth funds' changing investment strategies. International Forum of Sovereign Wealth Funds, London. Available at: https://www.ifswf.org/sites/default/files/IFSWF%20New%20Challenges%2C%20Private%20Markets.pdf
IFSWF & OPSWF (2021) In full flow: sovereign wealth funds mainstream climate change. International Forum of Sovereign Wealth Funds and One Planet Sovereign Wealth Funds, London; Paris
Jepson N (2020) In China's wake: how the commodity boom transformed development strategies in the global south. Columbia University Press, New York
Kimmitt RM (2008) Public footprints in private markets: sovereign wealth funds and the world economy. Foreign Aff 87(1):119–130
Kirshner J (2009) Sovereign wealth funds and national security: the dog that will refuse to bark. Geopolitics 14(2):305–316. https://doi.org/10.1080/14650040902827765
Knill A, Lee B-S, Mauck N (2012) Bilateral political relations and sovereign wealth fund investment. J Corp Finance 18(1):108–123
Kurlantzick J (2016) State capitalism: how the return of statism is transforming the world. Oxford University Press, New York
McCarthy MA (2019) The politics of democratizing finance: a radical view. Polit Soc 47(4): 611–633. https://doi.org/10.1177/0032329219878990
Mehrpouya A (2015) Instituting a transnational accountability regime: the case of sovereign wealth funds and "GAPP". Account Organ Soc 44:15–36. https://doi.org/10.1016/j.aos.2015.05.001
Meunier S, Nicolaidis K (2019) The geopoliticization of European Trade and Investment Policy. JCMS: J Common Mark Stud 57(S1):103–113. https://doi.org/10.1111/jcms.12932
Monk AHB (2009) Recasting the sovereign wealth fund debate: trust, legitimacy, and governance. New Polit Econ 14(4):451–468
Nölke A (2020) Financialization and the crisis of democracy. In: Mader P, Mertens D, Van der Zwan N (eds) The Routledge international handbook of financialization. Routledge, Abingdon; New York
Norton JJ (2010) The Santiago Principles for sovereign wealth funds: a case study on international financial standard-setting processes. J Int Econ Law 13(3):645–662. https://doi.org/10.1093/jiel/jgq034
Reed BJ (2009) Sovereign wealth funds: the new Barbarians at the gate-an analysis of the legal and business implications of their ascendancy. Va Law Bus Rev 4:97
Rietveld M, Toledano P (2017) The new frontiers of sovereign investment. Columbia University Press, New York
Roe MJ (2006) Political determinants of corporate governance. Oxford University Press, Oxford
Rose P (2008) Sovereigns as shareholders. North Carolina Law Rev 87:83
Rose P (2013) Sovereign investing and corporate governance: evidence and policy. Fordham J Corp Financ Law 18(4):913–962
Rozanov A (2005) Who holds the wealth of nations? Int J Central Bank 15(4):52–57

Schena PJ (2017a) Trends in transparency: Santiago Principle Self-Assessments 2016. International Forum of Sovereign Wealth Funds, London. Available at: https://www.ifswf.org/trends-transparency-santiago-principle-self-assessments-2016

Schena PJ (2017b) When states invest at home: the development role of sovereign wealth funds in public finance. Wake Forest Law Rev 52:917

Schena PJ, Gouett M (2022) Re-imaging development finance: sustainability, catalytic capital, and the role of sovereign wealth funds. In: Chaisse JL, Gorski J, Sejko D (eds) Regulation of state-controlled enterprises. Springer

Schena PJ, Braunstein J, Ali A (2018) The case for economic development through sovereign investment: a paradox of scarcity? Global Policy 9(3):365–376. https://doi.org/10.1111/1758-5899.12549

Schena PJ, Adhikari N, Manzi F, Sadri S (2020) 2019 IFSWF Member Self-Assessment Review. International Forum of Sovereign Wealth Funds, London. Available at: https://www.ifswf.org/publication/2019-ifswf-member-self-assessment-review

Thatcher M, Vlandas T (2022) Foreign states in domestic markets: sovereign wealth funds and the west. Oxford University Press, New York; Oxford

Treasury (2008) Treasury reaches agreement on principles for sovereign wealth fund investment with Singapore and Abu Dhabi. March 20. U.S. Department of the Treasury, Washington, DC. Available at: https://www.treasury.gov/press-center/press-releases/Pages/hp881.aspx

Truman EM (2010) Sovereign wealth funds: threat or salvation? Peterson Institute for International Economics, Washington, DC

Truman EM (2018) Perspective: sovereign wealth funds: building on a decade of progress. In: IFSWF (ed) The origin of the Santiago Principles: experiences from the past; guidance for the future. IFSWF, London, pp 39–51

Wigell M, Scholvin S, Aaltola M (eds) (2019) Geo-economics and power politics in the 21st century: the revival of economic statecraft. Routledge, London; New York

# Much Ado About Nothing?: State-Owned Enterprises Under Foreign Investment Control in the European Union

**Alexandr Svetlicinii**

## Contents



**Abstract** This paper explores the treatment of state-owned enterprises (SOEs) in foreign direct investment (FDI) control in the European Union (EU). Although the alleged security risks linked to SOE-led investments in the EU shaped the drafting and adoption of the EU FDI Screening Regulation, the key issues related to the definition of SOEs, determination of the foreign state's control/influence over foreign investors, and specific security risks stemming from foreign SOE-led investments have remained largely undefined at the EU level. The author makes the following three findings. First, the review of the national FDI screening regimes of the Member States shows no signs of a common approach towards the "SOE factor" in FDI screening. Second, as demonstrated by the example of EU merger control enforcement, the determination of the existence of state control and/or influence over particular investors proved to be a challenging task, as the investigation needs to go beyond traditional corporate structures. Third, the example of China's military-civilian fusion strategy demonstrates that the focus on the "SOE factor" will not be sufficient for the identification of security risks, and therefore, the state/private dichotomy of foreign investors should be abandoned in favor of more comprehensive asset-focused FDI screening.

A. Svetlicinii (✉)
University of Macau, Macao SAR, China
e-mail: alexandrs@um.edu.mo

 
J. Hillebrand Pohl et al. (eds.), *Weaponising Investments*,
Springer Studies in Law & Geoeconomics (2023) 1: 37–58,
https://doi.org/10.1007/17280_2023_16, Published online: 14 June 2023

## 1 Introduction

The recipient countries of FDI have been traditionally welcoming towards foreign investors that can bring much needed capital, technologies, employment, and other opportunities to the respective economies. However, this welcoming mood frequently switches to suspicion or outright concerns when foreign investors are state-owned or state-controlled entities. SOEs' lack of transparency and accountability, the market economy (or non-market economy) status of their home countries (Warchol 2021), their potential pursuit of non-commercial objectives, their ability to leverage the competitive advantages obtained from the home state, including subsidization, etc., are among the causes for these concerns (Enderwick 2017). It was noted among others that the "FDI by SOEs may be perceived as an extraterritorial tool and raise concerns about their non-business objectives" (Cuervo-Cazurra 2018). Hence, the financial support (deep pockets) of the SOEs and their potential role of the home countries' agents have been noted among the SOEs' characteristics that could present security risks for the recipient country (Esplugues Mota 2018).

The international community initially reacted to these concerns by encouraging the home states to streamline the corporate governance of their SOEs to ensure more transparency and accountability in their commercial practices overseas. For example, the Organisation for Economic Co-operation and Development (OECD) adopted corporate governance guidelines calling upon the states to "allow SOEs full operational autonomy to achieve their defined objectives and refrain from intervening in SOE management" (OECD 2015). On the other hand, it called upon the host states to apply the principle of non-discrimination to the investment policies related to national security, which would require to "treat similarly situated investors in a similar fashion" (Wehrlé and Pohl 2016).

Nevertheless, host countries increasingly view foreign SOEs as not "similarly positioned investors" in regard to national security. For example, when justifying the application of lower screening thresholds for SOE investors, the Canadian Prime Minister noted: "purchases of Canadian assets by foreign governments through state-owned enterprises are not the same as other transactions" because the "larger purposes of state-owned enterprises may go well beyond the commercial objectives of privately owned companies" (Harper 2012). Likewise, the Australian FDI screening legislation distinguishes "foreign government investors" that include SOEs as "corporation in which: a foreign government or separate government entity holds a substantial interest".[1] Even when SOE investments are completed as planned, they frequently face more regulatory hurdles and screenings than their private counterparts (Li and Xia 2017).

The European Union (EU) has a unique position in the field of investment controls based on security considerations. The freedom of capital is guaranteed by the Treaty on the Functioning of the European Union (TFEU) and extends to third

[1] Foreign Acquisitions and Takeovers Regulation [2015] SLI No. 217, Section 17.

countries but can be derogated from on the grounds of security.[2] The matters of defense and national security remain within the exclusive competence of the Member States.[3] As a result, the functioning of the EU internal market and the maintenance of the freedom of capital[4] in relation to foreign investors conditioned the establishment of a cooperation mechanism between the EU and its Member States. Such a mechanism was introduced by the EU FDI Screening Regulation,[5] whereby the Member States and the Commission coordinate the screening of FDI into the EU.

The uneasy relationship between the EU's commitment to its openness towards FDI and the increased need to protect national security of the Member States, along with the distribution of competences, renders the EU a distinctive example in regard to investment screening. In this context, the EU's approach towards SOE-led foreign investments merits particular attention. The present paper explores the role of SOEs in investment control in the EU in the following manner. First, it discusses how the "SOE factor" shaped the drafting of the EU FDI Screening Regulation (Sect. 2) and how foreign SOEs are treated under the cooperation framework established by the said regulation (Sect. 3). Second, it reviews the treatment of SOEs under the national FDI screening regimes of the Member States (Sect. 4). Third, it tests the viability of determining the existence and exercise of state ownership/control/influence, drawing valuable insights from EU merger control (Sect. 5). Finally, the author disputes the viability of distinguishing between state-owned and private investors in the context of China's military-civilian fusion strategy (Sect. 6).

## 2 State-Owned Enterprises and the Adoption of the EU FDI Screening Framework

From the early formation stages of the EU-wide FDI screening framework, foreign SOEs have featured as the "primary suspects" in the public discourse. They have been looked upon as foreign investors raising potential security concerns that could be addressed through the screening of foreign investments into the Union. In its 2017 resolution, the European Parliament urged the Commission "to pay more attention to

[2]Pursuant to Consolidated versions of the Treaty on European Union and the Treaty on the Functioning of the European Union [2012] OJ C326/1 (hereinafter TFEU), Article 65, Member States have a right "to take measures which are justified on grounds of public policy or public security".

[3]TFEU, Article 346(1)(b): "any Member State may take such measures as it considers necessary for the protection of the essential interests of its security which are connected with the production of or trade in arms, munitions and war material".

[4]TFEU, Article 63: "all restrictions on the movement of capital between Member States and between Member States and third countries shall be prohibited".

[5]Regulation (EU) 2019/452 of the European Parliament and of the Council of 19 March 2019 establishing a framework for the screening of foreign direct investments into the Union [2019] OJ L 79 I (hereinafter EU FDI Screening Regulation).

the role of foreign-based state-owned enterprises that are supported and subsidised by their governments in ways that the EU single market rules prohibit for EU entities" and "to screen third country FDI in the EU in strategic industries, infrastructure and key future technologies, or other assets that are important in the interests of security and protection of access to them, while bearing in mind that Europe depends to a large extent on FDI".[6] The Directorate-General for Trade official Martin-Prat further clarified that "[a]cquisitions by foreign state-owned or controlled companies in these strategic areas may allow third countries to use these assets not only to the detriment of the EU's technological edge but also to put our security or public order at risk" (Martin-Prat 2020).

Nevertheless, stakeholders' concerns in relation to the security risks posed by foreign SOEs were far from uniform. For instance, ten MEPs from the European People's Party who tabled their own proposal for a Union Act on the Screening of Foreign Investment in Strategic Sectors were primarily concerned about the lack of reciprocity for EU investors in third countries and distortion of the level-playing field in the case of state-subsidized foreign investments (Weber et al. 2017).[7] Similarly, in its communications, the European Council viewed FDI screening as an additional regulatory tool in the "levelling the playing field" toolbox (General Secretariat of the Council 2018). On the other hand, France, Germany and Italy attempted to formulate a common approach to investment screening whereby they suggested that "due consideration should be given to the extent to which the acquisition is part of a state-led industrial policy strategy geared towards making targeted direct investments in foreign companies in certain economic sectors in a bid to pursue overriding national interests" (Zypries et al. 2017). This pro-active stance towards strengthening the investment controls taken by several Member States prompted the observation that the EU FDI Screening Regulation "is not also the result of a genuine initiative of the Commission as it was primarily the request of France, Germany and Italy" (Bismuth 2020, p. 105). Likewise, it was argued that "the initiative was the result of a minority of EU Member States who are willing to tighten the control of non-EU FDI and have raised concerns as to the level playing field and reciprocity in international trade and investment" (Bismuth 2020, p. 106). On the other hand, it was expected that Member States with higher levels of technology intensive industries would be more supportive towards an EU-wide FDI screening framework, while those relying more heavily on foreign investments in the non-tech sectors would tend to oppose it (Chan and Meunier 2022).

Although several Member States had their security-based FDI controls in place prior to the adoption of the EU FDI Screening Regulation, the enforcement practices do not reflect any specific SOE-related concerns that would distinguish their

---

[6] European Parliament, Resolution of 5 July 2017 on building an ambitious EU industrial strategy as a strategic priority for growth, employment and innovation in Europe [2018] OJ C 334/124, paras 19–20.

[7] In the context of obtaining reciprocity for the European businesses abroad, the European Parliament also supported the adoption of the international public procurement instrument and the anti-coercion instrument. See Balázs (2022a, b).

acquisitions from those carried out by private entities. For example, the acquisition of the German industrial robot manufacturer Kuka by the Chinese home appliance producer Midea sparked concerns about technology transfer, but the transaction was ultimately cleared by the German authorities. Although Midea was a private company, the transaction was viewed as part of the Made in China 2025 strategy in terms of moving up the value chains by acquiring necessary technologies (Hooijmaaijers 2019, p. 460). In 2016, the Fujian Grand Chip Investment Fund made an attractive bid to acquire German chipmaker Aixtron, but the transaction was blocked by the US, as Aixtron's products could have military applications (U.S. Department of the Treasury 2016). Although this case did not involve any SOEs directly, the screening process raised concerns as to the possible links between the funding used for the acquisition and the Chinese government (Hooijmaaijers 2019, p. 463). In 2018, the German government vetoed another acquisition by a private Chinese investor—Yantai Taihai—of the German specialized manufacturing company Leifeld Metal Spinning (Deutsche Welle 2018). One common denominator observed in the specified transactions was not the state-owned status of the foreign investors but rather the importance of technologies that the target companies possessed.

As a result, even though the "SOE factor" has featured prominently in the public discourse around the need to adopt an EU-wide FDI screening framework, the stakeholders did not have a uniform position as to what are the particular security risks stemming from SOE-led FDI. The lack of consensus as to the precise risks posed by foreign SOEs vis-à-vis their private counterparts has also been reflected in the drafting process and deliberations on the EU FDI Screening Regulation, which are discussed in the following section.

## 3 State-Owned Enterprises in the EU FDI Screening Regulation

The European Commission tabled a proposal for an EU-wide FDI screening cooperation mechanism on 13 September 2017. When explaining the necessity of having EU framework on FDI screening, the Commission noted the "growing concerns regarding certain foreign investors seeking to acquire control of or influence in European firms whose activities have repercussions on technologies, infrastructure, inputs or sensitive information" while these risks are especially pronounced in cases "when foreign investors are state owned or controlled, including through financing or other means of direction." (European Commission 2021, question 1) In its working document accompanying the proposal, the Commission reasoned that foreign state-controlled investors "may seek to acquire control of or influence in European undertakings whose activities have repercussions on critical technologies, infrastructure, inputs or sensitive information".[8] Such investments would allow foreign states to use European assets "to the detriment not only of the EU's technological edge but also its security and public order".[9] While the Commission's working document provided information on the relative size, number, sectoral presence and other characteristics of the foreign state-controlled entities, it did not specify how exactly the existence of state control should be ascertained.

The European Economic and Social Committee (EESC), in its opinion on the Commission's proposal, noted that foreign SOEs "are strategically acquiring European businesses that possess key technologies, and that they are poised to take over infrastructure, important future technologies and other assets that are important to guaranteeing the security of the Member States and the EU as a whole".[10] More specifically, the EESC urged the Commission to expand the strategic sectors subject to screening, taking into account the Made in China 2025 industrial policy.[11] The EESC has even suggested "that the regulation should include a separate screening procedure for foreign direct investment made by third-country governments, or investors with close ties to such governments"[12] or "foreign direct investment can be restricted more comprehensively if an investor is controlled by, or has close ties to, a government"[13] or "regulation should include a separate screening procedure for foreign direct investment made by third-country governments, or investors with close ties to such governments".[14] The Committee of Regions was more cautious in that regard: "an FDI screening mechanism that restricts investments simply because the FDI is subsidised cannot be sufficient grounds for blocking an investment and that it has to prove that the FDI at hand is part of strategic or national industrial goals of a foreign state" (European Committee of the Regions 2018, para. 39).

The members of the European Parliament have also expressed their interest in specifically targeting the state-owned foreign investors and proposed to modify the Commission's initial wording of Article 4, "Member States and the Commission may take into account whether the foreign investor is controlled by the government

[8]Commission Staff Working Document accompanying Proposal for a Regulation of the European Parliament and of the Council establishing a framework for screening of foreign direct investments into the European Union [2017] SWD(2017) 297 final (hereinafter Commission Staff Working Document accompanying Proposal for FDI Screening), p. 6.

[9]Commission Staff Working Document accompanying Proposal for FDI Screening, p. 6.

[10]Opinion of the European Economic and Social Committee on the 'Proposal for a Regulation of the European Parliament and of the Council establishing a framework for screening of foreign direct investments into the European Union' [2018] OJ C 262/94 (hereinafter EESC Opinion), para 2.2.

[11]EESC Opinion, para 2.32.

[12]EESC Opinion, para 1.14.

[13]EESC Opinion, para 2.33.

[14]EESC Opinion, para 2.34.

of a third country, including through significant funding",[15] into a more detailed "whether the foreign investor is directly or indirectly controlled by the government, including state bodies or armed forces, of a third country, including through ownership structure or significant funding".[16] In the end, to allow the Commission and the screening authorities of the Member States ascertaining the links between a foreign investor and a third country, the final text of the EU FDI Screening Regulation required the foreign investors to provide information on their ownership structure and the origin of the funds used for the proposed investment.[17] The preamble of the EU FDI Screening Regulation further added foreign government subsidies and "State-led outward projects or programmes" to the list of factors that may be considered during investment screening.[18]

However, in the subsequent guidance documents issued by the Commission following the adoption of the EU FDI Screening Regulation, there is virtually no discussion on the specific risks associated with foreign SOE-led investments. For example, the Commission's 2020 Guidance issued in the midst of the COVID-19 pandemic focuses on protection of critical health care infrastructure and supplies and prevention of the sell-off of European businesses in times of economic downturn.[19] While it urged the Member States to adopt and/or expand their FDI screening legislation, it offered no further guidance as to particular security risks that would stem from the foreign SOEs' acquisitions in the internal market. The Member States have followed the Commission's guidance by strengthening their FDI screening systems and expanding their coverage (Ginevri 2020; Svetlicinii 2021).

In its 2022 guidance to the Member States, issued in the context of the Russia-Ukraine armed conflict, the Commission specified that "any investment directly or indirectly related to a person or entity associated with, controlled by or subject to influence by the Russian or Belarusian government into critical assets in the EU may give reasonable grounds to conclude that the investment may pose a threat to security or public order in Member States"[20] because "these governments have a strong incentive to interfere with critical activities in the EU and to use their ability to

---

[15] Proposal for a Regulation of the European Parliament and of the Council establishing a framework for screening of foreign direct investments into the European Union [2017] COM(2017) 487 final, Article 4.

[16] European Parliament legislative resolution of 14 February 2019 on the proposal for a regulation of the European Parliament and of the Council establishing a framework for screening of foreign direct investments into the European Union [2020] OJ C 449/673, Article 4(2).

[17] EU FDI Screening Regulation, Article 9(2).

[18] EU FDI Screening Regulation, recital 13.

[19] European Commission, Guidance to the Member States concerning foreign direct investment and free movement of capital from third countries, and the protection of Europe's strategic assets, ahead of the application of Regulation (EU) 2019/452 [2020] OJ C 99 I/01 (FDI Screening Regulation).

[20] Communication from the Commission Guidance to the Member States concerning foreign direct investment from Russia and Belarus in view of the military aggression against Ukraine and the restrictive measures laid down in recent Council Regulations on sanctions [2022] OJ C 151 I/01 (hereinafter Guidance Concerning FDI from Russia and Belarus), p. 1.

control or direct Russian and Belarusian investors in the EU for that purpose".[21] In its overview of the current Russian and Belarusian investments in the EU, the Commission offered the following statistics: Russian public authorities, State and the Government controlled 1.1% (or 343) of the companies with Russian influence or control,[22] for Belarus it was 0.41% (or 11) of the companies with Belarusian influence or control.[23] Needless to say, the SOEs from Russia and Belarus, many of which have been targeted by EU sanctions, will be unlikely to act as direct acquirers or investors in European companies. As a result, the focus of the FDI screening efforts by the Member States would have to focus on the links between the foreign investors and the respective governments, as well as tackling possible circumvention strategies of foreign investors who could seek investments through entities already established in the EU.

On 17 March 2021, the MEP Tom Berendsen inquired whether "the Commission [can] give an overview of Chinese investments and interests in European strategic infrastructures such as ports, airports and container terminals" and "how will the Commission set about obtaining it as soon as possible, given the strategic importance thereof" (Berendsen 2021). The Executive Vice President Dombrovskis replied that the Commission "is not in a position to give an overview of Chinese investments and interests in European infrastructures such as ports, airports and container terminals. Although the Commission is often aware of such investments, there is no obligation for Member States to report the presence of foreign investors in their territory" (Dombrovskis 2021). Dombrovskis' answer reiterates that due to the absence of foreign investment controls in several Member States and an EU-wide information-sharing framework, it is not possible to have comprehensive information on the extent of foreign SOEs' investment activities in the Union. However, even in situations where the Commission becomes aware of certain investments that are undergoing screening, one should not expect any case-specific explanations, as the following exchange indicates. Concerned about foreign acquisitions in the EU semiconductor industry, the Austrian MEP Othmar Karas inquired "[w]hat is the Commission's assessment of the impact of the proposed acquisition of Siltronic AG on the EU semiconductor industry, in particular as regards the competitiveness of the internal market, the EU's role as an industrial centre, security of supply in critical technologies, and intellectual property" (Karas 2021). The Commission's Executive Vice President Vestager replied that due to confidentiality considerations, "the Commission is not in a position to comment on any possible case that has been or could be brought to its attention under the EU cooperation mechanism on Foreign Direct Investment (FDI) screening" (Vestager 2021). As a result, the divergences of the national FDI screening regimes and the relevant confidentiality considerations may preclude both the EU institutions and the general public from grasping the

[21] Guidance Concerning FDI from Russia and Belarus, p. 2.

[22] Guidance Concerning FDI from Russia and Belarus, p. 4.

[23] Guidance Concerning FDI from Russia and Belarus, p. 6.

current state of affairs with the foreign SOE-led investments and the security risks they may generate in particular Member States.

## 4 State-Owned Enterprises in the National Investment Control Regimes

As demonstrated in the above discussion on the inclusion of the "SOE factor" in the security risk assessment under the EU FDI Screening Regulation, there is little EU-level guidance on how the state ownership over the foreign investor should be considered by the screening authorities of the Member States. While the EU FDI Screening Regulation includes a non-exhaustive list of factors that could be considered by the screening authorities, it will be instructive to understand how the "SOE factor" is addressed in the national FDI screening regimes of the Member States. As of 2 February 2023, 18 Member States (European Commission 2022)[24] have notified their screening mechanisms under Article 3(8) of the EU FDI Screening Regulation (Velten 2020).[25]

The Danish FDI screening legislation among the criteria used for assessing an investment undergoing screening reproduces verbatim the provision from the EU FDI Screening Regulation: "Whether the foreign investor is directly or indirectly controlled by a foreign government, including foreign government agencies or foreign armed forces of a third country, including through ownership or substantial financing".[26] The Austrian,[27] the Maltese,[28] and the Slovenian[29] legislators have included the same in the list of factors to be considered in FDI screening. Similarly, the German FDI screening authority would consider whether "the acquirer is directly or indirectly controlled by the government, including other state agencies or armed forces, of a third country", as this factor may have an effect on public order or security.[30] Nevertheless, the German Foreign Trade and Payments Ordinance (*Außenwirtschaftsverordnung*) further specifies that if direct or indirect control over a domestic company or certain investment in such company is transferred

---

[24] These are: Czechia, Denmark, Germany, Spain, France, Italy, Latvia, Lithuania, Hungary, Malta, Netherlands, Austria, Poland, Portugal, Romania, Slovenia, Slovakia, Finland.

[25] Essentially, the Member States have the following options in relation to the coverage of the FDI screening mechanisms: (1) no screening mechanism; (2) narrow screening mechanism as an exception to fundamental freedoms with limited scope for public policy/security; (3) wide screening mechanism following the EU FDI Regulation's notion of "critical assets"; (4) even broader screening mechanism covering "strategic assets" as provided in the EU Commission's Guidance.

[26] Act on screening of certain foreign direct investments, Act no. 842 of 10/05/2021, section 15(2).

[27] Federal Act on the Control of Foreign Direct Investments, No. 87/2020, section 3(2).

[28] National Foreign Direct Investment Screening Office, Act No. LX of 2020, Articles 11 and 12.

[29] Act Determining the Intervention Measures to Mitigate and Remedy the Consequences of the Covid-19 Epidemic, No. 80/20 of 30 May 2020, Article 72(4).

[30] Foreign Trade and Payments Ordinance of 2 August 2013, section 55a(3).

"between companies whose respective shares are held in full by the same controlling company, and all contracting parties have their headquarters located in the same third country", such transaction would not be subjected to FDI screening.[31]

The Spanish Decree on foreign investments (644/1999) specifies that public bodies (*entidades publicas de soberania extranjera*) are considered foreign investors within the meaning of FDI screening legislation.[32] Spanish Decree-Law 8/2020 specifically suspended the liberalization regime and subjected to FDI screening those investments where "the foreign investor is controlled directly or indirectly by the government, including public bodies or armed forces, of a third country".[33] The criteria being applied for the purposes of determining the existence of such control are laid down in Article 42 of the Commercial Code.[34] These include situations where a company has a majority of voting rights, has the power to appoint or dismiss the majority of the members of the governing body, and may dispose, by virtue of agreements entered into with third parties, of the majority of the voting rights.

In France, the Minister of Economy, which acts as a screening authority for the specific FDI, may take into consideration the fact that "the investor has links with a foreign government or public body".[35] To ascertain the existence of such links, the French FDI screening legislation specifically requires foreign investors to "mention any significant equity relationship or financial support from a State or public body outside the European Union over the last five years".[36] The Polish FDI screening procedures were also designed to establish the linkages between foreign investors and other entities by requiring the former to provide information on "legal and actual capital, financial and personal ties with other entities".[37] In Hungary, the FDI screening legislation expressly requires the minister carrying out the screening to ascertain among others whether "the notifier is controlled, directly or indirectly, by an administrative organ of a State not belonging to the European Union, including also state organs and armed forces, either due to its ownership structure or as a result of significant funding".[38]

The Italian FDI screening regime legislation covers a range of factors that may be relevant to the foreign SOEs' acquisitions in Italy: (a) the existence of links between the acquirer and third countries that do not recognize the principles of democracy or the rule of law, that do not respect the norms of international law or have engaged in

[31] Foreign Trade and Payments Ordinance, section 55(1).

[32] Royal Decree 664/1999 of April 23 on Foreign Investment, Article 2.

[33] Royal Decree-Law 8/2020 of 17 March on Extraordinary Urgent Measures to Deal with the Economic and Social Impact of Covid-19, Article 7a.

[34] Royal Decree of 22 August 1885 approving the Spanish Commercial Code, Article 42.

[35] France Monetary and Financial Code, Article R. 150-10.

[36] Decree No. 2019-1590 of 31 December 2019 relating to Foreign Investments in France, Article 1.

[37] Act of 24 July 2015 on the Control of Certain Investments, Article 6(4).

[38] Act No. LVIII of 2020 on the Transitional Rules related to the End of the State of Danger and Pandemic Preparedness, section 283.

risky behaviors towards the international community, derived from the nature of their alliances; (b) the acquirer is directly or indirectly controlled by public administration, including state bodies or armed forces, of a country not belonging to the European Union, including through the ownership structure or substantial financing.[39] The Portuguese legislation echoes this approach and refers to "the existence of links between the acquirer and third countries that do not recognize or respect the fundamental principles of the democratic rule of law, that pose a risk to the international community as a result of the nature of their alliances".[40] The Netherlands, which at the time of writing has not yet adopted a comprehensive FDI screening regime, refers to the acquirer that "has close ties with or is under the influence of a state... known or reasonably suspected of intent to influence a telecommunications company to facilitate misuse or intentional outages" (de Kok 2021).[41]

The Lithuanian FDI screening legislation appears more resolute in specifying that an investor would pose a risk to national security if "at the time of contacting the Commission, he or she has, or has had in the past, relations with the authorities of foreign states or natural or legal persons of those states which increase the risk or present a threat to national security".[42] The procedural rules in Lithuania require the investor to indicate whether the investor has concluded contracts and/or agreements with third country authorities and, if applicable, to provide information on the contents of such contracts and/or agreements.[43]

The above review of the SOE-related provisions in the national FDI screening regimes of the Member States demonstrates that although state ownership and/or control frequently appear among the factors considered during the security risk assessment of the notified investments, the national legislation largely goes no further than the EU FDI Screening Regulation in terms of defining the specifics of the relevant security risks. The national investment control regimes also differ somewhat in terms of determination of the existence of state control over a foreign investor. While some Member States following the principle of competitive neutrality determine the existence of control and/or material influence using traditional corporate indicators such as shareholdings and managerial appointments, others refer to a broader concept of "links" between foreign investors and governments. As a result, the consideration of potential risks stemming from state ownership/

---

[39] Rules on special powers on corporate assets in the defense and national security sectors, as well as for activities of strategic importance in the energy, transport and communications sectors, Decree law 15 March 2012, nr. 21, Articles 1(3) and 1(3bis).

[40] Decree-Law No. 138/2014 of 15 September, Article 3(3).

[41] Act of 19 October 1998 Laying Down Rules for Telecommunications, Article 14a.4.

[42] Law on Protection of Objects Important to Ensuring National Security of the Republic of Lithuania, No. IX-1132, Article 11.

[43] Annex of Resolution on the Rules of Procedure of the Commission for Coordination of Protection of Objects of Importance to Ensuring National Security Approved by the Government, No. 1540, para 1.9.

control will depend on the ability of the screening authorities to determine the existence of such ownership/control and/or material influence by a foreign state.

## 5 The Issue of State Control: From Merger Control to Investment Screening

As shown by the above review of national FDI screening practices, the concept of a state-owned, state-controlled or state-linked foreign investor under FDI screening rules remains to be clarified. Nevertheless, legislators and investment screening authorities could draw some inspiration from merger control regimes, which have been dealing with this concept both from procedural and substantive assessment perspectives (Svetlicinii 2019). As merger control seeks to ascertain the likely changes in competitive conditions in the relevant markets affected by the notified mergers/acquisitions, it becomes necessary to clarify whether the merging entities are independent from each other or belong to the same economic group and therefore can behave in a coordinated manner. For instance, EU merger control rules provide that if two merging SOEs "were formerly part of different economic units having an independent power of decision, the operation will be deemed to constitute a concentration and not an internal restructuring".[44] Normally, companies with the same controlling shareholder, which could be a state-owned holding company or a public institution, are viewed as members of the same "single economic unit", and this presumption could be rebutted if the companies have sufficient autonomy in their decision-making. In a number of cases, the Commission concluded that two SOEs with independent decision power that did not coordinate their economic activities in the past should be viewed as autonomous economic entities for the purpose of merger assessment.[45]

Apart from ascertaining the links between the SOEs and the controlling State for procedural reasons, the Commission has also estimated the likelihood of coordination among the SOEs. For example, in the *Rosneft/TNK-BP* case, the Commission considered a possibility that all Russian SOEs in the oil and gas sector would act as a "single economic unit".[46] In the *China National Bluestar/Elkem* case, the Commission attempted to ascertain "the possible power of the State to influence the companies' commercial strategy and the likelihood for the State to actually coordinate their

[44] Commission Consolidated Jurisdictional Notice under Council Regulation (EC) No 139/2004 on the control of concentrations between undertakings [2008] OJ C 095/01, para 52.

[45] See Case IV/M.511 *Texaco/Norsk Hydro*, Commission decision of 9 January 1995; Case IV/M.216 *CEA Industrie/France Telecom/Finmeccanica/SGS-Thomson*, Commission decision of 22 February 1993; Case IV/M.931 *Neste/IVO*, Commission decision of 2 June 1998; Case COMP/M.5549 *EDF/Segebel*, Commission decision of 12 November 2009.

[46] See Case COMP/M.6801 *Rosneft/TNK-BP*, Commission decision of 8 March 2013, para 9.

commercial conduct, either by imposing or facilitating such coordination".[47] Since at that time the Chinese SOEs accounted only for a small share of the relevant market (10–20%), the Commission has not reached any definitive conclusions on the SOEs' decision-making.

When analyzing the exercise of the shareholder's rights and corporate appointments, the Commission noted that the Chinese State's "influence may be exercised through formal channels such as the SASAC [State-owned Assets Supervision and Administration Commission of the State Council] but also in less formal ways".[48] Without ascertaining the existence of these channels of influence, the Commission on several occasions applied a "worst case scenario" approach by regarding all Chinese SOEs active on the relevant markets as parts of a "single economic unit".[49] Some commentators characterized this approach as "a well-defined practice in reviewing concentrations in which Chinese SOEs are involved" (Fountoukakos and Puech-Baron 2012) while others urged the Commission not to deviate from its previous practice and focus the determination of the "single economic unit" not on *de jure* powers of the State to exercise control over its SOEs but on *de facto* exercise of this control (Zhang 2017, p. 172).

The Commission has moved away from the "worst case scenario" assumption in the *EDF/CGN/NNB* case where China General Nuclear Power Corporation (CGN) sought to acquire joint control together with Électricité de France S.A. over three nuclear power plants in the UK.[50] The Commission's assessment arrived at the conclusion that the Chinese State, through the SASAC and the China Nuclear Industry Alliance, can effectively impose or facilitate the coordination of SOEs in the energy industry.[51] As a result, the Commission held that all Chinese SOEs in the energy sector should be regarded as members of a single economic group for EU merger control purposes. This allowed the Commission to aggregate the turnovers of CGN and other Chinese SOEs active in the energy sector, which have cumulatively reached the requisite notification thresholds and brought the transaction within the Commission's jurisdiction under the EU Merger Regulation. Although the Commission's conclusion did not prevent the clearance of the notified acquisition, it has set a precedent for the assessment of the state control over SOEs, which is particularly relevant for China, which granted the exercise of the state shareholder rights in all major SOEs to the single institution—the SASAC.

Before making any conclusions as to the applicability of the EU merger control standards to the screening of SOE-related FDI, one should make two important

---

[47] Case COMP/M.6082 *China National Bluestar/Elkem*, Commission decision of 31 March 2011, para 10.

[48] Case COMP/M.6113 *DSM/Sinochem/JV*, Commission decision of 19 May 2011, para 15.

[49] See, e.g., Case COMP/M.6141 *CNAC/Koor Industries/Makhteshim Agan Industries*, Commission decision of 3 October 2011; Case COMP/M.7643 *CNRC/Pirelli*, Commission decision of 1 July 2015.

[50] Case COMP/M.7850 *EDF/CGN/NNB Group of Companies*, Commission decision of 10 March 2016.

[51] Above Commission decision COMP/M.7850, para 49.

caveats that distinguish the two regulatory regimes. First, the EU Merger Regulation strictly adheres to the principle of ownership-neutrality embedded in Article 345 TFEU and stipulates that "arrangements to be introduced for the control of concentrations should…respect the principle of non-discrimination between the public and private sectors".[52] The EU Competition Commissioner Margrethe Vestager further emphasized that the Commission "must be impartial; it must be blind to the nationality of the companies we investigate; and it must be impeccable – if only because practically every decision we take must pass the muster of the European Court" (Vestager 2015).

Second, in ascertaining the likely behavior of the SOEs within its merger control assessment, the Commission primarily relies on economic factors encouraging or discouraging possible (anti)competitive behavior. For example, in a merger case involving China National Agrochemical Corporation, the Commission ruled out the likelihood of predatory practices to be adopted by the Chinese SOEs due to the current competitive conditions of the relevant markets: for predatory pricing to work, the merged entity would need to have enough market power so that it can reasonably expect to be able to raise prices once it has driven its rivals out of the market".[53]

The above two caveats do not apply to FDI screening based on security considerations that allow distinguishing foreign investors carrying certain security risks, while security risk assessment clearly goes beyond the mere profitability or economic rationale of the alleged conduct. Nevertheless, the merger control experience is instructive, as it demonstrates the difficulties in ascertaining the existence and/or exercise of state control, a factor that will certainly have to be considered in the context of FDI screening of SOE-related transactions (Du 2021).[54] Specifically, the EU merger control practice in relation to Chinese SOE-led mergers and acquisitions encountered numerous instances where state control/influence is exercised outside traditional corporate channels such as shareholder rights and managerial appointments. Therefore, for the "SOE factor" to be properly considered in the FDI screening process, as required by some national FDI screening regimes, the screening authorities would have to undertake a thorough investigation that would need to go beyond the review of the foreign investor's corporate structures. As a result, by ascertaining the "links" between the foreign investor and a foreign state, FDI screening would go beyond the mere establishment of foreign state ownership, which further reduces the meaning of the "SOE factor".

Foreign state ownership becomes even less pronounced in the context of investment control aimed at the identification and prevention of the "weaponized investments" defined by Carrai as "commercial investments aimed at acquiring a recipient

---

[52] Council Regulation (EC) No. 139/2004 of 20 January 2004 on the control of concentrations between undertakings [2004] OJ L24/01, recital 22.

[53] Case No. COMP/M.6141 *CNAC/Koor Industries/Makhteshim Agan Industries*, Commission decision of 3 October 2011.

[54] The difficulty of distinguishing between the state-led (exercise of governmental authority) and commercial conduct of the SOEs was also highlighted in the context of the investor-state dispute settlement.

country's technology, sensitive information, or other protected interests for the sake of strengthening the investor country's national security vis-a-vis the recipient one's" (Carrai 2020, p. 354). Such "weaponization" could be carried out although a variety of means including "intelligence services, academic collaboration, coordinated investments, joint ventures, mergers and acquisitions, talent recruitment programs, science and technology investments, and research partnerships" (Carrai 2020, p. 358). We shall address the screening of potentially "weaponized investments" and its implications for the SOEs using China's policy on combining civil and military development as a case study.

## 6 State Ownership in the Context of China's Military-Civilian Fusion Strategy

On 29 August 2014, the Political Bureau of the Communist Party of China (CPC) conducted a collective study on new trends in global military development and the promotion of military innovation. On that occasion, the CPC's general secretary Xi Jinping observed the increasing role of technological innovation in the maintenance of the effective military and articulated the need to reform the current approach towards military innovation, which should increasingly rely on the independent innovation generated by the private sector (Xinhua 2014). In 2015, at the meeting with the People's Liberation Army (PLA) delegation to the Third Session of the Twelfth National People's Congress, Xi Jinping called for further deepening of military-civilian integration, which should move from the "initial integration" to the "deeper integration" phase where military innovation would evolve in a state-led, demand-driven and market-oriented manner (People's Daily Online 2015).

In 2017, the Ministry of Science and Technology released the 13th Five-Year Special Plan for Science and Technology Military-Civil Fusion Development.[55] The plan provides, among others, for the sharing of military and civilian science and technology infrastructure, such as laboratories, testing facilities, large scientific installations, and scientific equipment centers. It offers support to research institutes, colleges, and universities in establishing science and technology transformation institutions for dual use technologies (Lafferty 2019, pp. 648–650). The provincial and municipal governments have moved to take advantage of the central government's support for military-civil fusion and formulated their own plans, pilot projects and initiatives.[56]

[55] Ministry of Science and Technology, Central Military Commission Science and Technology Commission, 13th Five-Year Special Plan for Science and Technology Military-Civil Fusion Development [2017] No. 85.

[56] For example, the city of Xianning in Hubei province included the development of the new energy vehicles, firefighting and rescue services, traditional Chinese medicine and military-use drugs, beverages and health products. Xianning Bureau of Economy and Information Technology

Similarly, the State Council's Opinions on promoting military-civilian integration call for integration of the civilian industrial base into the military supply chains whereby the non-defense companies are encouraged to supply directly to the PLA.[57] As a result, numerous actors, including state-owned defence contractors, PLA-supervised academic research institutes (including universities and think tanks), private investment funds and private dual-use manufacturers, are participating in different processes and carrying out different functions (Can and Vieira 2022). The two distinctive groups (Joske 2019) of defence-related universities have emerged: "Seven Sons of National Defence"[58] and the "Seven Sons of the Arms Industry".[59] Examples of industry-military collaborations in research and development include Alibaba and Norinco Group (SOE), which collaborated on the BeiDou navigation satellite system, and Baidu and China Electronics Technology Group (SOE), which established a joint lab for intelligent command and control technologies (Fritz 2021).

It was noted that this deeper integration of military and civilian innovation and production processes "inevitably necessitates the redirection of foreign technologies to support the modernization of the PLA" (Bitzinger 2021, p. 21). The acquisition of much needed foreign technologies became increasingly the task of the private sector since "civilian companies and other bodies have better access than their military peers to foreign sensitive, dual-use technologies" (Evron 2021, p. 35) and "the relatively easy access of China's civilian organizations and professionals to advanced dual-use foreign expertise provides them a certain advantage over their military peers" (Evron 2021, pp. 40–41). Therefore, some of the outward investments by Chinese companies could be motivated by the implementation of military-civilian integration objectives. While the National Security Law,[60] the Cybersecurity Law,[61] and the National Intelligence Law[62] refer to the whole society's participation in the protection of national security, "none of these laws creates the necessary

(2021) Xianning City Action Plan for In-Depth Development of Military-Civil Fusion (2021–2025) (Revised Draft). https://perma.cc/3KWG-VCVC.

[57] General Office of the State Council, Opinions of the General Office of the State Council on Promoting Closer Civil-Military Integration in the National Defense Science and Technology Industry, [2017] No. 91.

[58] Beijing Institute of Technology, Beihang University, Harbin Engineering University, Harbin Institute of Technology, Nanjing University of Aeronautics and Astronautics, Nanjing University of Science and Technology, Northwestern Polytechnical University.

[59] Beijing Institute of Technology, Changchun University of Science and Technology, Chongqing University of Technology, Nanjing University of Science and Technology, North University of China, Shenyang Ligong University, Xi'an Technological University.

[60] Standing Committee of the National People's Congress, National Security Law of the People's Republic of China [2015] order No. 29 of the President of the People's Republic of China.

[61] Standing Committee of the National People's Congress, Cybersecurity Law of the People's Republic of China [2016] order No. 53 of the President of the People's Republic of China.

[62] Standing Committee of the National People's Congress, National Intelligence Law of the People's Republic of China (2018 Amendment) [2017] order No. 6 of the President of the People's Republic of China.

groundwork for a regime of compulsory participation in MCF [military-civilian fusion] or compelled technology transfer" (Kania and Laskai 2021).

As a result, the implementation of China's MCF strategy would require a case-by-case assessment in the context of foreign investment control because there is no general obligation for SOEs or private companies to participate in specific industry-military projects. While diverging motivations may be present in individual cases, it would be important to ascertain how a particular company would balance between its own business objectives and possible non-business objectives pursued by the government (Cuervo-Cazurra et al. 2022). Naturally, both business and non-business objectives may be complimentary, as governmental policies and support could also be conducive to the attainment of economic objectives and profit targets (Li et al. 2022). For example, a study in high-tech and automobile manufacturing in China demonstrated that while the government provided significant subsidies to stimulate innovation in the respective sectors, internationalization through FDI has helped SOEs achieve a better effect in terms of innovation (Xie et al. 2022). The personal economic interests and incentives of the managers and other corporate officers should also be considered in terms of their influence on individual FDI-related decisions. A recent study on the effects of China's anti-corruption campaign on SOEs' investment practices suggested that the observed reduction in outward FDI is due to the reduced personal benefits available to managers and increased risks associated with FDI-related decisions (Qi et al. 2022).

As demonstrated by the overview of China's MCF strategy, the realization of government-set policy objectives is expected not only from SOEs but also from the private sector, particularly in relation to Sino-foreign cooperation and the acquisition of foreign technologies. In that regard, ascertaining the state ownership of a foreign investor in the context of FDI screening would not be sufficient for identifying potentially "weaponized investments". The focus on critical or dual use technologies in this context further diminishes the significance of the "SOE factor" in FDI screening.

## 7 Conclusion

As demonstrated in the above account of the drafting and adoption of the EU FDI Screening Regulation, SOEs have featured prominently in the calls for a more comprehensive EU foreign investment control system. Strongly advocated by multiple stakeholders, the "SOE factor" has been embedded in the screening standards of the EU FDI Screening Regulation and replicated in the national FDI screening regimes of individual Member States. At the same time, the broad wording of the screening standards and the confidentiality considerations related to the individual screening cases do not allow ascertaining how the "SOE factor" is being considered by the screening authorities.

In regard to the available enforcement data released by the Commission, contrary to the initial expectations generated by the public discourse, SOEs do not appear to be the primary targets of FDI screening in the EU. According to the Commission's first annual report on the enforcement of the EU FDI Screening Regulation, from 11 October 2020 to 30 June 2021, a total of 265 notifications were submitted by 11 Member States under Article 6 EU FDI Screening Regulation (more than 90% originated from Austria, France, Germany, Italy, and Spain).[63] The average public shareholding was a mere 4% for merger and acquisitions deals and greenfield investments, "so looking only at actual control would leave out a significant number of cases".[64] Interestingly, the largest number of foreign investors with public shareholdings (45% of cases) originated from the US, where the average stakes were below 1%.[65] The Commission noted: "The data on State influence depends on the reconstruction of ownership links among subsidiaries, sometimes very difficult for Chinese companies. Those companies often use offshore subsidiaries to enter EU, with little or no information on the links with Mainland China, or have complex nested structures…"[66] The situation remained largely the same when the Commission released its second annual FDI screening report covering the period 11 October 2020 to 30 June 2021. The average public shareholding in the notified FDI transactions was 3%, with the largest number of cases (47%) coming from the US, where the average stake was below 1%.[67] When discussing Russian investments in the EU, which involved more than 30,000 companies, the Commission noted that in 57.7% of cases, the control of influence was exercised by a natural person, while the Russian government held direct stakes only in 1.1% of the cases.[68] The above enforcement statistics indicate that thus far, SOEs appear as foreign investors only in a small number of transactions undergoing screening by Member States under the EU FDI Screening Regulation.

Furthermore, as shown by the EU merger control experience, the screening authorities may encounter substantial hurdles in appreciating whether and how foreign state control is actually exercised over the respective SOEs. Unlike the EU Merger Regulation, which demands from the Commission an ownership-neutral and economic evidence-backed assessment of the SOEs' likely market conduct, the EU

[63] See European Commission, First Annual Report on the screening of foreign direct investments into the Union [2021] COM(2021) 714 final (hereinafter First Annual Report on the Screening of FDI into the Union), p. 11.

[64] European Commission, Commission Staff Working Document Screening of FDI into the Union and its Member States accompanying the document First Annual Report on the screening of foreign direct investments into the Union [2021] SWD(2021) 334 final (hereinafter Staff Working Document Screening of FDI into the Union and its Member States 2021), p. 17.

[65] First Annual Report on the Screening of FDI into the Union, p. 14.

[66] Staff Working Document Screening of FDI into the Union and its Member States 2021, p. 18.

[67] See European Commission, Commission Staff Working Document Screening of FDI into the Union and its Member States accompanying the document Second Annual Report on the screening of foreign direct investments into the Union [2022] SWD(2022) 219 final (Commission Staff Working Document Screening of FDI into the Union and its Member States 2022), p. 14.

[68] See Commission Staff Working Document Screening of FDI into the Union and its Member States 2022, p. 16.

FDI Screening Regulation provides for a much lighter burden of proof that the screening authorities will be expected to satisfy. Indeed, while determining whether a given FDI is "likely to affect security or public order", Member States could resort to broad presumptions in relation to foreign SOEs that can potentially engage in "weaponized investments". At the same time, it was argued that investment control pursuing competitive neutrality objectives should be ownership-neutral, as both SOEs and private companies may benefit from the financial support of the host state and the exclusive focus on SOEs would be discriminatory and unjustified (Baumann 2022). Moreover, as demonstrated by the example of China's military-civilian fusion strategy, the distinction between state-owned and private investors that can be voluntarily engaged in the realization of government-set objectives may be less relevant for FDI screening purposes.

The above considerations suggest that the focus on the "SOE factor" would present practical difficulties for the screening authorities in ascertaining the existence and exercise of the state ownership/control/influence over foreign investors. Even if the executive discretion and lighter burden of proof in relation to the security risks would allow blocking or conditioning foreign SOE-led investments, the "SOE factor" will not be sufficient for identifying the potentially "weaponized investments". As a result, instead of concentrating on the ownership of foreign investors, the screening authorities should focus on the development of an asset-focused assessment, which would aim at protecting critical technologies and dual use items from unwanted acquisitions.

## References


Balázs E (2022a) International public procurement instrument: securing fairness for EU firms. News | European Parliament. https://www.europarl.europa.eu/news/en/press-room/20220603IPR32143/international-public-procurement-instrument-securing-fairness-for-eu-firms

Balázs E (2022b) MEPs back new trade instrument to protect the EU from economic blackmail. News | European Parliament. https://www.europarl.europa.eu/news/en/press-room/20221010IPR42635/meps-back-new-trade-instrument-to-protect-the-eu-from-economic-blackmail

Baumann P (2022) How host country governments can ensure competitive neutrality in cross-border M&As. Columbia FDI Perspect 336:1–3

Berendsen T (2021) Chinese investment in European strategic infrastructures | Question for written answer E-001464/2021 to the Commission. Parliamentary question | European Parliament. https://www.europarl.europa.eu/doceo/document/E-9-2021-001464_EN.html

Bismuth R (2020) Reading between the lines of the EU regulation establishing a framework for screening FDI into the Union. In: Bourgeois J (ed) EU Framework for Foreign Direct Investment Control. Kluwer Law International, pp 103–114

Bitzinger R (2021) China's shift from civil-military integration to military-civil fusion. Asia Policy 16:5–24

Can M, Vieira A (2022) The Chinese military-civil fusion strategy: a state action theory perspective. Int Spectator 57:85–102. https://doi.org/10.1080/03932729.2022.2080262

Carrai MA (2020) The rise of screening mechanisms in the global north: weaponizing the law against China's weaponized investments? Chin J Comp Law 8:351–383

Chan ZT, Meunier S (2022) Behind the screen: understanding national support for a foreign investment screening mechanism in the European Union. Rev Int Organ 17:513–541. https://doi.org/10.1007/s11558-021-09436-y

Cuervo-Cazurra A (2018) Host country concerns and policies toward state-owned MNEs. Columbia FDI Perspect 237:1–3

Cuervo-Cazurra A, Grosman A, Megginson WL (2022) A review of the internationalization of state-owned firms and sovereign wealth funds: governments' nonbusiness objectives and discreet power. J Int Bus Stud:1–29. https://doi.org/10.1057/s41267-022-00522-w

de Kok J (2021) Investment screening in the Netherlands. Leg Issues Econ Integr 48:43–46

Deutsche Welle (2018) Chinese takeover of Leifeld collapses. dw.com. https://www.dw.com/en/chinese-takeover-of-leifeld-collapses-ahead-of-expected-german-veto/a-44906055

Dombrovskis V (2021) Answer given by Executive Vice-President Dombrovskis on behalf of the European Commission. Parliamentary Question-E-001464/21. https://www.europarl.europa.eu/doceo/document/E-9-2021-001464-ASW_EN.html

Du M (2021) The status of Chinese state-owned enterprises in international investment arbitration: much ado about nothing? Chin J Int Law 20:785–815. https://doi.org/10.2139/ssrn.4003603

Enderwick P (2017) International investment by state-controlled enterprises: a source for concern? Strateg Change 26:261–271

Esplugues Mota C (2018) A more targeted approach to foreign direct investment: the establishment of screening systems on national security grounds. Revista de Direito Internacional 15:439–466

European Commission (2021) Frequently asked questions on Regulation (EU) 2019/452 establishing a framework for the screening of foreign direct investments into the Union. https://trade.ec.europa.eu/doclib/docs/2019/june/tradoc_157945.pdf

European Commission (2022) List of screening mechanisms notified by Member States. CIRCABC Library. https://trade.ec.europa.eu/doclib/docs/2019/june/tradoc_157946.pdf

European Committee of the Regions (2018) Opinion trade package. https://cor.europa.eu/EN/our-work/Pages/OpinionTimeline.aspx?opId=CDR-5423-2017

Evron Y (2021) China's military-civil fusion and military procurement. Asia Policy 16:25–44

Fountoukakos K, Puech-Baron C (2012) The EU merger regulation and transactions involving states or state-owned enterprises: applying rules designed for the EU to the People's Republic of China. Concurrences Rev 1:44–54

Fritz A (2021) At the nexus of military-civil fusion and technological innovation in China. The Diplomat. https://thediplomat.com/2021/07/at-the-nexus-of-military-civil-fusion-and-technological-innovation-in-china/

General Secretariat of the Council (2018) European Council meeting (28 June 2018) – conclusions. European Council. https://www.consilium.europa.eu/media/35936/28-euco-final-conclusions-en.pdf

Ginevri AS (2020) The Italian foreign direct investments screening in times of COVID-19: trends and perspectives. Law Econ Yearly Rev 9:122–132

Harper S (2012) Statement by the Prime Minister of Canada on foreign investment. Government of Canada. https://www.canada.ca/en/news/archive/2012/12/statement-prime-minister-canada-foreign-investment.html

Hooijmaaijers B (2019) Blackening skies for Chinese investment in the EU? J Chin Polit Sci 24: 451–470. https://doi.org/10.1007/s11366-019-09611-4

Joske A (2019) The China Defence Universities Tracker: exploring the military and security links of China's universities. Australia Strategic Policy Institute. http://www.aspi.org.au/report/china-defence-universities-tracker

Kania EB, Laskai L (2021) Myths and realities of China's military-civil fusion strategy. Center for a New American Security. https://www.cnas.org/publications/reports/myths-and-realities-of-chinas-military-civil-fusion-strategy

Karas O (2021) Planned acquisitions of EU semiconductor firms | E-002984/2021. Parliamentary Question-E-002984/2021. https://www.europarl.europa.eu/doceo/document/E-9-2021-002984_EN.html

Lafferty B (2019) Civil-military integrations and PLA reforms. In: Saunders P, Ding A, Scobell A, Yang A, Wuthnow J (eds) Chairman Xi remakes the PLA: assessing Chinese military reforms: National Defense University, pp 627–660

Li J, Xia J (2017) State-owned enterprises face challenges in foreign acquisitions. Columbia FDI Perspect 205:1–3

Li X, Bo L, Shen D, Soobaroyen T (2022) Bridging 'Home' political and economic rationalities with 'Host' demands and constraints: the case of regional Chinese state-owned multinational corporations. Br J Manag n/a:1–20. https://doi.org/10.1111/1467-8551.12605

Martin-Prat M (2020) The European Commission proposal on FDI screening. In: EU Framework for Foreign Direct Investment Control. Kluwer Law International BV, pp 95–98

OECD (2015) OECD guidelines on corporate governance of state-owned enterprises. https://www.oecd-ilibrary.org/governance/oecd-guidelines-on-corporate-governance-of-state-owned-enterprises-2015_9789264244160-en

People's Daily Online (2015) Xi Jinping: deeply implement the military-civilian integration development strategy and strive to strengthen and rejuvenate the army. http://opinion.people.com.cn/n/2015/0313/c1003-26686400.html

Qi Z, Kenderdine T, Tang T, Liu Q (2022) China's anti-corruption campaign and outward foreign direct investment by state-owned enterprises. World Econ 45:2950–2976. https://doi.org/10.1111/twec.13244

Svetlicinii A (2019) The interactions of competition law and investment law: the case of Chinese state-owned enterprises and EU merger control regime. In: Chaisse J, Choukroune L, Jusoh S (eds) Handbook of international investment law and policy. Springer, pp 1–21

Svetlicinii A (2021) Economic nationalism during COVID-19: is the EU merger control ready? Eur Competition Law Rev 42:69–74

U.S. Department of the Treasury (2016) Statement on the President's decision regarding the U.S. Business of Aixtron SE. https://home.treasury.gov/news/press-releases/jl0679

Velten J (2020) FDI Screening Regulation and the recent EU guidance: what options do member states have? Columbia FDI Perspect 284:1–3

Vestager M (2015) The future of competition. Competition speeches archive (1995–2020). https://competition-policy.ec.europa.eu/index/news/competition-speeches-archive-1995-2020-2020-01-01_en

Vestager M (2021) Answer given by Executive Vice-President Vestager on behalf of the European Commission. Parliamentary question | Answer for question E-002984/21 | E-002984/2021 (ASW). https://www.europarl.europa.eu/doceo/document/E-9-2021-002984-ASW_EN.html

Warchol J (2021) The birth of the EU Screening Regulation. YSEC yearbook of socio-economic constitutions 2020: a common European law on investment screening (CELIS) 53–75

Weber C, Saifi IW, Cicu P, Quisthoudt-Rowohl R, Schwab S (2017) Proposal for a Union act submitted under Rule 46(2) of the rules of procedure on the screening of foreign investment in strategic sectors. European Parliament. https://www.politico.eu/wp-content/uploads/2017/03/2017-03-20-Draft-Union-Act-on-Foreign-Investment.pdf

Wehrlé F, Pohl J (2016) Investment policies related to national security. OECD Publishing. https://www.oecd-ilibrary.org/content/paper/5jlwrrf038nx-en. Accessed 12 Jan 2023

Xie Y, Boadu F, Tang H (2022) Does internationalization encourage state-owned enterprises to utilize subsidies to innovate? Evidence from high-tech and automobile manufacturing industries of Chinese listed companies. Chin Manag Stud 16:803–829

Xinhua (2014) Xi Jinping: accurately grasp the new trend of world military development keeping pace with the times and vigorously promoting military innovation. http://www.xinhuanet.com//politics/2014-08/30/c_1112294869.htm

Zhang AH (2017) The antitrust paradox of China Inc. N Y Univ J Int Law Polit 50

Zypries B, Sapin M, Calenda C (2017) European investment policy: a common approach to investment control. https://www.politico.eu/wp-content/uploads/2017/08/170728_Investment-screening_non-paper.pdf

# Protection or Protectionism? Assessing the EU's New Investment Screening Measures Against State-Driven Foreign Investment Risks

**Naoise McDonagh**

**Contents**



**Abstract** Foreign direct investment (FDI) can be used by sovereign states for strategic goals, including as a mechanism for exploitation, technology transfers, espionage, and political influence. The EU's recently adopted foreign investment screening regulation (the Regulation) is a response to fears that state-led investment could strategically exploit the openness of the common market. The Regulation applies the concepts of '*security*' and '*public order*' as guidance to Member States restricting FDI. However, these concepts have no clear definition, raising concerns they may be abused for protectionist purposes. This article aims to contribute to the debate on whether these screening concepts are a reasonable response to state-based investment threats. It does so by taking a 'threats-based' approach to identifying relevant FDI risks for Member States' economic and national security. China, the world's second largest and heavily state-capitalist economy, is considered a key justification and yardstick for the EU's new investment screening measures. Hence, identifying risks relating to Chinese FDI is a good starting point for assessing the Regulation. Drawing on institutional analysis of China's economy, this article identifies unique threats arising from the country's *rule-by-law* socialist system of governance, where traditional public–private distinctions are heavily blurred, if not

N. McDonagh (✉)
School of Business and Law, Edith Cowan University, Perth, WA, Australia
e-mail: n.mcdonagh@ecu.edu.au



J. Hillebrand Pohl et al. (eds.), *Weaponising Investments*,
Springer Studies in Law & Geoeconomics (2023) 1: 59–78,
https://doi.org/10.1007/17280_2023_4, Published online: 16 June 2023

obliterated. The nature of those risks suggests that the undefined concepts of 'security' and 'public order' are reasonable to achieve the goals of the Regulation. Furthermore, a threats-based approach to screening Chinese FDI leans towards a presumption of risk for sensitive sectors, for both SOEs and nominally private firms, due to deep institutional public–private linkages.

## 1 Introduction

In September 2017 the European Commission proposed a Regulation[1] on establishing a common framework for the screening of foreign direct investment (FDI)[2] (hereafter the Regulation). The proposal was originally viewed with scepticism by some European Union (EU) Member States, with Finland describing it as 'unsuitable', while other Member States also voiced reservations.[3] These included concerns around restricting inbound FDI, which is valued for its role in boosting economic growth. The EU has long held a policy of principled economic openness,[4] which holds that unrestricted flows of capital 'can be directed to the places where it can be used most efficiently...contributing to an efficient squaring of demand and supply of capital within the community'.[5] This is expressed in the EU's legal prescription against any restrictions on the free movement of capital between Member States and between Member States and third countries, as outlined in the Treaty on the Functioning of the European Union (TFEU) (see Article 63). Principled openness is further reflected in Member State practice, as captured by data in the OECD's FDI Regulatory Restrictiveness Index (FDI RRI). This highlights that EU countries rank among the most open in the world.[6] Given this longstanding preference for minimal restrictions on FDI, the initial 2017 proposal of the Regulation was suggestive of a radical shift in thinking underway across the block. Furthermore, despite some initial reservations, the Regulation was adopted relatively quickly by March 2019,[7] coming into effect on 11 October 2020. What has driven this significant change in EU thinking around FDI?

---

[1]European Commission, Proposal for a Regulation of the European Parliament and of the Council establishing a framework for screening of foreign direct investments into the European Union COM (2017) 487 final, 13 September 2017.

[2]Graham and Krugman (1995), p. 8, define FDI as involving the 'ownership of assets in one country by residents of another for purposes of controlling the use of those assets'. Cf. Article 2(1) of the Regulation.

[3]Zwartkruis and de Jong (2020), p. 448.

[4]Grieger (2021); Nettesheim (2020), p. 498.

[5]Hindelang (2009), p. 19.

[6]OECD FDI Regulatory Restrictive Index, https://goingdigital.oecd.org/en/indicator/74.

[7]Regulation (EU) 2019/452 establishing a framework for screening of foreign direct investments into the Union [2019] OJ L 79 I/1.

Two points are noteworthy. First, there has been a long-running concern that countries investing in the EU could exploit its general market openness, and gaps in individual screening regimes across Member States, for achieving strategic goals such as illicit technology transfers. Economic exploitation of the EU's liberalized common market has long been possible through non-reciprocal investment access available to third countries sending EU-bound FDI.[8] Strategic vulnerabilities of FDI ranging from IP theft to political influence[9] are particularly contentious in a geopolitically tense world where FDI is no longer viewed as an unqualified good, but also as a tool for activities that have negative effects on national security.[10] The second major factor in the EU's changing perspective is the growing tensions between liberal democracies and authoritarian states, China being the most influential, on a broad array of issues relating to international order.[11] China is challenging liberal norms on human rights, the principle of rule of law, and competitive neutrality and represents a different model of state intervention in the economy. China is also an industrial powerhouse and technological leader in some spheres, such as 5G; while it extensive use of economic subsidies and weak environmental regulations combined with a low labour cost base means that developed countries are highly dependent on China for many critical goods, not least critical minerals vital to core twenty-first century technologies.[12]

Consequently, within EU Member States there is growing concern that authoritarian state-capitalist economies are exploiting the openness of the common market, while themselves engaging in selective and strategic forms of domestic liberalization that amount to a strategy of zero-sum economic gain.[13] The European Commission begin publicly alluding to this neo-mercantilist approach in a 2017 report that, while reaffirming the block's openness to FDI, reflected on the challenges of a changing investment landscape:

> [C]oncerns have recently been voiced about foreign investors, notably state-owned enterprises, taking over European companies with key technologies for strategic reasons. EU investors often do not enjoy the same rights to invest in the country from which the investment originates. These concerns need careful analysis and appropriate action.[14]

China's highly restricted variety of 'state-permeated' socialist market economy[15] is a core concern for the EU in this regard. Beijing's increasing willingness to use

---

[8] Meunier (2014).

[9] Meunier (2014), p. 1001.

[10] Lai (2021), p. 4; Moran (2017).

[11] Johnston (2019), McDonagh (2022), Weinhardt and ten Brink (2020) and Weiss and Wallace (2021).

[12] Leruth et al. (2022).

[13] Grieger (2021); Zwartkruis and de Jong (2020), p. 449.

[14] European Commission, Reflection Paper on Harnessing Globalization, COM (2017) 240, 10 May 2017, p. 15.

[15] Nölke et al. (2021) and Wu (2016).

economic relationships strategically and coercively to achieve political ends[16] poses new risks. Consequently, it is recognized in the literature that 'China serves as justification and yardstick for any investment screening measure'.[17] As a result, managing the economic relationship with Beijing in a manner that balances opportunities against growing risks is now paramount in Brussels. In establishing a common framework for investment screening, the Regulation is a central EU-wide policy aimed at achieving a better balance in terms of the risk side of the equation. As discussed further below, the Regulation applies the concepts of '*security*' and '*public order*' as guiding justifications for Member States seeking to restrict FDI that would otherwise be legally protected from such restriction. However, these concepts have no clear definition and have raised concerns that they may be abused for protectionist purposes. In particular, their definitional ambiguity has opened up a debate over how broad or narrow such concepts can, or ought to be, applied during screening assessments.[18] This debate reflects concerns within the EU Membership, with a broad split between countries such as Austria, Germany, France, and Italy seeking tighter screening and greater reciprocity, versus countries such as Netherlands, Finland, and Sweden who retain concerns about alienating FDI by way of excessively strict screening rules.[19]

The aim of this article is to contribute to the debate on how concepts with potentially very broad application should be applied in a context that does not permit hard and generalizable *ex-ante* rules. This can be usefully done by taking a 'threats-based' approach to identifying relevant risks for a given object to be 'secured';[20] in this case, EU Member States' economic and national security is to be secured from FDI-based threats. Since China is considered a key 'justification and yardstick' for new investment screening measures, identifying risks arising in connection to Chinese FDI is a good starting point. Drawing on institutional analysis of China's economic institutions, this article identifies unique threats arising from the country's rule-by-law socialist system of governance, where traditional public–private distinctions are heavily blurred if not obliterated. As argued below, the broad-based and non-transparent nature of those risks suggests that relatively undefined concepts such as *security* and *public order* are both reasonable and necessary to achieve the goals of the Regulation—protection of core economic national security interests. Lastly, the EU debate over FDI screening reflects a core political economy debate ongoing at the national level within liberal democracies, many of which are struggling to reconcile a liberal economic world view with the new geoeconomic world of

[16] Chen and Garcia (2016), McDonagh (2022) and Vekasi (2019).

[17] Wernicke (2020), p. 30.

[18] Nettesheim (2020) and Zwartkruis and de Jong (2020).

[19] See Simon (2020) for an overview of the EU's internal political economy of FDI screening; see National Board of Trade Sweden (2021) report 'An EU Trade Policy for Geopolitical Ends – clashing perspectives and policy recommendations' for a discussion of concerns about mixing economic and security goals in policy.

[20] See Collins (2016), p. 2.

power politics using economic means. In that context, this chapter holds insights not only for the EU debate over FDI risks from authoritarian state investment, but more broadly for all liberal democracies debating how to engage economically with China, while safe-guarding national security. Section 2 discusses the scope of the Regulation. Section 3 outlines the geoeconomic context in which the new EU FDI screening law was created. Section 4 discusses the unique risks posed by Chinese FDI. The final section offers a discussion and conclusion.

## 2 The Regulation, Its Scope, and What It Seeks to Protect Against

It is useful to begin this section by identifying what the EU's new FDI Regulation is not. It is not a mechanism authorising the European Commission to issue binding supra-national decisions on national FDI screening. Hence, it is not a version of the United States Committee on Foreign Investment in the United States Act (CFIUS) established in 1975,[21] which provides direct authority to CFIUS as well as to the American President to block FDI on national security grounds. Instead, EU Member States will remain final arbiters on FDI domestic market access. The operation of the Regulation, therefore, is somewhat different from direct screening authority in both form and function. Its function is to provide an EU-wide coordinating mechanism within a framework designed for collaboration, information sharing, and cooperation. Some examples of the legal form the Regulation adopts for ensuring the requisite degree of cooperation, will be helpful to illustrate its scope.

Information sharing is laid out in several Articles. Article 3 requires Member States to notify the Commission on existing or newly adopted screening mechanisms and provide updates on amendments within 30 days of entry into force. The Commission then aggregates and shares this information with other Member States. Article 5 addresses annual reporting requirements, including that Member States submit an annual report to the Commission on all FDI into their territory during the previous calendar year, and on all applications of national screening mechanisms. The Commission's role is again one of aggregation and information sharing, this time producing an annual Regulation report based on this information.[22]

Cooperative obligations include Article 6, which requires Member States that have applied FDI screening to notify the Commission and other Member States with specific information; the latter is laid out in Article 9(2) and relates to the nature of the FDI and the foreign investor involved. Article 6(1) encourages, but does not obligate, the notifying Member State to 'include a list of Member States whose

[21] CFIUS has been repeatedly updated legislatively and was notably broadened in scope and power by the Trump administration's 2018 Foreign Investment Risk Review Modernization Act (FIRRMA) in response to the economic-related security issues discussed in this article.

[22] The Commission released its first mandated annual report on FDI screening in November 2021.

security or public order is deemed likely to be affected' by the FDI under screening process. Article 6(2) in turn encourages Member States to provide comments to another Member State engaged in national FDI screening in cases where the FDI is considered to hold risks that may affect them. These comments must be simultaneously shared with the Commission, who in turn shares this with all Member States. Article 7 encourages Member States to communicate concerns relating to risks that may arise for them in relation to FDI occurring in other Member States, but which is not yet being screened. Again, comments must also be notified to the Commission, who shares the information with all Member States. The Commission can also issue opinions on all cases where comments and notifications are made in accordance with the Regulation's various articles.

The Regulation's framework should go a long way towards ensuring both the Commission and Member States have a far more integrated and up-to-date understanding of trans-European FDI activity and associated risks, thereby providing grounds for more robust cooperation as well as more coherent screening activities. The Regulation thereby goes some way towards overcoming the regulatory cacophony[23] that pre-existed the Regulation. However, while the overall framework is logical and largely uncontroversial,[24] the discussion now turns to the part of the Regulation that is controversial, that of Article 3(1), which states: 'In accordance with this Regulation, Member States may maintain, amend or adopt mechanisms to screen foreign direct investments in their territory on the grounds of *security* or *public order'* (emphasis added).

## 3 Security and Public Order: Bona Fide?

Article 2 of the Regulation contains a list of key terms and their definitions. However, one will not find detailed definitions of *security* or *public order*, despite these being critical concepts that determine the basis for the application of screening.[25] The lack of such detail accords with existing EU law on measures allowing capital movement restrictions in Article 65 TFEU. These cover a range of issues including tax and supervision of financial institutions, both for intra-EU capital flows and capital originating from third countries, as well as security issues.[26] On the latter, paragraph 1(b) of Article 65 TFEU allows Member States to 'take measures which are justified on grounds of public policy or public security'. Congruent with this

[23] On cacophony in pre-Regulation EU FDI governance see Meunier (2014).

[24] Wernicke (2020), p. 34.

[25] It is not the goal of this article to address how the Regulation relates to other EU legal texts, but for a discussion of consistency between the Regulation and existing European law, including CJEU interpretations of the Treaty on the Functioning of the European Union see Zwartkruis and de Jong (2020), pp. 455–457.

[26] See Chapter 4, Benyon (2010); Chapter VI, Hindelang (2009).

allowance is Article 52 TFEU, which states that measures prohibiting restrictions against freedom of establishment will not prejudice restrictions that can be justified on grounds of public policy, public security or public health. Instead of definitions and clear *ex ante* rules for application, Article 4 of the Regulation provides a non-exhaustive set of factors that '*may be taken into consideration by Member States or the Commission*' (Article 4). These include critical infrastructure, critical technologies and dual use items, supply of critical inputs, access to sensitive information and media pluralism and freedom (see Article 4(1)(a)-(e)).

According to Article 4, determining threats to public order and security should also consider the risk of criminal activity, the previous track record of an investor and 'whether the foreign investor is directly or indirectly controlled by the government. . .of a third country' (see Article 4(2)(a)-(c)). Since the criteria listed in the Article are non-exclusive, Member States have scope to add other factors they think are relevant. Additionally, the open-ended nature of these rules leaves room for interpretation, raising concerns that the Regulation could be used for purposes other than those originally intended. For example, critics such as Nettesheim accept that there are pressing issues arising from geopolitical competition that require new modes of investment screening. Nevertheless, he views the current legislation as insufficiently specified and thus prone to result in protectionism.[27] Wernicke similarly accepts the need for a revised and more coherent EU-wide FDI screening regime due to a changed geopolitical environment but is concerned that vaguely defined terms of security and public order may undermine 'transparency, predictability, and legal certainty'[28] that are critical to business investment.

These are reasonable concerns, but at this early stage in the life of the Regulation, open questions will necessarily remain. Nonetheless, some insight into whether a loosely defined security exception is likely to result in rampant protectionism can be garnered from both EU legal history, and the history of security exceptions in the General Agreement on Tariffs and Trade (GATT) multilateral agreement. Taking the EU first, both the TFEU and now the EU Screening Regulation allow Member States to apply restrictions on the right to free capital movement based on security, and other exceptions, with apparent leeway for Members to interpret the justifications for such derogation of a right. Yet, as the history of EU case law on exceptions concerning the four freedoms indicates, it is no simple task for a Member state to successfully justify a derogation, since these must pass muster in the European Court of Justice, a test often failed.[29] Barnard's study highlights that while the available derogations of EU law may seem to provide much scope for national regulatory autonomy, 'in practice the Court (ECJ) often says that, on the facts of a particular case, the Member State has failed to make out a justification'.[30] Even where a

[27] Nettesheim (2020), p. 483, p. 496.

[28] Wernicke (2020), p. 36.

[29] Barnard (2009) discusses the ECJ's authority to reject a justification of a derogation of EU law regarding the four freedoms, and lists numerous cases where such rejection is applied, including those involving capital.

[30] Ibid, p. 649.

justification may be possible, Barnard notes that the Court tends to further constrain state legal success with limitations grounded in concepts such as proportionality, fundamental rights, effective judicial protection and legal certainty. Aside from highlighting the steady shift of regulatory power away from Member States and towards the ECJ, it is also clear that the existence of exceptions to free movement of capital in no way opens the doors to runaway protectionism. In practice, there are existing checks within the EU to prevent such an outcome.

At the multilateral level, the history of GATT Article XXI indicates that security exceptions can be used sparingly and responsibly by actors who recognise the dangers of their unreasonable application. Article XXI came into force in 1947 and provides a broad interpretive framework for imposing national security restrictions on international trade. Article XXI states that '[n]othing in this Agreement shall be construed. . .(b) to prevent any contracting party from taking any action which it considers necessary for the protection of its essential security interests'. As Bhala notes, this is 'an all-embracing exception' where the invoking WTO Member has sole discretion to determine applicability.[31] Despite a lack of *ex ante* rules to guide its application, Article XXI has not become a protectionist blunderbuss and instead has been rarely used, and was rarely challenged when used, as GATT and WTO Members recognised the sensitivity of abusing a rule that overrides all others.[32] An example of concerns of protectionist misuse of Article XXI includes Sweden's 1975 invocation of the 'spirit' of the article to introduce a global import quota system for certain footwear, based on the premise low domestic production of said footwear undermined the nation's ability to provide for its defence forces during an international emergency.[33] Other signatories raised objections that this occurred at a time of high unemployment in Sweden, implying it was protectionist rather than security orientated. The issue became less salient after Sweden removed most of the items under restriction in 1977.[34] Voon notes that there has been a recent uptick in cases concerning Article XXI, such as Ukraine's case against Russian restrictions on traffic in transit from Ukraine to third countries via Russia.[35] The GATT's security exception has remained mostly unused, suggesting that there is no automatic link between a broad security exception and protectionism. This does not mean such a link cannot come into being, only that we need not assume it will. Although it should be noted that the GATT/WTO exception arguably has more potential for becoming an arbitrary protectionist tool. This is because contrary to the EU exceptions, where Member States' interpretation of a justification for placing restrictions on

[31] Bhala (1998), p. 267.

[32] Voon (2019).

[33] GATT 1947, Minutes of Meeting Held in the Palaise des Nations, Geneva, on 31 October 1975, GATT Doc. C/M/109, 9 (Nov. 10, 1975).

[34] GATT 1947, Sweden—Import Restrictions on Certain Footwear: Addendum, GATT Doc. L/4250/Add.1 (Mar. 15, 1977).

[35] Request for the Establishment of a Panel by Ukraine, Russia—Measures Concerning Traffic in Transit, WTO Doc. WT/DS512/3(Feb. 10, 2017).

fundamental rights must run the gauntlet of ECJ assessment and possible rejection, the GATT exception is considered wholly self-judging by a Member, which for the United States means the exception is 'non-justiciable'.[36] The WTO's role thereafter is only to recognize the application.

At this stage, it is worth considering why security exceptions are generally constructed in a broad manner that allows Member interpretation. This is largely a consequence of the combination of two facts. One, that a security issue can be existential for a state. Two, there are epistemological difficulties in defining security in the face of future uncertainty. Furthermore, 'security' as a concept is essentially contested, and one finds many definitions.[37] Collins points out that the concept of security presumes a referent object, in this case a WTO Member, and that 'despite the contested nature of security ... ultimately we are interested in how referent objects are threatened'.[38] Developing this idea, security scholars distinguish between risk-based and threat-based approaches to managing threats to referent objects.[39] Risk-based approaches rely on actuarial-style data modelling for probabilistic risk-management that may not require elimination of risks, but rather tolerating and embracing risk. Whereas threat-based approaches 'emphasize agency and intent between conflicting parties' and in cases such as national security is aimed towards elimination of identified risks.[40] The latter approach is more suitable for addressing inter-state geopolitical competition involving governments that act according to strategic goals, as well as various actors such as bureaucracies, state-owned enterprises and private firms that may be state agents, or at risk of state manipulation. Each of these actors have their own strategic goals, and the agency to act in favour of such goals. Dealing with actors and agency makes risk-assessment a far more dynamic calculation, that is not amenable in any certain sense to statistical modelling.

This does not imply a threats-based approach dealing with agents is arbitrary, since agents often signal their intent, for example through laws, discourse and actions,[41] and act within structural constraints, both social and physical. Therefore, a threat-based framework can be informed both by theory, and empirical evidence, to make informed, rational judgements about the degree and nature of threats to its given reference object, allowing for reasonably transparent application of an

[36] See Voon (2019), p. 47 for discussion of the United States' position on Russia—Measures Concerning Traffic in Transit, which states unambiguously that it is the Member's sole prerogative to determine applicability of Article XXI.

[37] Collins (2016) provides an overview on p. 3.

[38] Collins (2016), p. 2.

[39] Aradau et al. (2008), p. 148; Backman (2022), p. 6.

[40] Aradau et al. (2008), p. 148.

[41] See Economy (2018), Doshi (2021) for meticulous studies of China's intentions through detailed textual and discursive analysis of Xi Jinping's and other Chinese leaders speeches and reform agendas, followed by cross-referencing political discourse with actions designed to implement stated intentions. The latter includes institution-building, re-organization of power hierarchies, as well as the creation and enforcement of new laws.

otherwise loosely defined security exception. As a result, if we aim to better understand how security should be interpreted in the Regulation, a useful way to proceed is by using a threats-based approach to understand the nature of potential national security risks arising from FDI and, for this article's core concern, Chinese FDI in particular. Moreover, in discussing the Regulation, Zwartkruis and De Jong note that a focus on threats for interpreting a state's security needs is consistent with established European law.[42]

In that context, the remainder of this article will focus on contextualizing the geoeconomic environment in which FDI screening has become a crucial defensive tool for the EU and its Member States. This will be followed by identifying the unique security threats posed by FDI originating in China. Discussion of Chinese FDI risks will be grounded in a theoretical distinction between rule-of-law and rule-by-law economic governance systems, and then empirically grounded through analysis of China's recent legal evolution. The latter further dissolves an already tenuous legal distinction between the public and private domains of its economy.

## 4 The *Geoeconomic* Context for FDI Screening

The current international environment is marked by the increased exploitation of economic vulnerabilities arising from economic interdependencies, an outcome described as the *geoeconomic turn* in contemporary IPE.[43] Definitions of geoeconomics generally share the same following core idea, namely, that the concept refers to 'the application of economic means of power by states to realize strategic objectives'.[44] This type of action has long been described as economic statecraft. Yet while economic statecraft has existed for as long as have inter-state relations, the term 'geoeconomics' captures the use of such statecraft in the unique context of a hyper-Globalized twenty-first century world economy. It offers a conceptual foregrounding of the increasingly widespread use of economic statecraft in a highly inter-dependent global economy. Consequently, geoeconomics captures the fact that the modern globalized economy offers scope for states to leverage economic interdependencies for political and strategic ends that is historically unique. As a result, the lines between economics and security become blurred, radically transforming the international business environment. Norris terms the potential for security consequences arising out of economic interdependencies as *security externalities*.[45] Examples of such externalities include sensitive or dual use technology transfer, loss of strategic industries, industrial espionage, unfair competition through

---

[42] Zwartkruis and de Jong (2020), p. 450.

[43] Scholvin and Wigell (2018), see also Blackwill and Harris (2017) and Norris (2016).

[44] Scholvin and Wigell (2018), p. 74; Norris (2016), pp. 13–14.

[45] Norris (2016), p. 13.

subsidization, and dependencies arising from concentrated supply or demand of critical goods.

Additionally, states with large state-owned enterprises (SOEs) that are engaged in FDI activities will have a significant strategic advantage in an era of geoeconomic competition over countries that do not have such enterprises. Yet SOEs only account for a small portion of world trade and investment. Norris makes the important point that at the global level, most international business is carried out by commercial actors rather than government actors; thus, a potentially powerful policy tool for states seeking geoeconomic tools would be to create ways for influencing the behaviour of commercial actors to achieve strategic goals.[46] In principle, nations with strong rights protecting private property and individual rights will likely be precluded, or at least highly constrained from mobilising commercial actors for strategic state goals. Whereas states with authoritarian governance models will have opportunities and flexibility for such private sector mobilisation. Hence, while SOEs are an obvious risk for investment screening, effective screening must look beyond state-owned entities, to risks arising from *state-influenced private firms*. In returning to the question of how the concepts of security or public order should be applied in the Regulation, the answer very much depends on factors pertaining to the nature of the governance system in the country of origin (rule-of-law or authoritarian), its economic model (state-led or private-led market economy), and the willingness of a given state to use not only SOEs, but also private firms for geoeconomic activities.

Studies have already established that China is highly willing to engage in geoeconomic policy to achieve varied political and economic goals.[47] Examples include suddenly changing export quotas to withhold the delivery of rare earths to Japan when a territorial dispute over the Senkaku islands flared up in 2010; punishing Norway in 2010 by suspending trade talks and salmon imports as retribution for the privately run Norwegian Nobel committee awarding Chinese dissident Liu Xiaobao a Nobel peace prize; directing SOEs to stop buying Japanese goods over another Senkaku dispute flare-up in 2012, estimated to have cut 1% from Japan's 4th quarter growth that year;[48] banning group tourism to South Korea between 2017–2020 after American THAAD missiles were deployed on South Korea's territory; and most recently applying a mix of tariffs, countervailing duties and administrative bans on Australian wine, coal, barley and lobster since 2020, in response to growing political tensions between Canberra and Beijing. While China uses bilateral trade asymmetries for coercive means, FDI is a tool offering different geoeconomic opportunities for the Party, and in turn different risks for targeted economies.

FDI risks include illegal technology transfers, technology theft, espionage, and undesirable ownership of critical infrastructure, each of which can have negative

[46] Norris (2016), p. 14.

[47] See Kurlantzick (2016), chapter 10; Vekasi (2019); Chen and Garcia (2016).

[48] See Kurlantzick (2016), p. 207.

effects on national competitiveness, relative technological capabilities, and national security. Research highlights that China's industrial plan 'Made in China 2025' (MIC25) applies zero-sum strategies for boosting both technological leadership and economic self-sufficiency, with FDI a key tool for achieving these goals, thereby generating FDI-based security externalities.[49] Studies highlight that such externalities are a result of unfair Chinese business practices arising from its state-permeated economic system,[50] which provides politically sanctioned support, as well as politically sanctioned control, far beyond what private firms experience in liberal market economies. As analysts have noted, China's economic model is built around 'a strong government that effectively aligns business interests (state-owned as well as private)' with state and Communist Party interests.[51]

FDI is a central economic tool for operationalizing neo-mercantilist industrial policy, hence it is not surprising that in 2018 a full 58 percent of the value of Chinese FDI in Europe was related to core industries of the MIC25 strategy.[52] While SOE-driven investment is already heavily scrutinized from a security perspective, a key question regarding China's unique governance system is the degree of control Beijing can wield over private firms to achieve its strategic objectives. Understanding this capability is required for a comprehensive threat-based approach that can guide the applicability of the concepts of 'security' and 'public order' in ways that are proportional to actual risks. The next section focuses on China's institutional arrangements that allow unique forms of government control over the behaviour of private firms.

## 5 FDI Risks with Chinese Characteristics

### *5.1 Rule-by-Law Governance*

The constitution of the Chinese Communist Party (CCP) states that the CCP must 'develop a socialist rule of law system with Chinese characteristics, and build a socialist rule of law country'.[53] Furthermore, the term 'rule of law' appears four times in the document, the term 'in accordance with the law' also appears four times, while a commitment to 'law-based governance' is repeated on three occasions. This gives one the impression that China's governance framework has a rule-of-law underpinning equivalent to the terms meaning in liberal democracies. However, this is misleading, because in reality China is a *rule-by-law* rather than a *rule-of-law* law society. In a *rule-of-law* system that is typical in liberal democracies, the term

49 Wübbeke et al. (2016) and Zenglein and Holzmann (2019).

50 Nölke et al. (2021).

51 Zenglein and Holzmann (2019), p. 9.

52 Zenglein and Holzmann (2019), p. 13.

53 Communist Party of China (2017).

refers to a system where all persons stand equal before the given laws of the land, those laws are administered objectively by an independent judiciary, and laws are established free from arbitrary power or prejudice according to transparent, stable and legally protected procedures.[54] Where the CCP constitution and China's state constitution refer to rule-of-law, in practice this means *rule-by-law*, a formal system of rules enacted and used for governance and bureaucratic efficiency, but not necessarily for constraining the powerful from arbitrary acts.[55] As Du and Kong discuss, this formalistic approach to ruling with law is concerned primarily with systemic qualities of regularity and predictability rather than the moral substance of particular laws, or the equality of individuals before the law. This type of technical approach would allow for a 'rule of law' system to be in practice a form of rule-by-law authoritarianism.[56] China has a long tradition of such rule-by-law governance, in a political system predicated on the norm of formal inequality between social groups, as well as a paternalistic relationship between the ruler and the ruled.[57]

Today's CCP uses formal law to govern in a manner consistent with Chinese political tradition, with the Party and its chairman, rather than an Emperor, acting as the supreme rulers. As a result, the practice of China's constitutionalism is such that no legally enforceable limits are placed on its authority. Thus, while the Party's constitution does imply such limits, stating 'The Party must act within the scope of the country's Constitution and the law', this statement has little practical substance since the Constitution has never been enforced against the state or the Party. China, therefore, has a constitution without constitutionalism.[58] Instead, judges in China are appointed politically and disciplined politically to ensure they follow the Party line when and as needed. To illustrate, when an issue is deemed "politically sensitive", the Central Political and Legal Affairs Commission prescribe the legal outcome that must be delivered by the relevant authorities. If that is a judicial decision, then as noted in a 2009 National People's Congress, judges 'must remain loyal – in order – to the Party, the state, the masses and, finally, the law'.[59] The Party is likewise resolute in its rejection of the liberal democratic rule of law, as expressed in a 2017 speech by Chief Justice Zhou, the head of the Supreme People's Court of China, who stated "We should resolutely resist erroneous influence from the West: 'constitutional democracy', 'separation of powers', and 'independence of the judiciary'".[60] As Zhang notes, in China, it is impossible for a judge to resist political pressure in

[54] Bingham (2011).

[55] Zhang (2021), p. 585 ff.; Du and Kong (2020).

[56] Du and Kong (2020), pp. 887–888.

[57] On the long tradition of paternalism and a principle of unlimited state authority in Chinese political history see Jacques (2009), pp. 194–232.

[58] Zhang (2021), p. 586.

[59] McGregor (2012), p. 24.

[60] Michael Forsythe, 'China's Chief Justice Rejects an Independent Judiciary, and Reformers Wince', New York Times, 18 January 2017, https://www.nytimes.com/2017/01/18/world/asia/china-chief-justice-courts-zhou-qiang.html.

any court case in which the Party takes an interest.[61] This was true before Xi instigated political reforms designed to further reinforce political authority and Party discipline over all aspects of Chinese society.[62]

Consequently, *rule-by-law* governance in China means that not only SOEs, but also private firms can in principle be working directly for the Party's political goals if so directed, since they have no constitutionally enforceable right to maintain their autonomy. Instead, existing within a system of *rule-by-law* governance and arbitrary power, they are continually vulnerable to being influenced for political strategic ends. China's unique system of governance therefore means there are *risks with Chinese characteristics* when screening FDI from ostensibly private firms. Given that studies have previously documented extensive use by Beijing of SOEs for political purposes, including economic coercion,[63] it is logical to posit that the Party would also seek to use private firms for its goals. A number of recent reforms further indicate that this is the case, as discussed in the next section.

## 5.2 Legal Reforms for Strengthening Party Control Over the Private Sector

The key issue at stake from a threats-based approach to investment screening is the fact that Xi's reforms have eroded an already tenuous distinction between the public and private parts of China's economy, or as a recent study put it, 'it is difficult (if not impossible) to delineate with any precision where CCP influence ends and where firm autonomy begins'.[64] This is the result of Xi's efforts to develop a socialist, as opposed to a liberal, market economy,[65] and fits with his wider reform agenda aimed at strengthening the Party's presence and influence across all societal domains.[66] Hence, while the Party has recourse to arbitrary intervention, regular use of such an approach is inefficient and fails to establish a set of rules, procedures, and coherent bureaucratic governance frameworks. Consequently, to facilitate an efficient governance process to support types of desired interventions, as well as to create and regularize new legal obligations and norms, President Xi has presided over reforms to push his political agenda. From an investment screening perspective, noteworthy reforms include the 2017 National Intelligence Law, which requires private organizations and individuals to fulfil requests from state intelligence entities on national security grounds. Much like in the EU's Regulation, the latter is left undefined,

61 Zhang (2021), p. 590, see also McGregor (2012).

62 See Economy (2018) for a comprehensive discussion of Xi's political reforms.

63 Kurlantzick (2016), pp. 203–224; Vekasi (2019).

64 Blanchette (2020), p. 2.

65 I have outlined the institutional make-up of China's socialist market economy in McDonagh (2022), including how it generates systemic competition within the multilateral trade order.

66 Blanchette (2020), Economy (2018) and Minzner (2018).

meaning the Party can decide in any particular instance what counts as national security, while the private firm must then comply with the directive. However, the way the Party governs, as well as its lack of commitment to checks and balances on its authority, should be enough to dissuade anyone from claiming a moral equivalence on that point. Moreover, policies such as 'Made in China 2025' are politically driven, whole-of-society, policy programmes that the Party views as critical to China's overall economic and technological competitiveness.[67] Hence, it is reasonable to assume that the 2017 National Intelligence Law can be applied by Beijing to meet MIC 2025 needs, including requesting economic information from private firms relating to trade secrets, IP transfers, and other forms of industrial espionage.

Other recent laws are indicative of the manner in which the Party is shoring up bureaucratic efficiency for managing political oversight and influence directly within China's SOEs and the private sector. In 2017, the State Council formalized a requirement for establishing Party committees in SOEs, that would then be tasked with supervising Party members and overseeing ideological discipline and adherence to Party and state laws.[68] In 2018, the China Securities Regulatory Commission issued 'Guidelines for the Governance of Listed Companies', of which Article 5 requires private firms to 'provide for the activities of the Party committees',[69] including ensuring that medium and large firms establish Party cells who will conduct ideological training sessions as well as enforce Party discipline. These changes are part of Xi's goal laid out at the 2017 19th Party Congress to revitalize Party leadership across Chinese society. In Xi's speech titled 'Ensuring Party leadership over all work', he noted that 'The Party exercises overall leadership over all areas of endeavour in every part of the country...We must improve the institutions and mechanisms for upholding Party leadership'. Boosting the number of Party committees in SOEs and Party cells in private firms is part of the Party's efforts to increase political oversight and control across the economy. Figures claimed by the Party itself at the end of 2017 suggested that 1.88 million private firms, including foreign firms, had created such cells.[70] These cells provide the Party the means for informal executive influence over firm decision-making, as well as informational oversight of activities.

## 5.3 *The Investor Party-State*

Another reform of high importance to FDI screening policy is the Party's drive to evolve beyond its position as *owner* and *regulator* within the economy, to take on

[67] Wübbeke et al. (2016).

[68] Norris (2021), p. 25.

[69] Norris (2021), p. 25.

[70] Pearson et al. (2021), p. 209.

the role of core *investor* in the private sector.[71] China's new push into broad-based domestic investment 'entails widespread state investment capital and equity stakes in firms of all kinds, especially minority stakes in nominally privately owned firms'.[72] As discussed by Chen and Rithmire, this strategy poses new questions around the role of the Party-state in corporate decision-making, new issues around principle-agent tensions, and new risks for FDI screening, since widespread equity holdings in private firms offer 'an alternative means for states, especially authoritarian ones, to push political agendas through their majority or minority stakes in firms'.[73] This is known as 'policy channelling', whereby state ownership, or part thereof, of a business enterprise is used influence the business to carry out non-commercial objectives.[74] Party-state investment in non-SOE firm equities has provided significant new avenues for Beijing to engage in such policy channelling.

Chen and Rithmire devised one way to estimate the extent of China's state investment drive by assessing the ownership structure of all investment and asset management firms in China that held assets equal to, or above, 1 billion RMB. The number of which totals 1044 entities.[75] They found that of 18.45 trillion RMB managed by such entities, state-owned central- and local-level asset managers accounted for 46.51% and 45.18%, respectively, while private asset managers accounted for 8.31%. A single state-owned asset manager, Central Huijin, controlled over a fifth of the total stock of capital managed across the identified 1044 firms. In 2018, George Magnus estimated that if one added the share of China's economy controlled by SOEs with the share of assets controlled by state investment vehicles, the purely private part of the economy would likely be only approximately 20–30 percent of the economy.[76] Later studies, such as by Chen and Rithmire assessing the Party-state's investment activity and holdings, lend support to that estimation. The question of where China's public-owned or public-invested economy ends, and the private economy begins is increasingly an impossible question to answer. Likewise, the prevalence of Party cells even in nominally fully private firms further eviscerates any practical distinction and opens up a vista of an economy where the traditional public–private binary undergirding western political economy cannot be easily, if at all, applied.

[71] Blanchette (2020), p. 5; Chen and Rithmire (2020), pp. 260–270; Wu (2016), pp. 274–275.

[72] Chen and Rithmire (2020), p. 260.

[73] Chen and Rithmire (2020), p. 260.

[74] Milhaupt (2020), p. 363.

[75] Chen and Rithmire (2020), pp. 265–266.

[76] Magnus (2018).

## 6 Discussion and Conclusion

China's unique political economy offers a challenging set of threats for investment screening. The country's authoritarian governance system means that the Party has a latent capacity to oversee and intervene anywhere across the economy within a legal framework that in practice entails no constitutional checks on the Party's power. From a threats-based perspective, it is the hallmarks of the system that pose unique broad-based risks, these being (1) rule-by-law governance; (2) the Party as a paternalistic and ruler sitting above the law; and (3) a whole-of-society governance norm that dissolves boundaries between the public and private domains. In effect, all resources that fall within the boundaries of the Chinese state, be they public or private, exist within a norm of availability for the Party to utilize for its goals. This implies that in relation to FDI screening, private firms are as equally vulnerable to becoming Party agents, as SOEs. At the same time, given the plurality of mechanisms, both formal and informal, for policy channelling between the Party and a private firm, it is unlikely that precise *ex ante* rules could be devised for addressing the associated FDI risks. Aside from formal laws such as the 2017 National Intelligence Law, the Party has informal channels such as Party Cells for influencing the activities of private firms, as well as for accessing their confidential information without leaving any official paper trails.

A threats-based approach needs to recognize the fact that the risks posed by Chinese FDI are diffuse and systemic in quality. This means that the legal criteria specified for regulatory protection should be correspondingly flexible. *Security* and *public order* concepts offer a suitable flexible conceptual language. Their relatively undefined quality offers the flexibility needed to deal with the problem of future uncertainty in the high-stakes domain of national security. In a geoeconomic world where economic interdependency is increasingly weaponized, applying such concepts to FDI screening is appropriate, given the risks from China's whole-of-society approach to neo-mercantilist industrial policy include sensitive or dual use technology transfer, unfair competition and commercial espionage in strategic industries, as well as economic coercion. Policies such as MIC25 provide a roadmap for EU Members to identify core areas for enhanced screening efforts. Considering the above analysis, it is argued here that ostensibly private Chinese firms need to be considered as sitting in a similar risk category to SOEs. The interpretive quality of the concepts of *security* and *public order* are needed precisely because China's system demands such malleability. This is due to the legal and normative existence of a latent Party-state potential for activating executive influence over any private firm at any time.

The threats-based approach to screening Chinese FDI offers a non-arbitrary method to applying security concepts to FDI screening, so long as it draws on available research that can establish the goals, intent and capabilities of actors' risk profile. This can allay fears of protectionist misuse. In China's case, a threats-based approach leans towards a presumption of risk not only for SOEs but also for private firms, particularly for sensitive sectors and critical infrastructure. Thus, while FDI is something that all states rightly wish to incentivise, acting as if it is always an unqualified good is no longer a reasonable position in a post-Globalization reality. With the outbreak of renewed great power competition, FDI has become a potential economic good but also a potential strategic risk. Consequently, framing the debate around whether the Regulation is likely to result in protectionism misses the point. The EU is not the problem; it has long proven that it walks its talk concerning principled economic openness and fairness. Rather, the problem is that others have no such commitment and instead are willing to use FDI as a tool for state goals. The EU's new Regulation on investment screening is about protection, not protectionism, and the concepts of *security* and *public order* are appropriate to the nature of the risks its Member States now face.

**Acknowledgements** This article was developed from a conference paper presented at the 2022 CELIS Institute Annual Forum on Investment Screening, held at Uppsala University, Sweden. The author thanks the conference organizers for hosting an excellent interdisciplinary event that provided much food for thought. The author also thanks four reviewers who provided expert feedback on earlier drafts that helped greatly improve the article. Any remaining errors are the authors.

## References

Aradau C, Lobo-Guerrero L, Van Munster R (2008) Security, technologies of risk, and the political: Guest editors' introduction, vol 39. Sage Publications Sage CA, Los Angeles, pp 147–154

Backman S (2022) Risk vs. threat-based cybersecurity: the case of the EU. Eur Secur, pp 1–19

Barnard C (2009) Derogations, justifications and the four freedoms: is state interest really protected? In: Barnard C, Odudu O (eds) The outer limits of European Union law. Hart, London

Benyon FS (2010) Direct investment, national champions and EU treaty freedoms: from Maastricht to Lisbon. Bloomsbury Publishing, London

Bhala R (1998) National security and international trade law: what the GATT says, and what the United States does. Univ Pa J Int Econ Law 19:263

Bingham T (2011) The rule of law. Penguin, London

Blackwill RD, Harris JM (2017) War by other means: geoeconomics and statecraft. Harvard University Press, Cambridge

Blanchette J (2020) From "China Inc." to "CCP Inc.": a new paradigm for Chinese state capitalism. China Leadership Monitor 66:1–13

Chen X, Garcia RJ (2016) Economic sanctions and trade diplomacy: sanction-busting strategies, market distortion and efficacy of China's restrictions on Norwegian salmon imports. China Inf 30(1):29–57

Chen H, Rithmire M (2020) The rise of the investor state: state capital in the Chinese economy. Stud Comp Int Dev 55(3):257–277. https://doi.org/10.1007/s12116-020-09308-3

Collins A (2016) Contemporary security studies, 4th edn. Oxford University Press, Oxford

Communist Party of China (2017) Constitution of the Communist Party of China. Retrieved from http://www.china.org.cn/20171105-001.pdf

Doshi R (2021) The long game: China's grand strategy to displace American order. Oxford University Press, Oxford

Du M, Kong Q (2020) Explaining the limits of the WTO in shaping the rule of law in China. J Int Econ Law 23(4):885–905

Economy E (2018) The third revolution: Xi Jinping and the new Chinese state. Oxford University Press, Oxford

Graham EM, Krugman P (1995) Foreign direct investment in the United States. Institute for International Economics, Washington, DC

Grieger G (2021) EU–China comprehensive agreement on investment-levelling the playing field with China. Retrieved from Brussels

Hindelang S (2009) The free movement of capital and foreign direct investment: the scope of protection in EU law. Oxford University Press

Jacques M (2009) When China rules the world: the rise of the middle kingdom and the end of the western world. Allen Lane, London

Johnston AI (2019) China in a world of orders: rethinking compliance and challenge in Beijing's international relations. Int Secur 44(2):9–60

Kurlantzick J (2016) State capitalism: how the return of statism is transforming the world. Oxford University Press, Oxford

Lai K (2021) National security and FDI policy ambiguity: a commentary. J Int Bus Policy:1–10

Leruth L, Mazarei A, Regibeau P, Renneboog L (2022) Green energy depends on critical minerals. Who controls the supply chains? Peterson Inst Int Econ 22(12):1–35

Magnus G (2018) Red flags: why Xi's China is in jeopardy. Yale University Press, New Haven

McDonagh N (2022) How China challenges the liberal trade order: coercion, contestation and the socialist market economy. Institute for International Trade Working Paper Series, 08, pp 1–16

McGregor R (2012) The party: the secret world of China's communist rulers (Revised edition ed.). Penguin, London

Meunier S (2014) Divide and conquer? China and the cacophony of foreign investment rules in the EU. J Eur Public Policy 21(7):996–1016

Milhaupt CJ (2020) The state as owner—China's experience. Oxford Rev Econ Policy 36(2): 362–379

Minzner C (2018) End of an era: how China's authoritarian revival is undermining its rise. Oxford University Press, New York

Moran TH (2017) CFIUS and national security: challenges for the United States, opportunities for the European Union. Retrieved from Washington, D.C.: https://www.piie.com/commentary/speeches-papers/cfius-and-national-security-challenges-united-states-opportunities

National Board of Trade Sweden (2021) An EU trade policy for geopolitical ends – clashing perspectives and policy recommendations. National Board of Trade Sweden, Stockholm. Retrieved from https://www.kommerskollegium.se/en/publications/reports/2021/an-eu-trade-policy-for-geopolitical-ends/

Nettesheim M (2020) Screening for what threat: preserving "public order and security", securing reciprocity in international trade, or supporting certain social, environmental, or industrial policies? In: Hindelang S, Moberg A (eds) YSEC yearbook of socio-economic constitutions. Springer Nature, Geneva, pp 481–501

Nölke A, Ten Brink T, May C, Claar S (2021) State-permeated capitalism in large emerging economies. Routledge, Abingdon

Norris WJ (2016) Chinese economic statecraft: commercial actors, grand strategy, and state control. Cornell University Press, Ithaca

Norris W (2021) The party in the boardroom. In: Kennedy S, Blanchette J (eds) Chinese state capitalism: diagnosis and prognosis. Center for Stratetic and International Studies, Washington, D.C., pp 24–28

Pearson M, Rithmire M, Tsai KS (2021) Party-state capitalism in China. Curr Hist 120(827): 207–213

Scholvin S, Wigell M (2018) Power politics by economic means: geoeconomics as an analytical approach and foreign policy practice. Comp Strategy 37(1):73–84

Simon S (2020) Investment screening: the return of protectionism? A political account. In: Hindelang S, Moberg A (eds) YSEC yearbook of socio-economic constitutions. Springer, Berlin, pp 43–52

Vekasi K (2019) Politics, markets, and rare commodities: responses to Chinese rare earth policy. Jpn J Polit Sci 20(1):2–20
Voon T (2019) Can international trade law recover. The security exception in WTO law: entering a new era. AJIL Unbound 113(1):45–50
Weinhardt C, ten Brink T (2020) Varieties of contestation: China's rise and the liberal trade order. Rev Int Polit Econ 27(2):258–280
Weiss JC, Wallace JL (2021) Domestic politics, China's rise, and the future of the liberal international order. Int Organ 75(2):635–664
Wernicke SF (2020) Investment screening: the return of protectionism? A business perspective. In: Hindelang S, Moberg A (eds) YSEC yearbook of socio-economic constitutions 2020. Springer, Geneva, pp 29–41
Wu M (2016) The "China, Inc." challenge to global trade governance. Harv Int Law J 57:261–324
Wübbeke J, Meissner M, Zenglein MJ, Ives J, Conrad B (2016) Made in China 2025: the making of a high-tech superpower and consequences for industrial countries. Retrieved from Berlin
Zenglein MJ, Holzmann A (2019) Evolving made in China 2025: China's industrial policy in the quest for global tech leadership. Retrieved from Berlin
Zhang Q (2021) The communist party leadership and rule of law: a tale of two reforms. J Contemp China 30(130):578–595
Zwartkruis W, de Jong B (2020) The EU regulation on screening of foreign direct investment: a game changer? Eur Bus Law Rev 31(3):447–474

# The Concept of Security: Brief Genealogy of an Ambiguous Symbol

**Alejandra Torres Camprubí**

## Contents



**Abstract** The emergence of the notion of "security" in the 1920s in Western scholarly circles as an alternative concept to those of "war" or "defense", resulted from the involvement of civilian experts into an arena that had until then been exclusively reserved to the military statement. From that moment onwards, this highly contested notion fed the emergence of a new discipline, International Security Studies, which placed the notion of security at its core. Between the aftermath of the Second World War until the most recent Globalization era that followed the end of the Cold War, the notion of security progressively developed and was fundamentally transformed. The emergence of multiple layers of cumulative knowledge about the notion of security (proposing different referent objects of security as well as the inclusion of non-military factors within its scope) was brought about by the parallel foundation of several new schools of International Security Studies. This reveals the inherently ambiguous nature of the concept itself, as much as the disciplinary and political resistance to reaching a common understanding and shared methodological tools to apprehend this notion.

---

The contents of this article are of the author's sole responsibility and do not represent the views of any other person, company, State or institution.

---

A. T. Camprubí (✉)
Foley Hoag AARPI, Paris, France
e-mail: atorrescamprubi@foleyhoag.com

 
J. Hillebrand Pohl et al. (eds.), *Weaponising Investments*,
Springer Studies in Law & Geoeconomics (2023) 1: 79–94,
https://doi.org/10.1007/17280_2023_5, Published online: 24 June 2023

# 1 Introduction

Article 3(1) of the EU Foreign Direct Investment Screening Regulation ("the EU FDI Regulation") contemplates two grounds upon which Member States "may maintain, amend or adopt mechanisms to screen foreign direct investments in their territory."[1] Those are "security or public order."[2] In spite of their paramount importance and close connection to both the scope and core purpose of the Regulation, the text itself does not provide a clear-cut statutory definition of these central concepts.[3] Article 2 of the Regulation, which is devoted to the definitions that apply for the purposes of the Regulation, remains silent on them both. Instead, the Regulation adopts an oblique approach, providing in Article 4 a list of the "factors that may be taken into consideration" by Member States or the Commission in determining whether a direct investment "*is likely to affect* security or public order."[4] The array of elements incorporated in the list is vast and diverse—for instance, factors such as "energy," "water," "aerospace,"[5] "raw materials" or "food security,"[6] are included alongside "media," "data processing,"[7] or a broad category of "critical technologies."[8] Yet, an examination about the origins and evolution of the concept of security (the first of the two grounds cited in the Regulation), reveals in fact that the Regulation's elusive approach to this concept is unsurprising.

Security is a contested notion. It is *context-specific*—as it requires identifying the actors involved in the configuration of a specific evolution of its understanding. It is also *instrumental*—for it demands to unveil the underlying interests of its promoters; map the strategies of introduction, circulation and possible imposition of a new understanding of security in a particular time and place; and, ultimately, disentangle the purpose of such a move. Against this background, this article provides a brief reconstruction of the genealogy of the concept of security as reflected in the birth and development of the specific discipline that placed this notion at its core: International Security Studies.

[1] *Regulation (EU) 2019/452 of the European Parliament and of the Council of 19 March 2019, Establishing a Framework for the Screening of Foreign Direct Investments into the Union* (hereafter "EU FDI Regulation"), article 3(1): "In accordance with this Regulation, Member States may maintain, amend or adopt mechanisms to screen foreign direct investments in their territory on the grounds of security or public order."

[2] *Id.*

[3] Throughout this article, the expressions "notion" and "concept" of security are applied interchangeably.

[4] EU FDI Regulation, article 4(1): "In determining whether a foreign direct investment is likely to affect security or public order, Member States and the Commission may consider its potential effects on, inter alia . . ."

[5] *Id.*, article 4(1)(a).

[6] *Id.*, article 4(1)(c).

[7] *Id.*, article 4(1)(a).

[8] *Id.*, article 4(1)(b).

Section 2 traces back the emergence of the notion of security in Anglo-American intellectual circles during the twentieth century Inter-War period, and shows how since its inception the content of the concept of security proved to be variable. Section 3 then addresses how the notion of security was enthroned following the end of the Second World War, coinciding with the foundation of *Stategic Studies*, the first school of International Security Studies. Section 4 explains how the consolidation of the concept of security during the Cold War also led to its expansion in scope. The debate in western International Security Studies about political suitability of considering non-military threats within the notion of security preceded the end of the Cold War and was informed by the creation of new schools of thought devoted to this concept. Section 5 addresses how the Cold War ending brought about a structural crisis in the field of international security studies, giving rise to the "wideners and deepeners" movement, which called for an expansion in scope of the notion of security so as to consider non-military factors as phenomena *in their own right*. Finally, Sect. 6 closes this brief genealogical account recounting how in the era of globalization the critical school of International Security Studies proposed expanding the levels of analysis of the notion and considering the referent object of security beyond the State.

## 2 The Birth of the Concept of Security in the Inter-War Period

The notion of "security" emerged in the 1920s in Western intellectual circles as an alternative to the concepts of "war" or "defense". In the contemporaneous political analysis *The Twenty Years' Crisis*, Edwar Carr explained how the birth of the notion of security is intertwined with the parallel emergence of International Politics as a distinct social science, and resulted from civilian engagement into an arena that had been until then a *domaine réservé* of the military statement.[9] In the aftermath of the First World War, the popular demand to integrate the conduct of international relations into the realm of national politics became widespread—the decision to go to war would thereafter be subject to the public opinion's close scrutiny.[10] Similarly, the emergence of the concept of "security" in social sciences is the result of a sociological process initiated in Anglo-American intellectual circles of the twentieth century Inter-war period whereby the civilian, intellectual and political statements

[9] Carr (1939), Part I, Chapter 1. Carr contends that the reasons why American political class of the Inter-War period professed a sacred trust in both the power and the rightness of public opinion is to be found in the influence of the eighteenth century English rationalism.
[10] *Id.*

began to approach to "war" and "defense" issues.[11] That is the cradle of this notion, whose scope and meaning proved to be variable since its inception.

In 1952, Arnold Wolfers published an influential seminal article where he defined the "national security interest" as an "ambiguous symbol",[12] and provided an explanation of the basic structure of the notion as it was understood before the war. Four main conclusions that can be drawn from his analytical account on the notion of security:

(i) The Security Value has a *pivotal function*. It can be said to be the center of the security system, from which the other components find their respective places and define the relationships to one another. The security value is instrumental to the protection of other substantive "core values."[13]
(ii) The Core Values have an *ontological function*. They give both the sense and the justification to a security policy. Nonetheless, their essential character somehow contrasts with their variability in time and in space, which is linked to the fact that they originate in governmental decisions. The core values give a meaning and content to the "national security interest."[14]
(iii) The External Threats have in turn a *triggering function*. Whether considered from an objective sense (events), or from a subjective one (perception or fear), their existence is the conditio sine qua non for the acquisition or

[11] *Id.* Since the security notion resulted from the integration of defense issues in the scope of political parties, the existence of these indirectly became a condition for the development of "security" as a concept. Therefore, from a conceptual perspective, the notion evolved in democratic regimes. This is expressed, for instance, by Barry Buzan and Lee Hansen, who explained that "the centrality of the civilian element also reflects the fact that ISS [International Security Studies] has largely flourished in democratic countries", *see* Buzan and Hansen (2009), p. 2. See also, Amitva (1997), p. 300, who explained that "as with other concepts of International Relations, national security assumed a Eurocentric universe of nation-states and dwelled primarily on the responses of Western governments and societies, particularly the United States, to the problem of war. The issues and experiences within the other segment, collectively labeled as the Third World, were not fully incorporated into the discourse of security studies."

[12] Wolfers (1952), p. 502: "[n]ormative admonitions to conduct a foreign policy guided by the national security interest are no less ambiguous and misleading that the statement of fact concerning past behavior ... In order to be meaningful such admonitions would have to specify the degree of security which a nation shall aspire to attain and the means by which it is to be attained in a given situation ... Because the pendulum of public opinion swings so easily from extreme complacency to extreme apprehension, from utopian reliance on 'good will' to disillusioned faith in naked force only, it is particularly important to be wary of any simple panacea even one that parades the realist grab of a policy guided solely by the national security interest."

[13] *Id.*, pp. 484–485. Wolfers explains the instrumental function of the notion of security and qualifies it as a value as follows: "Security points to some degree of protection of values previously acquired. In Walter Lippmann's words, a nation is secure to the extent to which it is not in danger of having to sacrifice core values ... Security is a value, then, of which a nation can have more or less and which it can aspire to have in greater or lesser measure. It has much in common, in this respect, with power or wealth, two other values of great importance in international affairs."

[14] *Id.*, p. 489: "It would seem a fair guess that the efforts for security by a particular nation will tend to vary, other things being equal, with the range of values for which protection is being sought."

predetermination of the core values to be protected, which in turn inform the security value itself;[15] and

(iv) The National Security Interest has a *filtering function*. It is formulated through the determination of the national security policy targeting at the protection of the selected core values.[16]

With regard to the *content* of security (as opposed to its structure), Wolfers further explained that initially the meaning of security (more precisely, of "national security") during the Inter-war period admitted and included references to non-military factors. This was a reflection of the central role of welfare in the understanding of the "national interest" following the Great Depression.[17] Based on the analytical study that Charles Beard conducted at the time on the construction of the "national interest," Wolfers explained that the heart of the national interest during that time was the achievement of welfare and consequent social cohesion at a national level.[18]

The breakout of the Second World War tore apart this initial broad understanding of the notions of security and national interest. In the immediate aftermath of the conflict, the *Realist School* established itself as the most influential school of thought within the young discipline of International Politics. The axis and main contention of this school was that only balance-of-power could prevent national and international conflict—as opposed to the utopian legal principles and aspirations that had prevailed during the Inter-war period and had been epitomized by the creation of the League of Nations.[19] Such overarching and philosophical approach to the conduct of international politics correlatively forged a shift in the early

[15] *Id.*, p. 485: "Security, in an objective sense, measures the absence of threats to acquired values, in a subjective sense, the absence of fear that such values will be attacked. In both respects a nation's security can run a wide gamut from almost incomplete insecurity or sense of insecurity at one pole, to almost complete security or absence of fear at the other."

[16] *Id.*, p. 483: "While it would be wrong to say that the economic interest has ceased to attract attention, it is overshadowed by the national security interest. The change from a welfare to a security interpretation of the symbol 'national interest' is understandable. Today we are living under the impact of cold war and threats of external aggression rather than of depression and social reform. As a result, the formula of the national interest has come to be practically synonymous with the formula of national security today by the national security interest."

[17] *Id.*, pp. 481–483.

[18] Wolfers' account on the notion of "national security interest" departed from the work that Charles Beard devoted to the notion of the "national interest" in the early years of the New Deal. According to Wolfers' reading of Beard's work, during the Inter-War period the idea of the national interest was not yet "securitized" (or, as he put it "the security interpretation of the national interest symbol" had not yet taken place, *Id.*, pp. 481–483). See also, Beard (1934).

[19] Morgenthau (1948), p. 125, explaining balance of power as follows: "The aspiration for power on the part of several nations, each trying either to maintain or to overthrow the status quote, leads of necessity to a constellation which is called balance of power and to policies which aim at preserving it ... Balance of power and policies aiming at its preservation are not only inevitable, but an essential stabilizing factor in a society of sovereign nations; and [the] instability of the international balance of power is due not to the faultiness of the principle but to the particular conditions under which the principle must operate in a society of sovereign states."

understanding of the notion of security. Military factors regained their space in the notion's core, stressing the importance of defence power and strategy, and revealing the inherently malleable nature of the notion.

## 3 The Enthronement of the Notion of Security After the Second World War

The introduction of power as an analytical factor applied to the conduct of international relations found in the young notion of security a very useful and fertile tool—both conceptually and institutionally.

*First*, from a conceptual perspective, the previous belief that there is a common interest of all States to achieve and preserve peace, which effectively informs and structures the international order, was overshadowed by the formulation of the "security dilemma." This expression, coined in 1950 by John Herz, inaugurated the golden age of the notion of security. Thereafter, security became the cornerstone of analysis on the conduct of international relations until the Cold War ended four decades later. Herz explained the security dilemma as a situation in which:

> Groups or individuals . . . striving to attain security from an attack, they are driven to acquire more and more power in order to escape the impact of the power of others. This, in turn, renders the others more insecure and compels them to prepare for the worst. *Since none can ever feel entirely secure in a world of competing units, power competition ensues, and the vicious circle of security and power accumulation is on.*[20]

The "security dilemma" supposes that members of a society (devoid of a common entity that orders the system) have competing interests which materialize in their individual quest for absolute or relative power.[21] This leads to the emergence of the dilemma in which human societies have had to grapple since the dawn of history."[22]

*Second*, not only did the notion of security perfectly fit in the realist explanation of international politics; it also became the foundational concept for new schools of thought established by civilians that would be specifically dedicated to this concept. The beginning of the Cold War in the early 1950s, coupled with the lessons learned from the two World Wars and the profound disillusionment after the failure of the Wilsonian model, set up the conditions for the emergence of a specialized field of study which put at its heart the notion of security.

The institutionalization of the study of the notion of security first came about with the foundation of *Strategic Studies*, conceived as the instrumental and technical branch of the Realist school of International Relations. Strategic Studies emerged as

---

[20] Herz (1950), p. 157 (emphasis added).

[21] Morgenthau (1948), p. 21, explaining that: "Domestic and international politics are but two different manifestations of the same phenomenon: the struggle for power . . . a political policy seeks to either to keep power, to increase power or to demonstrate power."

[22] Herz (1950), p. 157.

a distinct field from that of International Relations, formally constituting the first school of a discipline which, in retrospect, has come to be known as International Security Studies. Although Strategic Studies approached the notion of security through militarized and Statist lenses, the military statement did not control this school of thought. Barry Buzan and Lene Hansen explain how it emerged as a way for civilian experts (particularly physicists and social scientists) who had made decisive contributions during the Second World War to participate in the progressive understanding of the balance of power that crystallized within the unfamiliar broad-spectrum of the Cold War.[23]

## 4 Consolidation and Expansion of the Concept of Security in the Cold War Era

As the Iron Curtain formed in Europe, the notion of security found in the Cold War a well-fitted historical habitat. Its prominence increased to a level leading to the emergence of a whole new "epistemic community,"[24] International Security Studies, specifically and entirely devoted to developing research and producing knowledge about the concept of security.[25]

The emergence of *Strategic Studies* in the 1950s first heralded an understanding of the notion of security characterized by its militarization and Statist level of analysis. Realism gave to the notion of security a solidly grounded habitat, a place where the notion could play a central role and serve the formulation of foreign policy strategies seeking to maintain the balance of power and ensure States' survival in the nuclear age. Yet, soon after it was enthroned by the realist paradigm, the quest for

---

[23] Buzan and Hansen (2009), p. 66: "Because of their crucial contributions during the Second World War, civilian experts, mainly physicists and social scientists, could now specialise in military issues under the heading of security, which unlike 'war' or 'defence' nicely bridged the military and non-military aspects of the subject. As well as having relevant technical expertise not possessed by the military, a large and influential civilian cohort helped to address specifically American concerns about the dangers of society becoming militarised by a long-term struggle."

[24] Hass (1992), p. 2. Hass defines epistemic communities as "networks of knowledge-based experts" who play an important role in "articulating the cause-and-effect relationships of complex problems, helping states identify their interests, framing the issues for collective debate, proposing specific policies, and identifying salient points for negotiation." He further contends that the analyses produced that these networks of experts demonstrate that control over knowledge and information is an important dimension of power and international policy coordination.

[25] Buzan and Hansen (2009), p. 67: "As it began to be clear that the Cold War could become a drawn-out, all-encompassing and existential struggle, the idea took hold that one needed a form of integrated understanding, where different forms of knowledge could be combined . . . This is a central part of the explanation for the rise of the term 'security' to cover mobilisation in more inclusive and 'civilian' terms, and it conditioned a particular space for civilian expertise in a military-centred universe. This nexus of peculiarly American concerns explains a lot about the origins of ISS [International Security Studies].

security under the realist view was somehow taken for granted and, therefore, no major theoretical developments of the notion itself were pursued.[26]

This would be challenged as early as in the mid-1950s by the school of *Peace Research*, which emerged in reaction to the "moral silence" or alleged objectiveness and neutrality of Political Realism. Since this new school was launched in a somewhat hostile environment, at a time when the dominance of the realist movement was overwhelming in Western intellectual circles, their founders originally named the school *Conflict Studies*, which sparked some initial confusion on this new school's tenets. Theo Lenz self-consciously and publicly re-labeled this new approach *Peace Research* in 1955,[27] whose differential characteristic was its unconditional commitment with pacifism. This was clearly encapsulated in the school's *moto*—the realization of peace by peaceful means—and in the close personal links which developed later between the peace movement and peace activists.[28]

The theoretical development that Peace researchers brought to the notion of security initially came with an "oppositional concept, which works through security but argues that it should be replaced by that of peace."[29] This school then offered a re-articulation of the notion of security by introducing a new dichotomy—"positive peace" and "negative peace"—first formulated in 1964 by Johan Galtung in the inaugural editorial of the *Journal of Peace Research*. The essence of the dichotomy is that:

> One may now look upon peace research as research into the conditions for moving closer to the state we have called GCP [General and Complete Peace], or at least not drifting closer towards GCW [General and Complete War]. *Thus, there are two aspects of peace as conceived of here: negative peace which is the absence of violence – and positive peace which is the integration of human society*. Correspondingly, there are two branches of peace research.[30]

Negative Peace Research became closely related to Strategic Studies, for both schools were concerned with the rapid technological advance leading to the arms race. They were part of a "single conversation", as they shared the same privileged

[26] *Id.*, p. 83, explaining that: "As the Cold War went on and Security Studies went through its so-called golden age between 1955 and 1965, these conceptual discussions receded and the sub-field became almost exclusively devoted to the study of nuclear weapons and bipolar rivalry ... The Strategic Studies understanding of the state, dangers and insecurities became institutionalised to such an extent that the majority of Strategic Studies literature felt no need to explicitly discuss its conceptualisation of security."

[27] Lenz (1955).

[28] Pacifist theories and tactics unsurprisingly made the object of several studies by Peace Research institutes. See, for instance, Klitgaard (1971), pp. 143–153.

[29] Buzan and Hansen (2009), p. 259.

[30] Galtung (1964), p. 2 (emphasis added).

object of study—military security, and the same key referent object from which military security was examined—the State.[31]

After Peace Research emerged as a new school challenging the Realist understanding of security, the notion went through an expansion in scope. This was prompted, most prominently, by the impacts of the 1973 Oil Crisis, which revived the original Inter-war period recognition that economic and security factors are in fact interdependent. The 1973 Oil Crisis exposed the fragility of Western economy and the fear of "resource wars."[32] As a result, the notion of "economic security" was introduced in the agenda of Strategic Studies,[33] and a new branch known as 'International Political Economy' was launched within the broader field of International Relations.[34] Besides, the Oil Crisis also exposed the interdependence existing in a world that was apparently divided in self-contained blocs,[35] a condition shared not only with regard to financial flows, but also by environmental factors. As a result, the same crisis also eventually paved the way to the emergence in the 1980s of the notion of "environmental security,"[36] as well as new formulations of the concept—such as "common security", and "comprehensive security", which reflected its expanded scope.[37]

[31] Buzan and Hansen (2009), p. 169: "There was a lot of substantive overlap, very similar drivers, a parallel profile of institutionalisation and not much in the way of epistemological differences, at least not in ways that correlate with Strategic Studies and Peace Research orientations. There were certainly disagreements, bordering at times on overt antagonism and contempt, about preferred priorities and policies, and at the extremes there were different views of how to define the problem. But across a broad middle range, both Strategists and Peace Researchers were responding to the same problem: how to pursue security in the context of a nuclear-armed bipolar superpower confrontation."

[32] Frédérick (1999), p. 93: "Over recent decades, events such as the oil crises of 1973 and 1979, the protectionist policies of certain trading powers, and the widening of inequalities between the North and the South underlines the impact of economic factors when formulating questions about security ... Strategic analyst experts thus had to face the truth and acknowledge that the 'non-military dimensions' of security would henceforth occupy a very important place in State behaviourism. This led them to redefined the concept of national security so as to broaden its scope, as the traditional approach reflected two narrow vision not only for the problems but also of the solutions available to cope with threats."

[33] See e.g., Nye (1974), pp. 584–598.

[34] Buzan and Hansen (2009), p. 85.

[35] Keohane and Nye (1977). See also, Lipschutz (1998), pp. 109–138, explaining that the emergence of "interdependence theory" tried "to account to what appeared to be the end of American dominance of the Free World after the dollar devaluations and the end of convertibility to gold and the oil embargo of the early 1970s."

[36] Tuchmann Mathews (1989), p. 162: "Environmental strains are beginning to break down the sacred boundaries of national sovereignty, previously rendered porous by the information and communication revolutions and the instantaneous global movement of financial capital." See also, e.g. Gledisch (2007), p. 178: "the concern for how environmental degradation may lead to insecurity is at the core of the question of scarcity of resources"; and Matthew (2000), pp. 33–48.

[37] See, e.g. Stern (1995), pp. 211–233. See also Williams (2008), p. 6, explaining that: "The second philosophy challenges the idea that security flows from power. . .Consequently, in the second philosophy, true or stable security does not come from cooperating to achieve security without

## 5 Constructing, Widening and Deepening Following the Cold-War Ending

The end of the Cold War had a significant impact on the Realist approach to the notion of security. It is frequently mentioned that one of the most surprising facts of the Cold War ending was that the realist analytical tools failed to predict it. Nor were they useful afterwards to explain or elucidate by a solidly structured theory the reasons why the Cold War had occurred. The end of the conflict thus gave rise to some important criticism of the realist basic tenets, which in turn affected the traditionalist notion of security from two main angles.

First of all, it put at stake the identity of the referent object of security, namely the (western) State. As Samuel Huntington famously remarked in his 1993 seminal article "The Clash of Civilisations", the end of the Cold War unveiled the "enemy syndrome" of both blocs and produced the following paradigm shift. It changed the nature of the conflicts ahead—which were previously based on class or ideological divisions, and would now be grounded on religious and ethnic grounds—as much as the self-identification of the Parties in conflict. As he put it, "in class ideological conflicts, the key question was: which side are you? And people could and did choose sides and change ideas. In conflicts between civilizations, the question is: what are you?."[38] Forced to face the big gap left by the end of "The Other," the attention of western intellectual circles consequently turned towards "The Self."[39]

In addition, the Cold War ending embodied the loss of an analytical superstructure. The obsolescence of a framework based on balance of power in a bipolar world generated the necessity of beginning an entirely new process that would enable the identification of the causes of war and instability. Thus, in the absence of what Barry Buzan and Ole Waever referred to as a "macrosecuritization event,"[40] most international relations theories developed under Strategic Studies underwent a thorough re-examination and revision. Multiple new branches adhered to what is known as the "widening and deepening movement" of International Security Studies, which were

---

depriving others of it. During the Cold War, such an approach was evident in Olaf Palme's call for 'common security', particularly his suggestion that protagonist must achieve security not against the adversary but together with him'."

[38] Huntington (1993), p. 27.

[39] Particular attention to the importance of "The Other" can be found, for instance, in the work of Campbell (1992). Besides, as Buzan and Hansen recall, the question of whether States needed enemies was confronted mainly by post-structuralism, one branch of the widening-deepening movement that was born before the end of the Cold War and which was indebted to the classical Realist tradition, arguing that state sovereignty and security are not easily transformed. Buzan and Hansen (2009), p. 218.

[40] Buzan and Waever (2009), p. 254. Macrosecuritizations such as the Cold War, allegedly the 'Global War on Terror', and possibly, climate change, are defined as "events which entered the realm of security policy and structured international politics on a larger scale beyond middle-range collectivities".

united by their challenge to military–State centrism and proposed constructing the notion of security on the basis of the perception and interpretation of external facts.

The main "wideners" that emerged after the end of the Cold War were the Constructivism movement, and the Copenhagen School. Barry Buzan explains that conventional constructivism was born out of Katzenstein's landmark work, and was the least radical widening approach to security, for it "fail[ed] to engage security critically" and embraced the same rationalist (rather than reflective) case-study research methodology as that of the traditionalists.[41] This is the cradle of the basic constructivist thought, whose core tenet holds that security is a theoretical construction based on an interpretation of external events by "The Self," rather than based on an interpretation of a situation which objectively constitutes a threat generated by "The Other."[42]

The Copenhagen School, which has been "the most concerted attempt to develop a theory or framework for the study of security in the constructivist tradition,"[43] produced conceptual innovations in the realist understanding of the concept of security. It created two main taxonomies—"securitization processes" and "security sectors", based on the idea that the meanings of security originate from intersubjective processes with political effect.[44] It thus places the study of linguistics at the centre of its research and, openly engaging with the notion of security, gives rise to a "discursive approach to security."[45] From there on, the Copenhagen School defines the new notion of "societal security" as "the ability of a society to persist in its essential character under changing conditions and possible or actual threats."[46] The Copenhagen School accepts two possible referent objects of security: the State and society, excluding both the individual level and the global level, a characteristic that places it in an eclectic trend between traditionalists and critical constructivists.

Furthermore, considering that the "possible or actual threats" are "linked to an objective definition," the Copenhagen School does not neglect how the identity of the referent object has an impact on the characterization of an objective situation as a threat. Such a relation is encapsulated in the notion of "securitization," according to

---

41 Katzenstein (1996). See also the explanation drawn by Buzan and Hansen (2009), p. 196.

42 Klein (1997), p. 363, who explains: "The theoretical construction around the notion of security born in part from the collapse of the narrative and subsequent need of the field to reinvent its own existence in a hostile environment … Security considerations are not objectively gleaned from a neutral road map of world politics, they are themselves socially constructed and discursively reproduced in ways that are contestable and subject to revision." See also, Deudney and Mathews (1999), p. 199, explaining that one of the consequences of this shifted focus was that it became necessary to rethink the referent object of security to be able to understand the connections drawn by such a subjective actor with any external fact that may subsequently be categorized under the "threat label." Deudney associated the growing awareness of the effects of environmental problems with the general effects of the 'enemy syndrome', for "environmental problems, at its basic level, ask us who we are and who "us" encompasses."

43 McDonald (2009), p. 68.

44 *Ibid.*, p. 68.

45 Buzan and Hansen (2009), p. 191.

46 Waever (1993), p. 23.

which, security results from a process whereby: (i) a securitizing actor (the referent object of security) defines a particular issue as an existential threat; (ii) such labelling is accepted by a relevant audience; which (iii) results in the introduction of the threat securitized in the (exceptional) realm of security policy.[47] Securitization theory is thus dependent upon the notion of "speech acts" found in J.L. Austin's language theory, since, during the securitization of a threat, security becomes a "site of negotiation between speakers and audiences".[48]

The Copenhagen School also puts forward the notion of "security sectors", defined as "fields of activity or arenas that entail particular forms of security interactions and particular definitions of referent objects."[49] Five different security sectors were listed by Buzan: the military sector (entailing relationships of forceful coercion); the political sector (entailing relationships of authority, governing status and recognition); the economic sector (entailing relationships of trade, production and finance); the societal sector (entailing relationships of collective security); and the environmental sector (entailing relationships between human activity and the planetary biosphere).[50]

Thus, far from becoming extinguished after the end of the Cold War, the notion of security re-emerged in the new World Order. Anything could, from this point onward, be subsumed in the realm of "security" (economic, environmental, humanitarian considerations, etc.) and not just as factors that can affect the military capacity of the State, but as factors that deserved to be considered as an element of security *in their own right*. However, the Copenhagen School did not escape the realist State-centred approach to security—the State remained the primary referent object for security, and State 'elites' (the political power) were the actors in the securitization process (that is, the 'relevant audience'). In addition, under this approach, security did not exist outside the "discourse" about it. Critical security studies would take on these points and develop further the theory of security within a radical new framework.

---

[47] Ole Waever first referred to securitization as a discursive construction of threat. See, Waever (1995), pp. 46–86. This idea was then developed in Buzan et al. (1998), p. 25, describing securitization as "[i]f by means of an argument about the priority and urgency of an existential threat the securitizing actor has managed to break free of procedures or rules he or she would otherwise be bound by, we are witnessing a case of securitization." Correlatively, 'de-securitization' is defined as the process whereby an issue re-enters the realm of normal politics.

[48] Buzan and Hansen (2009), p. 213. The authors also name the "Schmittian understanding of security and exceptional politics' and 'traditional security debates'" as the other two roots of the securitization theory. The discursive approach to security proposed by the Copenhagen School thus considers security as a 'thick signifier', and put the focus on the function of security in social life rather than in its inherent definition.

[49] McDonald (2009), p. 70.

[50] Booth (2007), p. 162.

# 6 Critical Thinking of Security in the Globalization Era

The more radical conceptual innovations of the notion of security were operated by Critical Security Studies. This branch was primarily conformed in the mid-1990s by the European Welsh School (also known as the Aberystwyth School), and was built up from the quest for a real new paradigm that would transform the existing understandings of the notion of security.[51] Critical theory opposed the realist perspective on security—which did not take into account the historical processes that have produced them—and rejected its alleged neutral morality which falls short of proposing alternative feasible transformations of the existing world they describe.[52] In contrast, the Welsh School aimed at finding the new grounds of a political order in which it will possible to identify referents and actors of security which are operative in today's globalized world. Bearing this principal purpose in mind, the critical school understood that "security is what we make of it."[53] It therefore reformulated the notion of security to encompass various aspects of human emancipation,[54] challenging Statism—the normative position that treats the State as the ultimate referent object and agent of security—and defying State-centrism—the consequent methodological choice of taking the State as the central actor and concentrating on its practices when studying international phenomena.[55]

On the one hand, it stressed the limits of Statism and State capacities to ensure security,[56] and considered that security ought to be defined globally, and practised locally. As the central focus of attention shifted away from the State, the Welsh School opened the door to proposals to redefine the notion of sovereignty in the new

[51] For an explanation of the origins and main tenets of the Welsh School (including its relation with the Frankfurt School), see Bilgin (2008), pp. 89–102; Buzan and Hansen (2009), pp. 205–208.

[52] See Horkheimer (1972), pp. 188–243. First published in 1937—and part of the philosophical and sociological movement that came to be known as the Frankfurt School—this article set up the founding layers and the agenda for critical theory, which developed most prominently, after the Second World Word, from the hands of Herbert Marcuse and Jürgen Habermas. "Non-critical" security thinking conceives security as a 'derivative concept' (i.e. which cannot be self-referential and therefore depends on the existence of a 'referent', an 'object' and an 'agent' to make it become a realm of study). Thus, from a realist perspective, 'security' does not exist on its own, without reference to whom is protected, how protection is ensured, and against what protection is needed. Despite the fact that critical security studies also consider that security is a derivative concept, it differs from the traditional perspective in so far as, in Mark Horkheimer's words, traditional theory leads to the "reification of ideas into institutions that are represented as immutable facts of life, whereas critical theory discards rigid distinctions between subject and object."

[53] See Krause and Williams (1997), p. xiii (Preface), who explain that the approach of critical security studies to security "is that of a stranger but not of an outsider".

[54] Booth (2007), p. 110: "Emancipation is at the heart of a critical theory of world security."

[55] Bilgin (2008), p. 94.

[56] Dalby (1999), pp. 155–185, who explains that "discussions of reformulating security also coincide with the widespread recognition of the limits of formal sovereignty in the modern world."

"ecological era."[57] In other words, the interconnectedness of the global ecology led to new understandings of the political community. This new assumption deeply challenged the traditional and the limited widening perspectives on the notion of security and constitutes a radical move within the discipline of International Security Studies. For until then, as explained by Michael Williams and Keith Krause, State sovereignty had embodied for security studies scholars "a coherent response to many of the central problems of political life."[58]

On the other hand, as a reaction to State-centrism, the critical approach put at the centre of the notion of security a concrete normative objective: the fulfilment of various aspects of human liberation. The individual is reified as the sole referent of security, and correlatively security is understood as instrumental to the function of security serving the achievement of the individual's higher goal: its own emancipation.[59] The notion of emancipation is defined by Ken Booth as "the freeing of people – as individuals and groups – from those physical human constraints which stop them carrying out what they would freely choose to do."[60] Critical theories thus argued that States are a means—rather than an end—of security policies.[61] Moreover, this approach to security is closely related to the emergence of the human security branch of International Security Studies, which mirrored the introduction of the notion of human security in United Nations institutions as well as in the policy agenda of some countries that eventually formed the Human Security Network.[62] As explained by Barbara Von Tigerstrom, the launch of the notion of human security "is

---

[57] Ecological security is seen as requiring a 'new cosmology' that incorporates a shift from a homocentric to a bio-centric approach to security. See e.g., Deudney (1991), p. 170. Deudney views as the need to reconstruct "many of the major institutions of industrial modernity, such as the State and the nation."

[58] Krause and Williams (1997), p. xiv (Preface).

[59] See Bilgin (2008), p. 92. The initiation and coining of the term 'critical security studies' comes from the seminal article of Booth (1991), pp. 313–326. Afterwards, what distinguished the Welsh School from other branches of critical security studies was its influence on the Gramscian and Frankfurt School tradition of critical theory.

[60] Booth (1991), p. 319.

[61] Buzan and Hansen (2009), p. 216.

[62] The introduction into the UN agenda of the human-centered approach came with the Human Development Report of 1993 elaborated by the United Nations Development Programme. The Report defined human security as "one of the five pillars of a people-centered world order" and pushed forward the use of the concept in the international discourse with the overall purpose for the UN system of maintaining international peace and security, and with the aim of reinforcing the impetus from military to development spending. Henceforth, clearly echoing the human-centered approach to security, the Report recognized that: "The concept of security must change, from one focused on nations, arms and territory to a greater concern with people, human development, food, employment and the environment," and considered in this context that: "[H]uman Security can be threatened in any of seven different areas, including threats to environmental security. Such threats include: degradation of local eco-systems, water scarcity, lack of sanitation, desertification, severe air pollution, nuclear or chemical accidents and natural disasters ... Threats to one dimension of Human Security often spread to others and many threats cross national borders." See United Nations Development Programme (1993), p. 2.

based on the argument that, because of its privileged moral position, individual human beings rather than States should be the primary referent objects of security."[63]

## 7 Concluding Remarks

Six decades after Arnold Wolfers defined security as "an ambiguous symbol", the basic tenets of his seminal article remain valid, as there is not a unique common understanding of what security constitutes and what it should encompass. Indeed, each of the stages the notion of security, developed through the flourishing of different schools of International Security Studies, brought about new layers of theoretical and empirical cumulative knowledge about it. The inherently ambiguous nature of the concept itself is thus a mirror of the disciplinary and political resistance to reaching a common understanding and shared methodological tools to apprehend this notion. All in all, the evolution of our approach to this notion appears to reflect the correlative transformations in our understanding of the conduct of international relations, as well as of our own identity.

## References

Amitva A (1997) The periphery as the core: the third world and security studies. In: Krause K, Williams MC (eds) Critical security studies: concepts and cases. University Minnesota Press, Minneapolis, pp 299–328

Beard CA with the collaboration of G.H.E Smith (1934) The idea of national interest: analytical study in American foreign policy. The McMillan Company, New York

Bilgin P (2008) Critical theory. In: Williams P (ed) Security studies: an introduction, pp 89–102

Booth K (1991) Security and emancipation. Rev Int Stud 17(4):313–326

Booth K (2007) Theory of world security. Cambridge University Press, Cambridge

Buzan B, Hansen L (2009) The evolution of international security studies. Cambridge University Press, Cambridge

Buzan B, Waever O (2009) Macrosecuritization and security constellations: reconsidering scale in securitization theory. Rev Int Stud 35:253–276

Buzan B, Waever O, De Wilde J (1998) Security: a new framework for analysis. Lynne Rienner, Boulder

Campbell D (1992) Writing security: the United States foreign policy and the politics of identity. University of Minnesota Press, Minneapolis

Carr EH (1939) The twenty years' crisis: 1919-1939. An introduction to the study of international relations. Macmillan Press Ltd., London

Dalby S (1999) Threats from the South? Geopolitics, equity and environmental security. In: Deudney D, Matthew R (eds) Contested grounds: security conflict in the new environmental politics, supra, pp 155–185

[63] Just as the critical theorists, proponents of the notion of human security mainly argue against the assumption that security is a negative force, instead of a condition under which Human Rights can flourish, *see* Von Tigerstrom (2007), p. 51.

Deudney D (1991) The mirage of eco-war: the weak relationship among global environmental change, national security and interstate violence. In: Rowlands I (ed) Environmental change and international relations. Palgrave McMillan, London
Deudney D, Mathews R (1999) Contested grounds: security and conflict in the new environmental politics. State University of New York Press, New York
Frédérick M (1999) A realist conceptual definition of environmental security. In: Deudney D, Matthew R (eds) Contested grounds: security conflict in the new environmental politics. State University of New York Press, Albany, pp 91–108
Galtung J (1964) An editorial. J Peace Res 1(1):1–4
Gledisch NP (2007) Environmental change, security and conflict. In: Crocker C et al (eds) Leashing the dogs of war: conflict management in a divided world. United States Institute of Peace Press, Washington, DC, pp 177–195
Hass PM (1992) Introduction: epistemic communities and international policy coordination. Int Organ 46(1):1–35
Herz J (1950) Idealist internationalism and the security dilemma. World Polit 2(2):157–180
Horkheimer M (1972) Traditional and critical theory. In: Horkheimer M (ed) Critical theory: selected essays. Crossroad Publishing Company, New York
Huntington S (1993) The clash of civilizations? Foreign Aff 72(3):22–49
Katzenstein P (1996) The culture of national security: norms and identity in world politics. Columbia University Press, New York
Keohane R, Nye J (1977) Power and interdependence: world politics in transition. Little, Brown & Co, Boston
Klein B (1997) Conclusion: every month is "security awareness month". In: Krause K, Williams M (eds) Critical security studies: concepts and cases
Klitgaard RE (1971) Gandhi's non-violence as a tactic. J Peace Res 8(2):143–153
Krause K, Williams M (1997) Critical security studies: concepts and cases. University of Minnesota Press, Minnesota
Lenz T (1955) Towards a science of peace. Bookman Associates, New York
Lipschutz R (1998) The nature of sovereignty and the sovereignty of nature: problematizing the boundaries between the self, society, state and system. In: Liftin K et al (eds) The greening of sovereignty in world politics. MIT Press, London, pp 109–138
Matthew R (2000) Integrating environmental factors into conventional security. In: Lowi MR, Shaw BR (eds) Environment and security. International political economy series. Palgrave Macmillan, London, pp 33–48
McDonald M (2009) Constructivism. In: Williams P (ed) Security studies: an introduction. Routledge, London and New York
Morgenthau H (1948) The politics amongst nations: the struggle for power and peace. Alfred A. Knopf, New York
Nye J (1974) Collective economic security. Int Aff 50(4):584–598
Stern E (1995) Bringing the environment in: the case for comprehensive security. Coop Confl 30(3): 211–233
Tigerstrom B (2007) Human security and international law: prospects and problems. Hart Publishing, Oxford and Portland
Tuchmann Mathews J (1989) Redefining security. Foreign Aff 68(2):162–167
United Nations Development Programme (1993) Human development report. Oxford University Press, New York
Waever O (1995) Securitization and desecuritization. In: Lipschutz R (ed) On security. Columbia University Press, New York, pp 46–86
Waever O et al (1993) Identity, migration and the new security agenda in Europe. Pinter, London
Williams P (2008) Security studies: an introduction. Routledge, London and New York
Wolfers A (1952) "National security" as an ambiguous symbol. Polit Sci Q 67(4):481–502

# Screening FDI in the EU: A Cornerstone of an Economic Security Agenda

**Francesca Ghiretti**

## Contents



**Abstract** Between 2017 and 2021 the European Union has transformed Chinese FDI from an economic means into a security threat. Yet very few scholars interrogated how the nexus between Chinese FDI, and security emerged in Europe. This chapter seeks to answer the question of how have actors and stakeholders transformed Chinese FDI from a purely economic matter into a security issue. The working hypothesis argues that if views of Chinese FDI as a threat emerge, then they induce the transformation of FDI from an economic to a security issue, and the evolution of the debate and policymaking in the EU confirms the hypothesis. The chapter demonstrates that security considerations related to traditional security were not the only reasons driving the process, economic considerations too played a central role in the securitisation process. Therefore, this chapters' contribution is foremost empirical. Empirically, firstly, it sheds light on the dynamics of the process that led Chinese FDI to becoming a security issue in Europe and clarifies the drivers of such a shift as not exclusively related to traditional security but also to economic considerations. Secondly, it reveals a trend of increasing interconnection between security and economy in Europe.

---

F. Ghiretti (✉)
Mercator Institute for China Studies (MERICS), Berlin, Germany
e-mail: francesca.ghiretti@merics.de

 
J. Hillebrand Pohl et al. (eds.), *Weaponising Investments*,
Springer Studies in Law & Geoeconomics (2023) 1: 95–108,
https://doi.org/10.1007/17280_2023_2, Published online: 11 July 2023

The debate on how to deal with inbound foreign direct investments (FDI) highlighted concerns about how to better defend European strategic assets. The concerns that emerged laid between the economy and security and triggered a process of securitisation of China's economic presence in Europe, first via direct investments and then more broadly.

This article argues that FDI screening forms the cornerstone of the EU's thinking on economic security. To substantiate such an argument, the article traces the path that led Chinese FDI to shift from being a (welcomed) economic tool to becoming a matter of security for the EU. This article interprets the shift as an important development in the broader EU-China relationship, which has set the scene for other areas of economic relations to go through the same transformation.

In this article, the EU is treated as one actor. The EU has competence in investments (Treaty on the Functioning of the European Union, Article 3). Since its foundation, the EU has had competence in trade, meaning trade agreements would be negotiated at the EU level rather than by member states. This was not the case for foreign direct investments, for which each member state held separate competences. It is with the Treaty of Lisbon, 2009, that the EU obtained competence in FDI. This means that it could now negotiate international investment agreements at the EU level (Bungenberg 2011, pp. 29–42). Despite the reticence of member states to accept this shift, thanks to this new competence, in 2013 the EU was able to launch and then in 2020, formally conclude negotiations with China for a comprehensive agreement on investments (CAI) (Meunier 2014; European Parliament 2021).[1] This article focuses on the EU screening mechanism for FDI, an outcome, of the competence acquired after the Treaty of Lisbon, which however operates on the basis of national security, a competence of member states. Therefore, after three years of negotiations, the final adoption of the EU framework for FDI screening required a vote in the Council (Warchol 2020). While the same conundrum does not necessarily appear to the same extent in other pieces of economic security legislation, it is meant to repropose itself more often as economy and security become increasingly entangled in the EU's policymaking.

While this article does not seek to contribute directly to a detailed description of the evolution of the relationship between the EU and China, it needs to be acknowledged that the whole of the bilateral relationship is undergoing a process of securitisation. The article contributes to the understanding of the EU and China by providing additional information in two areas. First, it analyses an instance where member state-EU-China relations interact. The article shows how both national and regional levels are necessary for the successful adoption and implementation of economic security policy. Furthermore, it shows how even a divisive policy such as

[1] In May 2021, the European Parliament adopted a resolution where it formally freezes the process of ratification of the CAI in reaction to the exchange of sanctions between the EU and China, which saw targeted five Members of the European Parliament as well as the subcommittee on Human Rights. European Parliament, 'MEPs Refuse Any Agreement with China Whilst Sanctions Are in Place', 20 May 2021, https://www.europarl.europa.eu/news/en/press-room/20210517IPR04123/meps-refuse-any-agreement-with-china-whilst-sanctions-are-in-place.

that of a defensive approach to FDI can trigger a Europeanisation process (Hadfield et al. 2017). Second, it illustrates the elements of the relationship that exist at the intersection of security and economy. The analysis of the process of securitisation will focus on three elements: the role of Chinese FDI, and the role of non-military considerations.

## 1 Chinese FDI in the EU in Context

Following the Euro Crisis, the EU began a slow, painful, and highly uneven recovery, which was still ongoing when in 2020, the COVID-19 pandemic and in 2022, Russia's invasion of Ukraine placed the European economy under further stress. Measures adopted after the Euro Crisis were often insufficient to recover the degree of growth to pre-crisis times (World Bank 2021). China was also severely hit by the 2008 global financial crisis, but its political response was to inject a stimulus into the economy, which led to a swift recovery. Such a decision not only pulled China's economy out of the crisis but also carried the recovery of the global economy (Lin 2011).[2] The government of China was then able to turn a debilitating event into a springboard for China's future economic growth and global presence. In fact, China's economy was already growing at an impressive pace before the financial crisis, but the crisis provided a great opportunity for the country's global outreach (Overholt 2010).[3] This outwards push accorded with the 'Going Global' strategy, elaborated by the Chinese government in the late 1990s, which actively incentivised its enterprises to occupy a more global role by entering foreign markets and investing abroad (Wang and Miao 2016). The struggling EU became one of the preferred destinations for foreign investment thanks to its globally renowned firms, know-how, (manufacturing) clusters, and the world's largest consumer market (Knoerich and Miedtank 2018). Both Chinese private and state-owned enterprises (SOEs) invested in the EU. Historically, SOEs accounted for the majority of investments: between 2010 and 2015, they accounted for more than 70 percent of investments. Now, that trend is changing, leaving larger space for private enterprises. Chinese investments have fluctuated over the years; recently, private enterprises have covered the majority of Chinese FDI in the EU (Kratz et al. 2021). The EU's economy found itself in a difficult situation post financial crisis and provided an opportunity for China to invest. Most investments made in the aftermath were auctions, which in most cases were solely attended by Chinese enterprises (Tu 2019).

[2] Lin (2011), pp. 1–14. Lardy (2011).

[3] Overholt (2010), pp. 21–34.

## 2 The Process: Adopting the EU Framework for Investments

The screening mechanism for FDI was not the first EU policy debate to directly involve issues with China. Looking specifically at the economic relations between the two actors since the early 2000s, two macro-areas emerged long before the debate on Chinese FDI in the EU, that on levelling the playing field and on reciprocity. The lack of a level playing field and reciprocity between the EU and China has emerged in policy proposals such as the international procurement instrument launched in 2013, as well as in anti-dumping tariffs and regulations that followed China's cheap production and large exports of products (initially, mostly textile) in the EU.

Thus lack of a level playing field and of reciprocity considerations will emerge in the debate on FDI screening as well as in subsequent policy debates that directly or indirectly involved China such as the EU's foreign subsidies regulation. However, it is with the debate on screening FDI that economic considerations, whether linked to macro areas mentioned above or not, meet with security considerations, beginning to shape economic security thinking in the EU.

China's SOEs are a good example of how an issue of lack of level playing field carries on in the debate on FDI screening and pick up elements with a security connotation. State-owned enterprises are a main feature of many Chinese companies but no longer EU ones. EU's companies must abide by the rules of anti-monopoly and state subsidies of the EU, which prevent them from creating large economic conglomerates such as China SOEs. The unfair competitiveness SOEs gain from such a situation has increasingly been perceived as problematic; SOEs have access to public capital, which gives them an advantage in competing with private enterprises, which tend to be smaller and more subject to market influences. The role of SOEs in the European economy is then further exacerbated by the fact that the majority of EU businesses are small and medium enterprises (European Commission 2017b). European grievances towards SOEs have grown to the point that in 2020, the European Commission published a new white paper on how to curb the action of state-subsidised companies in the EU (European Commission 2020a). At the same time, thanks to China's system, SOEs carry a direct connection to China's state and indirectly to China's Communist Party which raises questions over the scope of their actions abroad, including investments. Without arguing that all SOEs actions have a strategic objective and underlying that SOEs have commercia interests and pursue them, the structure in which they are embedded within China clearly highlights the potential for a strong strategic component to their economic endeavours.

SOEs connections to the Chinese state was one of the factors that contributed to the adoption of the EU's screening for FDI and the securitisation of investments, the other being the growth of China's economic presence in the EU, the growth of Chinese investments in the EU and the nature of the entities that Chinese investments were acquiring (Meunier 2019; Knoerich and Miedtank 2018).

In the years leading up to 2017, Chinese acquisitions in the EU grew significantly, and as an EU official put it, it became evident that China was coming to the EU and not simply the EU going to China.[4] The change in FDI flow with China investing in Europe rather than the other way around was representative of the changing economic relationship; China quickly became a strong economic partner, so strong that it could acquire a large number of European enterprises. It took the EU years to fully understand the implications of such a change, but when it did, it also realised that it was not well equipped to deal with a more economically powerful and present China.[5]

Between 2015 and 2020, Chinese enterprises procured a series of large acquisitions, e.g., ChemChina acquired the Italian tire-maker Pirelli in the largest European acquisition of 2015, that same year, the China General Nuclear Power Group (CGN) committed to building the nuclear plant Hinkley Point C in the UK, and COSCO acquired the majority shares in the Port of Piraeus in Greece in 2016. In 2017, ChemChina acquired Swiss Syngenta, the world's largest producer of agricultural chemicals, tourism investors focused on France, and most notably, 2017 is the year of the acquisition of the German robotic manufacturing Kuka by the Chinese Midea Group (Wenniges and Lohman 2019). The overall growth in acquisitions and high-level acquisitions in particular contributed to the realisation that China was heavily investing in the EU and the EU did not have means to protect its assets from them even if it wanted to. However, it was the acquisition of Kuka that this article, as others before, identifies as being the one that ultimately triggered the process in the EU. Other scholarly works and interviews confirm the importance of that particular transaction (Rabe and Gippner 2017).

The acquisition of Kuka is more relevant than the other acquisitions listed for the European process and for the argument present in this article for two reasons. First, Kuka is considered a strategic asset but not one with immediate security implications, but unlike the other examples listed, it triggered a series of concerns linked to security due to the dual-use nature of the technology it produced.[6] Second, it was in Germany, which this article identifies as being a fundamental actor in the EU process of adoption of the EU's FDI screening regulation.

Germany as a member state has been holding particular importance in shaping the EU's foreign policy and specifically the EU's China policy. Amongst others, Hugo Meijer provides a detailed description of how Germany has been shaping the China policy of the EU, and he also mentions the acquisition of Kuka as a pivotal moment for the adoption of the EU mechanism to screen FDI (Meijer 2022). The importance of Germany for the beginning of the process (adoption of an EU framework for FDI screening) is often downplayed. As the European country that benefits the most from the economic relationship with China, Germany holds great interest in maintaining a

---

[4] Interview EU September 2020.

[5] Interview EU January 2019d, gi; EU September 2019; EU September 2020.

[6] Godement and Vasselier (2017), pp. 1–127. Interview EU September 2019; EU January 2020; EU May 2020a, b; EU September 2020; EU December 2020; EU May 2021a.

positive economic and political relationship with China (Zenglein 2020). The decision to help trigger and back the adoption of a pan-European mechanism represents an important step for Berlin. Before 2017, both the government and industrial unions such as Bundesverband der Deutschen Industrie (BDI) were very sceptical.[7] Following the acquisition of Kuka and the coordination of Germany with two other large European economies in February 2017, France, Germany, and Italy sent a letter to the then EU Commissioner for Trade, Cecilia Malmström. The letter requested action at the EU level to protect the EU's strategic assets (Bundesministerium für Wirtschaft und Energie, Ministère de l'Economie et des Finances, and Ministero dello Sviluppo Economico 2017). The three countries were mainly concerned with know-how transfer and, as detailed above, had Chinese investments in mind when drafting it.[8] Several (former) EU officials have confirmed that Chinese investments and acquisitions were the main reason behind the proposal made by France, Germany and Italy and that Chinese FDI occupied an important position throughout the negotiation process that led to the adoption of the EU framework for FDI.[9]

Arguably, if Germany had not changed its position, the letter to the European Commission would have developed differently, by looking at other regulations with less political support from member states such as the international procurement instrument, it would have taken longer. When the letter arrived, the matter was already being discussed within the Directorate General for Trade. France had been raising the issue with the Commission several times in the past, but it took the acquisition of Kuka to get the German government to pay more attention to the issue. Germany was amongst the countries who sent the letter, and German Chancellor Angela Merkel personally raised the issue with the then President of the European Commission, Jean-Claude Juncker.

The acquisition of Kuka also mainstreamed the debate about the potential security risks of Chinese acquisitions. The argument went along two separate lines: one more concerned with security and one with competition. The former argument maintained that China was gaining access to sensitive assets (both material and immaterial) that could have implications for the security of the bloc (i.e., intelligence information and military and dual-use technology). The second argument was not entirely detached from the first, and it developed on the lines that China was successfully acquiring knowledge that could help its own companies and industries first, to catch up and then, to surpass those of Europe and other advanced economies (Rabe and Gippner 2017). The launch of China's industrial policy that aimed at increasing high-value added manufacturing production called Made in China 2025 fuelled many concerns and exacerbated the feeling that China would become an increasingly difficult competitor for the EU and that the European economic wellbeing could pay the

[7]Interview EU January 2019a; EU December 2020; EU May 2021b.

[8]Interviews EU January 2019a, b, c, d, f, gi; EU December 2020; EU May 2021a, b.

[9]Interviews EU September 2019; EU September 2020; EU May 2021b; IT September 2020b.

cost of such a competition (Breslin 2021).[10] Ultimately, only the more security-related concerns made it into the final legislation, but the debate over to what extent competition concerns should be included will continue even after the adoption of the policy.

## 3 After the Letter. Taking the Necessary Steps to Propose New Regulation

In March 2017, the European Commission published a White Paper on The Future of Europe. It became the starting point of a reflection made by the Commission on how a post-Brexit EU with 27 member states would move forward (European Commission 2017c). This first introductory paper was then followed by a series of issue-specific papers. Interestingly, the first follow-up paper issued in May 2017 was the reflection paper on 'Harnessing Globalisation', where the concerns expressed by France, Germany and Italy were mentioned for the first time in an official EU statement:

> Openness to foreign investment remains a key principle for the EU and a major source of growth. However, *concerns have recently been voiced about foreign investors, notably state-owned enterprises, taking over European companies with key technologies for strategic reasons.* EU investors often do not enjoy the same rights to invest in the country from which the investment originates. These concerns need careful analysis and appropriate action. (European Commission 2017c, p. 15 [emphasis added])

Three main concerns emerge from the quote: the lack of a level playing field, the takeover of key technologies for strategic reasons and the lack of reciprocity. All three of them lament the issue of unfair competition rather than more traditional security, and although China is not explicitly mentioned, the sentiment can be understood to be directed at China. The second element, the "takeover of key technologies for strategic reasons", describes the fact that European concerns were not regarding FDI in general but rather acquisitions. Furthermore, the sentence adds information on the nature of such concern: that the knowledge acquired could be used for strategic reasons. The text does not further elaborate on what these strategic reasons might have been. Interviewees, however, identified three main European strategic concerns linked to China's interest in acquiring European assets: achieving political influence in Europe, increasing China's military capabilities, and increasing the global and the EU's dependence on China.[11] In April 2017, the European Parliament presented a proposal for a Union Act on the Screening of Foreign Investment in Strategic Sectors (European Parliament 2017) in which they asked the Commission "non-EU investment can lead to the acquisition of entire European

[10] Interview EU January 2019a, b, c, d, e, f, gi, May 2020a, b, October 2020; Breslin (2021), pp. 148–154.

[11] Interview EU January 2019a, b, EU September 2019, EU May 2020b, EU September 2020.

companies as part of strategic industrial policies, potentially causing significant damage to the EU economy, particularly in sensitive areas as regards security or industrial policy" (European Parliament 2017). While these interests shed light on the direction of the screening framework, the description remained vague. As the new wording did not contradict the previously used language, the same reasoning proposed for the content of the letter and of the introductory paper can be applied here. The Parliament's proposal by explicitly referring to "damage to EU economy" and "industrial policy" of the EU confirms the hypothesis that since the beginning, European concerns about Chinese FDI were of an economic nature. In September 2017, during the State of the European Union, Juncker mentioned the mechanism to screen FDI as one of the means to protect the EU's strategic interests and once again explicitly mentions state-owned enterprises (Jean-Claude Junker, 2017). In that same month, the European Commission presented a communication for an EU Regulation to establish a mechanism for a European screening of FDI (European Commission 2017b). By doing so, the Commission officially commenced the European legislative process to adopt the new policy and set in motion the process. What followed was a series of 'speech acts' that framed FDI and implicitly framed Chinese FDI as a security threat. The Communication from the Commission to the European Parliament, the European Council, the Council, the European Economic and Social Committee and the Committee of the Regions with the title 'Welcoming Foreign Direct Investment while Protecting Essential Interests' was coupled with an official proposal for a Regulation Establishing a Framework to Screen Foreign Direct Investments from Third Countries on Grounds of "security and public order" in the EU (European Commission 2017a, p. 3). In these two documents, the wording which would then become part of the approved final regulation takes shape "in order to address the potential impact of *cross-border takeovers* on *security and public order*" (European Commission 2017a, p. 2 [emphasis added]).

It took a year of trilateral negotiations[12] and the determination of the leading negotiator from the Austrian Presidency of the Council to finalise the regulation text (European Commission 2019b). Many member states did not share the same position on the matter of regulating inbound FDI. An agreement was reached on 6 December 2018, and the final text was then voted on 5 March 2019. All member states voted in favour except for two abstentions: the UK and Italy. Following European regulations, the EU framework for FDI screening officially entered into force eighteen months after the vote in October 2020 (European Commission 2019b).

[12]Trilateral negotiations occur between the European Commission, the Council of the EU and the European Parliament.

## 4 The Difficult Marriage of Economy and Security

At the time of the proposal, first, the focus of the concerns remained takeovers/acquisitions rather than general FDI. Second, inbound FDI should be vetted on the grounds of 'security and public order'. However, at that stage, and even still, those terms were only broadly defined and only marginally elaborated in the list of sectors and criteria to be accounted for when screening FDI. When drafting the legal text, both the Commission and the Council wanted to make sure the regulation had strong legal ground and support from existing international regulation. Therefore, the proposed legal text was developed with the security exceptions of article XIV*bis* of the General Agreement on Trade in Services (GATS) in mind. In particular, article XIV*bis* b envisages acceptable exceptions to the established rules for the flow of trade and services to protect members' security interests. The aim was to create a tool that would safeguard the EU's strategic assets without risking adopting any protectionist measures that could undermine international rules and the openness of the European market. Coherence with international rules was essential for the EU, but at the same time presented a marginal fracture with the main purpose of the letter by France, Germany, and Italy, who were also concerned with the competitive advantage that China was gaining.[13] Such a concern would have required a limited quasi-protectionist response. The final text, with its broad and expanding list of sectors and criteria, ultimately manages to accommodate both inclinations. Ultimately, the question is whether preoccupations that shaped the process were more of a military or economic nature.

Ultimately, the competence of member states on national security shaped the framework, which in its current form functions as an information sharing mechanism that directs member states to share details with Brussels and other member states about FDI in the cases where (a) another member state or the European Commission requests information or (b) an investment is undergoing screening in the country. If a country does not have a national screening mechanism, it is not required to notify transactions to the European Commission but is expected to respond to requests for information from other member states and the Commission as well as to give due consideration to the comments of the other Member States and to the opinion of the Commission. Moreover, there is a possibility for a member state without an investment screening mechanism to ask other member states and the Commission to provide their opinion about an inbound FDI occurring within its borders. In the cases where FDI is reported to the European Commission, the European Commission and other member states can ask for further information and/or provide their

[13] It must be noted how of the three senders, Germany was the one who advocated a rigid adherence to the concept of security. To this day, the German regulation in matter of FDI screening rigidly limits the power to block investments to the security realm, which includes dual-use technology. France and Italy, on the contrary, were both more flexible in including matters related to competition. Federal Ministry for Economic Affairs and Climate Action. "Foreign Trade and Investment Law", 2021. https://www.bmwi.de/Redaktion/EN/Artikel/Foreign-Trade/investment-screening.html.

comments about the case at hand. These opinions must be considered by the member state in which the investment is happening when making a decision, but there is no 'hard' obligation[14] to follow the opinions provided, and consequently, no sanction can be imposed if the member state does not act upon this opinion (European Parliament and Council of the European Union 2019).

Article 4 of the EU framework for FDI screening better defines the criteria that can affect the security and public order and can in turn trigger FDI scrutiny (European Parliament and Council of the European Union 2019 Article 4). These are listed under 'inter alia', meaning the list can be expanded by Brussels or member states. Furthermore, the elements listed confirm a broadening of the concept of security beyond traditional security, which extends beyond the military sector. That is the case of energy and raw material, intended as what in the introductory section to this article was referred to as 'security of supply'. The underlying concern regarding "security of supply" relates to a situation where supply can be disrupted and have negative consequences over the functioning of the society and its safety. For example, the "security of supply" may be vulnerable to disruptions if a foreign company has acquired shares in a European energy provider, if the shares acquired provide the acquirer decisional or veto power over the acquired company, and if the energy provider is essential for the functioning of the country (i.e., the only provider, one of the few available, or manages core energy grids).

Furthermore, the expansion of the concept of security mirrored in the list of sectors presented in the final text of the regulation includes dual-use technologies. For example, elements such as semiconductors, artificial intelligence and robotics raise the issue of how to manage dual-use technology. Since dual-use technology can be applied both for military and civil use, the civil aspect of strategic assets has been securitised to adhere to a logic of 'better safer than sorry'. For example, a foreign company acquires a European company that produces semiconductors and has access to the technology used to produce them and then, transfers that technology to the home country of the acquirer. That technology can be used for civil and military purposes (there are case where it is not so, but it is not always possible to differentiate between the two), thus the technology as whole is protected to avoid a situation where European technology fuels the military capabilities of another country without explicitly agreeing to do so. Such fears are then further fuelled by China's official plan of civil-military fusions with the aim of strengthening the People's Liberation Army (Kania and Laskai 2021).

Finally, the inclusion of freedom of media is a case in point of the importance that safeguarding the EU's "way of life" (European Commission 2019a) played in the debate for adoption of the mechanism. This article does not deal with the topic of disinformation or information warfare, but the inclusion of media in the list highlights the importance the topic had for the EU when the regulation was approved.

[14]The general EU legal principle of sincere cooperation intervenes to require member states to act in good faith when considering the opinions. It can be viewed as a 'soft' obligation to not reject the Commission and/or other member states' opinions for no valid reason.

In March 2020 in the first months of the unfolding of the Covid-19 in Europe, the Commission issued the 'Guidelines to Protect Critical European Assets and Technology in Current Crisis', and Ursula von der Leyen, President of the Commission, in her speech directly mentioned "economic sovereignty" (European Commission 2020b).

While the Commission first adopted and consequently implemented the mechanism to serve security and public order, keeping security and economy separate appears to have become increasingly difficult. By 2020, the objective of the EU framework for FDI screening seemed to have gained one extra unofficial objective and become aimed at protecting the EU's security, public order, and economic sovereignty. In the context of the pandemic, the protection of economic sovereignty emerged not only in relation to investments but also in relation to supply chains (European Parliament 2021). The inclusion of value chains could amount to an expansion of the process to other areas of the economy and thus potentially exist in the EU of a broader process that is turning economic relations into a security matter. Confirming this is the acceleration in the EU's adoption of tools to protect its economic security that goes beyond FDI screening.

## 5 Beyond the EU Framework for FDI Screening: The Pandemic of COVID-19 and the War in Ukraine

The process of adoption of the EU FDI screening mechanism unlocked the policy connection between economy and security, which in the years that followed has become increasingly normalised and present in new policies. The pandemic of Covid-19 and Russia's invasion of Ukraine have then created tangible situations where the whole of the EU saw the risks connected with an open economic relation that left space for overdependencies and exposed EU's vulnerabilities. The two events also highlighted how economic relations could be instrumentalised to influence policies or diplomatic objectives, such as the case of the so-called mask diplomacy carried forward by China during the pandemic or the interruption of gas supplies to Europe by Russia in response to EU's sanctions against Russia. Both gifted the EU with the necessary momentum to increase attention and action towards better understanding how vulnerable the EU is and how to improve its own resilience. In 2021 and 2022, the EU carried on two assessments of dependencies proposed policies such as the Battery Regulation, the Chips act and the proposal for a Critical Raw Material Act to decrease EU's vulnerabilities and improve economic security.

Between 2019 and the beginning of 2022, the European Commission proposed ten new policies linked to economic security. 2022 also saw the proposal of new due diligence regulation, a regulation to fight force labour in EU's supply chains and the approval of a regulation to control foreign subsidies within the EU market.

Smaller, yet highly impactful, episodes include the use by China of its economic weight to adopt economic coercive measure in response to Lithuania's decision to open a Taiwanese permanent representation in Vilnius. The episode gave momentum to the EU's anti-coercion instrument (ACI), which however was born out of concern linked to the coercive use of economic ties by the US under the Trump administration.

Tab with policy timeline.

# 6 Conclusion

When views of Chinese FDI as a security issue emerged in the EU, they triggered FDI to transition from being an economic issue to becoming a security issue. The relationship between the EU and China was built on economic premises, and to this day, the core of the relationship remains economic. Therefore, the decision by the EU to defend strategic assets against Chinese acquisitions is an important change in the way the EU approaches China. The shift from opportunity to competition has played a role in shaping the relationship, but after the mid-2010s, security concerns strongly made their way into the economic agenda of the relations, starting with FDI. The issue of how FDI became a security concern in the EU remains underdeveloped and under researched. The chapter has demonstrated the difficulties that economically liberal institutions and governments face when turning an economic matter such as FDI into a security issue and adopting related policies.

Studying how the FDI screening mechanism in the EU has developed over time reveals some interesting aspects. First, the importance of the interaction between the regional and national levels. Both are fundamental to create the necessary political momentum to trigger relevant legislation and to get it fast-tracked and approved, especially for matters that are located in-between economy and security, where the former is largely competence of the EU and the latter of member states. Arguably, it led to what can be seen as a Europeanisation of the securitisation process of Chinse FDI. However, a second analysis of the dynamics also shows that while the EU needs member states' support to successfully securitise an item, it does not need them all to follow its example for the process at the EU level to be successful. The EU has securitised Chinese FDI even in a scenario where some member states have not. Overall, the EU framework for FDI screening not only represents a successful process of securitisation but also where a successfully adopted policy has caused a domino effect, pushing most EU member states to strengthen or adopt a screening mechanism for FDI for themselves and unlocking economic security thinking and policymaking.

A second important point is the special role that Germany played in the process. Once the German government recognised the security risks posed by Chinese FDI the process of securitisation received a vital impetus. At the same time, other member states have been fundamental for the success of the policy. To mention a few, France and Italy as co-signers of the letter to the European Commission making the case for a EU-wide investments screening. Austria who held the presidency of the Council that brought the negotiations and the instrument to a successful end.

Individual political actors, such as the then German Chancellor, Angela Merkel, as well as the President of the Commission, Jean-Claude Juncker, and the rapporteur Frank Proust, played an important role in setting the process in motion and in shaping its development. For example, Frank Proust's knowledge of FDI screening regulation in France shaped his way of approaching the issue and allowed him to bring the French experience as an example of what the mechanism is and how it could work.

Third, in the EU, FDI has been gradually managed as a security issue, but they have had to face numerous obstacles. With a few exceptions, the view of FDI as a security issue was completely new to the EU and many of its member states, and as such, the opposition was strong. Even more so, considering the EU—and some member states—strongly defends an open and liberal economy. Therefore, the securitisation process occurred gradually, not only in terms of numbers of supporters but also in terms of understanding what the security implications of FDI may be. After four years since the securitisation process began, it has become normal to talk about FDI in security terms and, more broadly, to discuss the security risks of economic interdependence. This chapter also shows how in the case of the EU, eventually, the concept of security takes a broad and rather flexible meaning. The meaning is often adapted to three elements: member states' needs, the developments in the relationship between the EU and China, and on a case-by-case basis of acquisitions. In general, the main concerns can be summarised as economic, e.g., a loss of competitiveness, a lack of a level playing field and reciprocity, and a risk of over dependency, as well as military, e.g., the use of dual-use technology for military purposes and access to intelligence data.

## References


Breslin S (2021) China risen? Studying Chinese Global Power, 1st edn. Bristol University Press, Bristol

Bundesministerium für Wirtschaft und Energie, Ministère de l'Economie et des Finances, and Ministero dello Sviluppo Economico (2017) Letter to Commissioner Malmström from France, Germany and Italy

Bungenberg M (2011) The division of competences between the EU and its Member States in the area of investment politics. In: Bungenberg M, Griebel J, Hindelang S (eds) International investment law and EU law. Springer, Berlin, Heidelberg, pp 29–42

European Commission (2017a) COM(2017) 494 Final Welcoming Foreign Direct Investment While Protecting Essential Interests

European Commission (2017b) FDI Proposal by the European Commission. 0224. http://www.europarl.europa.eu/RegData/docs_autres_institutions/commission_europeenne/com/2017/0487/COM_COM(2017)0487_EN.pdf

European Commission (2017c) White Paper on the Future of Europe

European Commission (2019a) European Commission and HR/VP Contribution to the European Council. EU-China, A Strategic Outlook

European Commission (2019b) Screening of Foreign Direct Investments

European Commission (2020a) White paper on levelling the playing field as regards to foreign subsidies

European Commission (2020b) EU foreign investments screening mechanism becomes fully operational

European Parliament (2017) Proposal for a Regulation of the European Parliament and of the Council establishing a framework for screening of foreign direct investments into the European Union

European Parliament (2021) Post Covid-19 Value Chains: Options for Reshoring Production Back to Europe in a Globalised Economy

European Parliament, and Council of the European Union (2019) (FDI Screening) Regulation (EU) 2019/452 of the European Parliament and of the Council of 19 March 2019 Establishing a Framework for the Screening of Foreign Direct Investments into the Union. OJ L 79I (21.3.2019), 1–14. 2019, no. March: 1–14. https://eur-lex.europa.eu/eli/reg/2019/452/oj

Godement F, Vasselier A (2017) China at the gates: a new power audit of EU-China relations. European Council on Foreign Affairs

Hadfield A, Ian M, Richard W (2017) Foreign policies of EU Member States continuity and Europeanisation, 1st edn. Routledge, London

Kania EB, Laskai L (2021) Myths and realities of China's military-civil fusion strategy. Center for New American Security. https://www.cnas.org/publications/reports/myths-and-realities-of-chinas-military-civil-fusion-strategy

Knoerich J, Miedtank T (2018) The idiosyncratic nature of Chinese foreign direct investment in Europe. Cesifo FORUM 19(4)

Kratz A, Zenglein M, Sebastian G (2021) Chinese FDI in Europe: 2020 Update

Lardy N (2011) Sustaining China's economic growth after the global financial crisis. Peterson Institute

Lin JY (2011) China and the global economy. China Econ J 4(1):1–14. https://doi.org/10.1080/17538963.2011.609612

Meijer H (2022) Awakening to China's rise European foreign and security policy toward the People's Republic of China. Oxford University Press

Meunier S (2014) Divide and conquer? China and the Cacophony of foreign investment rules in the EU. J Eur Public Policy 21(7):996–1016. https://doi.org/10.1080/13501763.2014.912145

Meunier S (2019) Beware of Chinese bearing gifts: why China's direct investment poses political challenges in Europe and the United States. In: Chaisse J (ed) China's three-prong investment strategy: bilateral, regional, and global tracks, Chapter 18. Oxford University Press, London

Overholt WH (2010) China in the global financial crisis: rising influence, rising challenges. Wash Q 33(1):21–34. https://doi.org/10.1080/01636600903418652

Rabe W, Gippner O (2017) Perceptions of China's outward foreign direct investment in European critical infrastructure and strategic industries. Int Polit 54(4):468–486. https://doi.org/10.1057/s41311-017-0044-x

Tu C (2019) Chinese outbound investments. In: Chinese FDI in the EU and the US. Springer, pp 1–13

Wang H, Miao L (2016) Going Global Strategy' and global talent BT - China goes global: how China's overseas investment is transforming its business enterprises. Palgrave Macmillan UK, London, pp 144–152. https://doi.org/10.1007/978-1-137-57813-6_6

Warchol J (2020) The birth of the EU screening regulation, Hinderlang & Moberg, YSEC Yearbook of socio - Economic Constitutions 2020, A Common European Law on Investment Screening (CELIS)

Wenniges T, Lohman W (2019) Chinese FDI in the EU and the US. Simple rules for turbulent times. Palgrave Macmillan, Singapore. https://doi.org/10.1007/978-981-13-6071-8

World Bank (2021) GDP (Current US$) - European Union, https://data.worldbank.org/indicator/NY.GDP.MKTP.CD?locations=EU

Zenglein M (2020) Mapping and recalibrating Europe's economic interdependence with China. Mercator Institute for China Studies

# The National Securitization of Foreign Direct Investment: A Strategic Futures Paradigm

**John Lash**

## Contents



**Abstract** The age of intelligent warfare has created a fully integrated cyber, economic, and information state of adversarial capabilities within an emergent threat landscape. The landscape is shaped by multidimensional strategic interactions of globalization, vis-à-vis foreign direct investment (FDI), that are not constrained by the traditional boundary conditions of national security or free trade. The complex concepts of power and influence within the broad scope of globalization and national security require an evaluation that adequately addresses the threat environment in the twenty-first century—a modernized model where investments, which create direct and indirect power over other nations, are weaponized.

Nations are required to make difficult, and at times zero-sum, decisions between enabling growth-oriented economic policies and national security determinations. All governments must consider their nations' place in progressing toward the next industrial revolution. This advancement includes evaluating how global competition creates technological and economic resilience, security, and innovation. Key reflection points include how to create consistent and transparent standards, evaluating to what extent governments participate in the capital markets, how and where capital and resources are allocated, and by what measure are the consequences of action or

J. Lash (✉)
Darkhorse Global, Pittsburgh, PA, USA
e-mail: jlash@darkhorseglobal.com



J. Hillebrand Pohl et al. (eds.), *Weaponising Investments*,
Springer Studies in Law & Geoeconomics (2023) 1: 109–116,
https://doi.org/10.1007/17280_2023_3, Published online: 14 June 2023

inaction judged over time. Nations must evaluate the positive and negative externalities on domestic industry that global competition creates by recognizing that placing limitations on the ability of companies to compete on a global scale directly impacts national security, technology, and economic policy.

## 1 Introduction

This article will discuss the developing variables related to the intersection of foreign direct investment and national security investment reviews, as well as establish a foundation to deliberate both the positive and negative externalities associated with national security investment reviews around the world. The observations were evaluated throughout the established foundational regulatory and policy domains for governments to consider in ensuring a harmonized economic policy and national security environment. In addition, this article evaluates the type and use of economic tools to further national security and foreign policy objectives, while challenging the theory that globalized free markets cannot self-regulate without government intervention.

Economic systems, founded on free markets and free trade, continue to underpin the broad domains of prosperity and security. The industrial policy of nations has evolved to directly map economic security as national security—a divergence from the narrower focus of national security within military capabilities and defense industries. This expansion toward a more comprehensive economic and technological strategy has created a paradigm wherein national security is utilized broadly into coordinated economic competition and industrial policy decisions. Today's global economic environment has benefitted greatly from competition, which provides the link between economic security and national security. Competition creates security, resilience, and innovation and provides cost-effective products and services.

However, by indirectly and directly mapping national security to industrial policy, nations have found themselves entangled in conflict over economic development, modernization, and how to address trade imbalances and adhere to and enforce global standards for world order. Nations must seek to evaluate the converging national security and industrial policy frameworks to evaluate the viability and consequences of the national securitization of global economies. Collaborative and competitive strategies establish effective models for security, reliability, resilience, and cost effectiveness while recognizing the potential negative externalities of regulatory barriers.

This article is structured to first examine the relationship between globalization and trade policy, then to explain the evolution of national interest and national security considerations in free markets, and finally exploring the practical implication of security nationalism within industrial policy.

## 2 Trade Policy & National Security

Trade policy integrates national economies into the global economic system. Globalization, through dynamic advancements of technology and the global expansion of trade, has created an irrevocably interconnected ecosystem for much of the global economy—from manufacturing to energy to the future of space exploration. The nature of these relationships creates economic, technological, and societal benefits but also establishes or exacerbates the potential risks related to national security.

National security issues most impacted by globalization fall into three primary categories: (1) the nature of security threats in a globalized world, (2) the effects of the phenomenon of globalization on the pursuit of national security, and (3) the erosion of the exclusivity of the state as a provider of national security (Phahlamohlaka 2008). The nature of threats are both constantly evolving and expanding as the world becomes more interconnected via technology and supply chains, which exasperbates some existing threats while creating novel threat environments. The effects of the phenomenon may present positive or negative externalities, or in many cases both, as countries become more secure via coordinated cooperation with allies while simultaneously expanding supply chain risks through offshoring. Lastly, the net effect is that private industry and commercial companies are now effectively providing and contributing to national security through various means of operation, including cybersecurity, supply chain resiliency, and research and development efforts.

The issues reflect the complexity of the new globalized security environment and require that the threats associated with the interconnected nature of the ecosystem be addressed in a multipolar manner—focusing on cybersecurity, supply chain risk management, and a coordinated approach to regulating markets.

Historically, nations concluded that the absolute benefits of globalization outweighed the costs and risks; however, in the current geopolitical and economic environment, some nations have moved toward a more protectionist posture globally, a concept known as "security nationalism." While these efforts often resonate as a domestic political narrative, both economic research and historical evidence illustrate that market-oriented policies (i.e., trade liberalization)—not security nationalism—boost the economy, discourage armed conflict, and help countries mitigate or recover from economic shocks (Lincicome 2021).

## 3 The Challenge of Globalization

Market-driven competition, a pillar of free and fair markets, has bolstered productivity while promoting dynamic industries, innovation, and economic growth. The economic dimension of national security is highly dependent on a nation's ability to harmonize with the evolving forces of the global ecosystem, which include the interdependent risks in goods, services, human capital, and information

(Constantinescu 2017). Inhibiting, prohibiting, or otherwise constraining the ability of certain domestic businesses or specific countries to compete under these global standards will negatively impact the progress of not only developed economies but also developing nations around the world, which would experience the consequences in an exponentially more impactful manner.

Nations must further evaluate the concept of hegemony in the current multipolar world and whether this "predominance" among economic, political, or military domains is an order that should be maintained as part of the vision of globalization. The American political scientists John Mearsheimer and Joseph Nye have argued that the U.S. is not a genuine global hegemon because it has neither the financial nor the military resources to impose a proper, formal, global hegemony (Nye 1993).

Evaluating the relationship between national power and commitments, the sources of that power (military, economic, political), means and commitments related to resources, and the characteristics of the contemporary international system must be considered—these vectors of change in the twenty-first century have created a new world order as it relates to the relationships between nations that have evolved through history (Hendrickson 2005).

Broad discretion around national security in economics can be found when evaluating issues such as intellectual property law, data rights, underselling or underbidding, or in the capital markets arena through investments, acquisitions, or joint ventures. While these issues are critically important to nations, there must be careful consideration to address potential national security issues contained therein with technical precision—not through broad national security determinations on trade policy issues. Foreign adversaries can further this influence through investment activities to pursue strategic objectives through diplomatic, informational, military, and economic capabilities that underpin their interests (Heffington et al. 2019).

## 4 The National Securitization of Foreign Direct Investment

The current thresholds for national security threats in critical infrastructure sectors are impacted by both technical and political considerations that are in a constant state of evolution. How nations operate in the gray zone using soft power or hard power methods is critically important to geopolitical relationships.

The gray zone is identified as being power competition and conflict existing within a hybrid threat environment elevated beyond normal steady-state diplomacy yet short of conventional war, which includes factors such as economic influence, sharp power, political warfare, malign influence, irregular warfare, and forms of modern deterrence (RAND 2019). These factors create dynamic forces where assessors must consider potentially competing issues on a global scale—the relative concepts of power and commitments.

First, it relates to commitments: How can nations preserve multilateral relationships, particularly with the United States, without jeopardizing key diplomatic, economic, intelligence, and military alliances? And second, as it relates to power:

How can nations comprehensively synthesize data and perform technical assessments to evaluate whether foreign direct investment has the potential to be used as "adversarial capital," meaning a direct threat to national security based in the range of influence the economic power will convey. This range of influence must be evaluated based on the type of control and governance over the business that the transaction conveys, not a theoretical construct that has not been contemplated within the deal structure.

In making these determinations, nations must seek to evaluate the converging national security and industrial policy frameworks to evaluate the viability and consequences of the national securitization of global economies. Collaborative and competitive strategies establish effective models for security, reliability, resilience, and cost effectiveness while recognizing the potential negative externalities of regulatory barriers. For example, there should exist a model for secure and mutually beneficial collaboration between the U.S. and China as it relates towards renewable energy and sustainability.

## *4.1 Investment Reviews: Competition or Conflict in Strategic Industries*

Traditional industrial policy can be broadly characterized by the policy actions of a government that supports particular domestic industries, whether via incentives or deterrents. The debate over the role of industrial policy exists because of the juxtaposition with free market economics, which is a self-regulating system that operates under the laws of supply and demand without forms of centralized government intervention.

Important questions remain around how to implement industrial policy beyond its theoretical constructs, with critiques that must be addressed, as illuminated by Dani Rodrick, a Turkish economist and Ford Foundation Professor of International Political Economy at the Kennedy School of Government at Harvard University—"-While the case for industrial policy is strong in theory, it is ambiguous in practice" (Rodrik 2014).

Sceptics raise two practical objections: (1) Informational objection: can governments accurately identify the relevant firms, sectors, markets subject to those market imperfections? This critique is often expressed by saying "governments cannot pick winners." (2) Political capture: can governments withstand lobbying from powerful firms and prevent industrial policy from becoming an instrument of rent transfer to incumbents?" (Rodrik 2019).

## 4.2 Industrial Policy as a Paradox

Throughout history, there had been broad consensus among economists that extoled the virtues of free trade or near-free trade. Over time, we have witnessed a shift in the approach and are firmly in a time of questioning the free trade consensus based on both theoretical developments and new empirical evidence. What has been observed during the rise of developed countries has often been the use of significant trade protection during phases of industrialization and rapid development, much of which blends the constructs of protectionism with competition.

One of the pillars of the free-market argument is that real-world states (the government) are even more imperfect than real-world markets. This is because government support for strategic industries can lead to the inefficient allocation of resources and a conflict of self-interests, such as when providing a subsidy to one sector implies a tax on others or creating circumstances that lead to a long-run shift in innovative behaviors and private sector risk-taking (Michalski 1991).

Although relatively untested directly, there is support for the meta-belief that imperfect markets are generally better than imperfect states—thus, states should withdraw from directly influencing resource allocation and protecting or giving preferential resources to certain sectors, known broadly as "industrial policy" (European Parliament 2012). The potential pitfalls of industrial policy have often been repeated, such as the argument that in a fragmented political structure such as the United States, a national industrial policy would be vague, confusing, politicized, and frequently ineffective (Philips 1992). However, regardless of political concerns, the majority of U.S. citizens have favored the federal government joining forces with industry in a national competitive strategy, as evidenced by the passage of multiple bills through Congress focused on competition, innovation, and the domestic manufacturing and production of key goods.

Responding to the resounding issues around the role that governments play in free markets and the debate over maximizing economic "efficiency," will play a vital role in how the theories of government intervention versus market-oriented policies can and should be effectively implemented into economic systems that are inherently globalized. Throughout history, the "invisible hand" of the markets has influenced both economic and political dynamics, and now the role of governments is becoming more overt and visible.

## 4.3 Strategic-Industry Competitiveness Policies

Beyond a generic government policy for industrial competitiveness, there is an argument for a policy specifically tailored to boost production and innovation capacity in strategically important industries—a strategic-industry competitiveness policy (Atkinson 2022). This type of policy is intended to be a more nuanced and explicit effort to identify the key industries in which the U.S. must maintain capabilities to be "secure" in the broad domains of national and economic security.

Critically important, however, is whether strategic-industry policy—which may also be termed "security nationalism"—functions as designed in practice. Empirical evidence exists for a similarly structured project SEMATECH (short for semiconductor manufacturing technology), a semiconductor R&D consortium with engagement by the U.S. government and the private sector that was funded by the U.S. Department of Defense via the Defense Advanced Research Projects Agency (DARPA) for USD 500 million.

Subsequent research on SEMATECH identified that "SEMATECH was able to borrow technology from private companies and reproduce results that private companies had achieved years before – and do it with taxpayer money; adding very little to what private industry was already capable of doing for itself" (Lindsey 1992). While researchers Douglas Irvin and Peter Klenow concluded that the "U.-S. government's contributions to SEMATECH do not induce more semiconductor research than would otherwise occur" (Irwin and Klenow 1996, p. 12739). Notably, there is consensus that the U.S. achievements during this time were due to the private sector's ability to outcompete and innovate effectively and was not attributable to the direct government intervention.

## 5 Conclusion

Industrial policy, economic competitiveness, and national security reviews of foreign direct investment are factors for political, economic, and military superiority at a global scale. The inherent ability of a government to influence private industry through industrial policy is based on the way the nation governs, with some nations actively subsidizing firms in sectors that are considered strategic, such as the technology sector in the twenty-first century.

Utilizing economics as an instrument of politics is a common tool within the operationalization of economic statecraft (e.g., economic forms of influence). These forms of influence can be wielded via distinct negative actions such as withholding economic advantages (e.g., sanctions) and positive actions such as offering economic benefits (e.g., direct government subsidies) (Delevic 1998).

However, the effectiveness and efficiency of using economic instruments to pursue foreign policy goals remains in dispute. Notably, economic sanctions are principally coercive tools whose effectiveness should be evaluated according to their ability to modify behavior, with research indicating that economic sanctions have rarely achieved coercive success.

Equally as critical as recognizing the potential negative externalities of economic statecraft, governments must avoid relying too extensively on economic benefits or regulation to carry companies to success. The role of government should be one that enables competitive and open global standards for innovation while protecting the key components of the ecosystem that rely on order such as intellectual property protections and cybersecurity.

The expansion of industrial policy to map to national security or national interests has created a paradigm wherein these considerations are utilized broadly to influence economic competition and traditional free trade interactions between nations. History and academic research show that freer markets can bolster national security and economic resilience and that "security nationalism," by contrast, has been not only unsuccessful but often based on an expansive and political definition of "national security" (Lincicome 2021). Nations must embrace the fundamental principles of globalization while addressing the new economic security challenges to pursue a vision of economic diplomacy in this new multipolar world.

## References

Atkinson R (2022) Computer Chips vs Potato Chips: the case for a U.S. strategic industry policy. ITIF. Retrieved from https://itif.org/publications/2022/01/03/computer-chips-vs-potato-chips-caseus-strategic-industry-policy

Constantinescu P (2017) Economic risks to national security, presented at the 12th International Scientific Conference Defense Resources Management in the 21st century. Romanian National Defense University, Regional Department of Defense Resources Management Studies, Brasov Romania

Delevic M (1998) Economic sanctions as a foreign policy tool: the case of Yugoslavia. Int J Peace Stud 3:1

Heffington S, Oler A, Tretler D (2019) A national security strategy primer. National Defense University Press, Washington, D.C.

Hendrickson D (2005) The curious case of American hegemony: imperial aspirations and national decline. World Policy J 22(2):1–22

Irwin D, Klenow P (1996) Sematech: purpose and performance. Proc Natl Acad Sci 93(23): 12739–12742

Lincicome S (2021) Manufactured crisis: deindustrialization, free markets, and national security. Policy Analysis no 907. Cato Institute, Washington DC

Lindsey B (1992) DRAM Scam. Reason

Michalski W (1991) OECD international futures program, strategic industries in a global economy. Support policies for strategic industries: an introduction to the main issues

Morris L, Mazarr M, Hornung J, Stephanie P, Binnendijk A, Keep M (2019) Gaining competitive advantage in the gray zone: response options for coercive aggression below the threshold of major war. RAND Corporation, Santa Monica

Nye JS Sr (1993) Understanding international conflicts: an introduction to theory and history. HarperCollins, New York

Phahlamohlaka J (2008) Globalisation and national security issues for the state: implications for national ICT policies. In: Avgerou C, Smith ML, van der Besselaar P (eds) Social dimensions of information and communication technology policy. HCC 2008. IFIP International Federation for Information Processing, vol 282. Springer, Boston

Philips K (1992) U.S. industrial policy: inevitable and ineffective. Harv Bus Rev 70(4)

Rodrik D (2014) Green industrial policy. Oxford Rev Econ Policy 30(3):469–491

Rodrik D (2019) Where are we in the economics of industrial policies. Retrieved from https://voxdev.org/topic/public-economics/where-are-we-economics-industrial-policies

# Economic Perspectives on FDI and Investment Screening

**Patrik Tingvall and Jonas Hallberg**

## Contents



**Abstract** It is proposed that in a future Swedish investment screening mechanism, it will become mandatory for the Inspectorate of Strategic Products to consult with the National Board of Trade. A key role for the Board will be to contribute with analysis

Valuable comments from conference participants at the 2022 CELIS Forum on Investment Screening (CFIS 22) are appreciated.

P. Tingvall
National Board of Trade, Stockholm, Sweden

Södertörn University, Stockholm, Sweden
e-mail: patrik.tingvall@kommerskollegium.se

J. Hallberg (✉)
National Board of Trade, Stockholm, Sweden
e-mail: jonas.hallberg@kommerskollegium.se

 
J. Hillebrand Pohl et al. (eds.), *Weaponising Investments*,
Springer Studies in Law & Geoeconomics (2023) 1: 117–140,
https://doi.org/10.1007/17280_2023_14, Published online: 24 June 2023

regarding the importance of the investment for the economy and the investment climate. We note a gap in the literature in the sense that the broad mass of economic analysis of foreign direct investments (FDI) focuses on the effects of production-oriented activities, while much of the security discourse also embraces ownership such as infrastructure and hospitals. It is shown that uncertainty is harmful to inward FDI. To minimize uncertainty and the potential FDI-dampening effects of an investment screening regulation, the range of affected sectors should be narrowly defined, accompanied by a swift and transparent review process that provides predictability to the transaction parties. Inward FDI in general and high-tech investments in particular can benefit innovation, stimulate investment, promote skill upgrading, improve resource allocation, sharpen competition, create high-wage jobs and increase economic growth. The literature has shown that many positive effects from FDI take place in the form of spillover effects that are difficult to measure directly. Many best practices attracting FDI include general policies rather than selective measures.

## 1 The Proposed Future Swedish Investment Screening Mechanism

A fairly recent amendment to the Swedish Protective Security Act gives the state the possibility to screen transfer of ownership of certain operations deemed to be of importance for Swedish national security.[1] However, this does not amount to a classic investment screening mechanism.

A substantive governmental inquiry (Screening of foreign investments, SOU 2021:87[2]) was handed over to the Government Offices in November 2021.[3] The inquiry suggests that the Inspectorate of Strategic Products (ISP) will be the governmental agency responsible for the screening of inbound direct investments. ISP is the national contact point for requesting and sending information about foreign direct investments (FDI) between the different EU Member States and the EU Commission, as required by the EU Investment Screening Regulation.[4] The inquiry suggests that ISP will screen both transfer of stock above 10% (brownfield

[1]Chapter 4, Paragraph 13–20, Protective Security Act (2018:545).

[2]Granskning av utländska investeringar, SOU 2021:87.

[3]In the following we will assume that the Government/Parliament follows the suggestions by the inquiry.

[4]Regulation (EU) 2019/452 of the European Parliament and of the Council of 19 March 2019 establishing a framework for the screening of foreign direct investments into the Union.

investments) and also start-ups of new companies (greenfield investments).[5] It's the sector to which the company belongs that will determine if the company will be screened and not the size of the company.

ISP was already before this assignment an agency dealing with issues related to Swedish security and was by the inquiry for this reason deemed most fit for the purpose. With this background, the likelihood that the Parliament will give ISP the proposed role as the responsible agency for investment screening is close to certain. The inquiry presumes that the bulk of inbound investments will be considered non-problematic, and ISP will, according to the proposal in these cases, not conduct an in-depth investigation. Instead, applications will be automatically cleared after a certain period. The period starts from the date the ISP receives a complete application.

In cases where ISP have information at hand that gives reason to take a more careful look at an investment, they will conduct an in-depth investigation. When doing so, ISP needs, according to the inquiry, to consult with appropriate governmental agencies and, in some cases, also regional agencies. Which agencies depend on the specific investment. However, it is also suggested that it will be mandatory for ISP to consult with four agencies no matter what kind of investment that seeks approval. The Swedish mandatory consultation agencies are the Swedish Security Service (Säpo), the Swedish Defence Forces (in practice MUST), the Swedish Civil Contingencies Agency (MSB) and finally the odd bird, the National Board of Trade.

Hence, the Swedish investment screening will at first instance not be conducted by the Government Offices such as is the case in most other countries, but instead by the governmental agency ISP, with the assistance of other agencies. The Swedish constitution generally prohibits the government from influencing decisions made by governmental agencies in individual cases. For this reason, when the ISP handles the case as the first instance, the government is not allowed to influence whether the specific investment should be allowed or not. This is especially true in this case, since a decision made by ISP, including a rejection/condition, may be appealed by the investor to the government. Supposedly, this will make a Swedish (future) investment screening mechanism more transparent in the first instance compared to countries where the decisions are taken directly by the government. A major reason behind the potentially increased transparency is that the Swedish agencies need to submit their opinion in writing to ISP.

Then, what is the National Board of Trades' role in this? Considering that the three other obligatory agencies are all security-oriented agencies, we might expect that the National Board of Trade will be given another role, which is what the inquiry suggests:

According to SOU (2021:87), it is suggested that "The National Board of Trade can contribute with analysis regarding the importance of an investment for the

---

[5] As opposed to mergers and acquisitions (brownfield), a greenfield is a type of FDI in which a parent company creates a subsidiary in a different country, building its operations from the ground up.

economy and the investment climate."[6] Furthermore, it is suggested that all applications be sent to the mandatory consultive agencies, who by that will be given an overview, and the possibility to share information to ISP on its own initiative. It is stated that:

> The assessment of the National Bord of Trade of the significance of an investment, from, among other things, economical and a political perspective, may be required as a basis for the review-agency when balancing different legitimate interests.[7]

With the National Board of Trade as one part of a future investment screening mechanism, there will be structural considerations taken that are complementary to security-related issues covered by other agencies when assessing whether to admit, reject or condition a foreign direct investment. ISP is not bound by the views of the consultation agencies and on paper the view of one consultation agency is not worth more than the view of another. Also, the consultation agencies have not been given independent rights to appeal a decision taken by ISP. Hence, in cases where there are diverging views if an investment should be accepted, rejected or linked to a condition it is always the view of ISP that will prevail.

## 2 The Need for an Economic Perspective

In many, if not most, countries, investment screening is conducted within the Government Offices. Often with the lead of ministries such as the Ministry of Justice or the Ministry of Economy or its equivalent. The EU Regulation 2019/452 on investment screening, which was adopted in March 2019 and has been applied since October 2020, states that if an investment poses a threat to the state's security or public order, the investment may be either forbidden or subject to conditions. If there is no such identified threat, the investment is allowed.

This starting point, focusing solely on security concerns, may lead to little or no weight being placed on the wide array of benefits associated with inward FDI. More precisely, the ministries may not put an economic price in their respective deliberations to a situation where a screened investment is stopped or conditioned.

A potential rationale to downplay the economic benefits from FDI is that the state does not wish to give the investor arguments to why the negative decision should be revoked by either the courts or the government, depending on who acts as an appellate body.

A diligent decision maker should ask how the home state may be affected by the stopping/conditioning of an investment. On the one hand, we may presume that there are situations where the perceived security threat is of such magnitude that the price for stopping or conditioning the investment is irrelevant. On the other hand, we

[6] Author's translation of "Granskning av utländska investeringar", SOU 2021:87, p. 35.

[7] Author's translation of "Granskning av utländska investeringar", SOU 2021:87, p. 456.

might also presume there are situations where the economic price is simply too high to stop or condition the investment considering the potential low level of threat a specific investment may pose. Then, how do we identify and separate such situations? Starting with the state needs to admit that these situations may occur and arrange institutional rules accordingly. And this is precisely the aim of including the National Board of Trade as an obligatory agency to consult with. It could be argued that in states where the screening is conducted by the Ministry of Economy, economic arguments are probably better received than in cases where the Ministry of Justice or the Ministry of Defence has the lead.

The question that arises is how to analyse the economic effects of a planned investment. This is not an easy task since it is inherently difficult to foresee future effects. Especially of greenfield investments. There is, however, a large body of literature that has investigated the economic effects of FDI. In addition, since the governmental inquiry for a Swedish screening mechanism suggests that only investments in certain sectors should be screened, we may at least work with the premise that only certain sectors need to be covered by a National Board of Trade analysis.[8] Even with this limitation, a screening will require the collection of substantial background information, especially since a screened sector may consist of many subsectors. To overview the economic effects of a specific FDI, we need to know the volume of FDI, the general effects of FDI, the mechanism behind these effects and the empirical challenges. This will all be helpful as a first guidance.

Below, we present an overview of factors that a decision-maker needs to consider when assessing the potential effects of a future investment. The complexity of such an exercise shows the difficulty for the state to put a hypothetical economic value to an investment. This may in turn explain why this aspect is rarely mentioned in connection to investment screening.

## 3 FDI Flows and Localization

*During the last twenty years, FDI has increased rapidly. Between 2000 and 2016, the share of FDI stock in global GDP increased from 22 to 35 percent.*[9] *Following a decline during the financial crisis, mergers and acquisitions recovered, peaking with a record value of USD 1.2 trillion in the first quarter of 2018. During the first year of COVID-19,* global foreign direct investment fell by one-third to $1 trillion, which is well below the low point reached after the financial crisis. Greenfield investments in industry and new infrastructure investment projects in developing countries were hit

[8] The sectors mentioned in the inquiry are suggestions, such as production of energy, financial services. In the end it will be the Swedish Civil Contingencies Agency in cooperation with other governmental agencies, including the National Board of Trade, who will decide exactly which sectors will be screened.

[9] Carill-Caccia and Pavlova (2018).

especially hard, but recent data from the OECD have shown a remarkable recovery during 2021.[10] During 2021, global FDI flows grew by 88%, reaching 37% above pre-pandemic levels. This growth was mainly driven by investments among the OECD countries where inward and outward FDI reached their highest levels since 2005. In 2001, the global top destinations were the United States and China. The currently ongoing war in Ukraine and distortions in global supply chains make the future economic outlook highly uncertain.[11]

## *3.1 Localization Theory*

There are many theories aiming to explain why multinational enterprises invest abroad. Surveys of the theoretical and empirical literature include but are not limited to Blonigen (2005), Iršová and Havránek (2013), Donnelly (2014), Paul and Singh (2017) and Teixeira et al. (2017).[12]

An early theory of FDI is MacDougall (1958), who built the analysis on a perfect competition model where the driver to FDI is cross-country differences in the return to capital. Along a similar line, Kemp (1964) showed how capital moves from capital-abundant to capital-scarce countries. The equilibrium outcome is that the return to capital will equalize across countries. Since then, new models of FDI have evolved that look beyond cross-country differences in the price of capital to explain investment patterns. The new theories of FDI take a broad firm decision-based approach, and we will briefly touch upon two of them.

Hymer (1960) developed a model on FDI stating that multinational enterprises (MNEs) must have some kind of "firm-specific" advantage. The idea is that domestic firms possess several home-market advantages in terms of knowledge about culture, language, legal system, etc. To compensate for this, Hymer (1960) stated that foreign firms must have some form of market power to compensate for these local factors. The Hymer (1960) hypothesis has gained support from many researchers (Lemafalussy 1961; Knickerbocker 1973; Knickerbocker 1973; Caves 1974; Dunning 1974; Vaitsos 1976). One weakness with Hymers' model, however, is that it fails to explain in which locations FDI takes place.

In the mid-1970s, a more general theory of the determinants of FDI was developed. Building on the assumption of imperfect competition and markets, Dunning (1977, 1979 and 1988) and Dunning and Lundan (2008) presented what has become known as the eclectic theory of FDI or the OLI theory. Dunning defines three groups

[10] Unctad (2022).

[11] OECD (n.d.), investment statistics.

[12] Being very brief, survey-based findings often put factors such as market size and market growth on the top of the list while theoretical models tend to empathize cost factors such as transportation cost, wages and capital cost. However, also risk factors such as risk of technological leakage suggesting that FDI is a safer choice than certain forms of outsourcing activities to an external firm are frequently put forward.

**Table 1** Motives for FDI

| Motive | Description |
|---|---|
| Market-seeking FDI | Closeness to customers.<br>– relates to horizontal FDI, tariff jumping. |
| Efficiency seeking FDI | Exploit benefits of specialization along the value chain.<br>– relates to vertical FDI and fractionized value chains. |
| Asset-seeking FDI | Exploits technological advantages.<br>– connected to inward FDI in developed countries. |
| Resource seeking FDI | Aiming to exploit (natural) resources in host countries.<br>– related to resource based comparative advantage |

Source: Minakshee (2020)

of determinants of FDI (O-L-I), where "O" stands for ownership, "L" stands for location and "I" stands for internalization. Starting with O, Dunning states that to invest abroad, the firm must possess some kind of ownership advantage; the "O" is therefore closely related to the firm-specific advantage discussed by Hymer (1960). This ownership, or firm-specific advantages, allows firms to overcome the costs of operating in a foreign country. Examples of firm-specific advantages include but are not limited to brand name, marketing, and organizational practices. The "L" or location advantages proposed by Dunning focus on where MNEs choose to locate. Hence, the localization part encapsulates a series of country-specific advantages a firm gains access when investing abroad (cheap labor, raw materials, etc.). Finally, the "I" or internalization advantages explain how and why firms choose to operate autonomously in the foreign country rather than outsource or licensing production to an external firm. Motives along this line of reasoning include the risk of technological leakage and firm-specific knowledge. Hence, there is a close link between internalization, technology, intellectual property rights (IPR) and the rule of law. Today, parts of the OLI paradigm have become integrated into the new economic geography (Fujita et al. 1999), the knowledge-capital model (Carr and Markusen 2001), and so forth. In addition to OLI, there are other factors that play a role in determining inward FDI. Table 1 follows Minakshee (2020), presenting four broad motives behind FDI.

## *3.2 Localization: The Evidence*

With the theory of FDI as a background, the objective of this section is to review the empirical evidence of host country determinants of inward FDI. The review begins with Table 2 and survey-based findings. In the survey, firms and experts were asked questions regarding FDI and localization. The respondents were asked to rank the determinants of FDI with regard to weight as a determinant for FDI. It should be noted that while foreign direct investors in certain cases may value a highly educated labor force, other investors may prioritize access to cheap labor. Hence, for specific investments, the ranking of determinants can deviate from the average view.

**Table 2** Determinants of inward FDI, survey evidence

| Rank | Variable | Note |
|---|---|---|
| 1 | Economic growth rate | Expected revenue |
| 2 | Market size | Scale |
| 3 | Expected profit | Expected revenue |
| 4 | Political and social stability | Uncertainty |
| 5 | Educational attainment of the labor force | Factor supply |
| 6 | Rule of law and IPR | Uncertainty |
| 7 | Infra structure | Transportation cost |
| 8 | Local supply of goods and services | Factor supply |
| 9 | Wage level | Cost factor |
| 10 | Access to high-tech | Technology |
| 11 | Financial market development | Other/mix |
| 12 | Fear of protection | Other/mix |
| 13 | Access to raw materials | Factor supply |

Source: United Nations (2001), International Investment Towards the Year 2001. Based on a survey targeting 311 companies and experts around the globe during the period June–October 1996

The survey-based findings are followed by a review of the econometric evidence. While the survey ranks the determinants of FDI, the econometric evidence divides the variables into four categories:

1. Macroeconomic variables
2. Industry attributes and infrastructure
3. Openness to trade and investment, and
4. Resources.

Each variable is thereafter marked as "positive", "negative", or "mixed" depending on its statistical significance as a determinant of inward FDI (Table 3).

A comparison of the survey-based evidence (Table 2) and econometric evidence (Table 3) lends at least three remarks to be made.

1. Economic growth and market size are important factors for attracting FDI. The size of the market is closely related to market-seeking FDI, while vertical FDI, where the production chain is split up, normally puts more value into factor prices and various conditions for production.
2. There are a number of factors related to the degree of uncertainty. This includes but is not limited to the quality of institutions, rule of law, and labor market conditions. *It is therefore plausible to assume that unclear rules regarding investment screening can be a deterrent to FDI.*
3. It is notable that on average, the wage level and per capita income rank relatively low. To some extent, this can explain why subsidies fail to make a significant

**Table 3** Determinants of inward FDI—econometric evidence

| Variable | Relationship to FDI | Note |
|---|---|---|
| Macroeconomic variables | | |
| Market size | Positive | Scale |
| Exchange rate | Mixed | Cost factor |
| Economic growth rate | Positive | Expected revenue |
| Per capita income | Mixed | Cost/level of development |
| Inflation rate | Negative | Uncertainty |
| Exchange rate stability | Positive | Uncertainty |
| Industry attributes and infrastructure | | |
| Competitive conditions | Mixed | Other/mix |
| Productivity growth | Positive | Uncertainty |
| Socio-political stability | Positive | Uncertainty |
| Protection of property rights | Positive | Uncertainty |
| Government efficiency | Positive | Uncertainty |
| Physical infrastructure | Positive | Transportation/information cost |
| Openness to trade and investment | | |
| Investment protection | Negative | Uncertainty |
| Restrictions to foreign ownership | Negative | Obstacles |
| Investment promotion agencies | Positive | Obstacles |
| Subsidies | Mixed | Cost factor |
| Requirements | Mixed | Obstacle/uncertainty |
| Openness to trade (trade/GDP) | Positive | |
| Tariffs and other barriers to trade | Mixed | Obstacles |
| Resources | | |
| R&D-intensity | Positive | Cost factor |
| Educational attainment | Positive | Factor supply |
| Total employment | Positive | Scale |
| Wage level | Negative | Cost factor |
| Unionization | Mixed | Other/mix |
| Large, liquid stock markets | Positive | Other/mix |
| Interest rate | Negative | Cost factor |

Source: Globerman and Zitian (2010)

Note: "Mixed" means that the positive and negative results for the variable in question were approximately equal in number, and/or the majority of the results for the variable in question were not statistically significant

mark on FDI attractiveness. However, it seems that investment promotion agencies can be effective instruments to encourage inward FDI, particularly if they focus on mitigating administrative costs and delays that confront foreign investors.

# 4 Economic Effects

Foreign direct investments are, for many countries, a key component in their growth strategy. Accordingly, there are a range of policies designed to attract and stimulate inward FDI. Behind this surge are the economic benefits associated with inward FDI. Numerous papers have shown that FDI can support economic growth and enhance capital accumulation (Alfaro et al. 2003) and boost productivity, both horizontally (within industries) (Haskel et al. 2002) and vertically up and down supply chains (Javorcik 2004). FDI can also stimulate innovation (Branstetter 2006), increase competition (Mastromarco and Simar 2012), and disseminate new management practices (Bloom et al. 2012). On top of this, there is an employment generating argument.

## 4.1 Employment

As an indication of the importance of inward FDI for Swedish employment, it can be noted that in 2019, out of 5.1 million employed workers, 683,149 were hired by foreign-owned firms. Out of these 683,149 workers, 64% were hired by investors originating from the EU single market. Comparing employment shares between investors from the single market and investors from third countries, we note that in the manufacturing sector, 52% of the workers were hired by firms that originated from the single market, while the corresponding number for the service sector was 68% (Table 4).[13]

**Table 4** Inward and outward FDI, Sweden 2019

| | Inward FDI | | Outward FDI | |
|---|---|---|---|---|
| Sector | # Employees in foreign owned firms | Single market share [a] (%) | Division of outward FDI | |
| Manufacturing | 204,705 | 52 | Total employment abroad | 1,421,879 |
| Service | 447,258 | 68 | Single market employment | 699,567 |
| Other | 31,186 | 88 | Single market, employment share, % | 49% |

Source: Growth Analysis. Utländska företag—Tillväxtanalys (tillvaxtanalys.se)
[a] Share of total number of employees working in foreign owned hired by firms originating from the single market

[13] Looking at Swedish outward FDI, during 2019 Swedish owned multinational enterprises had 1.4 million workers hired abroad, and out of these 49% were located on the EU single market.

The attractiveness of Sweden as a destination of FDI is further recognized by a survey conducted by Business Sweden (2021), in which Sweden ranked 14th in terms of attractiveness for FDI. Hence, Sweden is ranked as one of the world's most attractive sites for FDI.[14] One component behind this attractiveness is Swedish EU membership. According to Bruno et al. (2020), as a consequence of single market integration, external inward FDI to the single market has increased by 60%, and internal FDI across member state countries has increased by approximately 50%. Thus, it seems clear that the FDI-promoting effect of EU membership outperforms the impact of any other free trade agreement, including the *North American Free Trade Agreement* (NAFTA), *European Free Trade Association* (EFTA) and the Southern Common Market (Mercosur).

## *4.2 Documented Growth Effects*

As a brief overview of the recognized effects of inward FDI in a number of mostly European countries, Marchick and Slaughter (2008) give a brief survey of a series of evaluations of the economic effects of inward FDI. Below, we present the survey findings by Marchick and Slaughter (2008) and some of the Swedish experiences. These findings are rather representative of the body of literature on inward FDI in developed economies.

**Sweden**

- Firm R&D increases after foreign acquisition.[15]
- Firm level exports increase after foreign acquisition.[16]
- Firm-level employment increases after foreign acquisition.[17]
- Firm skill upgrading occurs after foreign acquisition.[18,19]
- After an acquisition, skill upgrading is particularly strong in small and medium sized non-MNEs active in the service sector.
- Foreign acquisitions are associated with increased productivity, skill-upgrading, increased average wage, and reduced job security.[20]

[14] Business Sweden (2021).

[15] Bandick et al. (2014).

[16] Karpaty and Kneller (2011).

[17] Bandick and Karpaty (2011).

[18] Bandick and Karpaty (2011).

[19] Bandick and Hansson (2009).

[20] Tillväxtanalys (2016).

**Denmark** The relative performance of firms acquired by foreign parents improved after takeover.[21]

**Finland** Foreign ownership raised the productivity of acquired plants by an average of approximately 10% and worker wages by approximately 4%.

**Indonesia** Large increases in average wages after foreign takeovers.[22]

**Italy** Foreign acquisitions raised the labor productivity of target firms, and these gains did not come via employment reductions.[23]

**Norway** Foreign owners tended to reverse a negative trend in productivity and employment in acquired plants, and employment increased.[24]

**Portugal** Wages rose after foreign acquisition by 3–12%.[25]

**United Kingdom** Acquired firms exhibited increased employment.

## *4.3 Spillovers and FDI*

A signature feature of the economic effects of FDI is that they to a large extent come in the form of technology spillovers. With spillover effects, we mean effects that are not encapsulated by the price mechanism. That is, the actors involved in the investment contribute to an effect that goes beyond the private return of the investment, and in the presence of technology spillovers, the market solution tends to under-invest in R&D activities. Technology spillovers have also been shown to be localized, suggesting that the largest benefits from FDI occur in the geographical hinterland of the investment. The diffusion of technological FDI spillovers has been categorized into five broad channels:

1. The demonstration effect,
2. labor mobility,
3. the competition effect,
4. trade and
5. backward and forward linkages.

*The demonstration effect* is arguably the most evident spillover channel (Wang and Blomström 1992). The idea is that the use of a new technology can be both costly and risky for a small domestic firm. If, however, a technology is used by a

[21] Gioia and Thomsen (2004).

[22] Lipsey and Sjoholm (2003).

[23] Piscitello and Rabbiosi (2004).

[24] Balsvik (2006).

[25] Almeida (2003).

multinational firm, this will work as a signal encouraging domestic firms to adopt the technology.

Spillovers by *labor mobility* have a geographical dimension in that they are related to the range of which workers commute and the range of which domestic firms hire workers with experience from an MNE (Fosfuri et al. 2001). The labor mobility argument can also invoke a negative effect of local firms in that multinational firms may attract the best workers (*brain drain*) and thereby negatively affect the competitiveness of local firms (Sinani and Meyer 2004). Related to the brain drain argument, competition for skilled labor is the general impact on *competition* that follows inward FDI. The idea is that local firms with low productivity either exit or increase their efficiency as competition increases. This leads to an overall increased productivity and overall higher wages (Markusen and Venables 1999). This kind of change may not always be appreciated since the exit of firms is associated with a (structural) change that can be costly and painful for individual workers and affected firms.

Several studies have established a positive impact of the entry of multinational firms on the *export capacity* of domestic firms (Kokko et al. 2001). One channel behind this export-spillover effect is the knowledge of export procedures, establishment of distribution networks, transport infrastructures, and even knowledge of consumers' tastes in foreign markets that can be transferred from foreign to local firms (Greenaway et al. 2004). Hence, by observing, cooperation or other types of learning from foreign firms, domestic firms may reduce their costs of entry into foreign markets.

A feature that has received increased attention is the impact of global value chains (GVCs) and forward and backward linkages (Markusen and Venables 1999). Multinational firms may benefit local suppliers directly by increasing demand. In addition, local suppliers can benefit from technical support, labor training, and help in creating various types of infrastructure (Lall 1980). On the user side (forward linkages), local firms benefit from the supply of higher quality inputs from foreign investors. A behind-the-scenes feature of the GVC argument is that bilateral trade diminishes with distance. Hence, having an international high-quality supplier at arms' length distance is beneficial for spillovers (Markusen and Venables 1999).[26]

## 4.4 Spillover Effects and Investment Quality

It is well known that technology diffusion does not occur automatically. Aside from a source of knowledge to tap from, the diffusion of technology requires the recipient to have the capacity to absorb the technology (Lapan and Bardhan 1973; Wang and

---

[26] Since many EU countries lacks abundant natural resources, instead market-seeking, efficiency-seeking and strategic asset-seeking motives predominate inward FDI to the EU (Kalotay 2006). In addition, the Single Market may stimulate FDI both from within and outside the EU.

**Table 5** Factors that determine the degree to which FDI has positive spillover effects

| Variable | Impact | Note |
|---|---|---|
| R&D | Strongly positive | Technology |
| Education and skill level | Weakly positive | Technology |
| Linkages to foreign firms | Mixed | Expected positive |
| Domestic competition | Mixed | Unrelated |
| Geographic density | Strongly positive | Agglomeration effects |
| Export orientation | Mixed | Market seeking vs resource seeking |
| Openness | n.a | More studies needed |
| Regulation of foreign affiliates | n.a | More studies needed |

Note: "Mixed" means that the positive and negative results for the variable in question were approximately equal in number, and/or the majority of the results for the variable in question were not statistically significant. "n.a." indicates that only a small number of studies reported results for the variable in question, such that no reliable inferences about the variable could be drawn
Source: Globerman and Zitian (2010)

Blomström 1992; Perez 1997; Kinoshita 2009). The size of the technology gap between sender and receiver therefore becomes relevant. One lesson learned is that domestic firms must not have a large technological gap vis-à-vis foreign investors. The results by Flôres Jr et al. (2002) suggest that spillover effects are maximized when the average level of domestic productivity is between 50–80% of the corresponding productivity level of foreign firms.

The concept of "absorptive capacity" comprises not only the technological level of local firms but also other factors that enhance the transmission of knowledge, such as the local infrastructure, communication and financial system (Hermes and Lensink 2003). Additionally, linkages between local suppliers and customers matter for how much the local market benefits from inwards FDI (Rodríguez-Clare 1996). There is also a difference between greenfield investments and mergers and acquisitions. When FDI occurs through greenfield investment, the introduction of the new technology is instantaneous (Braconier et al. 2001). If FDI instead takes place through a merger or acquisition, the MNE, due to its pre-integration into the local economy, is expected to establish wider intersectoral linkages with domestic firms (Scott-Kennel and Enderwick 2001; Belderbos et al. 2001).

It is evident that a series of factors are involved in the diffusion of investment spillovers. Although the existence of spillovers is well known, there are a limited number of studies analysing what determines the quality or the economic benefits of inwards FDIs on the host county. That is, what determines the extent of technology or productivity spillovers? Table 5 builds on Globerman and Zitian (2010), who summarize the empirical literature on the magnitude of spillovers.

From Table 5, it becomes evident that the strongest spillover effects occur in tandem with high-tech and R&D-intensive production. It is also noted that a dense environment promotes spillovers. Taken together, these results suggest that technology-intensive investment in R&D clusters such as Silicon Valley in the US and Kista in the Stockholm region creates a good environment for positive FDI spillovers.

### 4.5 Policy and the Evaluation Problem

When analysing effects of FDI, one needs to consider potential synergy-effects, and the economic literature provides strong evidence that know-how and technology spreads through FDI. However, recent studies have often concluded that the impact of FDI on the host country is weaker when the analysis is performed at the micro rather than the macro level (Gunby 2017). The gap in evidence between the micro and macro levels has very different policy implications. If FDI promotes national development, as the macro view suggests, policies should aim for openness and further inflows of FDI. If the operations of foreign investors instead have no impact on local firms, more neutral FDI policies might be appropriate.

There are several reasons why differences between the macro and micro perspectives may occur. While spillover estimations using aggregated data aim to distinguish the effects of FDI on the regions or sectors that are investigated, micro analyses look at the average effects at the firm level. Since estimations are rarely weighted by firm size and the "average" and relatively small firm may have a small impact on industry totals, estimation results may therefore indicate insignificant spillovers even if the largest and most important firms manage to learn from foreign investors.

Moreover, spillovers may originate from both horizontal and vertical relations with foreign investors: capturing vertical spillovers is a major challenge for microlevel studies but less of a problem for macro studies where the unit of analysis is a geographic region. These observations suggest that the evaluation of a specific investment project is challenging. One reason is that the benefit from a single investment is relatively small compared to the total stock of FDI and therefore easily becomes hidden by other factors.

In short, the specific effect and spillover channels from a specific investment are difficult to empirically capture.

## 5 FDI Policy: Days of Future Past

### 5.1 Classic FDI Policy

To reap the benefits of FDI, it is common for governments to offer incentives to foreign firms to invest in their countries. The incentives can be thought of as incentives that attract FDI and policies intended to maximize the economic benefit from an investment.

At the macro level, studies have identified a number of host country characteristics associated with attracting foreign investors. The most frequently investigated determinants include market size, government policies affecting entry costs, the cost of local production, wages, and the quality of infrastructure. Other measures that attract FDI are tax concessions, low interest loans, grants and subsidies (Blonigen 2005; Blonigen and Piger 2014).

In a survey study of the effectiveness of FDI policies, Globerman and Zitian (2010) note that many best practices attracting FDI include general policies. Hence, factors such as a well-functioning legal system, a well-educated workforce, well-functioning infrastructure (transportation and telecommunication), and policies that stimulate innovation are seen as factors promoting inwards FDI. On the other hand, Globerman and Zitian (2010) suggest that subsidies and tax breaks that specifically target foreign investors are not necessarily best practices for attracting investment. According to Globerman and Zitian (2010), such policies could even reduce productivity effects, particularly if subsidies and tax breaks result in FDI that geographically disperses industrial and scientific capacity (mitigating market-driven agglomeration effects). Recent research has also investigated policy tools leveraging collaboration between firms, resulting in mixed evidence.[27]

Reducing information uncertainty is beneficial for inwards FDI. Therefore, government agencies can be instrumental in informing foreign investors about locational advantages, administrative procedures, etc. In fact, in many countries, investment-promoting agencies are now part of national and local government strategies to attract foreign investment.

## 5.2 Recent Trends in FDI Policy

The above presented theoretical effects of FDI and the empirical analysis of inward FDI generally suggest that they are related with a series of positive economic effects for the receiving country. It is therefore interesting to look at actual FDI policies undertaken the last few years in this area.

During the 1990s and the first years into the millennium countries where competing for FDI, often offering generous tax redemptions and other privileges to foreign investors (OECD 2000). However, despite the seemingly positive picture painted above, many governments are now moving in a different direction. In recent years, several major countries have approved or are considering new laws that restrict certain types of FDI. Specifically, the range of sectors and technologies considered to fall within the scope of sensitive sectors in the context of the EU Investment Screening Regulation has become broader and does not only include military and defence interests. National security now includes factors such as critical infrastructure, energy, communication assets, advanced technology, and data security.[28]

Commonly used tools to restrict FDI are ownership limitations and performance requirements (Allen et al. 2022). Recent overviews of FDI policy measures taken

[27] Crescenzi et al. (2019).

[28] Compare Article 4(1) of the EU investment screening regulation.

can be found at the United Nations annual Conference on Trade and Development (UNCTAD), the global trade alert database, and the WTO data on trade and trade policy measures.[29] For further reference regarding recent trends, see also OECD Investment policy developments in 62 economies between 16 October 2020 and 15 October 2021.[30]

As FDI screening has become a common part of the regulatory framework, this shift has also resulted in a number of deals being blocked or unwound. Examples from 2021 include the new Australian FDI regime and the UK National Security and Investment Act (CFIUS Annual Report to Congress CY2020). In the EU already existing screening mechanisms has been updated to accommodate the new security environment.

An investor may receive information from a screening authority that an investment may be blocked. In such cases the often investor chooses to retract the application of screening. It appears as this was the case when Zhejiang Shuanghuan Transmission Machinery aborted the purchase of Schmiedetechnik Plettenberg, Werkzeugtechnik Plettenberg and VVP Vermögensverwaltung Plettenberg.[31] Another example of when a purchase is turned down is when Shenzhen Invenland Holdings Co. Ltd wanted to buy a controlling part of an Italian firm producing semiconductor equipment.[32] One driver behind stricter FDI policies is the increased inflow of Chinese investments that has been accompanied by complaints of unfair competition, risk of dominant position and threats against national security. For example, all four deals blocked by CFIUS under the Trump administration involved Chinese acquirers. However, China is not the only driver behind the movement towards stricter FDI regulation. In the US, 85% of the acquisitions reviewed by CFIUS in 2020 involved non-Chinese investors.[33]

At the same time, as the EU, US, and other major economies have moved towards stricter FDI regulation, some Asian countries have opened parts of their economies to inward FDI. One example from January 2020 is the new Chinese foreign investment law. Specifically, the new foreign investment law replaced three primary laws that had governed foreign investment in China for four decades. With unified provisions on market access, investment promotion, investment protection and foreign investment management, the goal was to attract more FDI investment. The law was, according to the Chinese authorities, promulgated to address international concerns regarding FDI into China. However, many important issues remain unresolved, and it is recognized that further actions are needed with regard to FDI in China (Zhang 2022). Other countries that have taken steps towards a more

[29] WTO Data—Information on trade and trade policy measures Global Trade Alert.

[30] OECD (2021) and earlier OECD papers.

[31] MERICS REPORT (2021) CHINESE FDI IN EUROPE 2020 UPDATE.

[32] NASDAQ, November 23, 2021.

[33] CFIUS Annual Report to Congress CY2020. Table I-13, page 36 of the report: Covered Transactions by Acquirer Home Country or Geographic Economy 2018–2020.

FDI-friendly regime include India and Vietnam, which also recorded pre-pandemic record levels of inward FDI (Allen et al. 2022).[34]

It is now clear that not all countries are going in the same direction. However, the overall trend (in particular among developed countries) regarding national security and FDI is clear—FDI restrictions are likely to rise. The increased restrictions against inward FDI are empathized by UNCTAD (2021) who notes that "*The number of investment policy measures of a regulatory or restrictive nature more than doubled in 2020*". UNCTAD (2020) also notes that the increased use of screening mechanisms is driven by national security concerns over FDI in sensitive industries and that most FDI liberalization measures were adopted by developing economies. Considering that many of these processes is recently implemented, it is still early to assess post-intervention estimates of how these new regulations actually impact FDI flows.

In sum, there is a movement pointing towards a more restrictive FDI environment. It has also been shown that inward FDI plays an important role for economic growth, technological progress and skill upgrading. We also noted that uncertainty, in its many different forms, is detrimental to FDI. A question of concern is therefore if FDI screening and new investment regulations will deter beneficial investments? Hence, it seems reasonable to assume that if new FDI restrictions are associated with an underlying uncertainty about the current and future framework regulating FDI, it will have a dampening effect on many types FDI, possibly even on attractive investments.

## 6 Conclusions and Recommendations

From this review, it becomes clear that foreseeing the economic effects of inward FDI can be a daunting challenge, while at the same time, existing evidence can provide some helpful guidelines.

First, in a number of studies inward FDI has been associated with a series of host country effects, including skill-upgrading, increased competition, increased productivity, higher wages, and improved resource allocation. Existing evidence suggests that R&D- and technology-intensive investments may be especially beneficial to a host country. It is also recognized that for many countries, including Sweden, employment in foreign-owned firms represents a substantial share of total employment.

A natural question therefore becomes, what decides if a destination is interesting for an investor? While some types of FDI require a highly educated labour force,

[34] Some examples: Interventions has been taken involving digital maps for the automotive industry (*Navinfo/HERE Technologies* (2017)) and digital apps (*Beijing Kunlun Tech Co Ltd/Grindr LLC* (2019) and *Beijing ByteDance Tech Co Ltd/Tik Tok* (2020)). In France, the *Couche-Tard/Carrefour* transaction was prohibited on the ground of food security.

other investments may prioritize access to cheap labour. Despite this heterogeneity, both survey-based and econometric evidence suggests that uncertainty is detrimental to FDI.

Uncertainty comes in many flavours and can among other things be related to unclear rules and regulations, weak rule of law and IPR but also a high inflation rate and uncertain labour market conditions.

As a corollary of the uncertainty paradigm, it becomes clear that if an investment screening mechanism introduces additional uncertainty, it can hamper beneficial inward FDI. Reducing uncertainty is therefore central. Uncertainty can, for example, be reduced by adhering to the transparency principles discussed below, but also by limiting the investment screening mechanism to a relatively small number of sectors. In the review of the economic effects of FDI we noticed that FDI in high technology sectors often are associated with economic benefits and positive spillover effects. At the same time, concerns regarding IPR is also part of the investment screening process. The challenge of balancing the economic effects of an investment screening mechanism against security concerns may therefore be especially difficult when evaluating FDI in high tech sectors. With these concerns as a backdrop, we adhere to the four principles suggested by Allen et al. (2022) to accommodate the need for a sharper investment screening while at the same time holding back the negative economic effects of restrictive regulations. The suggested principles are as follows:

1. Problems to target

   The investment review law should be narrowly tailored. Restrictions on foreign investments should be limited to the problems that the market itself cannot solve, such as anticompetitive impacts or threats to national security.
2. Predictability

   The investment screening process should provide predictability to transaction parties and facilitate reviews of most transactions in a short period of time.
3. Trust

   The investment screening process should ensure confidentiality to the transaction parties.
4. Limiting the number of affected sectors

   Countries should avoid broad sector-based lists requiring investment screening. If sector-based lists are used, such lists should be drawn as narrowly as possible and tailored to those transactions that are at the core of a government's national security interests.

Hence, the goal should be a clearly defined investment screening regulation, accompanied by a swift and transparent review process that provides predictability to the transaction parties while at the same time adding as little friction as possible to potential investors.

## Appendix

Examples of the definition of the expansion of sensitive sectors described by Allen et al. (2022).

- The list of 'sensitive sectors' in France was expanded in 2019 to include space operations and research and development (R&D) activities linked to sensitive technologies and activities (cybersecurity, artificial intelligence, additive manufacturing and semiconductors).
- Canadian 2021 added the acquisition of businesses with access to sensitive personal data, sensitive technology, or involved in producing critical minerals to the areas that could raise national security concerns.
- May 2021, Germany announced a filing obligation focused on acquisitions of high-technology enterprises, including companies developing automated or autonomous driving functions, specific nano electronic components and certain smart meter gateways.
- March 2020, Spain tightened its FDI regime, requiring acquirers who are not within the European Union or EFTA to obtain prior approval for an acquisition of a shareholding of 10% or more, or a management right, in a Spanish company in a broad range of sectors, including critical infrastructure and technology, healthcare, communications, energy and transport, media, the supply of key inputs such as energy, raw materials and food security, as well as any other sector with access to sensitive information (in particular personal data).

January 2020, the United Kingdom introduced a new mandatory notification regime (came into force on 4 January 2022) covering 17 specified sectors, including energy, transport, communications, artificial intelligence, data infrastructure and other high-tech sectors.

## Other Sources

CFIUS-Public-Annual-Report-CY-2020.pdf (treasury.gov)
Global Trade Alert
Monitoring investment and trade measures—OECD
WTO Data—Information on trade and trade policy measures

## References

Alfaro L, Chanda A, Kalemli-Özcan S, Sayek S (2003) FDI spillovers, financial markets, and economic development. IMF working paper no. 03/186

Allen R, MacGregor A, Roberts V (2022) Introduction: key current trends – global overview. Global Competition Review. Herbert Smith Freehills

Almeida R (2003) The effects of foreign owned firms on the labor market. Institute for the Study of Labor discussion paper no. 785, May 2003
Balsvik R (2006) Foreign direct investment and host-country effects. Norwegian School of Economics and Business Administration
Bandick R, Hansson P (2009) Inward FDI and demand for skills in manufacturing firms in Sweden. Rev World Econ / Weltwirtschaftliches Archiv 145(1):111–131
Bandick R, Karpaty P (2011) Employment effects of foreign acquisition. Int Rev Econ Finance 20(2):211–224
Bandick R, Goerg H, Karpaty P (2014) Foreign acquisitions, domestic multinationals, and R&D. Scand J Econ 116(4):1091–1115
Belderbos R, Capannelli G, Fukao K (2001) Backwards vertical linkages of foreign manufacturing affiliates: evidence from Japanese multinationals. World Dev 29(1):189–208
Blonigen BA (2005) A review of the empirical determinants of FDI. Atlantic Econ J 33(1): 383–403. https://doi.org/10.1007/s11293-005-2868-9
Blonigen BA, Piger J (2014) Determinants of foreign direct investment. Can J Econ 47(3):775–812
Bloom N, Sadun R, Van Reenen J (2012) Americans do IT better: US multinationals and the productivity miracle. Am Econ Rev 102(1):167–201
Braconier H, Ekholm K, Midelfart-Knarvik K (2001) In search of FDI – transmitted R&D spillovers: a study based on Swedish data. Weltwirtschaftliches Archiv 137(4):644–665
Branstetter L (2006) Is foreign direct investment a channel of knowledge spillovers? J Int Econ 68(2):325–344
Bruno RL et al (2020) The effect on foreign direct investment of membership in the European Union
Business Sweden (2021) Global upphämtning från krisnivå. Direktinvesteringar i den globala och svenska ekonomin
Carill-Caccia F, Pavlova E (2018) Foreign direct investment and its drivers: a global and EU perspective. ECB Econ Bull 4
Carr DL, Markusen JR, Maskus KE (2001) Estimating the knowledge-capital model of the multinational enterprise. Am Econ Rev 91(3):693–708
Caves RE (1974) Economic analysis and multinational enterprise. George Allen and Unwin, London. https://doi.org/10.1111/1467-8268.12039
Crescenzi R, Di Cataldo M, Giua M (2019) FDI inflows in European regions: what role for investment promotion agencies? Paper presented at the ERSA conference 2018
Donnelly D (2014) A review of literature regarding the determinants of foreign direct investment (FDI). Northern Ireland Assembly, Research and Information Service Briefing Paper
Dunning JH (1974) The distinctive nature of multinational enterprise. George Allen and Unwin, London. https://doi.org/10.1016/j.mulfin.2005.07.002
Dunning JH (1977) Trade location of economic activity and the MNE: a search of an eclectic approach. In: Ohlin B, Hesselborn PO, Wijkman PJ (eds) The international allocation of economic activity. Macmillan, London. https://doi.org/10.1007/978-1-349-03196-2_38
Dunning JH (1979) Explaining changing patterns of international production: in defense of the eclectic theory. Oxf Bull Econ Stat 41(4). https://doi.org/10.1111/j.1468-0084.1979.mp41004003.x
Dunning J (1988) The eclectic paradigm of international production: a restatement and some possible extensions. J Int Bus Stud 19:1–31. https://doi.org/10.1057/palgrave.jibs.8490372
Dunning JH, Lundan SM (2008) Multinational enterprises and the global economy. Edward Elgar, Cheltenham. https://doi.org/10.1016/S2212-5671(14)00341-4
Flôres Jr RG, Fontoura MP, Santos RG (2002) Foreign direct investment spillovers: additional lessons from a country study. FGV EPGE economics working papers (Ensaios Economicos da EPGE) 455, EPGE Brazilian School of Economics and Finance - FGV EPGE
Fosfuri A, Motta M, Ronde T (2001) Foreign direct investment and spillovers through workers' mobility. J Int Econ 53:205–222

Fujita M, Krugman P, Venables J (1999) The spatial economy: cities, regions and international trade. MIT Press, Cambridge

Gioia C, Thomsen S (2004) International acquisitions in Denmark, 1990–1997: selection and performance. Appl Econ Q 1:61–88

Globerman S, Zitian CV (2010) Best policy practices for promoting inwards and outwards foreign direct investment. The Conference Board of Canada, Report October 2010

Granskning av utländska investeringar, SOU 2021:87

Greenaway D, Sousa N, Wakelin K (2004) Do domestic firms learn to export from multinationals? Eur J Polit Econ 20(4):1027–1043

Gunby P (2017) Did FDI truly cause Chinese economic growth? A meta-analysis. World Dev 90 (C):242–255

Hansson P (2009) Inwards FDI and demand for skills in manufacturing firms in Sweden, med Roger Bandick. Rev World Econ 145(1):111–131

Haskel J, Pereira S, Slaughter M (2002) Does inwards foreign direct investment boost the productivity of domestic firms? Rev Econ Stat 89(3):482–496

Hermes N, Lensink R (2003) Foreign direct investment, financial development and economic growth. J Dev Stud 40(1):142–163

Hymer SH (1960) The international operation of national firms: a study of direct foreign investment. MIT Press, Cambridge. https://doi.org/10.18267/j.pep.337

Iršová Z, Havránek T (2013) Determinants of horizontal spillovers from FDI: evidence from a large meta-analysis. World Dev. https://doi.org/10.1016/j.worlddev.2012.07.001

Javorcik B (2004) Does foreign direct investment increase the productivity of domestic firms? In search of spillovers through backwards linkages. Am Econ Rev 94(3):605–627

Kalotay K (2006) The impact of EU enlargement on FDI flows. In: Batten JA, Kearney C (eds) Emerging European financial markets: independence and integration post enlargement, International finance review, vol 6. Emerald Group Publishing Limited

Karpaty P, Kneller R (2011) Demonstration or congestion?: Export spillovers in Sweden. Rev World Econ 147(1):109–130

Kemp MC (1964) The theory of international trade. Prentice Hall, London. https://doi.org/10.1016/j.worlddev.1098.12.891

Kinoshita Y (2009) R&D and technology spillovers via FDI: innovation and absorptive capacity, CERGE-EI working paper series no. 163

Knickerbocker FT (1973) Oligopolistic reaction and multinational enterprise. Division of Research, Harvard University, Cambridge. https://doi.org/10.1016/0305-750X(85)90002-6

Kokko A, Tansini R, Zejan M (2001) Trade regimes and effects of FDI: evidence from Uruguay. Weltwirtschaftlishers Archiv 137:124–149

Lall S (1980) Vertical interfirm linkages in LDCs: an empirical study. Oxf Bull Econ Stat 42(3): 203–226

Lapan H, Bardhan P (1973) Localized technical progress and transfer of technology and economic development. J Econ Theory 6:585–595

Lemafalussy A (1961) Investment and growth in mature economies. Basil Blackwell and Mott, Oxford. https://doi.org/10.1111/j.1475-4932.1960.tb00491.x

Lipsey R, Sjoholm F (2003) Foreign firms and Indonesian manufacturing wages: an analysis with panel data. National Bureau of Economic Research, working paper no. 9417

MacDougall GDA (1958) The benefits and cost of private foreign investment abroad: a theoretical approach. In: Economic record, vol 36

Marchick DM, Slaughter MJ (2008) Global FDI policy: correcting a protectionist drift, Bernard and Irene Schwartz Series on American competitiveness. Council on Foreign Relations. ISBN; 978-0876094075

Markusen J, Venables A (1999) Foreign direct investment as a catalyst for industrial development. Eur Econ Rev 43:335–356

Mastromarco C, Simar L (2012) Effect of FDI and time on catching up: new insights from a conditional nonparametric frontier analysis. J Appl Econ 30(5):826–847

Minakshee D (2020) Determinants of inwards foreign direct investments: comparison across different country groups. Appl Econ Int Dev 20(1):5–22

OECD (2000) Development centre studies. Policy competition for foreign direct investment: a study of competition among governments to attract FDI. Author, Charles Oman, OECD

OECD (2021) Investment policy developments in 62 economies between 16 October 2020 and 15 October 2021. Freedom of Investment Process

OECD (n.d.) Foreign direct investment statistics: data, analysis and forecasts investment statistics. Foreign Direct Investment Statistics: Data, Analysis and Forecasts - OECD

Paul J, Singh G (2017) The 45 years of foreign direct investment research: approaches, advances and analytical areas. World Econ. https://doi.org/10.1111/twec.12502

Perez T (1997) Multinational enterprises and technological spillovers: an evolutionary model. J Evol Econ 7:169–192

Piscitello L, Rabbiosi L (2004) More inwards FDI? Medium-term effects of foreign acquisitions on target company productivity. Appl Econ Q 1:21–40

Rodríguez-Clare A (1996) Multinationals, linkages, and economic development. Am Econ Rev 86:852–873

Scott-Kennel J, Enderwick P (2001) The degree of linkage of foreign direct investment in New Zealand Industry. Mimeo, Victoria University of Wellington

Sinani E, Meyer K (2004) Spillovers of technology transfer from FDI: the case of Estonia. J Comp Econ 32:445–466

Teixeira AAC, Forte R, Assunção S (2017) Do countries' endowments of nonrenewable energy resources matter for FDI attraction? A panel data analysis of 125 countries over the period 1995–2012. Int Econ. https://doi.org/10.1016/j.inteco.2016.12.002

Tillväxtanalys (2016) Utländska köp I svenskt näringsliv – hot eller möjlighet? PM 2017:12

Unctad (2021) World Investment Report 2021. Investing in sustainable recovery. United Nations, Geneva

Unctad (2022) World Investment Report 2021. United Nations, Geneva

United Nations (2001) International investment towards the year 2001 by United Nations Conference on Trade and Development (UNCTAD)

Vaitsos CV (1976) Power, knowledge and development policy: relations between transnational enterprises and developing countries. In: Helleiner GK (ed) A world divided: the less developed countries in the international economy. Cambridge University Press, London

Wang J, Blomström M (1992) Foreign investment and technology transfer: a simple model. Eur Econ Rev 36:137–155

Zhang S (2022) Protection of foreign investment in China: the foreign investment law and the changing landscape. Eur Bus Org Law Rev. https://doi.org/10.1007/s40804-022-00247-1

# From Principal Openness Towards Reciprocity: Reorienting the Normative Foundation of the EU Investment Screening Practice in Light of Geoeconomic Competition

**Thijs De Cuyper**

## Contents




**Abstract** Scholarly discourse has identified EU investment screening as revolutionary in recent years due to its shift away from principal openness to foreign capital. The screening framework was viewed as a step forwards in the development of a more assertive political and economic Union, which was deemed necessary in times of increasing geoeconomic competition. This contribution examines whether the EU and its member states are capable of effectively addressing the concerns and



T. De Cuyper (✉)
Catholic University of Leuven, Department of Economic Law, Leuven, Belgium
e-mail: thijs.decuyper@kuleuven.be





J. Hillebrand Pohl et al. (eds.), *Weaponising Investments*,
Springer Studies in Law & Geoeconomics (2023) 1: 141–168,
https://doi.org/10.1007/17280_2023_19, Published online: 3 August 2023

challenges that come with this new environment, particularly the lack of reciprocity. By considering the legal constraints as well as the political dimensions of investment screening, a grey zone between law and politics emerges where a discrepancy exists between the current legal argument and the political dynamics at play. This chapter identifies a function creep and seeks whether it is desirable to alter the standards that are used to shape investment relations with third countries in line with geoeconomics desires.

## 1 Introduction

The project of global economic liberalisation, with the aim of providing for economies open to trade and investment, is in distress. While the global economy may have never been structured better before in such a manner that products, services, and capital could freely flow across borders without the interference of the state, political and economic theories that reject the liberal premise are gaining favour. Indeed, elements of protectionist and neo-mercantilist discourse are being translated into internal and external economic policies around the world. This is to provide an answer to the negative spill-over effects associated with a globalised and interconnected economy.

The cause of this recent evolution can be partially traced back to a resurgent rivalry in the economic field between the great powers. The world is rapidly shifting from a setting with one dominant player (the U.S.) to a multipolar setting, where powers such as China, India and Russia claim their place. The use of trade and investment by foreign states with implicit political ends resulted in the introduction of security concerns in foreign and domestic economic policy. As a result, when considering how to manage economic relations with third states, an increasing number of countries adopt a different perspective on global liberalisation. In turn, the liberal system, which seeks to minimise government intervention, is now under pressure and must give way to the prepositioning of nation states' and supranational organisations' interests.

The European Union and its various Member States, traditionally an open market economy and a bastion of free trade, have not been immune to events where the effects of economic interaction with third countries proved to be detrimental rather than beneficial. Especially in times of crisis, economic dependency on third countries and their companies has been a cause for concern. The dependency on Russian gas and the resulting energy crisis, as well as the Sino-Lithuanian trade conflict, are examples of situations where the political system of the Member States is put under pressure. Furthermore, non-reciprocal trade relations with third countries, concerns about the competitiveness of European industry, the protection of vital processes and critical infrastructure, and a well-functioning internal market that is able to withstand disruptions from outside are issues that have received increased attention from EU institutions and Member States' governments.

How well positioned are the EU and its Member States to deal with these new challenges? With a principal focus on the area of foreign investment, this contribution aims to analyse the capacity of the EU and its Member States to adapt and face these challenges. To this extent, this paper will first try to provide a proper framework that explains the new dynamics that govern economic interactions between individual states or groups of states. For this, the concept of geoeconomics will be used. Second, this chapter will look at how the capacity to pursue geoeconomic objectives in investment screening is limited by the EU legal order. Acknowledging that the latter facilitates a principal openness towards non-EU investment on the basis of the erga omnes application of art. 63 TFEU, the focus will be on the legal limitations that determine the arguments that can *legally* be used in investment screening. Third, this contribution sheds some light on the *political* dimension of the practice of investment screening. In this part, the relativity of the legal discussion concerning the argumentative options will be discussed by using the case of the Hamburg port. Fourth, on the basis of the observations made in the previous part, the chapter will look into the possible alternatives for the erga omnes application of freedom of capital movement.

## 2 The Geoeconomic Relationship Between States

Nowadays, relationships between states are dual in nature. Not only are they characterised by economic partnership but also by rivalry. For example, it is accurate to say that the European Union and its member states are to a large extent economically entangled with the People's Republic of China (PRC). Regarding the EU's and China's largest trading partners in goods, both of these economic heavyweights are at the top of each other's list.[1] The economic relationship between the two blocs is not always an untroubled one, as there are significant and fundamental differences in how the state's influence on the economy is organised.[2] Principally, the European Union upholds a social market economy with an emphasis on economic competition between private parties, whereas in the Chinese approach, a state-driven economy is central.[3] This has resulted in the EU designating China as a systemic rival promoting different views on public–private economic organisation.[4]

---

[1] European Commission (Directorate-General for Trade) (2021) European Union, Trade in goods with China, 2.6.2021, https://webgate.ec.europa.eu/isdb_results/factsheets/country/details_china_en.pdf.

[2] Dadush et al. (2019), p. 18; European Commission (2019) Joint Communication to the European Parliament the European Council and the Council, EU-China – A strategic outlook, JOIN(2019) 5 final, 12.3.2019

[3] Katainen (2019), pp. 15–17.

[4] European Commission (2019) Joint Communication to the European Parliament the European Council and the Council, EU-China – A strategic outlook, JOIN(2019) 5 final, 12.3.2019.

To gain more insight into the duality at play, the notion of *geoeconomics* could *prima facie* provide for an explanatory guiding concept. The concept of geoeconomics, often associated with economic statecraft, was introduced to comprehend and apply structure to the complex but reciprocal relation between, on the one hand, politics and security and, on the other hand, global economic interactions. Geoeconomics builds a bridge between economic factors such as innovation, production and dependency and more (geo)political concepts such as the balance of power, spheres of influence, and national interests and security.[5] While the scientific value of this notion is (rightfully) debated, this paper will use geoeconomics as a guiding concept to better explain the relationships in which the EU currently finds itself. Indeed, its main contribution lies in the fact that it clarifies a set of key concepts that form the cornerstones of current EU-third country relationships and helps to understand the issues with regard to the altered perception of FDI not only as an economic reality but also as a politically charged instrument. Understanding geoeconomics, in turn, helps to better place and understand the broader policy context in which the investment screening practice was developed.

## 2.1 *Defining Geoeconomics*

Over the past decades, the notion of geoeconomics has received increasing attention in academia, governmental circles, and the international relations discourse. The forthcoming multipolarity through the rise of nations such as China, Brazil, Russia and others as major new economic powers sparked or revived the interest in interstate economic competition and how it should be waged.[6] Because of the increased association of commerce, trade, and investment with foreign policy and national security issues, geoeconomics has emerged as a critical concept in policy analysis.[7] To begin, it makes sense to provide an understanding of the concept by its "founding fathers," namely, Edward Luttwak and Pascal Lorot, who (re)introduced,[8] popularised and developed the concept of geoeconomics in its early stages.[9]

---

[5]Vihma (2018), p. 2.

[6]Mattlin and Wigell (2015), p. 126.

[7]Miosio (2018), pp. 22–23.

[8]There is much discussion in the literature about when geoeconomics as a concept took shape. Geoeconomics as a study and academic subject is definitely a more contemporary phenomenon as it is only recently that structured theories and understanding have been developed across a range of research fields and academic disciplines. Nevertheless, in certain fields of study such as law, geoeconomics has received little attention up to this present day. Whether the practice of geoeconomics in international relations is a recent phenomenon is much more debated. See for example: Domosh (2013), pp. 944–966.

[9]Vihma (2018), pp. 2–3.

The most significant idea that was put forwards by Luttwak was to identify the viability of economic power as an alternative to military power. Predominantly inspired by the events at the end of the Cold War period, Luttwak suggested that nation states compete for economic supremacy, as they see this as the new arena in which the struggles between states on the global theatre will take place.[10] According to Luttwak, states will tend to act geo-economically because of their *raison d'être*. He argues that, on the world scene, states are:

> ...spatial entities structured to jealously delimit their own territories, to assert their exclusive control within them, and variously to attempt to influence events beyond their borders, states are inherently inclined to strive for relative advantage against like entities on the international scene, even if only by means other than force.[11]

Luttwak's point of view is that of a state that serves as a defence structure against external foes. Following this logic, a nation will focus and organise itself around conflictual priorities and the need to prepare for interstate conflict.[12] If applied to the economic sphere, states will compete for resources and aim to overcome other nations to establish and consolidate a situation of economic welfare.[13] Nation states are thus partially established to delineate one group or entity against other equivalents and strive to gain a relative advantage over other states. As a result, when acting geoeconomically in the international economic sphere with other players, states will act competitively. However, this does not exclude that states will also seek cooperation if this serves their goal.[14]

Lorot takes a broader approach to geoeconomics based on the foundations laid down by Luttwak and describes the field of study as follows:

> ...the analysis of economic strategies (notably commercial), decided upon by states in a political setting aiming to protect their own economies or certain well identified sectors of it, to help their national enterprises acquire technology or to capture certain segments of the world market relative to production or commercialisation of a product. The possession or control of such a share confers to the entity - state or national enterprise - an element of power and international influence and helps to reinforce its economic and social potential.[15]

In his definition, Lorot emphasises the active role of the state as a relevant actor—if not a protagonist—in the practice that constitutes geoeconomics.[16] Geoeconomic strategies are mainly shaped by the political system of a state.[17] The state is a driving force behind the design and implementation of economic strategies that aim to

---

[10] Luttwak (1990), p. 17.

[11] Ibid., p. 19

[12] Luttwak has been inspired by the international relations' theory of realism. Certain elements, such as perceiving the state as inherently in competition with others while striving for its own survival, are clearly in line with realist theory.

[13] Wigell (2015), p. 138.

[14] Vihma (2018), p. 7.

[15] Lorot (2000), p. 15.

[16] Csurgai (2018) pp. 41–42.

[17] Szabo (2015), p. 84.

provide the state with (economic) power and influence in return. Together with other national economic actors, such as enterprises and investors, nations will develop and execute policies to increase their share of global economic power. Effectively using a geoeconomic strategy requires a certain synergy between the private sector and public or governmental agencies.

To establish a situation in which this cooperation can exist, a state needs to get a grip on the economic sphere and the actors that reside within. Among the means by which a government could attempt to achieve the goal of pursuing and implementing an effective geoeconomic strategy through its domestic economy are generally education and training, research and development, commercial strategy and policy, economic diplomacy, and economic intelligence. Each of these elements are individual parts that may shape and contribute to a greater geoeconomic strategy.[18]

## 2.2 Fundamental Geoeconomics Premises

A key shift in interstate relations, on the basis of geoeconomics, is the movement away from the idea that economic cooperation and interdependence are ultimately beneficial for all actors involved towards the presumption that the economic sphere is a place of competition and conflict. The latter relates to the positive- and zero-sum hypothesis, which help to understand the geoeconomic discourse.[19]

The assumption with economy, on the one hand, is that wealth is limitless and thus more of a positive-sum game. Consequently, a win or benefit for one party does not necessarily result in the loss for another party. On the other hand, the assumption on which Great Power competition and geopolitics are based is zero-sum, meaning that a certain state's or international actor's win necessarily results in another state's loss.[20] This is because power, in its geopolitical sense, is limited, and actors vying for power are thus in competition for a limited resource with one another.[21] Geoeconomics contributes to the discussion by situating economic means and processes

[18] Csurgai (2018), p. 43.

[19] Roberts et al. (2019), p. 659.

[20] Blackwill and Harris (2016), p. 24.

[21] Geoeconomics is often linked to geopolitical discourse and international relations (IR) realism theories. According to (classical) realism in international relations theory, states are continuously engaged in a struggle to increase their capabilities and will do everything in their power to protect their national security and to try to ensure their own survival. The realist vision is based on three assumptions. To begin with, states as cohesive units are the most powerful actors in global politics. Second, realists believe that force is a useful and effective policy tool. Other instruments may be used, but the most effective way of wielding power is to use or threaten force. Third, realists assume a hierarchy of issues in world politics, with military security at the top: "high politics" of military security dominates "low politics" of economic and social affairs, partly because of their second assumption. This message clearly fits within the context of geopolitical competition; Griffiths (2005), pp. 707–713; Keohane and Nye (1977), p. 19.

within the larger context of state power. The positive-sum aspect—one can win without inevitably impeding another—is being challenged when the economic means itself are being deployed for competitive ends in a greater struggle for power.[22] The modern (realist) interpretation of foreign economic policy is consequently perceived as based on zero-sum competition rather than on a positive-sum alternative.[23] It can be argued, however, that the re-emphasis of economics in political power not only creates competition but also forms new opportunities for cooperation between states.[24]

As seen in Luttwak's understandings of geoeconomics, states compete with one another to gain a relative advantage over others. This is related to the state's pursuit of power and wealth, as this is arguably the most effective way to position oneself in a position where an advantage can be realised. Power can be generally defined as an actor's ability to persuade others to do something they would not otherwise do (and at an acceptable cost to the actor), as well as the ability to influence outcomes.[25]

The post-war era has seen a dramatic transformation in the components, uses and exercise of power.[26] Indeed, in the new global economic rivalry, mastering trade, cross-border investment and finance, as well as leading in technological development, will prevail over military power.[27] Thus, from a geoeconomic perspective, power can be thought of as overall economic strength. When states disagree or pursue opposing strategies on economic issues, the outcome of the interaction is partially determined by the economic strength of the parties involved. The stronger a state's economic standing is, the higher its capability to harm or help other states. A strong domestic economy will continue to be a general requirement for any country's power projection in the long run.[28]

Currently, the question at which end of the international power distribution a state finds itself is mainly dependent on the overall state of its economy and, more specifically, its strategic autonomy. Indeed, in the pursuit of the national interest, economic performance is currently a top priority for most governments.[29]

More generally, "wealth" is used as a key factor when determining the economic potential of countries. In particular, to determine the economic power of a state, one will look at, e.g., the size of financial assets, the ability to accumulate capital, having a positive trade balance, developing the competitiveness of national companies, reducing dependency on other countries, and technological capability.[30] More concretely, relevant factors for determining economic power are human and

---

[22] Blackwill and Harris (2016), pp. 24–25.

[23] Mattlin and Wigell (2015), p. 126; Szabo (2014), p. 120.

[24] Grevi (2011), p. 28.

[25] Keohane and NYE (1977), p. 10.

[26] Hoffmann (1975), pp. 193–184.

[27] Csurgai (2018), pp. 38–39.

[28] Blackwill and Harris (2016), pp. 19–20.

[29] Grevi (2011), p. 28.

[30] Grosse (2014), p. 42; Subramian (2019), p. 67.

technological resources, availability of natural resources, production capacity of goods, intensity of research and development, percentage shares within the global economy, and influence or leverage over economic decision-making.

Perceiving power through an economic lens shows the essence of obtaining supremacy over these factors. For example, small nations that were irrelevant for the military power balance but that have monopolies or quasi-monopolies over natural resources or raw materials can have immense leverage over advanced economies.[31] These factors are, of course, only relevant to the extent to which a state is willing to use its economic power for political gain.[32] Power of economic nature will also be specific to certain issue areas. In a system of largely uncontrolled exchange, patterns of specialisation have developed, where specific economic activities take place in specific countries.[33] For example, despite its small size, Switzerland has a strong banking sector and can be seen as a sectoral authority. Similarly, the Netherlands and Taiwan are dominant in the semiconductor sector.[34] However, the influence these countries can exert on the basis of dominance in this sector is relative and not always easily translated to other sectors of the economy.[35] Moreover, as a consequence of the changing nature of power, the advantage provided by achieving and maintaining superiority over a component of power is temporary and relative.

## 2.3 *Self-Sufficiency and Reciprocity as Constituent Elements of Geoeconomic Power*

Building further on the foregoing general premise, the geoeconomic balance of the power game is mainly determined by a nation's strategic autonomy. Economic interdependence and interaction create economic efficiency gains; however, they also produce vulnerabilities such as dependency relationships on foreign states.[36] In principle, dependency between states starts from a division of capabilities, such as

[31] Keohane and Nye (1977), pp. 9–10.

[32] Hsiung (2009), pp. 113–114.

[33] Brown and Ainley (2009), p. 159.

[34] ASML in the Netherlands and Taiwan Semiconductor Manufacturing Company (TSMC in Taiwan) are both titans of the semiconductor industry. Especially in the case of Taiwan, its dominance in this vital industry is often seen as a reason for befriending the nation, as well as a wake-up call for ramping up domestic production capabilities (New York Times (2022, January 26) How the Computer Chip Shortage Could Incite a U.S. Conflict With China, https://www.nytimes.com/2022/01/26/us/politics/computer-chip-shortage-taiwan.html).

[35] See for example the end of Swiss banking secrecy under US pressure (Reuters (2018, October 5) Era of bank secrecy ends as Swiss start sharing account data, https://www.reuters.com/article/us-swiss-secrecy-idUSKCN1MF13O); Jackson and Sorensen (2013), p. 109.

[36] Roberts et al. (2019), pp. 659–660.

access to resources or technology, who exchange the latter, as this is—mostly, although not always—mutually beneficial. It is assumed that dependency is maintained by the fact that the opportunity costs of breaking or altering the relationship would be high.[37] Indeed, the most common understanding of maintaining dependency among international relations theorists is that in state-to-state relationships, countries are irreparably harmed by dissolving their relationships with one another.[38]

Furthermore, scholars tend to discuss dependency in terms of self-sufficiency, i.e., the capacity of a state to fulfil its own needs without external assistance. More concretely, self-sufficiency concerning natural resources and the absence of long-term dependency on external markets are factors that contribute to a favourable standing in the dependency hierarchy.[39] The degree of self-sufficiency is related to a state's vulnerability to changes in certain types of international economic relationships, particularly trade and foreign direct investment. A nation that does not possess the capacity to meet its own domestic needs without relying on flows of trade or capital with other international actors lacks self-sufficiency and is more vulnerable in its dependency on others. Quite simply, the costs of severing trade or investment relations will be lower for self-sufficient states than for dependent states.[40] Sectors that have the ability for self-sufficiency, thereby limiting a state's dependency, are thus of strategic importance in a geoeconomic context.[41]

In particular, asymmetries in economic interdependence are a source of power, i.e., control over resources and the ability to influence outcomes.[42] The consequent premise is that less dependent actors in interstate relationships thus have more power, as the change in relationship will be less costly for them.[43] In turn, this provides a number of advantages and benefits, such as having a better negotiating position and being able to resist pressure from external actors. An important nuance, however, is that favourable asymmetries in interdependency will not necessarily lead to similar patterns in the balance of power.[44] The resulting basis is that for many developed nations, securing the supply of raw materials has become a priority, for example, much more important than defending borders against external military threats.[45] The notions of national security or national interest have been stripped of

---

[37] Sir Norman Angell's "leaky boat" example, as described on page 17 of his book *The Foundations of International Polity*, is a simple but effective way to grasp the fundamental meaning of dependency; Baldwin (1980), pp. 483–484.

[38] This is commonly referred to as "vulnerability dependency"; Tanious (2019), p. 40.

[39] Hsiung (2009), pp. 114–115.

[40] Baldwin (1980), pp. 484–485.

[41] For similar argumentation, see Diesen (2021).

[42] Nye (2020), p. 8.

[43] Sattich and Inderberg (2019), p. 508.

[44] Keohane and Nye (1987), p. 728; Keohane and Nye (1977), p. 10; The same arguments can be found in Hirschman's *National Power and the Structure of Foreign Trade*, and in Waltz's *The Myth of National Interdependence*.

[45] Szabo (2015), p. 89; Roberts et al. (2019), p. 665.

their original meaning and should be reinterpreted in light of the new context in which economic security prevails. The key concern for states currently is economic wealth and prosperity, partially because this results in power according to the geoeconomic framework and less so with security in its traditional sense.[46]

To conclude, the key geoeconomics premises can be summarised as follows. First, the state interferes in the economic realm, and this intervention is driven by political ambition instead of the normal economic processes of the market. Second, economic interaction between nations is based on a zero-sum rather than a positive-sum hypothesis, which entails that competition will prevail over cooperation. Third, the goal of a state, or groups of states, is to create and consolidate state power via economic means, more specifically through the acquisition of "wealth" in all its aspects. Fourth, the balance of power is mainly decided by asymmetries in economic dependency, thus making self-sufficiency and autonomy key concepts. The minimum a state should thus aim to achieve in its economic relationships with other states is reciprocity.

The above-depicted understanding of geoeconomic competition highlights the new environment in which the EU and its Member States find themselves. Indeed, the latter are required to adapt to a new global setting in which trade and investment have a political-strategic connotation. Indeed, economic instruments such as trade and investment are widely used to achieve a variety of policy goals, including the advancement of political agendas.[47]

How do the EU and its Member States thrive in this competitive environment? This question relates essentially to the determination of the capacity of the EU and its Member States as geoeconomic actors. To that end, this contribution examines the latter's geoeconomic capacity in the field of foreign investment screening. Recognising that foreign investment control is a geoeconomic policy, the analysis seeks to answer the question of whether the current screening mechanisms and their underlying premises are appropriate in a geoeconomic environment. The approach is twofold. First, investment screening will be approached from a legal perspective to determine which limits exist for the EU and its Member States to use investment screening geoeconomically (under Sect. 3). Second, the contribution will look at the political dimension of investment screening mechanisms to determine whether these limits are respected or not (under Sect. 4).

[46] Szabo (2015), p. 84.

[47] Jacobs (2019), p. 114 and 117; Hindelang and Moberg (2021), p. 1429.

# 3 The Legal Dimension: Capacity of the EU to Engage in Geoeconomic Competition

It is assumed that effective geoeconomic action requires that a government can interfere in economic relations to rectify situations of dependency and asymmetry. In the case of foreign investment, the EU and its Member States should thus be able to use regulatory means in a way that these issues can be addressed. On the basis of the current EU legal order and the norms resorting within, can the EU and its Member States consider self-sufficiency, dependency and existing asymmetries–, i.e., reciprocity—as arguments to restrict inward non-European investment?

Answering this question requires us to start with identifying the legal fundaments upon which the EU and its Member States can control foreign investment flows. Indeed, the endeavour to determine the capacity of the EU as a geoeconomic actor relates closely to the norms and values upon which the EU and its Member States interact with third countries. In the realm of trade and investment, for the past decades, the baseline for almost every aspect of EU internal and external trade policy was to maintain a large degree of openness to the outside world.

## *3.1 The Normative Foundation: Principal Openness towards Foreign Investments*

For foreign investments, the aforementioned observation is also true. From a legal perspective, it is first and foremost important to highlight that foreign direct investments are considered capital movements. The latter are protected under one of the fundamental freedoms, the freedom of capital movement, as enshrined in art. 63 of the TFEU. Of particular relevance, however, is the fact that the application of this fundamental freedom extends towards third country situations. In essence, this erga omnes application of freedom makes this provision the backbone of foreign investment protection in the EU.[48]

Restricting these capital movements, and consequently non-EU investments, is only possible on exception grounds. In light of investment control, two relevant grounds exist. The first one is introduced by the Screening Regulation itself, as it states that Member States can adopt restrictive measures that allow to review foreign investment in light of the likely risk "security and public order". The second option is based on art. 65 (1)(b) TFEU, which states that measures that restrict the freedom of capital movement can be taken when justified on grounds of "public policy and public security".[49] As a result, the Member States do not enjoy a full discretionary competence in designing, adopting and operating an investment screening

[48] Velten (2022), pp. 116–117.

[49] Ibid., pp. 57–58.

mechanism. Indeed, foreign investment can thus only be screened within the limits of "security and public order" or "public policy and public security". The question now arises regarding which exact arguments can be considered when operating a screening mechanism on these grounds.

### 3.1.1 Security and Public Order

The European Investment Screening Regulation introduced a new screening ground, namely, "security and public order". The latter is similar in wording as the exception ground in art. 65 (1)(b) TFEU, although this is not the case. The European legislature intentionally introduced this new screening ground for Member States and only applied a subtle form of harmonisation in the interpretation of security and public order. In essence, the competence to give substance to these notions lies with the Member States.[50] Consequently, what is considered to be of relevance to security and public order is fragmented across the Member States that operate a screening mechanism on this ground. It is therefore difficult to provide a complete picture of the possible argumentation under all the mechanisms of EU Member States. While broad, the discretionary competence of the Member States is not unlimited.

First, limitations grounded in international economic law apply. As observed in the literature, WTO law allows for many arguments to be considered but excludes, for example, the consideration of reciprocity as an argument upon which a screening decision can be taken.[51] Essentially, analysis shows that an interpretation of security and public order in light of international economic law only allows for a partial meeting of FDI-related concerns, most notably those that are relevant in a geoeconomic context.[52]

Second, the case law on restricting the freedom of capital movement on the basis of art. 65 (1)(b) TFEU has to be taken into account. The fact that the Screening Regulation does not harmonise means that EU primary law—in particular the public policy and public security exception on the freedom of capital movement—still plays a role. Even though the Screening Regulation introduced a new screening ground, the interpretation of public policy and public security thus cannot be ignored.[53] The latter will be analysed in what follows. Moreover, an analysis of the argumentative leeway possible on the basis of art. 65 (1)(b) TFEU fits more within the objective of this subchapter, which aims to delineate the limits posed by the EU internal legal order.

---

[50] Hindelang and Moberg (2021), p. 843.

[51] Velten (2022), p. 101.

[52] Ibid.

[53] Hindelang and Moberg (2021), pp. 844–846.

### 3.1.2 Public Policy and Public Security

The provision that reflects the EU's philosophy has thus been identified as art. 63 TFEU and its erga omnes application. From a literal reading of the treaty, in the area of capital movement, the EU applies the same standards for foreigners as it does for Member States, which are part of an intimately linked political and economic Union. The latter has to be nuanced, as will become clear below.

Of particular relevance in the context of FDI screening are restrictions on this freedom permitted under art. 65 TFEU on the grounds of *public security* and *public policy*. On the basis of these provisions, as well as extensive case law from the Court of Justice of the European Union (CJEU), the requirements for exceptions under Article 65 TFEU were developed. The interpretation of these exception grounds in our European legal order indirectly establishes the boundaries within which the EU can operate.

The court states that the scope of the public security requirement, as a ground to derogate from the fundamental freedom of capital movement, cannot be determined unilaterally by each Member State without any control by the Community institutions.[54] First, according to the CJEU, to establish a restriction on these grounds, there must be a genuine and sufficiently serious threat to a fundamental interest of society.[55] Second, the restriction must be proportional with respect to its purpose.[56] Finally, art. 65 (3) TFEU stipulates that restrictive measures may not constitute a means of arbitrary discrimination or a *disguised* restriction on the free movement of capital.[57] These are consequently the parameters within which EU Member States must operate their screening practices and highlight the underlying spirit of retaining principal openness towards non-EU investment.

Building upon the foregoing, the next relevant question relates to the decisions Member States are legally allowed to take on the basis of their screening mechanisms in light of these restrictions. In other words, which arguments can a Member State invoke when determining whether a foreign investment poses a risk for public security or public order? The answer to this question, however, is not straightforward.

There is plenty of case law by the CJEU that outlines and clarifies the nature of the arguments that are allowed to be used when restricting the freedom of capital movement in an internal market situation under the banner of public security and public policy. In line with the strict internal market interpretation, the assessment of FDI for public security or policy reasons can be construed narrowly. The Court

---

[54] Hindelang (2009), p. 226.

[55] Judgment of the Court of 14 March 2000, Eglise de Scientology, C-54/99, ECLI:EU:C:2000:124, para 17; Judgment of the Court of 4 June 2002, Commission v. Belgium, C-503/99, ECLI:EU:C:2002:328, para 47; Judgment of the Court of 13 May 2003, Commission v. Spain, C-463/00, ECLI:EU:C:2003:272, para 72.

[56] Judgment of the Court of 13 July 2000, Albore, C-423/98, ECLI:EU:C:2000:401, para 19; De Jong and Zwartkruis (2020), p. 457.

[57] Warcholl (2021), p. 60.

already highlighted that purely economic grounds can never serve as justification to enact restrictions on the freedom of capital movement.[58] The Court also established that 'strengthening the competitive structure of the market concerned' or 'modernising and increasing the efficiency of means of production' are interests that cannot constitute valid reasons to restrict the freedom of capital movement.[59] Consequently, restrictions on the basis of economic grounds as well as on a reciprocity argument would be prohibited.[60] The strict limitations that the CJEU has defined on the basis of public security and order in the internal market context do not *necessarily* find parallel application to a third country context.[61]

The wording of art. 63 TFEU seems unambiguous, in that the scope of the freedom of capital movement in a third country context and an intra-EU context are the same. The latter, however, is not the case, as the interpretation in a third country context of the scope of this provision is not settled by the CJEU or by a divided legal literature.[62] Indeed, it is unclear whether the concepts of public security and public order as understood in an intra-EU context must be necessarily applied in parallel to a non-EU context.

Alternately, it can be argued that public security and order in the context of FDI should be interpreted in light of changing societal needs, as well as needs from secondary and national legislation when they represent a public interest.[63] In turn, this would result in a looser approach favouring discretionary competence for the member states to decide on public security and order.[64] Here, member states would enjoy more liberty, and certain arguments that would not be valid in an intra-EU context could be used in assessing inwards FDI from third countries.[65] An argument in favour of a broad interpretation of the grounds for restricting FDI, and thus the fundamental freedoms, is that the EU and its member states' mechanisms will be more capable of dealing with developments in the global FDI market, which formed the basis for the regulation's enactment in the first place.[66]

---

[58] Judgment of the Court of 4 June 2002, Commission v. Portugal, C-367/98, ECLI:EU:C:2002:326, para 52; Judgment of the Court of 27 February 2019, Associação Peço a Palavra e.a. v. Conselho de Ministros, C-563/17, ECLI:EU:C:2019:144, para 70; Hindelang (2009), p. 216-217.

[59] Judgment of the Court of 4 June 2002, Commission v. Portugal, C-367/98, ECLI:EU:C:2002:326, para 52.

[60] Jansen (2015), p. 307; De Jong and Zwartkruis (2020), p. 465.

[61] Wernicke (2021), p. 34.

[62] Hindelang and Maydell (2011), p. 2.

[63] Judgment of the Court of 22 October 2013, Staat der Nederlanden v. Essent, C-105/12 to C-107/12, ECLI:EU:C:2013:677, para 66.

[64] Judgment of the Court of 14 March 2000, Eglise de Scientology, C-54/99, ECLI:EU:C:2000:124, para 17.

[65] E.g.: the existence of an unlevel playing field with regard to FDI or the concern that the acquisition of a sensitive technology could affect national industrial policy; Jansen (2015), p. 309.

[66] *Infra* Sect. 4.3.

One important nuance that has to be made is that the CJEU may further develop the 'genuine and sufficiently serious threat to a fundamental interest of society' in light of societal and political needs by itself.[67] The latter, however, has not been the case since investment screening in the EU and its Member States more or less became 'common practice' in 2020.

The current situation is thus one where the EU and its Member States have investment screening mechanisms that were developed within the limits of its own legal system and whereby the legislative options were rather limited. The resulting investment screening mechanism that is in place thus only allows a limited set of considerations to be made within investment screening processes.

## *3.2 Geoeconomic Capacity on the Basis of the Current Legal Standards*

Does the current framework suffice, however, to address the concerns and challenges associated with foreign investment from a geoeconomic perspective? The legal literature is rather sceptical when considering this question. Important observations have been made in the literature stating that the current screening framework does not cover all concerns related to foreign investments. The fact that screening under the current framework is only possible on narrow grounds–, i.e., security and public order—makes one wonder whether other broader legal grounds are more useful.[68] To this extent, the literature observes that the alternative broader legal grounds upon which a screening mechanism could be established offer the same limited leeway, as significant legal barriers posed by European primary law and international investment commitments exist.[69] Ultimately, it seems fair to conclude that none of the available screening grounds that are used or could be used are broad enough to meet all the contemporary challenges with foreign investment.[70]

In other words, the EU legal system itself, with the third application of the fundamental freedom of capital movement, creates extensive limitations for imposing limits on inbound flows of foreign capital. Notwithstanding the international obligations that the EU or the Member States are bound to, the philosophy that is embodied in art. 63 and 65 TFEU limits the capacity of the EU and its Member States to adopt regulation that addresses reciprocity, or the lack thereof, and other geoeconomic concerns.

Having discussed the legal limitations in this subchapter, in what follows, a different perspective will be applied. In particular, this contribution will now focus

[67] Hindelang and Moberg (2021), p. 1453.

[68] Velten (2022), p. 121.

[69] Ibid., pp. 298–299.

[70] Ibid., p. 300.

on these limitations in light of the practical application of investment screening mechanisms.

# 4 The Political Dimension: Discrepancy Between Legal and Political Realities

While investment screening has been adopted under security exceptions, the question arises whether investment screening mechanisms are and will only be used within the legal limits associated with the latter. Because of the ambiguity of the concept of "security and public order" and "public security and public order" in the context of economic relations with third countries, as well as the wide range of interpretations that can be applied to it, there is a risk that screening decisions were or will be made that do not fall within the bounds of safeguarding and mitigating threats to security and public order. Despite the fact that the somewhat vague nature was intended to cover a wide range of situations, the question arises as to whether screening mechanisms in practice are used to achieve their primary goal, namely, the protection of security and public order.

To formulate an answer to the latter remains hard, as identifying the arguments upon which a screening decision has been taken is not straightforward. Consequently, whether certain arguments that were considered and taken into account fall outside the scope of what investment screening mechanisms ought to consider is equally troublesome to answer. The rather secretive and non-transparent manner in which screening decisions are taken does not contribute to the demystification of what happens at the Member States' Ministries of Economic Affairs when screening inbound investments.[71]

## *4.1 The Port of Hamburg*

On some occasions, however, the public is lucky and is granted a more detailed glimpse in the process of issuing a screening decision. The latter was the case with the Port of Hamburg saga. A proposed investment in a logistics company (Hamburger Hafen und Logistik AG—HHLA) that owns three terminals in the port of Hamburg was subject to scrutiny due to concerns with respect to the identity of the investor. The latter being China's Cosco, the investment fell within the scope of Germany's screening mechanism under the Foreign Trade and Payments Act (*Außenwirtschaftsgesetz*—AWG) and the Foreign Trade and Payments Ordinance (*Außenwirtschaftsverordnung*—AWV). A closer look at this investment review

[71] Bian (2021), p. 565.

process, with its exceptional publicity and controversy, gives a rather rare insight into how limited the clout of the legal argument is in a highly politicised policy area.

Reporting on Cosco's proposed investment triggered many reactions. While there were many that supported the investment, a large group of policymakers and government executives explicitly advised not to continue with the deal. The concerns were manifold. First and foremost, there was the usual debate in an investment review process about restricting Chinese ownership of critical port infrastructure because it could result in the instrumentalization of the Hamburg port during times of political crisis. Second, it is important to note that this argument does not appear to be the primary reason for the strong opposition to China's entry into HHLA. Indeed, the nature of the concerns extended beyond potential threats to security and public order.

In particular, other points of concern with respect to Cosco's investment had to do with an expansion of China's control over German and European transport infrastructure and the "strategic influence" it would obtain in its wake. Furthermore, commentators and policymakers pointed out that while China is permitted to make such investments in European ports, capital flows in the opposite direction are not permitted. The issue of non-reciprocity in investment relations with China, which is a common source of political and corporate resentment in Europe, was thus a source of contention in the case at hand.

Despite the outpouring of opposition to Cosco's acquisition of a stake in the Hamburg port, the German Ministry for Economic Affairs and Climate Action (*Bundesministerium für Wirtschaft und Klimaschutz*) continued to give the investment the go-ahead. Commentators believe German Chancellor Olaf Scholz's trip to China a few weeks after the deal was approved had something to do with allowing the Chinese to enter one of Germany's economic and logistical hubs.[72] However, some mitigation action was taken as the share Cosco acquired was reduced to a minority stake of 24.9%. The German Chancellor considers the latter insufficient to exert strategic influence over HHLA and promotes the outcome as a win–win solution for both parties. The German Ministry of Economic Affairs declared that the reduction in the stake to be acquired was due to the existence of a threat to public order and safety.[73] If one takes the German Ministry's words at face value, the limits within which a screening mechanism should operate were thus respected.

The German solution was praised and criticised. On the one hand, the United States of America welcomed the mandatory reduction of the stake acquired by the Chinese from 35% initially, down to 24,9%.[74] French policymakers, on the other hand, criticised the German decision, claiming that the investment, even if only

[72] Bundesministerium für Wirtschaft und Energie (2022), Bundeskabinett verabschiedet Teiluntersagung im Investitionsprüfverfahren Hamburger Hafen. Press release of 26.10.2022; Kohler (2022). The Chancellor doesn't want to alienate the Emperor. *Frankfurter Allgemeine Zeitung*.

[73] Euronews (2022). Germany agrees to controversial sale of Hamburg port terminal.

[74] Frankfurter Allgemeine Zeitung (2022b). USA warns Germany against Chinese influence on infrastructure.

granting a minority stake to Cosco, should not have taken place at a time when economic reliance on China is clearly no longer desirable.[75]

In Germany itself, the saga is seen as proof that Germany does not have a clear and functional vision, let alone policy, on how to deal with growing geopolitical tensions.[76] The Chancellor's coalition partners also voiced criticism over the investment, stating that German ports do not belong in Chinese hands, especially since German investment in Chinese ports is not possible.[77] Even the German Minister of Foreign Affairs, Annalena Baerbock, warned that Germany cannot repeat the same mistakes as it made with Russia and that Germany should not make itself dependent on a country that does not share the same values. Furthermore, the Minister also referred to the absence of a level-playing field in EU-China investment relations.[78]

## 4.2 Lessons Learned from the Hamburg Port Case: Function Creep and Investment Screening

There are two major observations to be made with respect to the Hamburg case. First, the screening procedures can become incredibly political. While this is obviously not always the case, a certain level of publicity will act as a catalyst for the review process to become a subject of political opportunism. Second, on the German and European sides, there are clear concerns with respect to non-reciprocity, dependency and the exertion of strategic influence at play. Notwithstanding the fact that the public only has limited information, it seems hard to imagine that those in power to ultimately deal with the case did not consider these arguments. Even given the uncertainty with respect to the interpretation of security and public order in third-country situations, it was not the intention of the legislator for those concerns to be within the limits of what can be legally considered in an investment review process under the current framework.[79]

In essence, investment screening under the current framework is susceptible to *function creep*. The latter is the phenomenon where an instrument is used for a different purpose than initially intended. The purpose of investment screening mechanisms was to protect against risks to "security and public order" and "public policy and public order". While the reciprocity argument, for example, does not fall within the original scope of what the legislator intended, it cannot be guaranteed that it will not be considered in a screening decision.

---

[75] Noyan, Bourgery-Gonse (2022). French policymakers irked by Chinese company's stake in Hamburg port. *Euractiv*.

[76] Braunberger (2022). Selbstvergessen. *Frankfurter Allgemeine Zeitung*.

[77] Deutsche Welle (2022, October 20). Scholz Criticised over China's Cosco Bid in Hamburg Port.

[78] Frankfurter Allgemeine Zeitung (2022a). Port Participation: Baerbock warns for dependency on China; Tamma (2022). Germany's Baerbock warns Scholz ahead of his China trip. *Politico*.

[79] Velten (2022), pp. 121–122; Nettesheim (2021), p. 485.

The aforementioned observations make one contemplate the interplay between the legal and non-legal dimension of investment screening. The whole debate concerning the substantive limits within which a screening decision can be taken on the basis of the legal framework seems only relative. This is true when considering the practical application of investment screening, which inevitably includes a level of political interference. Essentially, it appears that law ends where politics begins. This is not to say that the Hamburg port case is typical of EU investment control. In contrast, according to the EU Commission's most recent investment screening report, only a small number of investments were subject to screening, and an even smaller number were subject to conditions or were prohibited.[80] What the Hamburg port case demonstrates is that the political and legal worlds are not always on the same page with respect to investment screening.

## 4.3 *Investment Screening and Geoeconomics: The Case for Reciprocity*

The case of the Hamburg port reveals how investment control can be used as a geoeconomic instrument. On the one hand, the language of geoeconomics is easily discernible in the arguments and reactions surrounding the Hamburg case. The discourse concerning Cosco's proposed acquisition was intensely focused on issues such as dependency and reciprocity. Geoeconomic aspirations, on the other hand, are difficult to satisfy under the current legal framework, as demonstrated in subchapter 3.

Some of the reactions of public officials on the case show that there is some type of resentment present in the European political world. In essence, one could observe that there is a political movement that calls for more effective and direct means to tackle reciprocity and dependency issues. This is not something new, especially in the area of foreign investment control. While the investment screening framework has the protection of security and public order as its primary objective, the framework is clearly intended to play a role in the development of a wider foreign economic policy that tackles more than just the security issues associated with FDI.[81]

Few countries use the well-protected free flow of capital as a starting point for developing a policy on inbound foreign capital movements. As a result, given the scope and protection of the free movement of capital as provided for in the TFEU, the relationship between EU Member States and third countries in this regard is often asymmetric.[82] The interaction between economic systems that are based on different

[80] European Commission (2022) Second Annual Report on the screening of foreign direct investments into the Union, COM(2022) 433 final, 1.9.2022.

[81] Nettesheim (2021), pp. 485–486.

[82] Bakker (2021), pp. 12–13.

principles has led to the establishment of reciprocal economic relations as a political objective.[83]

What then, exactly, is understood under a lack of reciprocity? This asymmetry is often linked to the rise of unilateralism, regionalism and protectionism, which form a direct threat to the fundamentals of a free market system with fair competition and free flows of goods and capital.[84] China, for example, is clearly discontent with a US-led international economic system and often criticises the rules, institutions and practices that are associated with it.[85] With its state-capitalist system, China offers an alternative.[86] However, this system causes negative spill over effects that other major players perceive as distortive for the rule-based international trade order.[87]

Obviously, among those worried by the emergence of state capitalism is the EU for who's businesses this evolution did not exactly provide a level playing field. SOEs from third countries are often promoted to become not only domestic "champions of industry" but also international titans. These enterprises often receive favourable treatment from their respective governments to achieve this objective through subsidies and tax breaks.[88] In turn, when competing with European businesses that do not enjoy similar benefits, it is hard to speak of fair competition.[89] The reciprocity problem in investment relations is thus an issue that leads to frustration on the European side, as European businesses are restricted outwards due to market access restrictions in third countries, in addition to facing unfair competition by foreign state-backed investors at home.[90] Ultimately, the lack of reciprocity is one of the smouldering issues in investment and broader economic relations between China and a number of other countries.[91]

The current role of investment screening in promoting reciprocity is limited, at least when considered from a strictly legal perspective. As demonstrated with the Hamburg case, however, investment screening can play a role, although it is not within the limits of its original legal objective.

An interesting take in the literature is that while investment screening under the current framework is not directly aimed at resolving the reciprocity issue, the presence of an investment screening mechanism can serve as a bargaining chip for the EU in its wider economic relations with third countries.[92] By putting up barriers

[83] Nettesheim (2021), p. 498.

[84] Molthof et al. (2021), p. 9.

[85] Kim (2017), pp. 289–290.

[86] See for example the communiqué, also known as Document 9, that was sent in 2012 out by the CCP's leadership that warns for foreign (Western) ideas and values.

[87] European Commission (2021) Trade Policy Review - An Open, Sustainable and Assertive Trade Policy, COM(2021) 66 final, 18.2.2021, pp. 8–9.

[88] Bremmer (2009), pp. 42–43; Simon (2021), pp. 44–46.

[89] Bakker (2021), p. 26.

[90] Simon (2021), pp. 45–46.

[91] Chilton et al. (2020), p. 131.

[92] Nettesheim (2021), p. 498.

to market access, as done by other major economic powers,[93] the EU creates a level playing field that allows for the extraction of concessions of third states with regard to market access for FDI.[94] In essence, the dynamic is similar to the EU's international procurement instrument, which fosters reciprocity as a tool to gain access to foreign procurement markets.[95]

The question that rises is whether one should just accept this function creep of the current investment screening framework. Especially with the weight being given to the lack of reciprocity in investment relations—which was reaffirmed in the reactions to the Hamburg saga—it should be considered whether or not the investment screening framework should be reconfigured to facilitate this concern. From a geoeconomic perspective, one could argue that the EU legal framework that regulates economic interaction with third countries should adapt more to the new reality of geoeconomics. To a certain extent, this requires a change in the underlying premises, which now hinders the consideration of issues such as reciprocity, at least within the investment screening practice. Therefore, how fitting is the third country application of the freedom of capital movement in today's environment?

## 5 Changing the Normative Basis for Investment Screening: Reciprocity as a Standard

The new geoeconomic context in which the EU and its Member States find themselves should give rise to introspection with respect to the fundamental norms and standards underlying economic interaction with third countries. The obviousness of the free movement of capital vis-à-vis third countries is something that has been taken for granted, while many regulatory evolutions in the EU—including the adoption of an investment screening regulation—highlight the need to rethink the fundamental principles that underly our economic relations with third countries. Is reconfiguration desirable?

---

[93] E.g.: the practice of negative lists as adopted by China. On the one hand, there is a national "Negative List for the Access of Foreign Investments". On the other hand, there is a specific "Negative List for Access of Foreign Investments to China's Free Trade Zones". When a sector or asset is included in a negative list, foreign investment therein is prohibited or restricted. Both of the above lists apply only to foreign investors. Additionally, noteworthy is the existence of a Market Access Negative List. This list applies to domestic and foreign enterprises regardless of their nature (private as well as state-owned).

[94] Schill (2019), pp. 105–128.

[95] European Parliament (2022). International Public Procurement Instrument: Securing Fairness for EU firms. Press release of 9.6.2022.

## 5.1 Rethinking the Standard of Principal Openness

It should be noted that establishing the erga omnes application of the freedom of capital movement was not a walk in the park. Looking at the slow but steady historical development towards liberalising capital movements in the last half of the twentieth century,[96] the question of whether discriminatory treatment of third country capital movements was desirable had been subject of debate. Some Member States supported the principle, as it would attract foreign capital. Others, such as France, had a traditionally restrictive take on capital movements and were thus more sceptical.[97] France preferred a more privileged treatment for European states. The compromise that has been reached is still visible today. The freedom of capital movement applies to third countries, but Member States retain certain regulatory freedom to enact certain administrative measures directed at third countries.[98]

As observed in the literature,[99] the concerns with liberalisation in the past were mainly related to Japan. The latter applied a restrictive approach to foreign investors entering its domestic markets but practiced a rather aggressive outbound investment policy. The reason for the latter is to be found in Japan's limited domestic resources, which constrained Japan's growth at the time.[100] European and American counterparts, however, did not have the same access in the Japanese market, and this was a major cause for resentment.[101] Under foreign pressure and bi and multilateral initiatives, the playing field for capital flows was ultimately levelled.[102] Much of the European concerns back then sound similar to the concerns which exist vis-à-vis China today.

Some authors doubt that if art. 63 TFEU would be drafted today it would be similar to its current reading.[103] Given that, on the one hand, the EU is fundamentally open to foreign investment due to the broad scope of application of the freedom of capital movement principle and that, on the other hand, the absence of the same principle in other major economies is deemed unfair, the question of which alternatives exist for the erga omnes principle arises. Given that reciprocity is one of the major concerns in today's discussion of international investment flows, one might wonder if using this principle as a standard is a viable option. While changing the fundamental premise of capital inflows in the EU appears quite radical at first glance, the possibility of function creep that plagues the current investment screening framework—as demonstrated in the Hamburg case—shows that consideration of this issue is both necessary and relevant.

---

[96] OECD (2002), pp. 23–28.

[97] Ibid., p. 155.

[98] Bakker (2021). pp. 19–21.

[99] Ibid., pp. 21–23.

[100] Ozawa (1979), pp. 235–236.

[101] Chilton et al. (2020), pp. 131–132.

[102] Bakker (2021), pp. 21–22.

[103] Nettesheim (2021), p. 498.

## 5.2 *Reciprocity as a Sensible Option?*

Reciprocity is first and foremost a natural dynamic at play in international relations that upholds the sovereign equality between nations. Reciprocity essentially means that if a state asserts certain rights for itself, it should anticipate that other states may also assert those same rights. In fact, a state must admit that enforcing a unilateral policy is some type of norm-creation and that other states can generally adopt these norms.[104] Reciprocity functions as a default for cooperation when rules on interaction are absent.[105] Investment relations—and in particular, market access—are subject to this dynamic. In the absence of bi- or multilateral legally binding commitments on market access, a slow but steady convergence of market access policy is thus not surprising. This is the case, for example, with the perspective that Europe's embrace of investment screening is partially a response to China's closed market. Should the European Union and its member states, however, go further?

Reciprocity is not a legal rule in and of itself. Rather, reciprocity can refer to the conditionality under which a rule or conduct applies. It emphasises the interdependence of the expectations of behaviour that states owe each other.[106] If reciprocity is implemented as an element within the application of the freedom of capital movement, foreign investors originating from countries that do not provide the same level of access for European businesses will thus not be allowed to invest in European assets. Where should the reciprocity element be fitted within the current legal framework? Institutionalising reciprocity as a determining element for investment relations with third countries should necessarily take place on the European level, as the EU holds to competence with respect to FDI on the basis of the Common Commercial Policy. In essence, establishing reciprocity as a condition would replace the erga omnes application of the freedom of capital movement.

As previously stated, the mere existence of investment screening frameworks in their current form has been viewed as a means of overcoming market access asymmetries. However, the efficacy of the notion that by closing one's own market, one's foreign economic partners will open theirs is debatable. As the literature correctly points out, there is little evidence that restricting market access allows the other party to make concessions.[107] However, from the standpoint of geoeconomic competition, restricting market access to parties who do not provide equal opportunity makes far more sense, as reciprocity is a minimum requirement.

What would be the advantages and disadvantages of reciprocity as a standard upon which investment relations with third countries are shaped? First and foremost, it must be observed that reciprocity in international economic relations is not an alien concept. In contrast, the idea of engaging in exchange only when it is mutually beneficial is present on a multitude of levels, both theoretically and in practice.

---

[104] Whelan (2023), p. 47.

[105] Ibid., p. 68.

[106] Ibid., pp. 50 and 55–56.

[107] Nettesheim (2021), p. 499.

In theory, some authors argue that reciprocity is a necessary standard of behaviour to foster cooperation between states. Indeed, it is argued that "reciprocity seems to be the most effective strategy for maintaining cooperation among egoists".[108] When reciprocity is absent in bilateral economic relations, states will tend to resort to themselves. To some extent, the Hamburg case can be seen as an example of the latter dynamic, as German officials and commentators called for restricting Chinese access to German ports, especially because the opposite movement of capital was not possible.

From a more practical perspective, in the United States, some investment policies are explicitly designed around the concept of reciprocity.[109] In the EU, the same can be observed with, for example, the international procurement instrument, with which the EU intends to open up foreign procurement markets for European businesses. Essentially, the EU will deny foreign corporations' access to the European public procurement market if the state from which they came does not offer similar access to European businesses to compete in that state's domestic procurement procedures. Furthermore, reciprocity is also present in the management of trade relations between countries. Under the GATT/WTO, reciprocity can be identified when balancing tariffs between two trading partners.[110] It can be observed that reciprocity is a standard that is used within the field of regulating economic interaction.

There could be downsides to the use of reciprocity as well. For one, the use of the latter instead of the universal application of the freedom of capital movement would not send a message that inspires trust to foreign investors, which could in turn hamper the attractiveness of the EU as an investment destination. After all, economic liberalism was and continues to be a pillar of the European economic project. Furthermore, when policies with respect to market access are based upon reciprocity, there is a risk for escalation in times of crisis. The eye for an eye principle could be detrimental, especially in a highly politicised area such as foreign investment. Nonetheless, as seen in the Hamburg case, political escalation is also possible under the current framework. Once, however, one abandons the principal openness towards foreign investment, it might be hard to recover.

## 6 Conclusion

In the beginning of this chapter, it became clear in which environment the EU and its Member States currently resort. The concept of geoeconomics is abstract but provides direction to understand the dual nature of economic relationships between states. In the area of foreign investment, screening mechanisms play a major role in dealing with the challenges that arise out of this renewed perspective on foreign

---

[108] Keohane (1986), p. 2.

[109] Chilton et al. (2020), p. 132.

[110] Keohane (1986), pp. 1 and 7.

investment flows. A legal analysis of the current framework, however, showed that the capacity of the current framework is rather limited. At least within the legal limitations posed by the current investment screening framework, Member States cannot consider issues such as reciprocity due to strict interpretations of the screening grounds on which contemporary investment screening mechanisms are developed. A more practical view that incorporated the political dimension of investment screening, however, established that the latter can be used for other purposes that do not necessarily fall within the legal confines surrounding it.

Furthermore, it was revealed that the lack of reciprocity remains an important topic of debate—and a source of resentment—in international economic relations. Finally, the question is whether we should keep disguising our desire for reciprocity in terms of security and public order or public policy and public security. Geoeconomically, a more direct approach to dealing with reciprocity issues is preferable. This chapter considered whether it would be desirable to change the base standard of erga omnes openness to foreign capital to one that takes into account European companies' access to invest in third countries. To some extent, the investment screening framework could form a comprehensive geoeconomic tool if reciprocity could be taken into account. The practical implementation of introducing reciprocity into the normative framework upon which the EU and its Member States shape investment relations is still a big question mark. However, it is already clear that the need to enforce reciprocity exists and that it will continue to be relevant in the coming years. When focused on investment control, for now, one must accept that sometimes the clout of the legal argument is less convincing than political power plays.

## Cases

Judgment of the Court of 14 March 2000, Eglise de Scientology, C-54/99, ECLI:EU:C:2000:124

Judgment of the Court of 13 July 2000, Albore, C-423/98, ECLI:EU:C:2000:401

Judgment of the Court of 4 June 2002, Commission v. Belgium, C-503/99, ECLI:EU:C:2002:328

Judgment of the Court of 4 June 2002, Commission v. Portugal, C-367/98, ECLI:EU:C:2002:326

Judgment of the Court of 13 May 2003, Commission v. Spain, C-463/00, ECLI:EU:C:2003:272

Judgment of the Court of 22 October 2013, Staat der Nederlanden v. Essent, C-105/12 to C-107/12, ECLI:EU:C:2013:677

Judgment of the Court of 27 February 2019, Associação Peço a Palavra e.a. v. Conselho de Ministros, C-563/17, ECLI:EU:C:2019:144

## References


Bakker A (2021) The political economy of capital controls and liberalization in the European Union. In: Hindelang S, Moberg A (eds) YSEC yearbook of socio-economic constitutions 2020: a common European law on investment screening (CELIS). Springer International Publishing, Cham, pp 11–28

Baldwin DA (1980) Interdependence and power: a conceptual analysis. Int Organ 34:471–560

Bian C (2021) Foreign direct investment screening and national security: reducing regulatory hurdles to investors through induced reciprocity. J World Invest Trade 22:561–595

Blackwill RD, Harris JM (2016) War by other means: geoeconomics and statecraft. Harvard University Press, Cambridge

Braunberger G (2022, October 25) Selbstvergessen. Frankfurter Allgemeine Zeitung

Bremmer I (2009) State capitalism comes of age: the end of the free market? Foreign Aff 88:40–55

Brown C, Ainley K (2009) Understanding international relations. Palgrave Macmillan, Hampshire

Bundesministerium für Wirtschaft und Energie (2022), Bundeskabinett verabschiedet Teiluntersagung imInvestitionsprüfverfahren Hamburger Hafen. Press release of 26.10.2022

Chilton A, Milner H, Tingley D (2020) Reciprocity and public opposition to foreign direct investment. Br J Polit Sci 50:129–153

Csurgai C (2018) The increasing importance of geoeconomics in power rivalries in the twenty-first century. Geopolitics 23:38–46

Dadush U, Dominguez-Jimenez M, Gao T (2019) The state of China-European Union economic relations. Bruegel Institute (Working Paper) p 28

De Jong B, Zwartkruis W (2020) The EU regulation on screening of foreign direct investment: a game changer? Eur Bus Law Rev 31:447–474

Deutsche Welle (2022, October 20) Scholz Criticized over China's Cosco Bid in Hamburg Port

Diesen G (2021) Great power politics in the fourth industrial revolution: the Geoeconomics of technological sovereignty. I. B. Tauris & Company, London

Domosh M (2013) Geoeconomic imaginations and economic geography in the early twentieth century. Ann Assoc Am Geogr 103:944–966

Euronews (2022, October 26) Germany agrees to controversial sale of Hamburg port terminal

European Commission (2019) Joint Communication to the European Parliament the European Council and the Council, EU-China – A strategic outlook, JOIN(2019) 5 final, 12.3.2019

European Commission (2021) Trade Policy Review - An Open, Sustainable and Assertive Trade Policy, COM(2021) 66 final, 18.2.2021

European Commission (Directorate-General for Trade) (2021) European Union, Trade in goods with China, 2.6.2021, https://webgate.ec.europa.eu/isdb_results/factsheets/country/details_china_en.pdf

European Parliament (2022) International public procurement instrument : securing fairness for EU firms. Press release of 9.6.2022

Frankfurter Allgemeine Zeitung (2022a, October 31). Port Participation: Baerbock warns for dependency on China

Frankfurter Allgemeine Zeitung (2022b, November 3). USA warns Germany against Chinese influence on infrastructure

Grevi G (2011) Geo-economics and global governance. In: Martiningui A, Youngs R (eds) Challenges for European foreign policy in 2012: what kind of geo-economic Europe? FRIDE, Madrid, pp 27–37

Griffiths M (2005) Encyclopedia of international relations and global politics. Routledge, Abingdon

Grosse TG (2014) Geoeconomic relations between the EU and China: the lessons from the EU weapon embargo and from Galileo. Geopolitics 19:40–65

Hindelang S (2009) The free movement of capital and foreign direct investment: the scope of protection in EU law. Oxford University Press, Oxford

Hindelang S, Maydell N (2011) The EU's common investment policy - connecting the dots. In: Bungenberg M, Grieber J, Hindelang S (eds) International investment law and EU law. Springer, Berlin, pp 1–27
Hindelang S, Moberg A (2021) The art of casting political dissent in law: the EU's framework for screening of foreign direct investment. Common Mark Law Rev 57:1427–1460
Hindelang S, Moberg A (2021) A complex setting of cooperation and (potential) conflict: regulation (EU) 2019/452 in a doctrinal perspective. In: Hindelang S, Moberg A (eds) YSEC yearbook of socio-economic constitutions 2020: a common European law on investment screening (CELIS). Springer International Publishing, Cham, pp 837–852
Hoffmann S (1975) Notes on the elusiveness of modern power. Int J 30:183–206
Hsiung JC (2009) The age of Geoeconomics, China's global role, and prospects of cross-strait integration. J Chin Polit Sci 14:113–133
Jackson R, Sorensen G (2013) Introduction to international relations: theory and approaches. Oxford University Press, Oxford
Jacobs J (2019) Tiptoeing the line between National Security and protectionism: a comparative approach to foreign direct investment screening in the United States and European Union. Int J Leg Inf 47:105–117
Jansen P (2015) You can talk the talk but can you walk the walk? Niet-mededingingsrechtelijke nationale belemmerende maatregel, en met betrekking tot fusies en buitenlandse investeringen en het recht van de Europese Unie. Nederlands Tijdschrift voor Europees Recht 10:299–311
Katainen J (2019) Chinese investments in the EU. In: Wennings T, Lohman W (eds) Chinese FDI in the EU and the US: simple rules for turbulent times. Springer Singapore, Singapore, pp 15–20
Keohane R (1986) Reciprocity in international relations. Int Organ 40:1–27
Keohane RO, Nye JS (1977) Power and interdependence: world politics in transition. Little Brown, Boston
Keohane RO, Nye JS (1987) Power and interdependence: revisited. Int Organ 41:724–753
Kim DJ (2017) Trading with the enemy? The futility of US commercial countermeasures against the Chinese challenge. Pac Rev 30:289–308
Kohler B (2022) The chancellor doesn't want to alienate the emperor. Frankfurter Allgemeine Zeitung
Lorot P (2000) Introduction à la géoéconomie. Economica, Paris
Luttwak EN (1990) From geopolitics to geo-economics: logic of conflict, grammar of commerce. Natl Interest 20:17–23
Mattlin M, Wigell M (2015) Geoeconomics in the context of restive regional powers. Asia Eur J 14: 125–134
Miosio S (2018) Towards geopolitical analysis of geoeconomic processes. Geopolitics 23:22–29
Molthof L, Zandee D, Cretti G (2021) Unpacking open strategic autonomy: from concept to practice.Clingendael institute (Clingendael Report)
Nettesheim M (2021) Screening for what threat: preserving "public order and security", securing Reciprocityin international trade, or supporting certain social, environmental, or industrial policies? In: Hindelang S, Moberg A (eds) YSEC yearbook of socio-economic constitutions 2020: a common European law on investment screening (CELIS). Springer International Publishing, Cham, pp 481–504
Noyan O, Bourgery-Gonse T (2022) French policymakers irked by Chinese company's stake in Hamburg port. Eur Secur
Nye JS (2020) Power and interdependence with China. Wash Q 43:7–21
OECD (2002) Forty Years of Experience with the OECD Code of Liberalization of Capital Movements
Ozawa T (1979) Multinationalism, Japanese style: the political economy of outward dependency. Princeton University Press, Princeton
Reuters (2018) Era of bank secrecy ends as Swiss start sharing account data
Roberts A, Moraes HC, Ferguson V (2019) Toward a geoeconomic order in international trade and investment. J Int Econ Law 22:655–676

Sattich T, Inderberg T (2019) EU geoeconomics: a framework for analyzing bilateral relations in the European Union. J Common Mark Stud 57:502–514

Schill SW (2019) The European Union's foreign direct investment screening paradox: tightening inward investment control to further external investment liberalization. Legal Issues Econ Integr 46:105–128

Simon S (2021) Investment screening: the return of protectionism? A political account. In: Hindelang S, Moberg A (eds) YSEC yearbook of socio-economic constitutions 2020: a common European law on investment screening (CELIS). Springer International Publishing, Cham, pp 43–52

Subramian A (2019) The inevitable superpower: why China's dominance is a sure thing. Foreign Aff 90:66–78

Szabo SF (2014) Germany's commercial realism and the Russia problem. Survival 56:117–128

Szabo SF (2015) Germany, Russia and the rise of geo-economics. Bloomsbury Academic, London

Tamma P (2022). Germany's Baerbock warns Scholz ahead of his China trip. Politico

Tanious MI (2019) The impact of economic interdependence on the probability of conflict between states: the case of "American–Chinese relationship on Taiwan since 1995". Rev Econ Polit Sci 4:38–53

Velten J (2022) Screening foreign direct investment in the EU: political rationale, legal limitations, legislative options. Springer International Publishing, Cham

Vihma A (2018) Geoeconomic analysis and the limits of critical geopolitics: a new engagement with Edward Luttwak. Geopolitics 23:1–21

Warcholl J (2021) The birth of the EU screening regulation. In: Hindelang S, Moberg A (eds) YSEC yearbook of socio-economic constitutions 2020: a common European law on investment screening (CELIS). Springer International Publishing, Cham, pp 53–75

Wernicke SF (2021) Investment screening: the return of protectionism? A business perspective. In: Hindelang S, Moberg A (eds) YSEC yearbook of socio-economic constitutions 2020: a common European law on investment screening (CELIS). Springer International Publishing, Cham, pp 29–41

Whelan A (2023) Reciprocity in public international law. Cambridge University Press, Cambridge

Wigell M (2015) Conceptualizing regional powers' geoeconomic strategies: neo-imperialism, neo-mercantilism, hegemony, and liberal institutionalism. Asia Eur J 14:135–151

# Inward FDI Regulation in the UK: Closing the "Open Door"?

**Peter Muchlinski**

## Contents



**Abstract** In recent years, the UK has undergone major shifts in its international economic policy that challenge its traditional commitment to an "open door" to inward FDI. This article explores the reasons behind this shift. It begins with a brief overview of UK inward investment policy since World War II and then considers contemporary challenges to the "open door". The most prominent is growing concern over the role of inward investment, especially Chinese investment, for national security. This was the major factor leading to the adoption of the National

P. Muchlinski (✉)
SOAS, University of London, London, UK
e-mail: pm29@soas.ac.uk

 
J. Hillebrand Pohl et al. (eds.), *Weaponising Investments*,
Springer Studies in Law & Geoeconomics (2023) 1: 169–198,
https://doi.org/10.1007/17280_2023_6, Published online: 17 June 2023

Security and Investment Act 2021 (NSIA). The framework introduced by the NSIA is described, and then the paper will examine the wider policy context in which the NSIA will operate. This considers, first, factors pointing to a "light touch" approach to the application of the NSIA, including the effects of Brexit and the increased pressure to attract inward investment without the benefits of EU membership, and factors pointing to a more interventionist approach, including the continuing concern over foreign investment in sensitive and strategic sectors, as shown by recent ministerial decisions made under the old national security rules in the Enterprise Act 2002. Second, the NSIA has been criticised on a number of technical legal grounds. In particular, the lack of a clear definition of national security and the width of ministerial discretion under the Act have led some to consider that decisions under the NSIA risk "politicisation". Whether the right to judicial review contained in the NSIA is enough to safeguard against such outcomes, as well as the possible use of investor claims under international investment agreements, are assessed. Equally, the extraterritorial effects of the law, the inclusion of related party transactions and the application of NSIA to both domestic and foreign investors are highlighted and analysed. The paper will end by considering whether the national security focus of the 2021 law is sufficient. Other Commonwealth states, in particular Canada, Australia and New Zealand, have more general investment screening laws, raising the further question of whether the UK should follow suit and expand its investment screening regime to cover economic and social impacts.

## 1 Introduction

The UK is undergoing a sea change in its inward FDI policy. The twin impacts of perceived national security threats from foreign investors, especially from China and, more recently, Russia, coupled with Britain's hard exit from the EU Single Market and Customs Union have given rise to a new policy and legislative environment. Historically, since World War II, Britain has been a welcoming host state for FDI. The reasons for this approach will be briefly outlined in Sect. 2. This stance was increasingly put into doubt over the last decade or so through instances where the "open door" to FDI appeared to result in proposed, or actual, foreign acquisitions of UK firms that had negative economic, social or strategic consequences, leading to increased calls for stronger inward FDI controls. In particular, the spectre of strategic Chinese investment in the British economy, championed by the successive administrations of Prime Minister David Cameron, came to be seen as a potential threat to national security. These developments will be discussed in Sect. 3 as precursors to the adoption of the NSIA. The framework for screening strategically sensitive inward investments introduced by the NSIA will then be described in Sect. 4.

The NSIA is analysed in a wider policy and legal context in Sect. 5. The section first raises the core issue surrounding national security-oriented screening laws: how far is investment openness to be sacrificed in favour of protecting national security?

In the UK context, a number of factors point towards a "light touch" approach, including the need to attract inward FDI to counter any adverse impacts on such investment arising out of the decision to leave the EU Single Market and Customs Union after 1 January 2021; the historical legacy of a consistent political and administrative consensus that inward FDI is beneficial to the UK economy; the continuing emphasis on purely economic issues over social and political issues in UK mergers and acquisitions policy; and the generally permissive approach to national security reviews under the predecessor to the NSIA, the Enterprise Act. The key factor pointing to a more "interventionist" approach is the fact that Chinese FDI remains a potential national security threat. Indeed, the former Secretary of State for Business, Energy and Industrial Strategy, Kwasi Kwarteng, used his power to stop the sale of computer vision technology from the University of Manchester to a Chinese semiconductor company.[1]

Section 5 continues by examining some key legal issues arising out of national security screening laws that risk creating a more uncertain and less attractive investment environment, including the extension of the NSIA to related party transactions, the lack of a clear definition of "national security" and the imposition of significant criminal and civil penalties for violations of the law. Whether the availability of judicial review to challenge decisions made under the NSIA will provide adequate protection for foreign investors is discussed, as is the possibility of using international investment agreements (IIAs) to bring international claims against the UK founded on alleged breaches of investor guarantees in IIAs.

Finally, Sect. 5 concludes by discussing the interface between national security concerns and wider environmental, social and governance (ESG) concerns that are often involved in investment screening reviews. Although ESG concerns are not covered by the NSIA, the question is asked whether at some future point the UK government should follow the examples of other common law-based Commonwealth countries, namely, Canada, Australia and New Zealand, and amend the NSIA to turn it into a general FDI screening law.

## 2 UK Inward FDI Policy Since World War II: From Exchange Controls to an "Open Door"

British inward FDI policy in the immediate post-World War II years was characterised by concerns over the balance of payments at a time when the most significant impediment to reconstruction was a shortage of US dollars and a lack of resources caused by post-war shortages. Unrestrained dollar-based inward investment could undermine Sterling. Accordingly, a system of controlled entry for US dollars was required, one which would facilitate much needed inward investment by

[1] "First use of UK law to ban foreign deal marks 'stark' trend, warns ex-minister" *Financial Times* 21 July 2022 at https://www.ft.com/content/dee8c799-0bbb-4869-96c2-4a733e72bd83.

US companies but ensure that the sums approved for entry would not adversely affect the British balance of payments.[2] That system was enshrined in the Exchange Control Act of 1947.[3]

Under the 1947 Act, the initial establishment of a subsidiary, or the takeover of an existing British company, required specific permission from the Treasury, which may, or may not be, subject to conditions.[4] Permission would hinge on whether the investment made an "appropriate" contribution to foreign exchange reserves, requiring the amount of foreign currency brought in to finance the fixed assets of the British company to be proportionate to the interest of the foreign parent company in its British subsidiary and, in the case of an acquisition, at a purchase price that fairly reflected the market value of the acquired company. An exception could be made for investments in assisted areas where the foreign investor could raise additional capital locally.[5]

Exchange controls were administered by the Bank of England in cases where the amount was less than £500,000. For larger investments, the Treasury would have authority.[6] The screening process was effectively decentralised in that the investor would first contact a bank or legal adviser who would help the investor adopt a financial structure for the proposed investment that would conform to the approval criteria. It was then for the investor to apply to the Bank of England for permission or decide not to invest.[7] In cases of mergers between a British and foreign firm, consent was also conditional upon approval of the Monopolies Commission where the market share, or asset value, conditions that would trigger an investigation under the Monopolies and Mergers Act 1965 had been met.[8]

The Exchange Control Act provided a potentially strong regime for screening inward investment. In practice, it was applied with a light touch, and refusals of permission were extremely rare.[9] In appropriate cases, permission could be given subject to conditions relating to a variety of economic and social criteria, including technology transfer, board composition, production and export targets and labour arrangements. However, there was no legal mechanism to enforce such investor undertakings.[10]

From the 1950s onwards, successive British governments eased controls over inward investment.[11] While such controls made sense in the early post-war years,

---

[2]On which see further Rooth and Scott (2002).

[3]Exchange Control Act 1947 available at https://www.legislation.gov.uk/ukpga/1947/14/enacted. See further Steuer et al. (1973) especially ch 9 on which this account draws.

[4]Steuer et al. (1973) para 9.7.

[5]ibid para 9.8.

[6]ibid paras 9.13–9.15.

[7]ibid paras 9.13–9.15.

[8]ibid para 9.16.

[9]ibid para 9.17.

[10]ibid paras 9.18–9.19. See too Rooth and Scott (2002).

[11]See for analysis up to the 1990s Bailey et al. (1994b) ch 6 "Britain".

when resource scarcity required investments that could give the highest social and economic returns and resulted in enhanced quality inward investment, particularly from US firms, they could, over time, become barriers to valuable inward investment.[12] One important factor was the establishment of the European Economic Community (EEC), which helped enhance Western Europe as a competitive destination for US FDI. The UK needed to maintain a competitive advantage over the EEC in terms of FDI attraction, which led the Conservative Government of the period to engage in early investment promotion policies and the Bank of England to loosen exchange controls.[13]

This approach continued through the 1960s in what my late friend and colleague Michael Hodges called "a case of benign neglect".[14] Successive Conservative and Labour Governments followed an increasingly open policy towards inward FDI. Writing of the Labour Government in power between 1964 and 1970, Hodges concluded that, despite growing concerns on the left about the rising power of multinational enterprises (MNEs), the Government did not perceive inward FDI controls as a salient political issue due to a number of interlocking factors, including the need to protect British overseas investment from retaliatory restrictions; cross-party political consensus that inward FDI was beneficial to the economy; a similar conviction among civil servants; not distinguishing between domestic and foreign investment in policy-making; a relative lack of systematic and reliable information on the impacts of FDI on the British economy;[15] the absence of a centralised administrative body responsible for FDI controls; and the progressive liberalisation of exchange controls.

A further factor moving Britain towards an "open door" to inward FDI was membership of the EEC. The 1972 Budget lifted exchange controls for subsidiaries of EEC-based, Danish and Norwegian investors to ensure conformity with EEC directives on capital movements.[16] The progressive removal of all exchange controls was on the horizon. The election of Margaret Thatcher's Conservative Government of 1979 led to the suspension of the Exchange Control Act.[17] The Exchange Control Act was itself repealed in 1987, removing the most significant restrictions on inward and outward investment.

Apart from certain provisions in the Enterprise Act 2002 and the NSIA, discussed in Sect. 4, the other remaining powers for the control of inward investment are those given to the Secretary of State for Business, Energy and Industrial Strategy under the scheme of "golden shares" in privatised companies and under the Industry Act of

[12] Rooth and Scott (2002), p. 158.

[13] Rooth and Scott (2002), pp. 144–152.

[14] See Hodges (1974) especially ch 7 on which this paragraph draws.

[15] On which see further Bailey et al. (1994a) who argued in the 1990s for the establishment of a UK authority to gather useful information on the effects of inward FDI as an input to better policy-making.

[16] Steuer et al. (1973) para 9.9.

[17] See Part III of the Exchange Control Act 1947; suspended by S.I. 1979/1333 and S.I. 1979/1660.

1975.[18] The government holds "golden shares" for certain defence-related firms privatised in the 1980s to prevent them from falling under foreign control, as in the case of Rolls Royce.[19] More recently, in 2016, the UK government announced that it would retain a special share in the Hinkley Point nuclear power plant project and in other future nuclear new-build projects to ensure that national security concerns are met.[20] In addition, under the Industry Act 1975 sections 11-20, the Secretary of State may prevent the transfer of control of "important manufacturing undertakings" to non-residents, where they build up a share of over 30% in the undertaking. These powers have never been used.

The general policy of the UK government remains one of welcoming inward FDI.[21] UK policy on inward investment has involved not only the removal of regulatory barriers but also the positive encouragement of investors through the activities of regional and national investment promotion agencies, the selective use of industrial aid, and the establishment of enterprise zones and free ports.[22] The Conservative Government of Boris Johnson, like its predecessor under Theresa May, was determined that this open approach would continue, seeing the UK as "Global Britain" open to both inward investment and as a major outward investor in its own right. This is coupled with a commitment to levelling up the less affluent regions of the UK through increased investment both domestic and foreign and the establishment of a new "Office for Investment" to act as a "single front-door" investment promotion body.[23]

---

[18] See further Muchlinski (2021) at 182 on which this paragraph draws.

[19] See Rolls Royce Articles of Association (adopted by Special Resolution passed on 2 May 2013 and amended by special resolutions passed on 8 May 2015, 4 May 2017 and 3 May 2018) Article18 "The Special Share" at https://www.rolls-royce.com/~/media/Files/R/Rolls-Royce/documents/about/2018-rr-holdings-plc-articles-of-association.pdf.

[20] "UK gives go-ahead for 'revised' £18bn Hinkley Point plant" *Financial Times* 15 September 2016 at https://www.ft.com/content/466704e6-7a4b-11e6-b837-eb4b4333ee43.

[21] See HM Government *UK Industrial Strategy: A Leading Destination to Invest and Grow* (14 December 2017) 4 available at https://www.gov.uk/government/uploads/system/uploads/attachment_data/file/672468/uk-industrial-strategy-international-brochure-single-pages.pdf See further HM Government White Paper *Industrial Strategy: building a Britain fit for the future* (27 November 2017) at https://www.gov.uk/government/publications/industrial-strategy-building-a-britain-fit-for-the-future.

[22] On which see further Muchlinski (2021), pp. 215–217.

[23] See Prime Minister Teresa May's Foreword to *UK Industrial Strategy: A Leading Destination to Invest and Grow* (14 December 2017) 1; HM Treasury "Build Back Better: Our Plan for Growth" 3 March 2021 at https://www.gov.uk/government/publications/build-back-better-our-plan-for-growth/build-back-better-our-plan-for-growth-html#build-back-better-our-plan-for-growth-at-a-glance and see UK Government "Office for Investment" at https://www.gov.uk/government/organisations/office-for-investment.

## 3 Challenges to the UK's "Open Door"

The traditional UK "open door" approach to inward FDI has been periodically tested in cases where foreign investments have not lived up to their promise. For example, in the 1960s, concerns were expressed over foreign ownership in the car manufacturing and computer industries.[24] In Scotland, a series of highly public and controversial divestments by foreign multinationals during the 1970s questioned whether the British government could control inward investors and ensure that they lived up to their promises of stable investment and secure jobs.[25] In 1988, the takeover of the confectioner Rowntree-Macintosh by Swiss food producer Nestlé generated a major national debate over whether competition policy should protect major national firms against foreign takeover in the public interest, including to protect jobs, or whether only competition considerations should be relevant.[26] The latter view prevailed.

In recent years, concerns have once again surfaced over the wider economic, social and national security implications of foreign takeovers of UK firms.[27] For example, in 2010, following the takeover of the UK confectionery manufacturer Cadbury's by US food firm Kraft, controversy arose when Kraft closed Cadbury's plant at Somerdale despite assurances, given at the time of the takeover, that the plant would be kept open.[28] A wide public debate ensued about whether foreign takeovers should be subject to greater scrutiny and whether undertakings made by the foreign acquirer should be legally enforceable.[29]

In May 2014, the proposed bid for UK pharmaceuticals firm AstraZeneca by Pfizer of the US raised concerns that it would risk the closure of R&D facilities in the UK, adversely affecting the country's science base. In a public letter to the Prime Minister, the then leader of the Opposition, Ed Miliband, called for a stronger public interest test.[30] Pfizer withdrew its bid on 26 May, before the four-week deadline set

---

[24] See Hodges (1974) chs 5 and 6.

[25] See Hood and Young (1982) covering divestments and job rundowns by Singer in Clydebank, Chrysler and Peugeot at Linwood, Hoover in Cambuslang, NCR in Dundee, Honeywell in Lanarkshire and Goodyear in Drumchapel, Glasgow.

[26] See Bailey et al. (1994b), p. 174.

[27] This summary is taken from Muchlinski (2021), pp. 458–460.

[28] See House of Commons Business, Innovation and Skills Committee Mergers, *Acquisitionsand Takeovers: the Takeover of Cadbury by Kraft* Ninth Report of Session 2009–10 (HC 234 6 April 2010) available at http://www.publications.parliament.uk/pa/cm200910/cmselect/cmbis/234/234.pdf.

[29] See "Government Response to the Business, Innovation and Skills Committee's Report on "Mergers, Acquisitions and Takeovers: The Takeover of Cadbury by Kraft" CM 7915 July 2010 available at http://www.official-documents.gov.uk/document/cm79/7915/7915.pdf. The Government agreed that companies should be more responsible in their takeover strategies and commitments but there were no plans to reintroduce a public interest test into merger law. Vince Cable, then Business Secretary, was reported as wishing to reopen the debate about foreign takeovers, "Cable sets out to stop investors making a quick killing" *The Guardian* 25 October 2010 27.

[30] Quoted in Seely (2016), p. 30.

by the Takeover Code for potential bidders to make a firm bid, or secure agreement from the potential target company for more talks, the so-called 'put up or shut up' rule, which had been introduced into the Code following the Cadbury/Kraft case.[31]

A number of other takeovers and investments have raised national security concerns. Such concerns are not new to the UK authorities. The predecessor to the Competition and Markets Authority (CMA), the Monopolies and Mergers Commission, took strategic and security considerations into account when applying the "public interest" test for mergers and acquisitions under the now repealed Fair Trading Act 1973, either rejecting the bid on public interest grounds or making it subject to certain security undertakings.[32]

Security concerns have also been raised in bids involving UK-based investors, which explains why the NSIA applies to all acquisitions of strategically sensitive entities or assets regardless of the nationality of the acquirer. In 2018, the hostile bid by UK-based Melrose for GKN raised concerns about the survival of GKN as a leading engineering firm with significant defence and aerospace business, including the manufacture of wings for Airbus aircraft, raising potential national security and strategic economic security issues.[33] In response, the then Defence Secretary, Gavin Williams, intervened to demand assurances from Melrose about its plans for GKN's defence businesses.[34] Melrose replied with assurances to the Business Secretary, Greg Clark, that it would not dispose of GKN's defence businesses in the short term without government consent.[35] Mr Clark also demanded assurances over GKN's workforce, R&D and pension schemes.[36] The GKN Board recommended the acceptance of Melrose's offer on 29 March 2018.[37] Again, the issue of whether the UK

---

[31] Seely (2016), p. 31. This change was introduced in 2011. Other changes introduced into the Takeover Code at that time include: strengthening the target company board's position by allowing it to consider longer-term considerations, not just the offer price; inducement fees were banned; transparency was improved through greater disclosure of the bidder's plans, offer related fees, and the financing of the offer; and greater recognition of the interests of employees and employee representatives was introduced through improved ability to make their views known: see Seely (2016), p. 36.

[32] See, e.g., *Kuwait/British Petroleum plc* (Cm 477 1988) where the MMC rejected the acquisition by the Kuwait Investment Office of some 22% of the stock of British Petroleum (BP) on the grounds *inter alia* that future conflicts of interest between Kuwait, as a member of OPEC, and BP and the British Government were foreseeable. In *GEC plc and Siemens AG/Plessey plc.* (Cm 676 1989) the MMC held unanimously that the joint bid of GEC and Siemens for Plessey should be allowed to proceed subject to certain security undertakings that would be negotiated with the Secretary of State: para.6.85 and Appendix 6.1. The merger of BAE and Marconi was cleared after undertakings were offered: DTI *Press Release* P/2000/220 28 March 2000.

[33] Dan Sabbagh "Unprotected GKN left to brave the cold corporate winds alone" *The Observer* 28 March 2018 at 58. Summary taken from Muchlinski (2021), pp. 459–460.

[34] "GKN deal faces defence challenge" *Financial Times* 31 March/1 April 2018 1.

[35] GKN deal faces defence challenge" *Financial Times* 31 March/1 April 2018 1.

[36] "Test for May as GKN fate hangs in the Balance" *Financial Times* 28 March 2018 15.

[37] "Melrose victorious in hostile bid for GKN" *Financial Times* 29 March 2018 at https://www.ft.com/content/c6afe24c-3356-11e8-b5bf-23cb17fd1498.

should have a general public interest test for mergers and acquisitions was raised, and whether the government could legally enforce assurances made by bidders.[38]

As already noted, in 2016, the proposed Hinkley Point C nuclear power plant project was reviewed on national security grounds. The project involves investments by EDF, the French energy company that is 83% owned by the French government, and China General Nuclear Power Group, a state-run Chinese energy company. The project was given the go-ahead subject to the retention of a special government share to prevent possible future control by Chinese interests.[39] The project was widely criticised as a bad deal.[40]

The Hinkley Point case is but one illustration of growing concerns over the strategic and national security impact of Chinese FDI in the UK. The British approach to inward Chinese FDI has moved from the so-called "golden era" of UK-China relations, promoted by the government of David Cameron and George Osborne, which favoured open Chinese inward investment, towards following the lead of the US in treating Chinese investment in strategically sensitive industries with caution.[41] This shift came to a head in July 2020 when Boris Johnson announced a ban on the Chinese telecom company Huawei supplying 5G technology to UK telecom firms, a move that was badly received by Beijing.[42]

In light of concerns over foreign bids, such as the above, the UK government launched a review of its powers over takeovers involving national security and infrastructure issues.[43] This found that the Enterprise Act 2002 was insufficient to ensure that national security risks received the appropriate level of scrutiny and that the necessary powers to ensure the national security of the UK were lacking. In 2018, the government amended the turnover thresholds and share of supply tests in the Enterprise Act, allowing it to examine and potentially intervene in mergers in two areas: dual-use and military use technologies and parts of the advanced technology sector. For these areas only, by Order in Parliament, the Government lowered the

[38] "Test for May as GKN fate hangs in the Balance" *Financial Times* 28 March 2018 15.

[39] See "UK gives go-ahead for 'revised' £18bn Hinkley Point plant" *FT.Com.* 15 September 2016 at https://www.ft.com/content/466704e6-7a4b-11e6-b837-eb4b4333ee43 and "National security concerns keep closer scrutiny of foreign investment on table" *Financial Times* 24 July 2017 3.

[40] Holly Watt "The 'dreadful deal' behind the world's most expensive power plant" *The Guardian* 21 December 2017 at 31; House of Commons The Committee of Public Accounts Hinkley Point C Third Report of Session 2017–19 (HC 393, 22 November 2017) at https://publications.parliament.uk/pa/cm201719/cmselect/cmpubacc/393/393.pdf.

[41] See Jonathan Ford and Laura Hughes "UK-China relations: from 'golden era' to the deep freeze" *Financial Times* 14 July 2020 at https://www.ft.com/content/804175d0-8b47-4427-9853-2aded76f48e4.

[42] George Parker, Nic Fildes, Helen Warrell and Demetri Sevastopulo "UK orders ban of new Huawei equipment from end of year *Financial Times* 15 July 2020 at https://www.ft.com/content/997da795-e088-467e-aa54-74f76c321a75.

[43] UK Government *The National Security and Infrastructure Investment Review* (Green Paper, 17 October 2017) and *Government response to its consultation on short-term proposals* (15 March 2018) at https://www.gov.uk/government/consultations/national-security-and-infrastructure-investment-review on which this paragraph draws.

target's UK turnover threshold from £70 million to £1 million and removed the requirement for the merger to increase the share of supply to or over 25%.[44]

This fell well short of a general public interest test, let alone the kinds of "benefit to the national economy" tests used in other Commonwealth jurisdictions.[45] The focus remained strictly toward strategic national security concerns and followed earlier rejections of a general investment screening approach.[46] In the meantime, the government committed itself further to assessing risks in other sectors, including emerging technologies, to consider if additional legislation might be required.[47] Additionally, the assessment of competition impacts remained the primary function of merger reviews under the Enterprise Act.[48] The risk of undermining the UK's openness to inward investment was not one that regulators were willing to bear easily.[49]

However, by 2021, the NSIA had been adopted. Never before had the UK passed an explicit FDI screening law. The NSIA had been clearly motivated by a desire to control inward Chinese investments in strategic sectors and, given its timing after the Huawei decision and growing controls over Chinese nuclear investments, it created "some confusion" in China over UK policy towards Chinese investments.[50] It remains unclear whether the NSIA will be a major barrier to such investments in the future. Indeed, Mr. Johnson asserted his desire to encourage economic engagement with China, saying he would not "pitchfork away" Chinese inward investment but would retain the right to review strategically sensitive investments under the NSIA, leaving the precise ambit of UK policy on trade and investment with China uncertain.[51]

---

[44]The Enterprise Act 2002 (Share of Supply Test) (Amendment) Order 2018 (2018 No. 578) 14th May 2018 at http://www.legislation.gov.uk/uksi/2018/578/introduction/made; Enterprise Act 2002 (Turnover Test) (Amendment) Order 2018 (2018 No. 593) at http://www.legislation.gov.uk/uksi/2018/593/introduction/made. See further Department for Business, Energy & Industrial Strategy *Enterprise Act 2002: Guidance to Changes to the Turnover and Share of Supply Tests for Mergers* (July 2018) at https://assets.publishing.service.gov.uk/government/uploads/system/uploads/attachment_data/file/715174/EA02_guidance.pdf.

[45]See further Muchlinski (2021), pp. 197–206 discussing Australia, Canada and New Zealand.

[46]See further Seely (2016), pp. 33–44 outlining the discussion of the public interest test after AstraZeneca/Pfizer and more recently.

[47]*Government response to its consultation on short-term proposals* (15 March 2018) n 43 para 115.

[48]This paragraph adapts Muchlinski (2021), p. 461.

[49]See further Alex Chisholm, CMA Chief Executive, "public interest and competition-based merger control" (Speech given at the Fordham Competition Law Institute Annual Conference, published 11 September 2014) at https://www.gov.uk/government/speeches/alex-chisholm-speaks-about-public-interest-and-competition-based-merger-control.

[50]See House of Lords International Relations and Defence Committee 1st Report of Session 2021–22 "The UK and China's security and trade relationship: A strategic void" (HL Paper 62, 10 September 2021) paras 319–26 at https://committees.parliament.uk/publications/7214/documents/75842/default/.

[51]See Jim Pickard "Boris Johnson seeks to forge closer economic ties with China" *Financial Times* 11 February 2022 at https://www.ft.com/content/321ffeaf-58b7-4ed5-a367-4d175edbab8a; "UK

## 4 The Framework of the NSIA and Its Relation to the Enterprise Act

Since the early 1980s, successive UK governments have taken a predominantly market-based position on mergers and acquisitions.[52] The Enterprise Act 2002 Part 3 introduces the "substantial lessening of competition" (SLC) test. The CMA is under an obligation to refer qualifying mergers for review, which in its view have resulted or may result in a substantial lessening of competition.[53] The SLC test replaces the wider "public interest" test under s 84 of the Fair Trading Act 1973.[54] In practice, the promotion of competition has, for many years, been the primary regulatory goal of the UK competition authorities and became known as the "Tebbit Doctrine" after the policy adopted in 1984 by former Secretary of State for Trade and Industry, Norman (now Lord) Tebbit.[55] The CMAs predecessor, the Monopolies and Mergers Commission, generally followed this approach when considering whether a merger or acquisition between a UK and non-UK firm was in the public interest but, as noted above, did consider strategic factors within the "public interest" test as well as other factors, including employment and balance of payments effects, capacity to

---

will not 'pitchfork away' China investment, PM Minister Boris Johnson says" *Hong Kong Free Press* 19 October 2021 at https://hongkongfp.com/2021/10/19/uk-will-not-pitchfork-away-china-investment-pm-minister-boris-johnson-says/. Mr Johnson's successors have perpetuated this uncertainty with Liz Truss taking a hard line on Chinese economic ties while Rishi Sunak has sought to abandon designating China as a "national security threat" to the UK, amid opposition from his own party, thus bringing him closer to Mr Johnson's position: see Eleni Courea "Rishi Sunak ditches plan to class China as a 'threat' to UK security" *Politico* 15 November 2022 at https://www.politico.eu/article/rishi-sunak-ditches-plan-to-class-china-as-a-threat-to-uk-security/.

[52] See Muchlinski (2021), pp. 455–461 on which this account draws.

[53] Enterprise Act 2002 s.22 and 33. See generally UK Government "Mergers: detailed information" at https://www.gov.uk/topic/competition/mergers. See further Graham (2004); CMA *Merger Assessment Guidelines* (CMA 129, 2021) available at https://www.gov.uk/government/publications/merger-assessment-guidelines.

[54] Fair Trading Act 1973 s 84 stated that, in considering whether a merger operates or may operate against the public interest, the Monopolies and Mergers Commission (predecessor to the CMA) shall take into account, "all matters which appear to them in the particular circumstances to be relevant and, among other things, shall have regard to the desirability - (a) of maintaining and promoting effective competition between persons supplying goods and services in the United Kingdom; (b) of promoting the interests of consumers, purchasers and other users of goods and services in the United Kingdom in respect of the prices charged for them and in respect of their quality and the variety of goods and services supplied; (c) of promoting, through competition, the reduction of costs and the development and use of new techniques and new products, and of facilitating the entry of new competitors into existing markets; (d) of maintaining and promoting the balanced distribution of industry and employment in the United Kingdom; (e) of maintaining and promoting competitive activity in markets outside the United Kingdom on the part of producers of goods, and of suppliers of goods and services, in the United Kingdom."

[55] See House of Commons written answer by the Secretary of State for Trade and Industry (5 July 1984) reproduced in Annex 2 of the Office of Fair Trading Guide *Mergers* (HMSO, 1987, and 1991) and see Seely (2016), p. 9.

regulate an offshore parent company and the implications of bids by foreign state-owned enterprises.[56]

Notwithstanding the dropping of the public interest criterion, the Enterprise Act (the Act) did not completely exclude public interest considerations. The Secretary of State for Business, Energy and Industrial Strategy was empowered, by Section 58(1) of the Act, to consider national security interests and, by Section 58(3), any other interests that they have designated by order, as involving public interest concerns, through the adoption by Parliament of a Statutory Instrument. The s 58(1) power has now been superseded by the NSIA. The s 58(3) power was used in 2008 to designate the need to maintain the stability of the UK financial system as an issue of public interest in the aftermath of the financial crisis.[57] In addition, the Secretary of State retains the right to review newspaper and other media mergers as a matter of public interest.[58]

## 4.1 The Basic Scheme of the NSIA

The Secretary of State is empowered to prohibit a foreign investor acquiring a firm based and/or operating in the UK—the "qualifying entity"—or acquiring an asset based in the UK, or used in connection with commercial or other activities in the UK—the qualifying asset"—where this comes within the definition of a "trigger event" indicating a risk to national security.

The "qualifying entity" is defined as "any entity, whether or not a legal person, that is not an individual, and includes a company, a limited liability partnership, any other body corporate, a partnership, an unincorporated association and a trust."[59] A "qualifying entity" may also be formed or recognised overseas but which carries on activities in the United Kingdom or supplies goods or services to persons in the

[56] For a full analysis of MMC decisions in this area see Whish (2001), pp. 826–830 and see Muchlinski (2021), pp. 456–457.

[57] The Enterprise Act 2002 (Specification of Additional Section 58 Consideration) Order 2008 (2008 No. 2645) at http://www.legislation.gov.uk/uksi/2008/2645/pdfs/uksi_20082645_en.pdf. This was prompted by the Lloyds/HBOS merger on which see further Louise Smith "The Lloyds-TSB and HBOS Merger: Competition Issues" (House of Commons Library Standard Note: SN/BT/4907 Last updated: 15 December 2008) at http://researchbriefings.parliament.uk/ResearchBriefing/Summary/SN04907#fullreport.

[58] Enterprise Act 2002 s 69; Communications Act 2003 sections 375–388. In 2010 the proposed bid by Rupert Murdoch's NewsCorp for full ownership of Sky News was challenged: see Seely (2017). In 2012 the Competition Commission decided that Global Radio Holdings Limited should sell radio stations in seven areas of the UK following its completed acquisition of Real and Smooth Limited (formerly GMG Radio Holdings Limited) on purely competition grounds as no public interest issues of media plurality arose: Global Radio/GMG merger inquiry at https://www.gov.uk/cma-cases/global-radio-gmg-merger-inquiry.

[59] NSIA n 1 s 7(2).

United Kingdom.[60] A "qualifying asset" includes "(a) land, (b) tangible (or, in Scotland, corporeal) moveable property, (c) ideas, information or techniques which have industrial, commercial or other economic value."[61] Examples falling into category (c) include trade secrets, databases, source code, algorithms, formulae, designs, plans, drawings, specifications and software.[62] Land or moveable property situated outside the UK may also be a "qualifying asset" if it is used in connection with activities carried out within the UK or the supply of goods or services to persons in the UK.[63]

The "trigger event" is defined by the acquisition of control over a qualifying entity or asset.[64] Control over an entity is defined in Section 8. This distinguishes four cases. The first is where the percentage of shares, or percentage of rights to capital or profits, or in the case of a limited liability partnership the percentage of any surplus assets on winding up, held by the foreign investor increases from 25% or less to more than 25%, from 50% or less to more than 50%, or from less than 75% to 75% or more.[65] The second case is where the percentage of voting rights increases by the same margins.[66] The third case is where the voting rights enable the foreign investor to secure or block resolutions governing the affairs of the entity. The fourth case is where the acquisition creates a capacity for the foreign investor materially to influence the policy of the entity where there has not been any pre-existing capacity to do so.[67]

Control over an asset arises where the foreign investor, as a result of its acquisition, is able, "to use the asset, or use it to a greater extent than prior to the acquisition, or to direct or control how the asset is used, or direct or control how it is used to a greater extent than prior to the acquisition."[68] The use of an asset includes its exploitation, alteration, manipulation, disposal or destruction.[69] Acquisitions other than land, or which fall within a number of designated regulatory provisions, made by an individual for purposes that are wholly or mainly outside the individual's trade, business or craft are exempt.[70]

---

[60] ibid s 7(3). On the extraterritorial aspects of the NSIA see further UK Government Guidance "How the National Security and Investment Act could affect people or acquisitions outside the UK" (20 July 2021 entered into force 4 January 2022) at https://www.gov.uk/government/publications/check-if-an-acquisition-outside-the-uk-will-be-in-scope-of-the-national-security-and-investment-act#full-publication-update-history.

[61] ibid s 7(4).

[62] ibid s 7(5).

[63] ibid s 7(6).

[64] ibid s 5 (1) (a) (b).

[65] ibid s 8(2)-(3).

[66] ibid s 8 (5).

[67] ibid s 8(8)-(9).

[68] ibid s 9(1).

[69] ibid s 9 (2).

[70] ibid s 11.

## 4.2 *The Mandatory Notification Procedure*

The review power is activated through a notification procedure. Prospective investors must assess whether their proposed acquisition involves a trigger event requiring notification.[71] Such "notifiable acquisitions" will be void if completed without the approval of the Secretary of State.[72] The foreign investor must give notice of the proposed acquisition as soon as they gain control of the qualifying entity or asset.[73] The Secretary of State must determine whether the notice fulfils the conditions of a valid notice as soon as reasonably practicable after receipt of the notice.[74] If the mandatory notice is accepted, a 30-day review period is activated from the date that the Secretary of State notifies the foreign investor of acceptance.[75] Before the end of the review period, the Secretary of State must give a "call-in notice" in relation to the proposed acquisition or notify the foreign investor and any other appropriate persons that no further action will be taken.[76]

## 4.3 *The "Call-In Notice"*

The "call-in notice" is the formal acknowledgement that a trigger event has taken place in relation to the qualifying entity or asset and that this has given rise to a national security risk or that the proposed arrangements will result in a trigger event giving rise to a national security risk if carried into effect.[77] The "call-in" power is not limited to cases of mandatory notification. A "call-in notice" can be issued by the Secretary of State in any case where there are reasonable grounds to suspect that a qualifying acquisition has given, or may give, rise to a risk to national security or that a contemplated transaction, if carried into effect, will result in an acquisition that may give rise to a risk to national security.[78]

---

[71] ibid s 6. Some guidance has recently been given by the Government on how this should be approached: Department for Business, Energy and Industrial Strategy "National Security and Investment Act: Market Guidance Notes" (19 July 2022) at https://www.gov.uk/government/publications/national-security-and-investment-nsi-act-market-guidance-notes/national-security-and-investment-market-guidance-notes-july-2022.

[72] ibid s 13(1).

[73] ibid s 14(1).

[74] ibid s 14(5). The form and content of the mandatory notice is outlined in The National Security and Investment Act 2021 (Prescribed Form and Content of Notices and Validation Applications) Regulations 2021 at https://www.legislation.gov.uk/uksi/2021/1272/made.

[75] ibid s 14(9).

[76] ibid s 14(8).

[77] ibid s 1(1) (a) (b).

[78] UK Government Notice National Security and Investment Act 2021: Statement for the purposes of Section 3 (2 November 2021) para 1 at https://www.gov.uk/government/publications/national-security-and-investment-statement-about-exercise-of-the-call-in-power.

The Government Notice covering this power is at pains to stress that it will not be used to promote any objectives other that solely to "safeguard the UK's national security" and that, "The NSI Act is not a system for screening all acquisitions in the economy.[79] According to the Notice,

> 4. The Act intentionally does not set out the circumstances in which national security is, or may be, considered at risk. This reflects longstanding government policy to ensure that national security powers are sufficiently flexible to protect the nation.
>
> 5. Each qualifying acquisition will be assessed on a case-by-case basis, taking account of all relevant considerations and with regard to the risk factors set out below. This applies to all qualifying acquisitions, whether they involve parties only within the UK or involve parties overseas.
>
> 6. The call-in power will not be used to arbitrarily interfere with investment. The UK has a proud record as one of the most open economies in the world, and the Secretary of State's use of the call-in power will not change that. The UK remains firmly open to investment, and the government wants the UK to be the best place in the world to work and do business.[80]

## *4.4 Relevant Risk Factors*

According to the Government Notice covering the application of the "Call-in Power", there are three key risk factors:

> **a. Target risk**
>
> This concerns whether the target of the qualifying acquisition (the entity or asset being acquired) is being used, or could be used, in a way that raises a risk to national security.
>
> **b. Acquirer risk**
>
> This concerns whether the acquirer has characteristics that suggest there is, or may be, a risk to national security from the acquirer having control of the target.
>
> **c. Control risk**
>
> This concerns the amount of control that has been, or will be, acquired through the qualifying acquisition. A higher level of control may increase the level of national security risk.[81]

Normally, all three risk factors will be present, but calling in an acquisition on the basis of fewer risk factors is possible.[82] For most qualifying acquisitions, the overall consideration of these risks is expected to indicate a low risk to national security.[83] The Notice identifies seventeen areas of the economy that are considered more sensitive and that are subject to mandatory notification requirements. They are also more likely to generate a call-in notice from the Secretary of State.[84]

---

[79] ibid paras 2 and 7.

[80] ibid. On the powers to obtain information and related issues see NSIA n 1 s 19–22.

[81] ibid para 20.

[82] ibid para 21.

[83] ibid para 22.

[84] ibid paras 7–13. The seventeen areas of the economy are: Advanced Materials; Advanced Robotics; Artificial Intelligence; Civil Nuclear; Communications; Computing Hardware; Critical

## 4.5 Voluntary Notification

Apart from the mandatory notification scheme, voluntary notifications can be made in relation to otherwise non-notifiable acquisitions, but where the seller, acquirer or qualifying entity concerned considers that a triggering event has occurred or is likely to occur if the arrangements in question will be carried into effect.[85] If accepted, a voluntary notification also gives rise to a 30-day review period.[86] The Secretary of State will also be able to call in or accept voluntary notifications in relation to transactions falling below a 25% control threshold where there is "material influence". This can mean acquisitions of shareholdings as low as 10-5%.[87]

## 4.6 Orders Under the NSIA

The review process will lead the Secretary of State either to make a final order or give a final notification to each person to whom the call-in notice was issued that no further action will be taken in relation to the call-in notice.[88] A final order will be made where the Secretary of State is satisfied, after considering any representations made to them and on the balance of probabilities, that a trigger event has taken place or that arrangements which, if carried into effect, will result in a trigger event, and this results in a risk to national security.[89] In addition, the Secretary of State must reasonably consider that the provisions of the order are necessary and proportionate for the purpose of preventing, remedying or mitigating this risk.[90]

The final order may contain requirements on the foreign investor to do or not do particular things; not to disclose the contents of the order except to the extent permitted by the order; provide for the appointment of a person to conduct or supervise the conduct of activities on such terms and with such powers as may be

Suppliers to Government; Cryptographic Authentication; Data Infrastructure; Defence; Energy; Military and Dual-Use; Quantum Technologies; Satellite and Space Technologies; Suppliers to the Emergency Services; Synthetic Biology; Transport. See further UK Government "National Security and Investment Act: Guidance on Notifiable Acquisitions" (4 January 2022) https://www.gov.uk/government/publications/national-security-and-investment-act-guidance-on-notifiable-acquisitions.

[85] NSIA n 1 s 18 (1)-(2).

[86] ibid s 18(9).

[87] See Gibson Dunn "UK Government Issues Further Updates on National Security Regime: A Comprehensive State of Play For Investors" (8 September 2021) at https://www.gibsondunn.com/wp-content/uploads/2021/09/uk-government-issues-further-updates-on-national-security-regime-a-comprehensive-state-of-play-for-investors.pdf.

[88] NSIA n 1 s 26(1)-(2). The Secretary of State is also empowered to make interim orders during the review period: ibid s 25.

[89] ibid s 26(3) (a) (i)-(ii); s 26(4).

[90] ibid s 26(3) (b).

specified or described in the order; and any consequential, supplementary or incidental provisions.[91]

The final order may apply extraterritorially to any person who is a UK national, an individual ordinarily resident in the UK, a body incorporated or constituted under the law of any part of the UK, or carrying on business in the UK.[92] The Secretary of State must keep the final order under review and act as soon as practicable on any request by the foreign investor to vary or revoke the order unless there has been, in the Secretary of State's opinion, no material change of circumstances.[93]

## 4.7 Criminal and Civil Sanctions

The NSIA is backed up by a range of criminal and civil sanctions. New offences are created to deter the completion of a notifiable acquisition without approval, failure to comply with an order made under the NSIA, failure to appear as a witness or failure to comply with information and attendance notices issued by the Secretary of State as part of the review process and sharing information in violation of the disclosure of information requirements under s 54 and 55(1) of the NSIA.[94] The NSIA establishes joint and several liability for legal bodies and their officers.[95] The above offences carry the alternative penalties of imprisonment or a fine.[96] In the alternative, the Secretary of State may issue a penalty notice for a civil monetary penalty in cases where the above offences have been committed.[97] This penalty cannot be imposed while criminal proceedings are taking place or where a conviction has been secured, and it excludes subsequent criminal proceedings.[98]

## 4.8 Interaction Between the NSIA and Other Regulatory Requirements

Finally, the interaction between the NSIA and other regulatory requirements that apply to foreign acquisitions of UK firms or assets needs to be described. Most importantly, the NSIA continues to interact with competition rules under the Enterprise Act. To this end, the NSIA clarifies that when a final order is in force or a final

---

[91] ibid s 26(5).

[92] ibid s 26(6).

[93] ibid s 27.

[94] ibid s 32–35.

[95] ibid s 36.

[96] ibid s 39.

[97] ibid s 40.

[98] ibid s 43.

notification has been given where a merger of takeover covered by Part 3 of the Enterprise Act is the triggering event, the Secretary of State may direct the CMA "to do, or not to do, anything under Part 3 of the 2002 Act in relation to the trigger event if the Secretary of State reasonably considers that the direction is necessary and proportionate for the purpose of preventing, remedying or mitigating a risk to national security."[99] The direction must be issued in a public notice, and the Secretary of State must consult the CMA and any other appropriate persons before issuing such a direction.[100] The CMA is dutybound to comply with such a direction regardless of any other duty imposed upon it.[101]

Interactions with the Export Control Joint Unit (ECJU) may arise where items specified on its "control list" are also assets acquired in a situation where a national security risk is reasonably suspected. Here, the Investment Security Unit, the body responsible within the Department for Business Energy and Industrial Strategy for administering the NSIA, will take account of any controls or licences issued by the ECJU.[102]

Further interactions will arise with the Takeover Code in cases of foreign acquisitions of UK businesses. The Takeover Code provides a framework to allow acquirers (offerors) awaiting a decision under the NSIA to suspend or pause the offer timetable prescribed by the Code.[103]

In relation to financial services, both the Financial Conduct Authority (FCA) and the Prudential Regulation Authority (PRA) may find themselves regulating transactions coming within the NSIA and placing obligations on entities. According to the UK Government's Guidance, "[i]t is possible, but highly unlikely, that orders under the NSI Act could have an impact on other obligations, and the NSI Act is not intended to prevent persons complying with their statutory obligations."[104] Thus, NSIA reviews will not prevent financial regulation from taking its proper course and will generally not interfere with obligations imposed by the FCA or PRA.

[99] ibid s 31(1)-(2). See further for a more detailed statement of the relationship between the NSIA and CMA: UK Government Notice "Memorandum of Understanding between BEIS and the CMA on the operation of the National Security and Investment Act 2021" (16 June 2022) at https://www.gov.uk/government/publications/operation-of-the-national-security-and-investment-act-2021-memorandum-of-understanding.

[100] ibid s 31(3)-(4).

[101] ibid s 31(5).

[102] See UK Government Guidance "The National Security and Investment Act Alongside Regulatory Requirements (4 January 2022) at https://www.gov.uk/government/publications/the-national-security-and-investment-act-alongside-regulatory-requirements.

[103] ibid.

[104] ibid.

# 5 Future Prospects for the NSIA

The NSIA is a landmark law. For the first time, a UK law sets out a detailed regime for the screening of acquisitions of entities and assets that raise possible national security risks. In this regard, it follows an increasing trend in national laws and EU law.[105] It is still too early to assess its impact empirically. However, this concluding section of the article will set out a framework for such an assessment taking into account the wider legal, economic, social and political environment in which the NSIA will be operating.

The NSIA raises a well-known issue that other jurisdictions have already encountered, most notably the US with its national security review law, first adopted in 1988.[106] How far should considerations of national security restrict open access for foreign investors? This question involves both issues of policy and a number of technical legal questions that may affect how the authorities approach actual or proposed foreign acquisitions of sensitive firms or assets.

## *5.1 Policy Factors Conducive to a Light Touch Approach*

The current situation in the UK points to a number of factors conducive to a "light touch" approach. First, Brexit makes the attraction of inward FDI essential for future economic health. However, at the same time leaving the EU has made the UK less attractive to EU-based investors and to non-EU investors who seek easy access to the Single Market.[107] Investments focusing on the acquisition of UK firms may therefore be focused on a stake in the UK domestic economy. It may prove hard in practice to exclude them even if there is a possible national security dimension to the investment if the result is new capital investment and jobs. Second, as noted above, the predominant approach remains one of openness towards inward FDI. This will affect how ministers view national security concerns and what constitutes a trigger event. Third, experience under the Enterprise Act national security review process suggests a broadly permissive policy. Since the entry into force of that law, only thirteen national security interventions were undertaken, ten resulted in formal remedies, one was abandoned without formal remedies being imposed, and one

[105] On which see generally Muchlinski (2021) chs 5 and 6; Cheng Bian (2021).

[106] See Exon-Florio amendment to the Defence Production Act 1950, now Section 721 of the Defense Production Act of 1950 as revised by the Foreign Investment and National Security Act of 2007 (FINSA) and the Foreign Investment Risk Review Modernization Act of 2018 (FIRRMA), codified at 50 U.S.C. 4565 at https://www.govinfo.gov/content/pkg/USCODE-2017-title50/pdf/USCODE-2017-title50-chap55-subchapIII-sec4565.pdf.

[107] On the benefits of EU membership for inward FDI flows see Bruno et al. (2021).

case, the bid by Cobham—a British-based but US-owned aerospace firm—for Ultra Electronics, was ongoing.[108]

## 5.2 Policy Factors Conducive to a More Interventionist Approach

There are also factors pointing to a more interventionist approach. In 2020, for the first time, two proposed acquisitions by a Chinese-owned investor of a UK aerospace manufacturer were abandoned following formal national security interventions by the UK government under the Enterprise Act rules.[109] Interim orders preventing the integration of the merging parties were issued by the Secretary of State in both transactions. Furthermore, after the deals were abandoned, the acquirers were asked to provide additional assurances that the transaction would not proceed.

More recently, the former Secretary of State for Business, Energy and Industrial Strategy, Kwasi Kwarteng, intervened in the proposed acquisition of Ultra Electronics by Cobham, a rival owned by a US private equity group Advent International.[110] On 18 August 2021, the Secretary of State issued a Public Interest Intervention Notice (PIIN) with respect to the acquisition under the Enterprise Act, which applies to this transaction as the intervention arose prior to the entry into force of the NSIA.[111] The Secretary of State held talks with the parties over national security undertakings prior to deciding whether to refer the proposed transaction to the CMA or to accept the transaction on the basis of such undertakings.[112]

On 6 July 2022, the acquisition was cleared subject to detailed conditions.[113] Two new "SecureCos" are to be created as UK-incorporated entities to deliver strategically sensitive capabilities to the UK government. The government will also have significant control over the governance of these new entities. These comprise the following: a government appointed Non-Executive Director on the Board of each

---

[108] Potter and Long (2021).

[109] Potter and Long (2021) on which this summary draws. See *Aerostar/Mettis* (2020) at https://www.gov.uk/cma-cases/aerostar-mettis-merger-inquiry and *Gardner/Impcross* (2020) at https://www.gov.uk/cma-cases/gardner-aerospace-holdings-limited-impcross-limited-merger-inquiry.

[110] See "Defence specialist bid tests Britain's foreign takeovers stance" *Financial Times* 19 January 2022 at https://www.ft.com/content/93986b38-bebe-483a-ac9c-9babfdbe6a7b.

[111] Proposed Acquisition Of Ultra Electronics Holdings Plc By Cobham Ultra Acquisitions Limited Public Interest Intervention Notice (Updated 28 April 2022) at https://www.gov.uk/government/publications/proposed-acquisition-of-ultra-electronics-holdings-plc-by-cobham-ultra-acquisitions-limited-public-interest-intervention-notice.

[112] ibid.

[113] UK Government Press Release "Update on the proposed acquisition of Ultra Electronics Holdings plc by Cobham Ultra Acquisitions Limited" 6 July 2022 at https://www.gov.uk/government/news/update-on-the-proposed-acquisition-of-ultra-electronics-holdings-plc-by-cobham-ultra-acquisitions-limited on which this paragraph draws.

SecureCo, "to protect UK national security interests and provide oversight of any disinvestment or divestment of sensitive capabilities"; the right to approve the Articles of Association of each SecureCo and to "draft their strategic objectives which would transfer to any future owner, locking that protection in" with any changes subject to the government Director's agreement; strong step-in rights, "(similar to a 'special share'), enabling transfer of ownership of the SecureCos on national security grounds, either to a third party or the government"; the power to access intellectual property and/or to transfer knowledge or training necessary for the Government to exercise its step-in rights effectively; and the institution of a Government approved control plan to prevent International Traffic in Arms Regulations controls applying to ITAR-free products designed and manufactured by Ultra. These are extensive interventions by any measure and suggest that the UK government will be active in overseeing strategically sensitive activities in foreign-acquired British firms under the NSIA as well.

## 5.3 Legal Risks to Investors

In addition to these recent cases, suggesting a more cautious attitude towards foreign acquisitions in sensitive sectors, the NSIA itself contains a number of legal risks to investors that can contribute to a more interventionist environment and thus to a less open and attractive investment climate. The first and obvious risk is that if the investor fails to comply with the regulatory requirements of the NSIA, they face the significant criminal or civil penalties introduced by the NSIA and outlined earlier. More particular legal risks relate to the definitions of sensitive sectors covered by mandatory notice powers, the lack of a clear definition of national security, the extraterritorial scope of the NSIA, and the extension of the law to related party transactions and to national and foreign investors. Given the resulting broad discretions contained in the law, there is also a risk that specific cases will become "politicised" and decided according to factors outside strict legal analysis.

The definition of sensitive sectors has been criticised for being too broad, making it difficult to draw clear lines between products and technologies from which national security implications could arise and those where this could not conceivably be the case.[114] In the US, this issue has been approached by moving on from sector-based codes to controls based on "specific export-controlled technology."[115] This replaces the former mandatory declaration process based on the North American Industry Classification System (NAICS) codes that identified 27 industries requiring a mandatory declaration regarding critical technology. The basic principle is that a

[114] See House of Commons International Trade Committee *Inward Foreign Direct Investment* Third Report of Session 2021–22 (HC 124, 23 September 2021) para 135 at https://committees.parliament.uk/publications/7423/documents/77694/default/.

[115] ibid para 137.

transaction falls within the scope of a mandatory declaration if it involves the use of a critical technology that would require US export control licensing or authorisation prior to its export to the foreign investor's home state.[116]

Turning to the extraterritorial elements of NSIA, while this widens the net of review, its application is clearly related to significant connecting factors between the acquirer and the UK jurisdiction based on the conduct of activities or the supply of goods and services to the UK. In this, the NSIA is a domestic regulation that has extraterritorial impacts, but it is not a direct assertion of jurisdiction over the foreign conduct of individuals and companies unconnected to the UK.[117] It is the latter that carries the greatest risk of inter-state conflict due to the lack of a substantial connection between the conduct and the regulating state.

Regarding related party transactions, while the focus of the NSIA is on third-party acquisitions, intra-group reorganisations may also fall within the new regime, potentially even requiring mandatory notification.[118] The published guidance provides a number of examples where the NSIA procedure should apply, including the case of an overseas supplier of critical components to a UK company working in a sector of the UK economy that falls under mandatory notification; a proposed takeover of such a supplier by another foreign company; or the acquisition by a foreign company of a foreign parent company of a UK-based subsidiary operating in a sector falling within mandatory notification.[119]

## *5.4 "Politicisation" of NSIA Reviews and Legal Responses*

The government's call-in power has raised concerns about how it may be used.[120] As noted above, the Secretary of State has broad discretion to call in an investment that has not been notified under mandatory or voluntary declaration routes but nonetheless raises significant national security concerns. This, coupled with the absence of a comprehensive definition of "national security", raises the risk that this power will

[116] See U.S. Department of the Treasury, Office of Investment Security Final Rule Provisions Pertaining to Certain Investments in the United States by Foreign Persons (31 CFR Part 800 RIN 1505–AC68 15 September 2020) at https://www.federalregister.gov/documents/2020/09/15/2020-18454/provisions-pertaining-to-certain-investments-in-the-united-states-by-foreign-persons#print.

[117] See Zerk (2010).

[118] See Norton Rose Fulbright "The UK's new NSI regime: What do you need to know?" (June 2022) at https://www.nortonrosefulbright.com/en/knowledge/publications/c8b20a65/the-uks-new-nsi-regime-what-do-you-need-to-know.

[119] UK Government Notice National Security and Investment Act 2021: Statement for the purposes of Section 3 (2 November 2021) at https://www.gov.uk/government/publications/national-security-and-investment-statement-about-exercise-of-the-call-in-power.

[120] See House of Commons International Trade Committee n 114 paras 138–40.

be used arbitrarily to block proposed investments that are deemed politically unpopular using national security as a justification.[121]

It is correct for the government to say that it cannot fetter its discretion by having a detailed definition of national security, as it may in practice render the review process ineffective against new and unforeseen national security risks that do not fit into the definition. However, some clarification is required to ensure that investors can identify the types of transactions that commonly raise national security issues without these acquiring the status of exclusive definitions. Guidance through hypothetical examples, as already used in the initial Government Notice on the application of s 3 of NSIA, can be further evolved in light of experience.[122]

In particular, the government must clarify the boundary between threats to the UK economy and threats to national security. Lord Callinan, a minister at the Department of Business Energy and Industrial Strategy, in reply to questioning about the meaning of national security under the NSIA before the House of Commons Committee on International Trade asserted, "[w]e are determined that this is precisely focused on threats to the UK economy by a small minority of hostile actors, and we will be flexible about how we interpret the regime, but there is no attempt to politicise it."[123] The reference to the "UK economy" is concerning as it connotes a broad concept of national security that includes "national economic security". Such an approach is consonant with a general screening law, not a specifically focused national security screening law. The remark may be no more than a casual use of language, but it suggests that some transactions will indeed be screened because of wider economic concerns. Inevitably, it may be impossible to draw clear "bright lines" between strategic security and economic concerns in a given case, but a fluid concept of national security can always evolve into a hybrid of strategic and economic concerns, with the latter eventually becoming dominant.[124]

This concern may be illustrated by one of the first "call-ins" under the NSIA.[125] In December 2021, Patrick Drahi's telecoms group Altice increased its ownership of the leading UK telecoms firm BT from 12 to 18%, fuelling speculation about a takeover attempt and triggering a six-month standstill obligation under the Takeover Code, which expired at the end of June 2022. The government decided to review this

---

[121] ibid paras 141–3.

[122] See n 119 above and see too "National Security and Investment Act: Market Guidance Notes" n 72. See further for a detailed analysis of the concept of national security as applied to foreign mergers and acquisitions Thomas Lenihan (2020), pp. 32–38.

[123] International Trade Committee *Oral evidence: Inward Foreign Direct Investment*, HC 124 Wednesday 16 June 2021 Q 148 at https://committees.parliament.uk/oralevidence/2394/pdf/.

[124] See further Thomas Lenihan (2020), pp. 32–38; Muchlinski (2021), pp. 171–177 focusing on US s 721 Defense Production Act of 1950 as amended n 107.

[125] See Nicole Kar, Mark Daniel and Elisha Kemp "Five months with the NSIA – what have we learnt?" Linklaters (10 June 2022) at https://www.linklaters.com/en/insights/blogs/foreigninvestmentlinks/2022/june/five-months-with-the-nsia-what-have-we-learnt on which this paragraph draws.

proposed acquisition even though it was below the 25% level that gives rise to a mandatory notification under the NSIA.

According to a Linklaters blog on this case, "[w]hile BT is clearly sensitive in terms of UK national security, the decision to review may also be in part driven by concerns that Altice may increase its stake. . .rather than solely by concerns that the incremental 6% stake in BT is a threat to national security." It would appear that in this case national security may well be used to protect a "national champion" from foreign takeover, even though the acquirer would be from a friendly country.[126]

More recently, the then Business Secretary, Grant Schapps, blocked the sale of Newport Wafer Fab to Chinese owned Nexperia, requiring the latter to divest 86% of the company leaving it with its original 14% stake held before the launch of its takeover in 2021.[127] The government's reasoning is that the company is located in a high-tech semiconductor cluster in South Wales and that the acquisition creates the risk of Chinese access to it. In addition, a Chinese presence could prevent other companies within the cluster from engaging in future projects relevant to national security.[128] These reasons appear to be somewhat speculative.[129] Previous reviews of Newport Wafer Fab revealed no national security risks given that its main activity, the manufacture of silicon wafers for export, is not cutting edge. The mere fact of being located in a cluster that might in future become engaged in sensitive work also appears an insufficient ground for barring the acquisition in the absence of any government plans to locate such work there. The most plausible explanation is that the mere fact of Chinese ownership was sufficient to block the acquisition even if the actual risk to national security was small. The company plans to appeal the ruling.

The risk of administrative abuse of discretion under the NSIA may be mitigated by the availability of judicial review under s 49. Judicial review is not usually available under foreign investment screening laws given the uniqueness of each decision and the need to maintain wide discretionary powers in cases involving vital national interests.[130] That said, fuller accountability for and transparency of investment screening decisions can enhance the investment climate in the regulating state.

---

[126] The use of national security reviews in cases where the acquirer is from a friendly country can be understood as a form of internal balancing of state power by non-military means, hence making it useful in cases involving potential threats to that power from acquirers located in strategically allied countries as well as those located in strategically unfriendly countries. See further Thomas Lenihan (2020).

[127] See Department of Business, Energy and Industrial Strategy, "Acquisition of Newport Wafer Fab by Nexperia BV: notice of final order" (16 November 2022) at https://www.gov.uk/government/publications/acquisition-of-newport-wafer-fab-by-nexperia-bv-notice-of-final-order.

[128] See Anna Gross and Jim Pickard. "Newport Wafer Fab's sale to Nexperia blocked by UK ministers" *Financial Times* (16 November 2022) at https://www.ft.com/content/cdaddf62-72f7-4789-890c-69f1ce196748.

[129] See Helen Thomas "Welsh chip mess is a lesson in strategy" *Financial Times* (22 November 2022) at https://www.ft.com/content/7467ec0e-9819-4a92-bd69-ca1d0b7762e2 on which this paragraph draws.

[130] See Muchlinski (2021), pp. 205–206 for a discussion of the availability of judicial review in New Zealand, Canada and Australia.

In this respect, the availability of judicial review under the NSIA is a welcome development. However, the bringing of a judicial review claim places the burden of proof and costs upon the claimant foreign investor and thus may not be as valuable a defence of their rights as might at first appear. Equally judicial review under English law is generally limited to procedural issues only and thus offers little help even where the decision shows procedural errors, as it will be returned to the decision-maker to reconsider without committing the same errors. Judicial review will not help to overturn decisions on substantive grounds, as it is not an appeal process.

An alternative approach may be to use the investor protection provisions of IIAs in force between the UK and the investor's home state to bring an international claim before an investor-state dispute settlement tribunal. However, the process will be costly, lengthy and hard to prove given the wide margin of discretion inherent in investment screening decisions. Other legal obstacles can emerge.

First, there may be an issue concerning subject-matter jurisdiction if the IIA in question applies only post-entry. The majority of first-generation BITs were generally of this type, and many remain in force. Newer agreements tend to extend the protection of anti-discrimination provisions to the pre-entry stage, and here, an investor may be able to argue that a negative screening decision has discriminated against them, resulting in less favourable treatment compared to a domestic investor under the national treatment standard or an investor from a third state whose investment was approved under the most-favoured-nation standard. The main issue is whether the claimant investor can prove that the comparator investor was in similar circumstances to them. Given the highly case-specific nature of national security reviews, this may prove very difficult.

Reliance on the fair and equitable treatment standard (FET) may also prove hard to apply in practice. It requires proof that the decision breaches the standard of treatment, which may be very difficult to show in a case involving national security concerns, especially as the control of entry and establishment for aliens is an inherent right of a sovereign state. In this connection, the tribunal in *Global Telecom Holding S.A.E. v. Canada*, which considered a claim from an Egyptian-owned telecom company that had complained *inter alia* that the national security review it had been subjected to by Canada violated the FET standard, held that FET was much broader than the minimum standard of treatment required by customary law, rejecting Canada's argument and referring to the approaches of tribunals in *Vivendi v Argentina* and *C.M.S. v. Argentina*.[131] This finding may be controversial, as many recent IIAs expressly refer to the international minimum standard of treatment as definitive of the FET standard.

On the application of FET, the tribunal found that Canada's national security review did not violate the standard, as Canada had provided GTH with an adequate opportunity to make its case and so did not violate due process. The tribunal considered that due process

[131] *Global Telecom Holding S.A.E. v. Canada*, ICSID Case No. ARB/16/16 Award of Tribunal 27 March 2020 at https://www.italaw.com/sites/default/files/case-documents/italaw11434.pdf.

> should be deemed satisfied where the subject of the investigation is afforded a fair opportunity to make its case in relation to readily identifiable issues, and that opportunity is afforded reasonably ahead of an administrative decision being made based on objectively verifiable factors and after an appropriate time period which is not unnecessarily rushed.[132]

This case covered the extension of an existing investment, so the application of FET to the screening of a new investment was not considered.

Disputes over national security review decisions may be excluded from review under a national security exception in the IIA, especially if it is deemed to be self-judging as where it empowers the state to take "any measure the state deems necessary..." to protect its "essential security interests". The precise scope of such exceptions remains uncertain in light of conflicting arbitral interpretations regarding the applicability of the customary international standard of necessity. Clear language is needed. Thus, in *Devas v India,* use of the phrase "directed to" in the national security exception was insufficient to make it self-executing.[133] Routine national security reviews will not constitute a state of emergency or crisis, so the applicability of a self-judging exception would have to reflect this in its wording. If the exception is limited to emergencies, it will not exclude such reviews from the IIA's coverage.

In cases of non-self-judging national security exceptions, a wide margin of appreciation will be granted to the respondent state. If, on the facts, the national security review comes within the states "essential security interests", the claim will fail. According to the Tribunal in *Devas v India*:

> An arbitral tribunal may not sit in judgment on national security matters as on any other factual dispute arising between an investor and a State. National security issues relate to the existential core of a State. An investor who wishes to challenge a State decision in that respect faces a heavy burden of proof, such as bad faith, absence of authority or application to measures that do not relate to essential security interests.[134]

The tribunal held that India had a legitimate essential security interest to reserve military access to the space segment capacity of its satellites. This applied to up to 60% of such capacity. The remaining 40% of such capacities had been allocated to other sectors and so did not fall within the exception. Accordingly, the claimant whose agreement to lease spectrum capacity was cancelled by the government on national security grounds could recover 40% of its losses under the expropriation provisions of the applicable BIT.

Finally, in some IIAs, investment screening decisions are expressly excluded from the subject matter jurisdiction of the treaty. For example, under the Comprehensive and Progressive Agreement for Trans-Pacific Partnership (CPTPP),

[132] ibid para 608.

[133] *Devas v India* PCA Case No. 2013-09 Award on Jurisdiction and Merits 25 July 2016 paras 233–243 at https://www.italaw.com/sites/default/files/case-documents/italaw9750.pdf.

[134] ibid para 245.

Australia, Canada, Mexico and New Zealand have excluded their foreign investment review powers from the scope of the investor-state dispute settlement clause.[135]

In light of the limited capacity of law to control national security screening decisions, a scheme of investor insurance against adverse screening decisions may be used.[136] This can mitigate the loss caused to the investor from an adverse screening decision and assist the host state by ensuring that it remains an attractive FDI destination.

## 5.5 *Administrative Concerns*

A final concern surrounding the NSIA is that the inclusion of both domestic and foreign investors within its review powers will lead to an overload of notified cases, the majority of which will raise no actual national security concerns.[137] The UK Government estimated approximately 2000 notifications per year, which when compared to the very limited number of notifications made under the Enterprise Act is a significant sum.[138] The government's first annual report into the working of the NSIA notes that in the first three months of operation, 222 deal notifications were received.[139] This caseload is expected to fall once revised guidance is available based on the initial experience of the new regime. It is also important that all government agencies involved in national security, investment and trade co-operate and co-ordinate their activities to ensure an efficient process that does not require multiple and repetitive reviews by different departments. Here, the relationship between the new Office of Investment, Department of International Trade and BEIS needs further development and review.[140]

## 5.6 *Beyond the NSIA?*

Finally, should the NSIA one day evolve into a general screening law? It remains open to discussion whether a narrow national security focus is sufficient to deal with

[135] See CPTTP 21 February 2018 Chapter 9 Annex 9-H at https://www.mfat.govt.nz/assets/Trade-agreements/TPP/Text-ENGLISH/9.-Investment-Chapter.pdf.

[136] Hagemeyer and Hillebrand Pohl (2021).

[137] House of Commons International Trade Committee n 114 paras 146–151.

[138] ibid para 151.

[139] Department for Business, Energy and Industrial Strategy "National Security and Investment Act 2021 Annual Report 2022" 4 January 2022–31 March 2022 (June 2022) at https://www.gov.uk/government/publications/national-security-and-investment-act-2021-annual-report-2022. Of these 17 were called in for further assessment, three were cleared and the remaining 14 were continuing to be assessed.

[140] ibid paras 156–61 and 165.

the myriad policy implications that foreign acquisitions of UK entities and assets raise. In particular ESG concerns are clearly not covered under NSIA. Screening for ESG concerns is at present very unlikely, although there is some discussion as to whether the Modern Slavery Act should extend to financial investments, including inward investments.[141] Canada, Australia and New Zealand have a general screening law that includes a broad national environmental, economic and social benefit test.[142] It would not be difficult to amend the NSIA into a general screening law. As noted earlier, NSIA is essentially a recasting of the original power in s 58(1) of the Enterprise Act. A parallel development involving the recasting of the general public interest powers of intervention under s 58(3) of that Act could be done through the adoption of a general screening law, evolving the NSIA into a "National Security and Public Interest Investment Review Act". This may ensure a wider ESG focus on screening, but of course, the problems inherent in screening laws do not go away, and at present, there is virtually no debate along these lines in the UK. However, that does not preclude future debate, and as past examples show, it may only take one high profile inward investment to go badly wrong to rekindle such a debate.

## References

Bailey D, Harte G, Sugden R (1994a) Making transnationals accountable: a significant step for Britain. Routledge, London

Bailey D, Hare G, Sugden R (1994b) Transnationals and governments: recent policies in Japan, France, Germany, the United States and Britain. Routledge, London

Bian C (2021) Foreign direct investment screening and national security: reducing regulatory hurdles to investors through induced reciprocity. J World Invest Trade 22:561–595

Bruno RL, Ferreira Campos N, Estrin S (2021) The effect on foreign direct investment of membership in the European Union. J Common Mark Stud 59(4):802–821. https://doi.org/10.1111/jcms.13131

Graham C (2004) The Enterprise Act 2002 and competition. Mod Law Rev 67(2):273–288

Hagemeyer TM, Hillebrand Pohl J (2021) Managing the risk of self-judging security exceptions through insurance: how recent mergers and acquisitions practice copes with investment screening. J World Invest Trade 22:596–625

Hodges M (1974) Multinational corporations and national government; a case study of the United Kingdom's experience 1964-70. Saxon House, Farnborough

Muchlinski PT (2021) Multinational enterprises and the law, 3rd edn. Oxford University Press, Oxford

Potter A, Long K (2021) The foreign investment regulation review: United Kingdom. The Law Reviews at https://thelawreviews.co.uk/title/the-foreign-investment-regulation-review/united-kingdom

[141] See further Anthony Mangnall MP Q38 in International Trade Committee Oral Evidence n 123; House of Commons Library "Investment Industry Exposure to Modern Slavery" Commons Library Research Briefing, 25 October 2021 at https://researchbriefings.files.parliament.uk/documents/CBP-9353/CBP-9353.pdf.

[142] See for detailed analysis Muchlinski (2021), pp. 197–206.

Rooth T, Scott P (2002) British public policy and multinationals during the "Dollar Gap" Era, 1945—1960. Enterp Soc 3(1):124–161. https://www.jstor.org/stable/23699999

Seely A (2016) Mergers and takeovers: the public interest test (House of Commons Library Briefing Paper Number 05374, 1 September 2016) at http://researchbriefings.parliament.uk/ResearchBriefing/Summary/SN05374

Seely A (2017) Media ownership and competition law - the BSkyB Bid in 2010-11 (House of Commons Library Briefing Paper Number 6028, 23 June 2017) at http://researchbriefings.parliament.uk/ResearchBriefing/Summary/SN06028#fullreport

Steuer MD et al (1973) The impact of foreign direct investment on the United Kingdom. Department of Trade and Industry, London

Thomas Lenihan A (2020) Balancing power without weapons: state intervention into cross-border mergers and acquisitions, paperback edn. Cambridge University Press, Cambridge

Whish R (2001) Competition law, 4th edn. Butterworths, London

Zerk JA (2010) Extraterritorial jurisdiction: lessons for the business and human rights sphere from six regulatory areas. Corporate Social Responsibility Initiative Working Paper No. 59. John F. Kennedy School of Government, Harvard University, Cambridge, MA. Available at https://www.hks.harvard.edu/sites/default/files/centers/mrcbg/programs/cri/files/workingpaper_59_zerk.pdf

# The EU Foreign Subsidies Regulation: The Final Piece of the Regulatory Puzzle to Ensure Competitive Neutrality in Cross-Border M&A?

**Phil Baumann**

## Contents



**Abstract** State-owned enterprises (SOEs) that have undue competitive advantages can distort the market in cross-border mergers and acquisitions (M&A transactions) and consequently lead to economic inefficiencies and welfare losses. Nevertheless, the issue of competitive neutrality regarding international M&A transactions has been left largely unaddressed in international trade and investment law as well as domestic competition, investment screening and anti-subsidy regimes. The new Regulation on Foreign Subsidies distorting the Internal Market (FSR) aims to fill this regulatory gap by introducing a kind of merger control regime for transactions facilitated by foreign subsidies. The tools provided in the FSR will allow the Commission to investigate M&A transactions undertaken by companies that benefit from foreign subsidies. In cases where the Commission finds that the foreign subsidy irremediably distorts the internal market, the concentration may even be prohibited. The tools of the FSR are generally well suited to prevent undue competitive advantages enjoyed by foreign SOEs in M&A transactions. However, as the tools are not mirroring those under EU state aid law, they potentially distort the level

P. Baumann (✉)
University of Lucerne, Faculty of Law, Lucerne, Switzerland
e-mail: phil.baumann@unilu.ch



J. Hillebrand Pohl et al. (eds.), *Weaponising Investments*,
Springer Studies in Law & Geoeconomics (2023) 1: 199–218,
https://doi.org/10.1007/17280_2023_9, Published online: 22 June 2023

playing field. Several recently concluded international investment agreements (IIA) address the issue of competitive neutrality. In contrast to the FSR, they focus mainly on requirements for SOEs and deal only to a limited extent with subsidies in the context of cross-border M&A. To increase coherency and to reduce unpredictability and uncertainty regarding its new regulatory tools, the EU should aim to include general principles on subsidies and prohibitions of specific subsidies in its IIA. Finally, the extent to which the tools of the FSR are compliant with the EU's national treatment obligations as stipulated in its IIA must be carefully examined.

# 1 Introduction

Legislators usually justify the need for foreign investment screening mechanisms on the grounds of security and public order.[1] Apart from these concerns, investment controls may also be advocated for reasons of competitive neutrality, a principle according to which all enterprises are to be provided with a level playing field with respect to a state's ownership, regulation or activity in an economic market so that no enterprise operating in such market is subject to undue competitive advantages or disadvantages.[2] In particular, SOEs may dispose over undue competitive advantages that are unavailable to their competitors. For instance, such non-efficiency based competitive advantages can take the form of preferential financing from state-backed institutions, preferential regulatory treatment, tax exemptions or a privileged market position conferred by the government.[3] While this concern is typically raised in the context of SOEs, it is also possible for private firms to benefit from support measures by their governments. Home country governments may grant their firms outward foreign direct investment (FDI) incentives (e.g., loans or financial guarantees), placing them in an advantageous competitive position.[4]

Undue competitive advantages can have negative economic consequences. Particularly, they help to finance cross-border M&A transactions by enabling the unduly advantaged company to outbid firms that do not benefit from such state support but could use the assets more efficiently.[5] This leads to an inefficient allocation of resources and prevents competitors from reaching their full potential of economic

[1] See Bian (2021), p. 562; Gordon and Milhaupt (2019), pp. 226 et seq.

[2] OECD (2022), p. 5; OECD (2012), p. 17.

[3] See for an overview of (undue, government-created) competitive advantages of SOEs Capobianco and Christiansen (2011), p. 2 et seq.; see also European Commission, Proposal for a Regulation of the European Parliament and of the Council on foreign subsidies distorting the internal market, COM(2021) 223 final, p. 2; Nielsen (1981), p. 57 et seq.; see further Enderwick (2017), p. 268.

[4] Sauvant et al. (2014), p. 98.

[5] See Gordon and Milhaupt (2018), p. 247; European Commission, White Paper on levelling the playing field as regards foreign subsidies, COM(2020) 253 final, p. 7; OECD (2016), p. 53; see further Trapp (2020), p. 965.

efficiency or accessing key tangible and intangible assets.[6] Consequently, both allocative and productive efficiency decrease, causing welfare losses.[7]

Against this background, the Commission has established a need to ensure a level playing field for the acquisition of EU targets.[8] In particular, the Commission has identified a regulatory gap where foreign subsidies facilitate the acquisitions of EU undertakings.[9] The reason for this regulatory gap is that the existing tools of the EU state aid regime and the EU merger control rules cannot be applied to foreign subsidies, providing an unfair advantage to their recipients when acquiring companies active in the EU.[10] Furthermore, *Regulation (EU) 2019/452, establishing a framework for the screening of foreign direct investment into the EU,* addresses potential risks to security and public order but does not address the issue of causing distortions through undue advantages for foreign SOEs in the investment process.[11] Finally, the EU's trade policy instruments under the WTO Agreement on Subsidies and Countervailing Measures and under the EU anti-dumping and anti-subsidy rules only apply to trade in goods but not to investments in the EU.[12] The European Commission argues that the new FSR addresses this regulatory gap by introducing a kind of merger control regime for transactions facilitated by foreign subsidies.[13] In this regard it should be noted, that the FSR addresses not only distortions that arise in concentrations but with respect to any economic activity.[14]

The new instruments introduced by the FSR come up against a complex, multifaceted and multilevel set of existing rules on state-owned enterprises, subsidies and competition neutrality. These include EU state aid law, the EU framework for the screening of foreign direct investment, WTO rules on subsidies, rules on state-owned enterprises and subsidies in international investment agreements, and soft law such as the OECD guidelines on corporate governance of state-owned enterprises.[15] By addressing the regulatory gap, the FSR could thus be considered the last piece of the regulatory puzzle to ensure a level playing field in cross-border M&A transactions to the EU.

---

[6] See European Commission, White Paper (fn. 4), p. 7; Gordon and Milhaupt (2018), p. 247; OECD (2012), p. 19.

[7] See Geddes (2004), p. 29.

[8] European Commission, White Paper (fn. 4), p. 7.

[9] European Commission, White Paper (fn. 4), p. 9.

[10] European Commission, White Paper (fn. 4), p. 9; see also Kühling et al. (2021), pp. 5 et seq.

[11] European Commission, White Paper (fn. 4), p. 9; see also Baumann (2020), pp. 86 et seq.

[12] European Commission, White Paper (fn. 4), pp. 9 et seq.; see also Crochet and Gustafsson (2021), pp. 347 et seq.

[13] See European Commission, Proposal (fn. 2), p. 10.

[14] Article 1(1) FSR.

[15] See for an overview of existing rules Biau et al. (2016), pp. 7 et seq.; Chaisse (2016a), pp. 240 et seq.; Krenek and De Smijter (2021), pp. 7 et seq.; Nagy (2021), pp. 150 et seq.; OECD (2016), pp. 49 et seq.; see for the aim of the OECD guidelines on corporate goverance of state-owned enterprises OECD (2015), p. 11.

However, this only holds true if, first, the new instruments fit as seamlessly as possible into the existing regulations and, second, the new instruments themselves do not lead to any undue competitive (dis-)advantages. This article cannot provide an in-depth analysis of the fulfillment of these two conditions. Its aim is to provide an initial assessment of the FSR regarding some potential conflicts with competitive neutrality and its relationship to the existing rules in international investment law. For this purpose, this article will briefly describe two tools under the FSR that concern cross-border M&A transactions (Sect. 2). The article then discusses certain aspects of the new tools that potentially hamper the pursued objective of establishing a level playing field (Sect. 3). Subsequently, the new tools are assessed in relation to their consistency with current approaches in international investment law to ensure competitive neutrality (Sect. 4).

## 2 New Tools to Ensure a Level Playing Field

The FSR introduces three tools to address the distortive effects of foreign subsidies: a general market investigation tool, which the Commission may use *ex officio* (Tool 1); a notification-based tool to investigate certain mergers and acquisitions (Tool 2); and a notification-based tool to investigate bids in public procurements (Tool 3).[16] This article is not the place to describe the three instruments comprehensively. Rather, it aims to provide a brief overview of the tools that concern cross-border M&A transactions. For this reason, Tool 3 will not be discussed in further detail.

Tool 2 is intended to prevent distortions of the internal market and impairments of the level playing field in the Union caused by takeovers of Union undertakings that are financed through foreign subsidies.[17] For concentrations above certain thresholds, Tool 2 provides for a compulsory notification mechanism and an *ex-ante* review by the Commission. Pursuant to article 20(3) FSR, concentrations (as defined in article 20(1) and (2) FSR) have to be notified to the Commission if (i) the acquired undertaking—or at least one of the merging entities—is established in the EU and generates a turnover of at least EUR 500 million in the EU; and if (ii) the undertaking concerned received from third countries an aggregate financial contribution of more than EUR 50 million in the three years prior to the conclusion of the agreement, the acquisition of a controlling interest or the announcement of the public bid. Furthermore, the Commission has the right to request the prior notification of concentrations that do not meet the described thresholds where it suspects that the undertakings concerned may have profited from foreign subsidies in the previous three years.[18] Concentrations that were wrongly not reported may be reviewed by the

[16] European Commission, Proposal (fn. 2), p. 10.

[17] See recital 4 FSR.

[18] Article 21(5) FSR.

Commission *ex officio*.[19] As long as the review of the Commission is pending, the transactions falling in the scope of Tool 2 may not be closed.[20] At the end of the in-depth investigation, the Commission may prohibit the transaction if it finds that a foreign subsidy distorts the internal market and such distortions cannot be fully and effectively remedied by commitments or redressive measures (such as divestment of certain assets, repayment of the foreign subsidy, etc.).[21]

Under Tool 1, the Commission may investigate *ex officio* distortive foreign subsidies.[22] In particular, the Commission will be able to use this tool for concentrations below the thresholds set by Tool 2.[23] Therefore, the Commission has the power to investigate, on its own motion and outside the scope of any merger procedure, foreign subsidies of any amount granted to companies, even if they have only a small EU turnover. If the commission finds a distortion that cannot be remedied by behavioral measures or structural measures or the repayment of the subsidy, it may even decide to order the undertakings concerned to dissolve the concentration.[24]

## 3 The Tools' Effect on Competitive Neutrality

The issue of competitive neutrality regarding international M&A transactions has been left largely unaddressed in international trade and investment law, as well as the competition law, investment screening and anti-subsidy regimes of the EU.[25] Therefore, the need for new regulatory tools can hardly be disputed.[26] The new tools of the FSR are supposed to fill the identified legal gap and actually prevent the risk of non-subsidized companies being outbid by foreign-subsidized undertakings (in particular foreign SOEs) in the acquisition process.[27]

The FSR's tools build on the concept of foreign subsidies, which is similar to the concept of state aid under EU state aid law.[28] State aid law is designed to prevent

[19] Article 21(4) FSR.

[20] Article 24(1) FSR.

[21] Article 25(3)(c) FSR. See Article 7 FSR regarding commitments and redressive measures.

[22] Article 9 FSR.

[23] European Commission, Proposal (fn. 2), p. 10.

[24] See recital 25 FSR.

[25] See Baumann (2020), p. 82 et seq.; European Commission, White Paper (fn. 4), p. 9; Krenek and De Smijter (2021), p. 7 et seq.; Svetlicinii (2018), p. 14.

[26] See recital 6 FSR; see further Briguet (2018), p. 857; Cunha Rodrigues (2021), p. 200 et seq.

[27] See European Commission, Impact assessment accompanying the Proposal for a Regulation of the European Parliament and of the Council on foreign subsidies distorting the internal market, SWD(2021) final, p. 55.

[28] See Article 3 FSR; see further Kühling et al. (2021), p. 8; Zöttl and Werner (2022), p. 476. However, there are also some noticeable differences between the definitions of "foreign subsidy" and intra-EU state aid (Luja (2021), p. 188).

distortions of competition in the internal market due to selective advantages granted by national authorities and not to establish general competitive neutrality between SOEs and private companies.[29] Nevertheless, EU state aid law is an overarching competitive neutrality framework that captures nearly all undue advantages commonly enjoyed by SOEs.[30] Therefore, by quasi adapting the state aid rules for cross-border M&A transactions, the FSR applies and enforces indirectly the principle of competitive neutrality in this area.[31] Naturally, in extending the state aid rules to foreign subsidies, it is not possible to apply the identical set of legal instruments. Rather, an equivalent regime needs to be developed.[32]

However, ensuring a level playing field by introducing new obligations for certain actors is a delicate undertaking. It runs the risk of creating new disadvantages for specific market participants and thereby impairing the objective pursued. In particular, foreign SOEs—as common beneficiaries of foreign subsidies—may be adversely affected in future M&A transactions in the EU by certain aspects of the FSR.

## *3.1 Uncertainties Arising from the Notification Duty*

Tool 2 provides for a compulsory notification mechanism and an *ex-ante* review by the Commission for concentrations above certain thresholds. Upon receipt of a notification, the Commission may initiate an in-depth investigation, potentially including fact-finding visits at the Union premises of the undertaking concerned.[33] Further, if the Commission finds that a foreign subsidy distorts the internal market, it may prohibit a concentration or—where the concentration has already been implemented—require the undertakings concerned to dissolve it.[34] Consequently, foreign SOEs, whose competitive position in the acquisition process of an undertaking in the EU has been improved by a foreign subsidy, may be prohibited from completing the transaction. Incidentally, the notification requirements and the possibility of prohibiting an acquisition under the FSR do not only apply to classic cross-border transactions in which a foreign company—with the help of subsidies—acquires an EU target. Rather, this is also the case where the acquisition of the Union company is made through a subsidiary of the foreign buyer that is already domiciled in the EU or where a joint venture is created in the EU.[35]

---

[29] OECD (2012), p. 83.

[30] Baumann (2019), p. 342; OECD (2012), p. 83.

[31] See Cunha Rodrigues (2021), p. 224.

[32] Hahn (2021), p. 184; see also Kühling et al. (2021), p. 8.

[33] Article 25(1) in connection with Article 14(2)(a) FSR.

[34] Article 25(3)(c) and (6)(a) FSR; see also Luja (2021), pp. 196 et seq.

[35] See with regard to joint ventures article 20(2) FSR; see article 20(1) FSR for the different concentration constellations.

In contrast, under the EU state aid regime, aid has not to be notified by the undertaking but by the respective EU Member State to the Commission.[36] Further, acquisitions by companies subsidized by EU Member States may not be prevented, even if such concentrations have been facilitated by subsidies that distort the internal market. Although under EU state aid law the subsidy is likely to be reclaimed from the company, the completed company takeover remains unaffected.[37]

It follows that takeovers of EU companies intended by SOEs (as well as private actors, for that matter) benefitting from foreign subsidies are subject to potentially greater procedural burdens and restraints than those of companies receiving subsidies from EU Member States.[38] This consequence does not seem inevitable. Instead,—in line with the rules of EU state aid law—it could have been provided that while foreign subsidies must be repaid, acquisitions of EU companies financed through them remain unaffected.[39] It seems, however, that the legislator did not want to be presented with a *fait accompli* with respect to subsidized takeovers of EU companies.

It can be argued, however, that the undertakings concerned might prevent a prohibition of the concentration if they offer commitments that fully and effectively remedy the distortion caused by the foreign subsidy.[40] Such an argument disregards the procedural burdens imposed on the respective companies and the fact that legal certainty is of the essence in M&A processes. Recent research in the U.S. M&A market seems to indicate that policy risks and uncertainty related to mergers disproportionately deter foreign investors.[41] At the beginning of an EU-M&A process, it may be highly uncertain for a foreign investor whether it is considered to be the recipient of a distortive foreign-subsidy[42] and what legal consequences this would entail for the intended acquisition of an EU company: Is the foreign investor going to have to offer certain commitments,[43] or is the Commission going to impose

---

[36] Article 108(3) TFEU.

[37] Article 108 TFEU does not stipulate any consequences in this regard. However, capital market rules may provide for a takeover not to be completed, while the examination under EU state aid law is still pending. In such cases, if the particular state aid is finally found to violate EU state aid law, the takeover bid would be withdrawn.

[38] It must be noted in this respect, that in certain cases also under EU State Aid Law, companies subsidized by an EU Member State haven been required to divest certain assets or to refrain from acquiring a company (see European Commission, Impact Assessment (n 27), p. 55). Particularly, this is the case regarding to undertakings benefiting from restructuring aid (see Guidelines on State aid for rescuing and restructuring nonfinancial undertaking in difficulty (2014/C 249/01), para. 78 and para. 84).

[39] See Monopolkommission (2020), para. 924, for a proposal in this regard.

[40] See recital 23 FSR. According to the European Commission, White Paper (fn. 4), p. 23, the prohibition of an acquisition should only be used as a last resort.

[41] See Clougherty and Zhang (2021), p. 472 et seq.

[42] See article 3 and 4 FSR; see also European Commission, Impact Assessment (fn. 27), p. 54.

[43] See article 7 FSR.

redressive measures such as the divestment of certain assets[44] or even prohibit the takeover? Due to these high degrees of legal uncertainty regarding the concentration process and outcome, foreign investors may refrain from acquiring EU companies.[45] To reduce these uncertainties for all market participants, the Commission shall issue guidelines providing details regarding the criteria for determining the distortive nature of a subsidy.[46]

## *3.2 Exceptions, Thresholds and Balancing Test*

Due to the very broad scope of EU state aid law, there are wide-ranging exceptions to the prohibition of state aid to take into account the economic policy competences of the Member States. In particular, the exemptions under article 107 (2) and (3) TFEU—which have been widely relied upon during the COVID-19 pandemic—were further specified by the Commission by means of the General Block Exemption Regulation (GBER).[47] In the GBER, certain types of state aid that fall into the categories of article 107 (2) and (3) TFEU are exempted from the notification requirement. In contrast, the notification of concentrations under Tool 2 of the FSR is subject to specific thresholds but does not provide for exemptions from the notification requirement for certain kinds of foreign subsidies.[48] Due to limited information and lack of practice in applying the new legislation on foreign subsidies, the Commission considered it impossible to replicate the sophisticated system of guidelines and block exemptions for foreign subsidies.[49] Article 4(4) FSR merely provides that foreign subsidies making good damages from "natural disasters" or "exceptional occurrences" may be considered not to distort the internal market. However, this does not affect any obligation to notify the transaction when the specified thresholds under Tool 2 are exceeded. Therefore, competitive advantages may arise for companies subsidized by EU Member States if the subsidies fall under the State aid exemption criteria. While in the cases covered by the GBER, EU state aid does not have to be notified, the companies receiving foreign subsidies are potentially subject to notification requirements and related burdensome review procedures. This difference takes on particular significance considering that 95% of the state aid awarded in the EU are block exempted.[50]

---

[44] See article 7(4)(f) FSR.

[45] See Clougherty and Zhang (2021), pp. 471 et seq.; see further Zöttl and Werner (2022), p. 486.

[46] Article 46(1)(a) FSR; see also recital 73 FSR.

[47] Commission Regulation (EU) No 651/2014 of 17 June 2014 declaring certain categories of aid compatible with the internal market in application of Articles 107 and 108 of the Treaty.

[48] Crochet and Gustafsson (2021), p. 362.

[49] European Commission, Impact Assessment (n 27), p. 65.

[50] European Commission, Impact Assessment (n 27), p. 65.

Furthermore, concentrations that fall below the thresholds for Tool 2 may still be investigated under the *ex officio* review in Tool 1. However, when applying Tool 1, a foreign subsidy shall be considered unlikely to distort the internal market if it stays below EUR 4 million over a period of 3 years.[51] This threshold is considerably higher than the *de minimis* exemption applied in EU state aid law. The higher threshold is intended to take account of the fact that – as mentioned above—foreign subsidies do not benefit from an equivalent system of block exemptions as EU state aid.[52] Thereby, the objective is expressed, as in the case of EU state aid, to focus on the largest and hence potentially most distortive foreign subsidies.[53] However, it seems questionable whether the higher threshold can compensate for the described disadvantages caused by the lack of block exceptions. First, in quantitative terms, it is unclear whether 95% of foreign subsidies fall under this threshold as it is the case for EU state aid that is block exempted.[54] Second, the EUR four million threshold is also not framed as a *de minimis* exemption, meaning that the Commission can still act when a foreign subsidy is below this amount if, contrary to the presumption of article 4(2) FSR, a distortion of the internal market seems likely.[55] At least, foreign subsidies that would qualify as *de minimis* under EU state aid law are by definition not distortive, leaving no room for further examination by the Commission.[56]

In addition, the FSR enables the Commission to conduct a balancing test by balancing the negative effects of a foreign subsidy in terms of distortion in the internal market with positive effects on the development of the relevant economic activity.[57] In case the scales tip in favor of the positive effects, the Commission may even conclude that no redressive measures shall be imposed, even if a distortive foreign subsidy has been established.[58] The balancing test as set out in FSR seems to be inspired by the balancing test that is used to assess the compatibility of state aid under article 107(3)(c) TFEU.

However, it would not be adequate to simply assume an analogous application of the balancing test under EU state aid law in the FSR. First, there is an extensive body of practice under EU state aid law as well as detailed guidelines and regulations which contain specific rules and criteria to be used when conducting the balancing test.[59] In contrast, the balancing test under the FSR is of a much more general and superficial nature.[60] Second, recourse to the detailed EU state aid balancing rules are limited in practice, as they are not suitable for controlling foreign subsidies in the

[51] Article 4(2) FSR.

[52] European Commission, Impact Assessment (n 27), p. 65.

[53] See Hornkohl (2023), p. 143.

[54] Hornkohl (2023), p. 143.

[55] Krenek and De Smijter (2021), p. 17; Luja (2021), p. 190.

[56] Article 4(3) FSR.

[57] Article 6 FSR.

[58] See recital 21 FSR.

[59] Hornkohl (2023), p. 145; Zöttl and Werner (2022), p. 482.

[60] Hornkohl (2023), p. 145.

context of M&A transactions.[61] For instance, under EU state aid law only positive effects of the aid that impact the internal market are to be considered in the compatibility assessment whereas the positive effects in third countries are not taken into account. In many cases, the aim of the foreign subsidy will be to benefit the policy goals of a third country (for example, the promotion of renewable energy sources in a third country). In this respect, it has been justifiably argued that the Commission should also consider whether the foreign subsidy pursues a policy objective in a foreign country that has positive externalities for the EU (i.e., environmental protection, research and development).[62] At this point, it remains uncertain what methodology the Commission will use to conduct the balancing test under the FSR. In particular, it is unclear whether only the effects on the internal market will be considered or whether the positive effects of the foreign subsidy on third countries (i.e., the subsidizing country) may also be taken into account. The wording included in the final version of article 6(1) FSR seems to favor the above-explained approach allowing the Commission to consider broader positive effects in relation to the relevant policy objectives in third countries, apart from positive effects on the internal market.[63] However, the question remains as to how such foreign positive effects must be balanced against possible negative effects on the internal market.[64]

To clarify the criteria and the procedures for applying the balancing test, the Commission has to issue guidelines.[65] At best, such guidelines can resolve some legal uncertainties with regard to the balancing test, whereby a detailed and nuanced practice as under EU state aid law will only emerge over time. In the meantime, foreign subsidized companies will face considerable ambiguity about how the foreign subsidies at issue will be assessed in M&A transactions. Furthermore, if the positive effects in third countries are not appropriately considered, additional concerns for competitive neutrality may arise. A company receiving foreign subsidies may be subject to redressive measures that companies subsidized by EU Member States do not have to bear.

---

[61] See in detail Hornkohl (2023), pp. 145 et seq.; Zöttl and Werner (2022), p. 482.

[62] See joint statement by the American Chamber of Commerce to the EU, the Europe India Chamber of Commerce, the European Australian Business Council, the Japan Business Council in Europe, the Korea Business Association Europe and the Swiss-American Chamber of Commerce, Foreign Subsidies Regulation: key EU trade and investment partners raise concerns, 1 June 2022, http://amchameu.eu/position-papers/foreign-subsidies-regulation-key-eu-trade-and-investment-partners-raise-concerns (last accessed 20 November 2022).

[63] See recital 21 FSR according to which positive effects outside the internal market "should be taken into account, where appropriate, in order to avoid that the balancing gives rise to unjustified discrimination."

[64] See Zöttl and Werner (2022), p. 483.

[65] Article 46(1)(b) FSR.

## 3.3 Redressive Measures

Under EU state aid rules, unlawful state aid must be recovered from the recipient by the EU Member State concerned.[66] Measures other than reimbursement are only permitted in cases where reimbursement is not suitable or feasible to restore equal competition conditions.[67] In contrast, pursuant to article 7(4)(h) FSR, the repayment of the foreign subsidy is only one of several possible redressive measures. Further redressive measures to remedy the distortion in the internal market caused by a foreign subsidy include, for example, reducing capacity or market presence, refraining from certain investments or divestment of certain assets.[68] The Commission believes that these alternative redressive measures are necessary, as "it may be difficult in practice to establish that the foreign subsidy is actually and irreversibly paid back to the third country."[69] For this reason, the Commission shall accept the commitment of an undertaking to repay the foreign subsidy only, "where it can ascertain that the repayment is transparent, verifiable and effective, while taking into account the risk of circumvention."[70]

The German Monopolies Commission (Monopolkommission) fears in this regard that the wide range of alternative redressive measures might be misused for industry-policy purposes.[71] Therefore, the Monopolkommission argues that foreign subsidized companies should be obliged to effect redressive payments to the Member States or to the EU in cases where it is difficult to establish whether the foreign subsidy has actually been repaid to the third country.[72] To the extent that instead of actual repayments to third countries, Member States or the EU alternative redressive measures are imposed to remedy distortions caused by foreign subsidies, there is a risk that foreign-subsidized companies will be treated differently than their EU counterparts.[73] As a result, the FSR's objective of restoring the level playing field on the internal market would be impaired.[74]

---

[66] See European Commission, White Paper (fn. 4), p. 19.

[67] ECJ, Judgment of 26 June 2003, C-404/00 – Commission/Spain, 2003, I-6695, ECLI:EU:C:2003:373, paras. 45 ff.

[68] See article 7(4) FSR.

[69] European Commission, White Paper (fn. 4), p. 19.

[70] Article 7(6) FSR; see also recital 24 FSR.

[71] Monopolkommission (2020), para. 892; see also Kühling et al. (2021), pp. 9 et seq. For example, a foreign company could be ordered to reduce capacity in a certain EU market in order to protect EU companies operating in this market.

[72] Monopolkommission (2020), para. 892.

[73] See Crochet and Gustafsson (2021), p. 362.

[74] See European Commission, Proposal (fn. 2), p. 48, for the objective of FSR.

### 3.4 General Concerns

In general, it can be argued that the FSR's set of tools is not suitable to ensure a level playing field, as it deviates significantly from the corresponding regulatory framework of EU state aid law.[75] To ensure the same regulatory treatment between state aid according to article 107 TFEU and equivalent foreign subsidies, providing a uniform instrument with respect to all subsidies may be deemed sufficient. According to the Monopolkommission's idea of such a uniform instrument, foreign subsidies above a certain amount would have to be notified to the Commission. The Commission could then intervene if the subsidy were classified as prohibited state aid according to the standards of EU state aid law. As a result, the undertaking concerned could be charged with a compensation levy corresponding to a maximum of the amount of the subsidy received, payable to the EU budget or it could be ordered to repatriate the economic advantage received to the third country that granted it.[76] Such levy could be smaller than the subsidy received, in cases where full repayment would be inappropriate or disproportionate.[77] Following these considerations, it can also be argued that *ex-officio*-Tool 1 is sufficient to address the concern of foreign subsidies in takeovers of Union companies and that no specific merger control instrument (as stipulated under Tool 2) is necessary at all. In fact, companies would not be burdened with extensive notification procedures, while the Commission would still be able to investigate foreign subsidies and to impose redressive measures if warranted.

It is now clear that the FSR is not limited to a uniform tool but also includes a specific merger control instrument. As outlined above, this places considerable administrative burden on the respective companies (i.e., foreign SOEs) and is associated with uncertainties that may prove to be crucial in takeover battles over Union companies. In addition, there are significant deviations from EU state aid law with regard to redressive measures, exemptions and the balancing test. These differences and their potential negative effects on a level playing field should be kept in mind when concretizing and applying the FSR.

## 4 The Tools' Consistency with Current Approaches in International Investment Law

How do the relevant tools of the FSR relate to the existing rules on SOEs, competitive neutrality and subsidies? This far-reaching question addresses an important concern of policymakers: to establish as much coherence as possible between the

[75] See Monopolkommission (2020), para. 889 et seq. and para. 924 et seq; see also Kühling et al. (2021), pp. 8 et seq.

[76] See Monopolkommission (2020), para. 889 et seq., para. 924 et seq. and para. 987.

[77] See Monopolkommission (2020), para. 940.

fragmented regulations dealing with these issues.[78] However, it cannot and does not need to be answered comprehensively in this article. For instance, it has been noted elsewhere that the compatibility of the FSR's tools with WTO law seems questionable.[79] Rather, this article aims to contextualise the new tools within the ongoing efforts of international investment law in dealing with state-owned enterprises, subsidies and competitive neutrality. Foreign direct investment—such as the acquisition of an EU company by a foreign investor—falls within the scope of international investment law. In recent decades, investment law has developed mainly around international investment agreements (IIA).[80]

## 4.1 Current Approaches

Several recent multilateral trade and investment agreements address issues regarding SOEs and competitive neutrality. The recently concluded "Comprehensive and Progressive Agreement for Trans-Pacific Partnership" (CPTPP) contains a whole chapter on SOEs.[81] These binding rules shall ensure that SOEs benefitting from undue competitive advantages do not impede the trade and investment activities of other companies.[82] In particular, the contracting parties must ensure that SOEs act in accordance with commercial considerations.[83] Further, non-commercial assistance provided to SOEs (such as loans that are provided to SOEs on better terms than those commercially available to SOEs) are not generally prohibited but shall not cause adverse effects to the interests of the other parties.[84] However, the obligations described apply only with regard to the purchase and sale of goods and the supply of services but not with respect to the SOEs' foreign investments.[85]

[78] See Chaisse (2016a), p. 258.

[79] See Crochet and Gustafsson (2021), pp. 361 et seq.; Nagy (2021), pp. 156 et seq.; see further Trapp (2020), p. 969 et seq.

[80] Subedi (2016), p. 8. Two major types of IIAs are to be distinguished: bilateral investment treaties (BITs) and multilateral preferential trade and investment agreements (see Chaisse [2016b], p. 604, for a description of these two types).

[81] Matsushita (2017), p. 188. The chapter on SOEs in the CPTPP is the same as in the initial Trans-Pacific Partnership Agreement (TPP).

[82] Matsushita (2017), p. 190.

[83] Article 17.4(1)(a) CPTPP; see further Matsushita (2017), pp. 190 and 193; Willemyns (2016), p. 671; Yun (2016), pp. 8 et seq. Commercial considerations are factors such as price, quality, availability, marketability, transportation, etc., that a privately-owned enterprise in the relevant business or industry would normally take into account when taking a commercial decision (article 17.1 CPTPP).

[84] See article 17.6 CPTPP; see Fleury and Marcoux (2016), pp. 459 et seq. and Yun (2016), pp. 10 et seq., for a discussion of non-commercial assistance as defined under article 17.1 CPTPP.

[85] Article 17.6 CPTPP; see Kawase and Ambashi (2017), p. 19.

The "United States-Mexico-Canada-Agreement" (USMCA), the successor to the "North American Free Trade Agreement" (NAFTA), follows the approach of the CPTPP with regard to SOEs and non-commercial assistance.[86] The USMCA goes further than the CPTPP by declaring certain forms of non-commercial assistance to be prohibited entirely.[87] In particular, SOEs, such as state-owned banks, may not grant loans or loan guarantees to an uncreditworthy SOE.[88] This prohibition applies regardless of whether non-commercial assistance is provided in connection with the purchase and sale of goods or services or with respect to foreign direct investment.

The aim of a level playing field has also been a main concern in the recently negotiated IIA of the EU. The "EU-China Comprehensive Agreement on Investment" (CAI), which has been confirmed in principle by the parties, contains several provisions aimed at leveling the playing field.[89] As the CPTPP, the CAI also obliges each party to ensure that its SOEs act according to commercial considerations in their purchases or sales of goods or services in the territory of the respective other party.[90] Furthermore, the CAI improves the transparency regarding subsidies by extending the current WTO transparency rules on subsidies related to goods to also cover service sectors.[91] Although these obligations do not directly affect the issue of foreign subsidies distorting the EU internal market, they should be read together with the objectives of the FSR. Changing the behavior of SOEs through specific obligations in IIA moves them closer to the model of private firms and thereby reduces the risk that they might take over Union undertakings facilitated by undue competitive advantages (i.e., foreign subsidies).[92] Furthermore, higher transparency obligations on subsidies and SOEs as included in the CAI may help the Commission's investigation of foreign subsidies under the FSR. The same applies for the "Comprehensive Economic and Trade Agreement" (CETA) between the EU and Canada, which also includes an obligation to ensure that SOEs act in accordance with commercial considerations and set out similar transparency requirements regarding subsidies.[93]

---

[86] See Borlini (2020), pp. 329 et seq., for a critical appraisal of the commitments regarding SOEs under the CPTPP and the USMCA.

[87] Article 22.6(1) USMCA; see Borlini (2020), pp. 330 et seq.

[88] Article 22.6(1)(a) USMCA. The contracting parties must ensure that their respective SOEs comply with this obligation (article 22.6(3) USMCA).

[89] See Xu (2022), pp. 103 et seq.

[90] Section II. article 3bis CAI. In Section II article II CAI China has for the first time agreed on a precise and comprehensive definition of SOEs in an international agreement (see Mavroidis and Sapir (2022), p. 18).

[91] Section III article 8(1) CAI. See further Mavroidis and Sapir (2022), p. 18; Xu (2022), pp. 104 et seq.

[92] See Enderwick (2017), p. 269.

[93] Article 7.2 and 18.5(1) CETA.

## 4.2 Future Approaches

Inconsistencies between domestic measures to ensure a level playing field and those provided for in IIA are of concern.[94] In connection with foreign direct investment screening mechanisms on grounds of national security, it has been argued that unpredictability and procedural uncertainty could be reduced by establishing certain symmetry constraints in IIA.[95] Such symmetry constrains provide a binding set of rules or an overarching framework regarding a certain issue that the contracting parties have to comply with.[96] This approach could also represent a possible future path for the EU to establish more coherence between its tools pursuant to the FSR and its IIA. Actually, by shaping its international agreements (i.e., free trade agreements) accordingly, the EU has already succeeded in the past in achieving better alignment of international subsidy rules with EU state aid law.[97] Therefore, it might be appropriate for the EU to include prohibitions of certain governmental support measures in its IIA. Furthermore, principles could be incorporated stating that other non-commercial assistance measures must not result in a distortion of the other party's internal market.[98] The greater the terms are aligned with those of the FSR, the greater the consistency achieved.

In fact, in the negotiations of an EU-Australia trade agreement the EU has tabled proposals that move in this direction. Apart from a chapter on SOEs that focuses on the issues of non-discriminatory treatment and commercial considerations,[99] the EU has also proposed a chapter that addresses subsidies. Particularly, the latter enshrines the principle of competitive neutrality (article X.2) and lists certain kinds of subsidies that are prohibited (article X.12). Furthermore, it provides for a consultation process in cases where a party considers that a subsidy is negatively affecting its trade or investment liberalization interests (article X.11).[100]

In relation to the EU-Australia trade agreement, it has been suggested to include provisions in the agreement that provide for procedural facilitation regarding the EU's new tools under the FSR.[101] Such arrangements would ease the burden for Australian companies, for example, by allowing faster individual procedures, higher

---

[94] See Chaisse (2016a), p. 258.

[95] Bian (2021), pp. 566 et seq.; Willemyns (2016), p. 680, also argues for including SOEs-specific obligations in international investment and trade agreements.

[96] See Bian (2021), pp. 566 et seq. With further references.

[97] Neumann (2019), p. 267 et seq.; Reinhold (2022), p. 208; see further Kühling et al. (2021), p. 9, mentioning the example of the EU-Singapore FTA in this regard.

[98] The term "noncommercial assistance" is based on the language in the SCM Agreement (Willemyns (2016), p. 671).

[99] See EU text proposal on State-owned enterprises, available at <https://trade.ec.europa.eu/doclib/press/index.cfm?id=1865>.

[100] See EU text proposal on Anti-competitive conduct, merger controls and subsidies, available at <https://trade.ec.europa.eu/doclib/press/index.cfm?id=1865>.

[101] Reinhold (2022), pp. 216 et seq.

thresholds or even exemptions from the application of the FSR. The FSR does allow for such deviations in international agreements.[102] Including respective arrangements in the EU-Australia trade agreement seems appropriate, as the agreement—as outlined above—itself is likely to contain several provisions on SOEs, competitive neutrality and subsidies. Furthermore, Australia has a domestic competitive neutrality regime in place that is at least comparable to EU state aid law.[103]

In general, offering facilitations with regard to the FSR in IIA may be a convincing incentive for other countries to agree on specific subsidies and SOEs obligations in IIAs and to implement their own subsidy control systems. It has been argued that in case such agreements are reached or similar unilateral subsidy control measures are established by third countries, the Commission should be able to issue a recognition decision stating that such subsidy control is equivalent to the state aid control system of the EU.[104] While the FSR does not provide the Commission with such a possibility, at least, it seems to leave the door open for possible future recognition of third countries' subsidy control systems. Pursuant to article 52(2) FSR the Commission shall report in 3 years on developments in international relations with regard to subsidy control systems by third countries.

Finally, it should also be considered whether the tools of the FSR comply with the obligations contained in the current IIA of the EU. In this regard, article 44(9) FSR provides that no measure shall be adopted that would be contrary to the international obligations of the EU. However, IIA typically contain national treatment clauses[105] that may be of concern. Such clauses require contracting parties to accord to investments or investors from other parties no less favorable treatment than they accord to nationals. The EU's IIA tends to extend the national treatment to the pre-establishment phase combined with a negative list approach.[106] As the previous section has shown, foreign-subsidized companies are being treated differently under the FSR's tools than undertakings subsidized by EU Member States. It seems that the tools would not lead to a de jure violation of national treatment, as they would apply to both domestic and foreign beneficiaries of foreign subsidies. However, the tools may constitute a de facto discrimination, as foreign companies are more likely to

[102] See article 44(9) FSR; Reinhold (2022), p. 216.

[103] See for an overview of the Australian competitive neutrality regime Baumann (2019), pp. 269 et seq.; Healey (2015), pp. 9 et seq.

[104] Kühling et al. (2021), p. 9; see further Reinhold (2022), p. 217. Amendment 35 proposed by the European Parliament (COM(2021)0223 – C9-0167/2021 – 2021/0114(COD)), wanted to enable the Commission to consider "whether the third country has a system for the review of subsidies in place, which the Commission has found to provide guarantees, in law and in practice, that the level of protection against undue state intervention into market forces and unfair competition is at least equivalent to the level of protection within the Union, whether the subsidy has been cleared under that system and whether that clearance appears relevant also for the effects on the internal market." However, this amendment has not made it into the final version of the FSR.

[105] Bjorklund (2018), n. 21.01.

[106] Bian (2021), p. 588. Whereas CETA extends national treatment to the pre-establishment phase (article 8.6 CETA), article 2.3 of the EU – Singapore Investment Protection Agreement does not.

receive foreign subsidies than EU companies.[107] To determine if there is indeed a violation of the national treatment obligations, it must be examined in each case whether the respective IIA of the EU provides for applicable reservations and exceptions regarding national treatment.[108] For future IIA of the EU, it might prove necessary to adjust the scope of application of the national treatment obligation as well as the corresponding exceptions accordingly.

# 5 Conclusion

With the FSR, the EU is addressing the legitimate concern of ensuring competitive neutrality in the takeovers of Union companies. This issue has been left largely unaddressed in international trade and investment law as well as domestic competition-, investment-screening and anti-subsidy-regimes. The FSR justifiably aims to fill this regulatory gap by introducing a kind of merger control regime for transactions facilitated by foreign subsidies. The FSR will provide the Commission with the necessary tools to prevent competitive distortions caused by takeovers financed with foreign subsidies. In particular, the tools of the FSR are for the most part well suited to prevent undue competitive advantages enjoyed by foreign SOEs in cross-border M&A transactions.

While an improvement in ensuring competitive neutrality can thus be recognized in principle, some reservations are warranted. On the one hand, the extent to which the new tools are put into effect, depends on the Commission's capacities. On the other hand, the application of the tools may impair the objective of competitive neutrality, as the tools do not mirror the rules under EU state aid law. Several potential competitive neutrality concerns with regard to the new tools are outlined in this article. Particularly, these concerns originate from a specific notification procedure, more extensive redressive measures (i.e., prohibition of the take-over), adverse application of the balancing test and limited exemptions. Not all of them seem unavoidable for the implementation of an effective foreign subsidies regime. Only further concretization and application of the tools will show whether they prevent more distortions of competition overall or whether they lead to unjustified competitive disadvantages for foreign companies in the acquisition of EU companies.

---

[107] See Crochet and Gustafsson (2021), p. 358, for a similar analysis under article XVII GATS; see further Bjorklund, n. 21.02, regarding de jure and de facto discriminations. Nagy (2021), p. 157, argues that based on the decisional practice of the Dispute Settlement Body, the EU may have a good case that the new tools do not violate the requirement of national treatment, but that it depends on how the tools are specifically shaped.

[108] See Bian (2021), pp. 587 et seq.; see also Bjorklund (2018), n. 21.94; see further Bungenberg and Reinisch (2021), p. 459, regarding the broad exception from national treatment in article 8.2 CETA for "activities carried out in the exercise of governmental authority".

The issues of competitive neutrality, SOEs and (foreign) subsidies are dealt with in a multifaceted and multilevel regime which needs coordination. The FSR must fit into this existing set of rules. As far as IIA are concerned, this article showed that several recent IIA address the issue of competitive neutrality. In contrast to the FSR, they focus mainly on specific obligations concerning commercial activities by SOEs and deal only to a limited extent with subsidies in the context of cross-border M&As. To increase coherency and to reduce unpredictability and uncertainty regarding its new regulatory tools, the EU should aim to include general principles on and prohibitions of certain subsidies in its IIA. In the future, third countries that enter into such agreements and/or introduce unilateral subsidies and SOEs control systems could be granted facilitations with regard to the FSR. Finally, the extent to which the tools of the FSR are compliant with the EU's national treatment obligations as stipulated in its IIA must be carefully examined.

## References


Baumann P (2020) When state enterprises have deeper pockets: ensuring competitive neutrality in cross-border M&A. In: Fach Gómez K, Gourgourinis A, Titi C (eds) International investment law and competition law. Springer, Cham, pp 73–95

Baumann P (2019) Wettbewerbsverzerrungen durch privatwirtschaftliche Staatstätigkeit. Schulthess, Zurich/Basel/Geneva

Bian C (2021) Foreign direct investment screening and national security: reducing regulatory hurdles to investors through induced reciprocity. J World Invest Trade 22:561–595

Biau C et al. (2016) Governments as competitors in the global marketplace: options for ensuring a level playing field. E15Initiative, Geneva

Bjorklund A (2018) The national treatment obligation. In: Yannaca-Small K (ed) Arbitration under international investment agreements: a guide to success. Oxford University Press, Oxford, pp 532–561

Borlini L (2020) When the leviathan goes to the market: a critical evaluation of the rules governing state-owned enterprises in trade agreements. Leiden J Int Law 33:313–334

Briguet J (2018) The state's invisible hand: Chinese SOEs facing EU antitrust law. J World Trade 52(5):839–858

Bungenberg M, Reinisch A (2021) A paradigm change: the CETA investment chapter. Zeitschrift für Europarechtliche Studien 23:437–484

Capobianco A, Christiansen H (2011) Competitive neutrality and state-owned enterprises: challenges and policy options. OECD Corporate Governance Working Papers No. 1

Chaisse J (2016a) Untangling the triangle: issues for state-controlled entities in trade, investment, and competition law. In: Chaisse J, Lin T (eds) International economic law and governance. Oxford University Press, Oxford, pp 233–258

Chaisse J (2016b) Demystifying public security exception and limitations on capital movement: hard law, soft law and sovereign investments in the EU internal market. Univ Pennsylvania J Int Law 37(2):583–646

Clougherty J, Zhang N (2021) Foreign investors reactions to risk and uncertainty in antitrust: U.S. merger policy investigations and the deterrence of foreign acquirer presence. J Int Bus Stud 52:454–478

Crochet V, Gustafsson M (2021) Lawful remedy or illegal response? Resolving the issue of foreign subsidization under WTO law. World Trade Rev 20:343–366

Cunha Rodrigues N (2021) Filling the regulatory gap to address foreign subsidies: the EC's search for a level playing field within the internal market. In: Cunha Rodrigues N (ed) Extraterritoriality of EU economic law: the application of EU economic law outside the territory of the EU. Springer, Cham, pp 197–227
Enderwick P (2017) International investment by state-controlled enterprises: a source for concern? Strateg Chang 26(3):261–271
Fleury J, Marcoux JM (2016) The US shaping of state-owned enterprise disciplines in the trans-Pacific partnership. J Int Econ Law 19(2):445–465
Geddes R (2004) Case studies of anticompetitive SOE behavior. In: Geddes R (ed) Competing with the government: anticompetitive behavior and public enterprises. Hoover Institution Press, Stanford, pp 27–58
Gordon JN, Milhaupt CJ (2019) China as a 'National Strategic Buyer': towards a multilateral regime for cross-border M&A. Columbia Bus Law Rev 192(1):192–251
Hahn M (2021) Aktuelle Entwicklungen im EU-Aussenwirtschaftsrecht «Offene strategische Autonomie» und EU-Aussenwirtschaftsrecht: Legitimer Durchsetzungswille oder Unilateralismus? In: Epiney A, Zlatescu P (eds) Schweizerisches Jahrbuch für Europarecht 2020/2021. Schulthess, Zurich, pp 157–187
Healey D (2015) Competitive neutrality: addressing government advantages in Australian markets. In: Drexl J, Bagnoli V (eds) State-initiated restraints of competition. Edward Elgar Publishing, Cheltenham, pp 3–39
Hornkohl L (2023) Protecting the internal market from subsidisation with the EU state aid regime and the foreign subsidies regulation: two sides of the same coin? J Eur Compet Law Pract 14(3): 137–151. https://doi.org/10.1093/jeclap/lpad005
Kawase T, Ambashi M (2017) Disciplines on state-owned enterprises under the Trans-Pacific Partnership Agreement: overview and assessment. ERIA Discussion Paper Series No. 13
Krenek F, De Smijter E (2021) From a white paper to a proposal for a regulation on foreign subsidies: filling a regulatory gap in protecting the EU internal market. In: Asian Yearbook of International Economic Law, Springer, Cham. https://doi.org/10.1007/16517_2021_3
Kühling J, Weck T, Reinold P (2021) Third-country state aid regulation: the European debate on foreign subsidies. In: Asian Yearbook of International Economic Law, Springer, Cham, https://doi.org/10.1007/16517_2021_4
Luja R (2021) The foreign subsidy regulation: countering state aid beyond the European Union. Eur State Aid Law Q 20(2):187–199
Matsushita M (2017) State-owned enterprises in the TPP agreement. In: Chaisse J, Gao H, Chang-fa L (eds) Paradigm shift in international economic law rule-making. Springer, Singapore, pp 187–203
Mavroidis P, Sapir A (2022) What is so special about CAI? Asia Pacific Law Rev 30(2). https://doi.org/10.1080/10192557.2022.2085414
Monopolkommission (2020) Chinese state capitalism: A challenge for the European market economy, Chapter IV of the Biennial Report XXIII of the Monopolies Commission ("Competition 2020") pursuant to Section 44 (1) sentence 1 of the Act Against Restraints on Competition
Nagy C (2021) Foreign subsidies, distortions and acquisitions. Central Eur J Comp Law 2(1): 147–162
Neumann F (2019) Export des europäischen Beihilferechts: Eine Analyse der Europäisierung des internationalen Subventionsrechts durch bilaterale Handelsabkommen. Springer, Wiesbaden
Nielsen R (1981) Competitive advantages of state owned and controlled businesses. Manag Int Rev 21(3):56–66
OECD (2022) Recommendation of the council on competitive neutrality, Paris
OECD (2016) State-owned enterprises as global competitors: a challenge or an opportunity? , Paris
OECD (2015) OECD guidelines on corporate governance of state-owned enterprises, Paris
OECD (2012) Competitive neutrality: maintaining a level playing field between public and private business, Paris

Reinhold P (2022) European trade policy and the regulation of subsidies: what can we expect from the EU-Australia FTA? In: Bungenberg M, Mitchell A (eds) The Australia-European Union Free Trade Agreement. Springer, Cham, pp 203–218

Sauvant K et al (2014) Trends in FDI, home country measures and competitive neutrality. In: Bjorklund A (ed) Yearbook on International Investment law & policy 2012–2013. Oxford University Press, New York, pp 5–117

Subedi S (2016) International investment law: reconciling policy and principle. Hart Publishing, Oxford

Svetlicinii A (2018) The acquisitions of the Chinese state-owned enterprises under the EU merger control regime: time for reflection? Revue Lamy de la concurrence 67:30–36

Trapp P (2020) Das Weissbuch der Kommission zur Gewährleistung fairer Wettbewerbsbedingungen bei Subventionen aus Drittstaaten. Europäische Zeitschrift für Wirtschaftsrecht:964–970

Willemyns I (2016) Disciplines on state-owned enterprises in international economic law: are we moving in the right direction? J Int Econ Law 19(3):657–680

Xu Q (2022) Scoping the impact of the comprehensive agreement on investment: liberalization, protection, and dispute resolution in the next era of EU-China relations. Asia Pac Law Rev 30(1):93–122

Yun M (2016) An analysis of the new trade regime for state-owned enterprises under the trans-Pacific partnership agreement. J East Asian Econ Integr 20(1):3–35

Zöttl J, Werner P (2022) Vive l'Industriepolitik – M&A unter der neuen Drittstaatensubventionsverordnung. Neue Zeitschrift für Kartellrecht:475–486

# Fair Play? The Politics of Evaluating Foreign Subsidies in the European Union

**Robert Basedow, Sophie Meunier, and Christilla Roederer-Rynning**

## Contents



**Abstract** The European Union (EU), for decades a pillar of openness and multilateralism, has recently shifted towards a more assertive commercial policy relying on the development of new geoeconomic instruments designed to level the playing field and deal with the increasing blurriness between economy and national security. Alongside the new EU FDI screening framework in place since 2020, the EU has proposed a new FDI screening mechanism to tackle market distortions arising from foreign subsidies in the context of European mergers and acquisitions. Why is the EU introducing this new policy instrument right now? What political economy

The authors would like to acknowledge financial support by the Independent Research Fund Denmark (#1028-00003B) for the project: 'Beauty Contests: The Changing Politics of Foreign Investment in Europe').

R. Basedow (✉)
London School of Economics, London, UK
e-mail: J.R.Basedow@lse.ac.uk

S. Meunier
Princeton University, Princeton, NJ, USA

C. Roederer-Rynning
University of Southern Denmark, Odense, Denmark



J. Hillebrand Pohl et al. (eds.), *Weaponising Investments*,
Springer Studies in Law & Geoeconomics (2023) 1: 219–238,
https://doi.org/10.1007/17280_2023_12, Published online: 4 July 2023

forces shape the institutional design? And why does this instrument enjoy broad support in the Commission, Council of Ministers and European Parliament despite its likely redistributive impacts on Member State economies? Our paper uses process tracing, expert interviews, media research and secondary literature to trace the history of this policy project from its inception to today. In particular, we question why the decision was made to embed this policy under the competition arm of the European Commission, unlike FDI screening which is managed by the trade policy arm. The paper finds that framing foreign subsidies as a competition issue insulated the policy from accusations of disguised protectionism and ensured political support across the EU. Whereas more activist Member States, services of the European Commission and Members of the European Parliament see the instrument as a steppingstone toward a European industrial policy and more assertive foreign policy, vis-à-vis notably China, others perceive it as a long overdue measure to close regulatory gaps and to strengthen EU competition and state aid policy as well as relevant WTO rules. The paper contributes to the growing literature on EU foreign economic policy at the nexus between International Political Economy and Security Studies by shedding light on one of the most prominent new policy initiatives in these domains.

## 1 Introduction

"We are not naïve free traders. Europe must always defend its strategic interests" (European Commission 2017). So Jean-Claude Juncker, then president of the European Commission, declared in 2017. This speech addressing the State of the European Union (EU) represented a strategic and political shift in the way the European Union had long conducted its trade policy. For decades, the EU pursued a liberal free-trade agenda predicated on achieving true freedom of movement within its internal market and using access to its market as both carrot and stick for the rest of the world. While the Chinese economy was growing, thanks in part to its accession to the World Trade Organization (WTO) and to strong state involvement that constrained foreign access to its own market, and while the United States (US) was first gradually and then abruptly turning away from multilateralism, the EU continued carrying the torch of liberal globalisation and playing by the multilateral rules. By 2017, however, the Commission, European Parliament, and several Member States had come to acknowledge that if other countries were not 'playing fair', the EU had to stop leading through example and adopt more aggressive defensive and offensive trade instruments while also acknowledging the new geopolitical dimension of economic relations (see European Parliament 2016).

One area where the EU seems particularly disadvantaged is in regard to the unfair competition stemming from foreign subsidies. The EU has long ensured a level-playing field internally by severely limiting state aid given by its Member States and externally by using so-called countervailing duties that seek to nullify the cost advantages of imports benefiting from foreign subsidies. State aid policy and trade defence measures, however, inadequately address a new, increasingly salient type of market distortion tied to foreign subsidies—subsidies paid by third countries to companies active in the Single Market. The EU indeed faces a regulatory gap: it has no policy instrument available to effectively address relevant market distortions. This risks putting European companies at a competitive disadvantage at home and in world markets. Concretely, foreign companies can build market power in the EU through participating in mergers and acquisitions, bidding in public procurement, or participating in other business transactions, thanks to state subsidies that are not allowed in the EU—in turn undermining the competitiveness of EU companies. Such distortive subsidies are a serious problem given the economic significance of Foreign Direct Investment (FDI) in the EU. The EU currently receives one-fourth of all inbound FDI in the world, and the more than 100,000 foreign companies operating in the single market are responsible for approximately 16 million jobs in the EU (European Parliament 2021).

In May 2021, the European Commission issued a legislative proposal designed to eliminate the use of "unfair" foreign subsidies that may cause market distortions (European Commission 2021a). After comparatively short discussions, the Council of Ministers and the European Parliament came to a political agreement in Summer 2022 followed by its formal adoption by Parliament by an overwhelming 598 votes to 5 in November 2022 (European Parliament 2022). The aim of this Foreign Subsidies Regulation (FSR) is to use new instruments and procedures allowing the EU to monitor FDI transactions, investigate potentially distortive subsidies, and, if necessary, adopt remedial measures. The FSR is meant to enable companies operating in the EU 'to compete on the basis of merit' regardless of nationality (European Commission 2021a). It is potentially very significant. Economically, the FSR encompasses any economic activity in the EU, including the sensitive areas of mergers and acquisitions and participation in public procurement. Politically, the FSR gives the EU's state aid and merger control regime an international arm. Administratively, this entails a significant enhancement of the European Commission's responsibilities in the area of competition policy. From a broader European integration perspective, the FSR proposal is one of several initiatives fleshing out a new EU foreign investment policy regime, straddling internal market policies and external commercial policies (see Basedow 2020; Meunier and Chan 2021). Internationally, the FSR creates an instrument that has no equivalent at the national or multilateral level and that will certainly attract global attention.

This article asks why the new EU policy that is finally closing a long-standing regulatory gap regarding foreign subsidies arises now, and how it has been shaped. We trace and analyse the genesis of this FSR, map out the preferences of the various European actors involved (including the Commission, the European Parliament, and the Member States), and discuss its potential policy significance in Europe and beyond. As Parliament's vote evidenced, the FSR is an overall consensual issue in the EU, in large part because of the collective characterisation of China as a systemic rival and the EU's new assertiveness in trade policy. Yet some details of the policy were controversial between the Member States, between the various EU institutions, and even within the European Commission.

We argue that European societal demands cannot account for the EU's recent activism on foreign subsidies. European firms, associations, and trade unions alike have been welcoming EU action yet have not been proactively pushing for it. Instead, EU activism reflects top-down dynamics in that EU policymakers have come to see the rise of Chinese state capitalism and subsidies as a challenge that requires mitigation. To deflect criticism of EU protectionism from predominantly China but also the US, EU policymakers have sought to present their efforts as updating competition and state aid policy rather than trade policy. Internal power struggles within the European Parliament have, however, somewhat counteracted this attempt and pulled the initiative partly back under the umbrella of trade policy.

We derive this argument from combining process-tracing and interest-mapping, drawing on interviews and policy archives, and, where it exists, secondary literature. The chapter proceeds in three steps. First, we trace the history of how the issue of foreign subsidies was put on the EU agenda and turned into a legislative proposal. Next, we map the political economy of preferences of the various actors on the foreign subsidies issue. Finally, we explore the politics of reconciling these diverse preferences into legislation and actionable policies.

## 2 From Agenda to Proposal: A Complex and Convoluted Process

The idea of an FSR emerged in a turbulent international context, shaped by new geopolitical actors and tensions, challenges to the global rules-based order, and the rise of protectionist and unfair trading practices. From 2015 onwards, EU institutions began to rethink and justify "who these policies are for" (European Commission 2015) and "modernize" these policies to make them better fit the changing global realities and societal expectations (European Commission 2017).

To understand how often diffuse discussions gave birth to the foreign subsidies proposal, we distinguish between the agenda-setting phase, during which the issue was labelled a policy problem and became an EU priority, and the phase of policy formulation, during which the menu for choice was developed and the intentions of the regulators crystallised. The Commission plays a prominent role in the latter phase given its formal monopoly over the legislative initiative. However, its role in this process and, a fortiori, in the agenda-setting phase (which is more informal) is constantly tested, sparking recurrent scholarly debates on a putative decline of the Commission. In the case of the FSR, *agenda-setting* was particularly long and protracted as it lasted almost a decade and covered two very different phases: from the mid-2010s to 2019, a largely incremental and consensual characterisation of the problem, which culminated with the EU-China strategy of March 2019; and from April 2019 to January 2020, a much more conflicted phase during which the "problem" became a concrete "legislative priority" on the Commission's work program. The main problem during this phase was to find the proper venue for addressing the issue of foreign subsidies. This difficulty had both an internal and an external dimension. Internally, the issue of foreign subsidies became intertwined with competing national visions of economic policy and the separate controversy over national champions. Externally, the difficulty lay in deflecting looming criticisms of protectionism coming from the United States and particularly China. Once the Commission overcame these difficulties in January 2020, it could devote itself to the *formulation of a policy*, which culminated with the publication of a proposal for the FSR in May 2021. Although contestation decreased, it never fully disappeared.

## 2.1 From Diffuse Discussions to the Decision to Act (Mid-2010s-March 2019)

Although it is difficult to date the starting point of this phase, there is some evidence that several Member States experienced growing public concerns about the distortive impact of foreign subsidies already in the mid-2010s, when the issue first acquired salience in Dutch politics (Interview II). Notably, following complaints from the Dutch coach and bus manufacturer VDL Group that the European arm of the Chinese competitor BYD enjoyed unfair advantages in European public tenders and markets due to subsidies from the Chinese state, the Dutch Ministry of Economic Affairs and Climate investigated the issue and identified a regulatory gap in European competition and state aid policy (Ministerie van Economische Zaken en Klimaat 2020). Moreover, in 2017, foreign subsidies started attracting considerable attention in the political arena during coalition negotiations for forming a new government. The Dutch Liberals (PVV) and the Christian Democrats (CDA), in particular, problematized foreign subsidies and demanded that the coalition agreement committed the incoming government to create policy instruments to tackle related market distortions. While the issue was framed as a China-related challenge in the Dutch political discourse, technocrats in the Dutch Ministry of Economic Affairs and Climate perceived and treated market distortions arising from foreign subsidies as a generic regulatory gap in the EU and Member States' competition and state aid policy toolkit. The Ministry continued its work throughout 2018, briefed the Dutch Parliament about progress (Tweede Kamer der Staten-Generaal 2019), and finally published a non-paper and draft regulation in September 2019 that sketched potential instruments to address foreign subsidies (Permanent Representation of the Netherlands 2019). Both documents were not only meant to advance Dutch discussions but also to trigger broader reflections on the reform of EU competition and state aid policy in Brussels and Member State capitals.

At the EU level, policy-makers at first focused on the distortive effects of subsidised imports (see Cicu 2016). In Spring 2019, however, the issue of distortive foreign subsidies flowing directly to EU-based entities occurred in the policy debate just as the new EU FDI screening regulation was being successfully passed (Meunier and Chan 2021; Warchol 2020). The context was the EU's new strategy towards China. In March 2019, ahead of the 21st EU-China Summit in April bringing together European Commission President Jean-Claude Juncker, European Council President Donald Tusk, and China's Premier Li Keqiang, the Commission published a rather blunt assessment of EU-China relations, contrasting with its formerly diplomatic tone. The EU identified the rising giant as "a cooperation partner," an "economic competitor," and a "systemic rival." Furthermore, the strategic communication outlined ten actions intended to address the Chinese strategic challenge—combating distortive foreign subsidies was one of them listed prominently under title V, devoted to "Strengthening the Union's Competitiveness and ensuring a level playing field" (Box 1).

It is important to note that discussions on China's Non-Market Economy (NME) status following the end of China's accession transition period in 2016 played no direct role in these developments. China's WTO accession protocol of 2001 provided for a transition period during which some degree of discrimination against China was considered legal. This arrangement was meant to allow WTO members and China to adjust to the competitive pressures arising from the country's accession to the global trade regime. However, when the transition period drew to an end in 2016, the US, the EU and other industrialized economies refused to recognise China as a market economy and phase out notably the use of controversial anti-dumping methodologies as provided in the accession protocol. To justify their stance, they pointed to China's failure to liberalize its economy in accordance with WTO law and argued that China had instead consolidated its state capitalism and use of subsidies (Fig. 2). European thinking on the need for a regulation to mitigate foreign subsidies clearly illustrated this challenge, yet China's NME status did not play an explicit and prominent role in relevant discussions in Brussels and Member State capitals.

**Box 1 Agenda-Setting Decision (March 2019): The Decision to Act**

*Action 8: to fully address the distortive effects of foreign state ownership and state financing in the internal market, the Commission will identify* ***before the end of 2019*** *how to fill existing gaps in EU law.*

Source: European Commission and High Representative of the European Union for Foreign Affairs and Security Policy (2012; emphasis added).

In reality, the path to identifying "how to fill existing gaps in EU law" was much slower and more strenuous than expected, and it took the European Commission more than two years to do so. The main problem was that there was "no natural home" for this initiative (Interview III). Internationally, it was a very sensitive topic. Domestically, it was caught up in a rapidly developing spiral of contestation about Europe's industrial and competition policies from February 2019 onwards.

## 2.2 *Finding a 'Natural Home' for the Proposal (April 2019 – January 2020)*

A second agenda-setting period, running from April 2019 to January 2020, was an interlude phase during which a new European Commission, under the presidency of Ursula von der Leyen, took ownership of the issue by formally making it a part of its work priorities. This period was very intense politically, as various Member States sought to shape the solution by issuing statements and (non-) papers on the question and related issues. Adding to the political tumult was the growing entanglement of the issue of distortive foreign subsidies with the overarching issues of the modernization of the EU's competition policy and the controversial development of an EU industrial policy. This entanglement was bound to be political given longstanding principled differences between Member States on issues such as the role of the state and the need for European champions. However, this discussion reached a paroxysm after the February 2019 decision of the European Commission, through its Executive Vice-President Margrethe Vestager, to veto the strategic Alstom-Siemens merger championed by the French and German governments (European Commission 2019). In response to the veto, French Minister for the Economy Bruno Le Maire countered that "the role of the Commission is to defend Europe's economic interests," whereas "the veto will serve the economic and industrial interests of China"—while his German counterpart Peter Altmaier declared on Twitter that the EU veto "demonstrates with urgency the need for a European industrial strategy. We are talking about orders for more than 100 billion dollars in the whole world. This is why we need true European champions. France and Germany agree" (Euractiv 2019).

In October 2019, the French and German governments in their Toulouse Declaration jointly called for an overhaul of EU competition and state aid rules to adapt them to the new realities of world markets (Elysée 2019). Shortly after, Italy and Poland came out in support of the French-German initiative. The new alliance between Berlin, Paris, Rome and Warsaw gave further impetus to Dutch calls to modernize EU competition and state aid policy. However, their positions differed fundamentally. The Dutch government sought to close a regulatory gap in EU competition and state aid rules to ensure their effective application in an evolving global market environment. It did not, in other words, question or seek a reform of existing EU competition and state aid rules. It merely sought to complement existing rules to prevent their erosion through strategic circumvention by third countries. The French-German initiative, in turn, advocated a far-reaching reform and subsequent softening of strict EU competition and state aid rules. At that point, Paris and Berlin questioned the appropriateness of existing rules for promoting European competitiveness and welfare and pleaded for a rebalancing of industrial and competition policy objectives. French and German politicians argued that it may be necessary to equip the EU with new defensive instruments—such as the FSR under discussion here—and promote the consolidation of European industry and high-tech so that Europeans might withstand geoeconomic competition with the Chinese and US economies (Bruegel 2019; Elysée 2019). However, this would challenge EU competition and state aid policy geared towards highly competitive and atomistic market structures.

On 29 January 2020, this phase culminated with the publication of the Commission's Work Program, which listed the 'White Paper on an Instrument on Foreign Subsidies' as a priority item, with a delivery scheduled for the Second Quarter 2020. Interestingly, the White Paper was part of a cluster of initiatives devoted to 'A New Industrial Strategy for Europe' (Cluster 14). Structural choices were made during this phase as the new Commission president defined the priorities of the new Commission and the mission of individual Commissioners and included the 'foreign subsidy' files in its 2020 Commission work program. These structural choices can be identified as follows (Box 2).

**Box 2 Agenda-Setting Decision II (December 2019 – January 2020): How to Act**

1. Decision to grant the responsibility of the file to Executive Vice-President Margrethe Vestager (Leyen 2019), "working with" Executive Vice-President Valdis Dombrovskis (An Economy that Works for People) and DG Trade (von der Leyen 2019).
2. Decision to associate Commissioner for Internal Market Thierry Breton (and DG Grow) "to contribute to the work addressing the distortive effects of foreign subsidies, *in particular in relation to public procurement*" (von der Leyen 2019).
3. Decision to develop a legal instrument on distortive foreign subsidies: as evidenced by the announcement of "White Paper on an Instrument on Foreign Subsidies," scheduled for the second quarter of 2020 (European Commission 2020).

Sources: European Commission (2020); Leyen (2019).

While these structural choices may appear to be of secondary importance, they had politically significant ramifications. Putting DG Competition in the lead—rather than DG Trade—signalled that EU action on foreign subsidies was meant to close a regulatory gap in EU competition and state aid rules to level the playing field on the Single Market. The European Commission, in other words, sought to signal to international observers that the EU was not embracing protectionism but, on the contrary, deepening norms of non-discriminatory treatment. What is more, it suggested that the European Commission was critical of demands to soften EU competition and state aid rules in light of an increasingly anarchic and confrontational world economy. DG Competition and its Commissioner Vestager—unlike DG Grow and Commissioner Breton—were known to be sceptical of demands to instrumentalise EU competition and state aid policy for industrial policy purposes (FAZ 2021). Finally, these choices also announced the Commission's intention to frame Europe's 'new industrial policy', with which the White Paper was associated, around the idea of restoring competition by ensuring that the EU's state aid rules applied to all firms active in the Single Market.

In sum, by February 2020, the initiative had now found a natural home: The new Commission had made it clear that it had no intention of "undermining the bloc's long-standing rules on open markets and fair competition"—even though "not everyone in Brussels shares Vestager's philosophy" (Scott 2020). A group of countries, led by France, Germany, Italy, and Poland, continued to pressure the Commission to pursue a more interventionistic competition policy to protect European companies (Scott 2020).

## *2.3* 'Closing the Regulatory Gap': Formulating and Adopting the Instruments (February 2020 – November 2022)

The third phase, during which the policy proposal was formulated, took place from February 2020 until June 2022 (at the time of writing). The COVID-19 pandemic, which initially led to worries that EU companies would face economic hardship and be easily taken over by foreign actors subsidized by their home government, publicly highlighted the urgency of the foreign subsidies issue and accelerated the process. However, as we clearly gathered from our process tracing, the pandemic was by no means the proximate cause of the new EU policy.

The Commission Communication on 'A New Industrial Strategy for Europe,' published in early March 2020, yielded new important clues about the intentions of the Commission by emphatically insisting that "Europe's response" to the new changing geopolitical realities "cannot be to erect more barriers, shield uncompetitive industries or mimic the protectionist or distortive policies of others. **Being competitive requires competition – both at home and in the world"** (European Commission 2020, 3; original emphasis). The Communication made it clear that it was with this overarching intention in mind that the White Paper would be framed as "a trade defence mechanism," enabling Europeans to restore competition on their own single market and thereby giving their industry a fair chance (European Commission 2020, p. 6).

In June 2020, the European Commission presented its White Paper on Foreign Subsidies jointly prepared by DG Competition, DG Trade and DG Grow. The paper revolved around three "modules:" the general instrument (Module 1), foreign subsidies and acquisition of EU companies (Module 2), and foreign subsidies in public procurement procedures (Module 3). In line with the competition frame, the White Paper outlined "the regulatory gap," policy options, and enforcement procedures. Additionally, in line with the competition frame, DG Competition played a key role in formulating the blueprint, working very closely with DG Trade in an informal taskforce to devise the policy model and develop Modules 1 and 2. DG Grow took the lead on Module 3, which explains the difference in style between this module and the other ones (Interview III).

The publication was followed by a 14-week-long phase of consultation with stakeholders, Member States, and foreign governments (closing on 23 September 2020). In October 2020, the Commission was ready to move to the final phase of policy formulation, with the file now one of the 56 legislative priorities for 2021. Several internal hurdles needed to be resolved, including the impact assessment and the green light from the internal inter-service consultations. In March 2021, the Regulatory Scrutiny Board delivered a positive opinion with some reservations. Some of these reservations were technical, while others were more political in anticipation of the legislative process. Among the latter, for example, the Board highlighted "the need to design options that are large enough to reflect positions likely to emerge in legislative process."

In May 2021, the European Commission finally published its draft FSR (Box 3). The proposal entered the phase of examination in the legislative bodies amid a background of confusion in the European Parliament and internal contestation within the European Commission. On the day of the publication of the proposal, French media reported about a discord between Commissioner Vestager and Commissioner Breton regarding the EU's industrial strategy, referring to their "irreconcilable visions" of the Old Continent's future (La Croix 2021). In the European Parliament, protracted discussions took place to designate the lead committee. A November 2020 briefing of the European Parliament Research Service (EPRS) had anticipated that the Committee on International Trade (INTA) would be the lead committee, without a need for other committees. However, in the end, MEPs agreed that the INTA Committee should be the dominant body but assisted by the Committee on Monetary and Economic Affairs (ECON) as well as the Committee on Internal Market and Consumer Protection (IMCO).

**Box 3 Overview of Foreign Subsidies Regulation (FSR)**

The FSR seeks to nullify the distortive effects of foreign subsidies paid to firms active in the Single Market and engaged (1) in mergers and acquisitions and (2) public procurement tenders. The legal basis for the draft FSR is the EU's exclusive competence in trade policy (Art. 207 TFEU) and its shared competence regarding the Single Market (Art. 114 TFEU). Foreign subsidies are defined broadly as any direct or indirect financial contribution, for instance, in the form of financial incentives, loans, guarantees or tax breaks provided by public and private entities, whose actions are attributable to a state.

The FSR foresees that the Commission investigates distortions arising from foreign subsidies to ensure that the regulation is applied consistently across the Single Market. It further proposes both *ex ante* and *ex officio* investigations. First, businesses are to *ex ante* notify the Commission of mergers and acquisitions resulting in market concentration, where the turnover of the EU target

(continued)

**Box 3** (continued)
exceeds EUR 500 million and foreign financial contributions exceed EUR 50 million. Second, businesses of foreign partial/full foreign ownership are to *ex ante* notify the Commission when bidding for public procurement contracts exceeding EUR 250 million. Last, the Commission may initiate *ex officio* investigations in case these thresholds are not met yet there is evidence pointing to distortive effects of foreign subsidies. Any foreign subsidy not exceeding EUR 5 million shall be considered non-distortive. When conducting investigations, the Commission will be held to balance negative effects arising from market distortions tied to foreign subsidies with any beneficial effects of relevant firm activities in the European public interest. Firms under investigation are under a legal obligation to notify, share information and cooperate with the Commission regarding operations inside and outside the EU. A breach of this obligation may result in financial penalties.

Depending on whether and to what extent the Commission finds distortive effects tied to foreign subsidies, the Commission may impose redressive measures. The Commission's toolkit of redressive measures is the same as for EU competition and state aid policy. The Commission may, for one, force firms to stop a merger or acquisition, to sell off certain operations in the Single Market to limit market concentration, to grant fair access to any infrastructure acquired, to publish research and development findings or repay foreign subsidies to level the playing field. As in EU competition and state aid policy, the Commission shall benefit from significant autonomy in investigating and determining redressive measures. Affected parties will, however, have the right to have recourse to the European Court of Justice in case of dispute over Commission actions and decisions.

Sources: European Commission (2021a).

The European Parliament's involved committees and the Council of Ministers started scrutinising the draft FSR. Member States and members of the European Parliament showed continuous broad support for the measure yet differed over some technical details. The European Parliament (2022b) adopted its mandate—consolidated through inter-committee deliberations—as part of the ordinary legislative procedure in April 2022. Its amendments to the draft FSR called for shorter investigation timeframes and lower investigation thresholds. The European Parliament, in other words, wanted the Commission to scrutinise more potential cases of distortions linked to foreign subsidies at a higher speed. The Council of Ministers, in turn, adopted its mandate in May 2022; contrary to Parliament, it sought to limit the application of the regulation (Consilium 2022). It proposed a balancing test to weigh public benefits and disadvantages tied to acting against foreign subsidies, to increase thresholds for investigations and, last, to curtail the Commission's ability to investigate foreign subsidies retroactively.

On June 30, 2022, on the last day of the French EU presidency, the European Parliament and the Council of Ministers found a political agreement on the FSR (European Commission 2022). Under the FSR (Box 3), companies will be obligated to notify the Commission in two cases: (1) "Concentrations where the acquired company, one of the merging parties or the joint venture generates an EU turnover of at least €500 million and the transaction involves a foreign financial contribution of at least €50 million"; and (2) "Tenders in public procurements procedures, where the estimated contract value is at least €250 million and the bid involves a foreign financial contribution of at least €4 million per third country." In both cases, the Commission must clear the transaction; it can impose fines or prohibit the transaction. The Commission will also be empowered to investigate other transactions on an *ad hoc* basis.

Following the political agreement, the European Parliament voted in favour of the FSR in November 2022 with an overwhelming majority of 598 votes against 5. Once the Council of Ministers has formally signed the act, the FSR will enter into force through publication in the EU's Official Journal in early 2023.

## 3 The Political Economy of the FSR: Theorising and Mapping Preferences

Even though there was a broad European consensus on the need to close the long-standing regulatory gap on distortive foreign subsidies, there was disagreement between the various actors involved on the specifics of the policy. This section discusses the political economy of the FSR.

The FSR aims to nullify the distortive effects of foreign subsidies on (1) mergers and acquisitions and (2) public procurement tenders. Focusing exclusively on the FDI screening component of the draft regulation, several income effects on stakeholders are likely.

First, non-subsidised investors in merger and acquisition proceedings meeting the minimum threshold for review will have a greater chance of being successful and of purchasing companies at a lower price. Owners of companies seeking to sell, in turn, may have to settle for lower prices, as purchasers benefiting from foreign subsidies will be removed from the bidding process.

Second, assuming the investors benefiting from foreign subsidies are more active in some Member States than in others, the FSR may have an asymmetric income effect on capital owners in capital-importing and capital-exporting Member States and thus accordingly sway Member State preferences. Chinese investment peaked in 2016 and has since then decreased, as shown in Fig. 1 (Merics 2019). In a similar vein, Chinese investment by Member State has shifted. Whereas in the mid-2010s Eastern and Southern European Member States received close to 50% of Chinese FDI, Chinese investors redirected their capital to Germany, France and Northern European Member States in recent years. In terms of FDI stock, Northern European

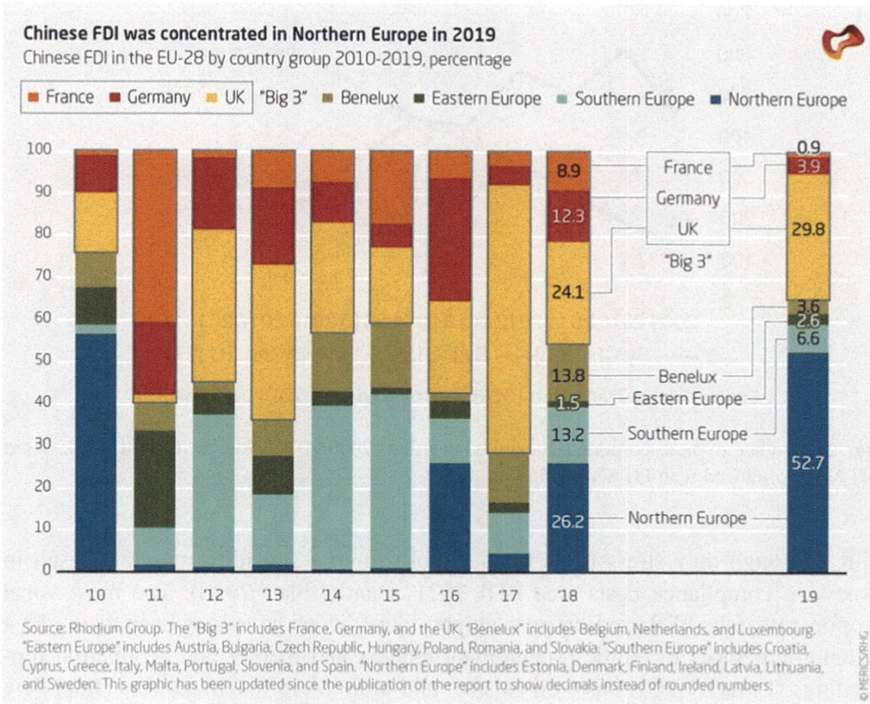


Note: Reproduced with the Rhodium Group's permission.

**Fig. 1** Chinese FDI flows and stocks per Member State over time. Note: Reproduced with the Rhodium Group's permission

countries are by far the largest hosts for Chinese investors, accounting for more than 53% (Fig. 1). While capital owners in capital-importing Member States are likely to see a negative income effect due to lower merger and acquisition prices, capital owners in capital exporting Member States (and third countries) may see less competition in merger and acquisition bids and benefit from lower prices for purchases. In short, one may expect Member State preferences to align to some degree with their capital account positions.

Third, consumers are thought to indirectly benefit from the FSR in that it maintains market competition, resulting in lower prices, higher quality goods and services and innovation. However, due to collective action challenges (Olson 1965), consumers are unlikely to shape the preferences of political decision-makers apart from independent regulatory agencies with consumer-focused mandates. In the following, we briefly scrutinise these political economy assumptions about actor preferences.

**Societal Interests** Consumer interests and organisations, as anticipated, have thus far not played a central role in discussions on the FSR. European business associations, including BusinessEurope and the European Services Forum, welcome the

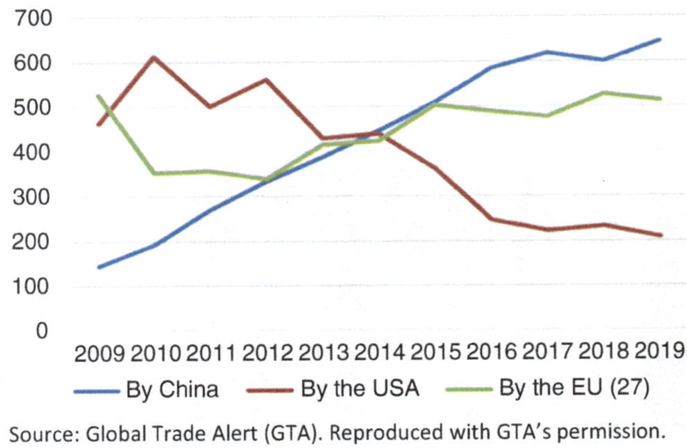


**Fig. 2** Number of new corporate subsidies awarded, 2009-2019. Source: Global Trade Alert (GTA). Reproduced with GTA's permission

FSR, although they stress that efforts to curb foreign subsidies must not result in excessive compliance costs (see BDI 2021; Handelsblatt 2020). The most vocal proponents of the FSR are European shipbuilders, which have long been facing East Asian competitors in public procurement tenders and merger and acquisition proceedings (Euractiv 2021) as well as steel and aluminium manufacturers (Interview IV). SMEs have not been much involved thus far (Interview IV). Unsurprisingly, the most vocal sceptic of the FSR is the Chinese Chamber of Commerce in Europe, which represents Chinese firms active in the Single Market. The Chinese Chamber of Commerce warns of a protectionist turn in EU foreign economic policy and stresses that Chinese subsidies mostly serve the attainment of environmental policy objectives (Xinhua 2020).

**EU Member States** While the Council of Ministers showed from the beginning interest and was generally supportive of the FSR, it took many Member States time to form detailed preferences on this dossier. The Portuguese Council presidency in the second half of 2021 indeed did not prioritise the FSR and it was only during the French presidency in the first half of 2022 that the Council started deliberating on the FSR in detail thus requiring all Member States to develop a detailed understanding of the dossier and their preferences. As discussed above, however, a small group of Member States had well-defined preferences on the FSR from the beginning. The Netherlands, France, and Belgium reportedly strongly supported the Commission's FSR (Interviews II, IV, V). The German government also supported it, yet its preferences have markedly shifted over time (Interviews IV & V). The German political leadership initially backed the French call to engage in an encompassing reform of EU competition and state aid rules to address foreign subsidies and, more generally, the evolving global competitive landscape. German technocrats, however, convinced their political leadership that this course of action would not be in Germany's best interest. The German government consequently realigned itself with the Dutch government in promoting the adoption of an instrument that limits itself to closing the regulatory gap in EU competition and state aid rules regarding foreign subsidies. Luxemburg, Ireland, Sweden and the Czech Republic, in turn, have occasionally voiced criticisms, although of different natures (Interviews II, IV, V). Luxemburg and Ireland seem concerned about potential implications for tax policy, while the Swedish and Czech positions seem predominantly driven by foreign policy considerations. These observations do not neatly fit political economy expectations that predict political cleavages depending on Member States' capital account positions. For instance, capital exporters, who are often heavily involved in extra-EU trade, seem concerned that the FSR may further weaken the WTO and antagonise the US because of long-standing transatlantic trade disputes over subsidies for aircraft (Interview V). Capital importers from Southern, Central and Eastern Europe, in turn, have had difficult experiences with Chinese investments and are generally supportive of the European Commission (Interviews II, IV). In short, other political economy and geopolitical considerations currently overshadow the theorised capital-exporter/importer cleavage in the Council and European Parliament.

**Members of the European Parliament (MEPs)** As representatives of their home states, one would assume that MEPs' preferences broadly align with the capital-importer/exporter cleavage. Parliamentary discussions on FSR since October 2021, however, paint a very different picture (European Parliament 2021). All party groups—from left to right—welcomed the FSR as a long-overdue step to tackle a regulatory gap in EU competition and state aid policy and to address unfair competition, notably through Chinese state-owned enterprises. The majority of MEPs further voted for amendments that seek to extend the applicability of the regulation to crack down on market distortions tied to foreign subsidies. The final vote in Parliament was highly consensual.

**European Commission Services** While the European Commission is naturally in favour of its FSR, preferences slightly vary across Commission services. DG Competition shares the assessment of the Dutch government that existing competition and state aid rules contain a regulatory gap that ought to be addressed to maintain a level playing field on the Single Market (Interview I). DG Competition does not see the need for a general reform of EU competition and state aid policy in view of industrial policy objectives as proposed by the French and German governments (FAZ 2021). It was indeed noted that DG Competition's press statement 'A competition policy fit for new challenges' of 18 November 2021 remained silent on relevant French-German proposals (European Commission 2021b). DG Trade, in turn, shares the assessment of a regulatory gap yet sees the FSR as part of its more geopolitical "open strategic autonomy" approach that seeks to enable the EU to push back against unfair trading practices (Interview III). Hence, DG Trade—unlike DG Competition—does see the FSR as functionally related to the EU's new FDI screening mechanism for national security. Finally, DG for Internal Market, Industry, Entrepreneurship and SMEs (DG Grow) led the work on the FSR's public procurement provisions and reportedly is sympathetic to French-German calls to strengthen the EU's industrial policy capacity. Commissioner Breton—at times described as a "champion of national champions" (FAZ 2021)—indeed advocates a softening of competition and state aid rules and EU action to build European production capacity in critical domains, including battery technology and semiconductors.

**Foreign states:** Many foreign states are interested in the FSR. Western states are reportedly thinking about enacting similar legislation. They study EU legislation and follow EU-internal discussions in view of developing their own toolkits to address foreign subsidies. The US, while interested in drafting similar legislation, looks at the FSR also with some suspicion that the EU might use this instrument in transatlantic trade disputes in the future (Interview V). Some US companies and business groups have expressed concern that they would, at best, face heavy compliance costs and, at worst, be targets of the FSR (Mackrael 2022). It remains to be seen how Russia's invasion of Ukraine in early 2022 and the consequent rapprochement of Western states may shape transatlantic discussions on these issues. The Chinese government, in turn, has been highly critical of the FSR and sees it as an anti-Chinese protectionist device (South China Morning Post 2020). Russia, India and Turkey have raised similar concerns that their firms are likely to be targets.

## 4 From Legislation to Implementation

In this last section, we explore the likely implementation and operation of FSR in the light of the diverse preferences articulated by policymakers and stakeholders in the last years. Several issues are likely to take centre stage in the coming years: (1) the administrative burden that the FSR will impose on stakeholders and bureaucracies; (2) the impact of the FSR on trade, investment and the WTO regime; and (3) the effect of FSR—and more generally of the EU's new 'open strategic autonomy' approach—on geopolitics.

The main disagreements within and between the Council of Ministers and the European Parliament during the ordinary legislative procedure concerned the scope and investigative powers of the EU. Whereas the European Parliament sought to increase both, the Council sought to limit the applicability of the FSR. Germany, in particular, was worried that the FSR may trigger a high number of requests and investigations with considerable resource implications for both businesses and bureaucracies (Interview V). Taking into consideration the extensive powers of the Commission under the final FSR, it remains to be seen how proactively the Commission will use its *ex officio* powers and how strenuous the FSR will show to be for stakeholders. First experiences with the EU's FDI Screening regulation indeed point to a potentially significant administrative burden (European Commission 2022).

It remains unclear, moreover, how the FSR will interact with the EU's FDI Screening regulation. It seems possible that transactions may get scrutinised under both measures. If investigations produce diverging verdicts and conditions for transactions, it may create legal uncertainty and complexity that are difficult to navigate for both businesses and bureaucracies.

Discussions notably in the Council of Ministers revolved around the WTO compatibility of the FSR. Several Member States emphasised that the FSR must not weaken the WTO regime and breach WTO law, in particular the WTO's Subsidies and Countervailing Measures Agreement. To address this concern, the FSR contains provisions that limit its application to domains and transactions not covered by WTO law and, furthermore, reiterates its non-discriminatory nature as a measure designed to close a regulatory gap in the EU's state aid regime in relation to foreign subsidies (Nagy 2021). The Commission holds that the FSR thereby conforms to WTO law, yet some Member States fear that the WTO membership may disagree and interpret the FSR as European disregard for WTO law, which could further weaken the WTO regime. Whether these concerns materialise will depend a lot on how the EU operates the FSR.

In a similar vein, some Member States—such as Sweden—fear that the FSR may limit trade and investment flows and intensify existing tensions between the EU and other economies. Third countries may indeed develop equivalent instruments and use them to the detriment of European firms.

Last, the FSR—like many other new EU measures—has a latent geopolitical and foreign policy dimension. While the European Commission has been emphasising the measure's technical nature and sought to dissuade worries of rising protectionism and geopolitical contestation, Russia's invasion of Ukraine and related tensions between Western and non-Western powers cast the measure in a geopolitical light. It remains to be seen what role the FSR will play in EU policy in the next years in the light of geopolitical turmoil.

## 5 Conclusion

The new FSR is likely to have several implications in the short and medium term.

First, the FSR is part of a panoply of other unilateral trade and investment instruments. Each one that is successfully adopted increases the likelihood that the next ones will be adopted as well. The quick passage of the FDI screening regulation, negotiated in the short time span of fourteen months, has paved the way for the FSR. Other related policies include the new International Procurement Instrument (IPI) to help ensure a level playing field in the global procurement market and the proposed anti-coercion instrument, designed to respond to attempts by third countries to force Member States into adopting certain policy positions. It remains to be seen how this new assertive toolkit will affect EU trade and investment relations and third country perceptions of the EU.

Second, other countries may be interested in adopting a similar foreign subsidies instrument, perhaps leading to progress on this at the multilateral level. A reform and modernisation of the WTO's Subsidies and Countervailing Measures Agreement has been on the agenda of global economic governance for many years.

Finally, the mechanism is likely to have implications for EU-China relations. The Chinese government perceives the FSR as a protectionist instrument to sanction Chinese firms and investors. Depending on how strenuously (and effectively) the FSR will be operated, Beijing is likely to push back and take actions against European firms.

## List of Interviews

Interview I (4 October 2021, Commission COMP)
Interview II (20 October 2021, Member State NL)
Interview III (26 October 2021, Commission TRADE)
Interview IV (9 November 2021, Member State FR)
Interview V (23 November 2021, Member State DE)

## References

Basedow JR (2020) The EU's international investment policy ten years on: the policy-making implications of unintended competence transfers. J Common Mark Stud

BDI (2021) Protection of the single market: Commission wants to control third-country subsidies [WWW Document]. URL https://english.bdi.eu/article/news/protection-of-the-single-market-commission-wants-to-control-third-country-subsidies/

Bruegel (2019) The Alstom-Siemens merger and the need for European champions [WWW Document]. Bruegel | The Brussels-based economic think tank. URL https://www.bruegel.org/blog-post/alstom-siemens-merger-and-need-european-champions

Cicu S (2016) REPORT on the proposal for a regulation of the European Parliament and of the Council amending Regulation (EU) 2016/1036 on protection against dumped imports from countries not members of the European Union and Regulation (EU) 2016/1037 on protection against subsidised imports from countries not members of the European Union | A8-0236/2017 | European Parliament [WWW Document]. URL https://www.europarl.europa.eu/doceo/document/A-8-2017-0236_EN.html

Consilium (2022) Regulating distortive foreign subsidies in the internal market: Council adopts position. https://www.consilium.europa.eu/es/press/press-releases/2022/05/04/reglementer-les-subventions-etrangeresgenerant-des-distorsions-sur-le-marche-interieur-le-conseil-adopte-sa-position/

Elysée (2019) Déclaration franco-allemande de Toulouse

Euractiv (2019) Les six arguments pour le rejet de la fusion Alstom-Siemens [WWW Document]. www.euractiv.fr. URL https://www.euractiv.fr/section/concurrence/news/six-takeaways-from-siemens-alstom-rejection/

Euractiv (2021) SEA EUROPE CEOs Open Letter to the Comission [WWW Document]. Euractiv. URL https://www.euractiv.com/section/economy-jobs/opinion/sea-europe-ceos-open-letter-to-the-comission/

European Commission (2015) Trade for all, Brussels

European Commission (2017) State of the Union 2017 - Trade Package: European Commission proposes framework for screening of foreign direct investments [WWW Document]. European Commission - European Commission. URL https://ec.europa.eu/commission/presscorner/detail/en/IP_17_3183

European Commission (2019) C(2019) 921 final
European Commission (2020) A new industrial strategy for Europe, Brussels. https://commission.europa.eu/strategy-and-policy/priorities-2019-2024/europe-fit-digital-age/european-industrialstrategy_en
European Commission (2021a) Proposal for a Regulation of the European Parliament and the Council on foreign subsidies distorting the internal market (COM(2021) 223 final)
European Commission (2021b) A competition policy fit for new challenges
European Commission (2022) EU investment screening and export control rules [WWW Document]. European Commission - European Commission. URL https://ec.europa.eu/commission/presscorner/detail/en/ip_22_5286
European Parliament (2016) A forward-looking and innovative future strategy for trade and investment [WWW Document]. URL https://www.europarl.europa.eu/doceo/document/TA-8-2016-0299_EN.html
European Parliament (2021) INTA Committee hearing on Foreign Subsidies Draft Regulation. Brussels
European Parliament (2022) Texts adopted - Distortive foreign subsidies [WWW Document]. URL https://www.europarl.europa.eu/doceo/document/TA-9-2022-0379_EN.html
FAZ (2021) Berlin und Paris laufen ins Leere. Frankfurter Allgemeine Zeitung 17
Handelsblatt (2020) EU-Binnenmarkt: Ein Türsteher für Europa: Vestager forciert Subventionskontrolle
La Croix (2021) À Bruxelles, « guerre d'influence » autour de la stratégie industrielle de l'Europe, 5 May 2021. https://www.la-croix.com/Economie/A-Bruxelles-guerre-dinfluence-autour-strategie-industrielle-lEurope-2021-05-05-1201154189
Mackrael K (2022) EU Foreign-subsidy limits target China but also hit U.S. companies, Wall Street Journal, 28 December 2022. https://www.wsj.com/articles/eu-foreign-subsidy-limits-target-china-but-also-hit-u-s-companies-11672234980
Merics (2019) Chinese FDI in Europe: 2019 Update Special Topic: Research Collaborations [WWW Document]. URL https://merics.org/en/report/chinese-fdi-europe-2019-update
Meunier S, Chan Z (2021) Behind the Screen: Understanding National Support for a Foreign Investment Screening Mechanism in the European Union. Review of International Organizations
Ministerie van Economische Zaken en Klimaat (2020) Beantwoording Vragen over Het Bericht "VDL Groep Verliest Busorder Aan Chinees Bedrijf". https://www.rijksoverheid.nl/binaries/rijksoverheid/documenten/kamerstukken/2020/04/24/beantwoordingkamervragen-over-het-bericht-vdl-groep-verliest-busorder-aan-chinees-bedrijf/beantwoording-kamervragen-overhet-bericht-vdl-groep-verliest-busorder-aan-chinees-bedrijf.pdf
Nagy CI (2021) Foreign subsidies, distortions and acquisitions: can the playing field be levelled? Cent Eur J Comp Law 1(2):147–162
Olson M (1965) The logic of collective action - public goods and the theory of groups. Harvard University Press, Cambridge
Permanent Representation of the Netherlands (2019) Non-paper strengthening the level playing field on the internal market The Netherlands
Scott M (2020) Vestager's next big fight will be with Europe. POLITICO. https://www.politico.eu/article/europeancommission-margrethe-vestager-next-big-fight-will-be-with-europe-regulation-competition-big-tech. Accessed 29 Jun 2022
Tweede Kamer der Staten-Generaal (2019) Raad voor Concurrentievermogen; Brief regering; Kabinetsinzet voor het realiseren van een gelijk speelveld op de Europese interne markt voor alle ondernemingen (level playing field instrument). Officiële publicatie, 2 December 2019. https://zoek.officielebekendmakingen.nl/kst-21501-30-470.html
Warchol J (2020) The birth of the EU screening regulation. In: YSEC Yearbook of Socio-Economic Constitutions 2020. Springer, Wiesbaden
Xinhua (2020) Chinese chamber expresses concern over potential legal barriers by EU scrutiny, 25 September 2020. http://www.xinhuanet.com/english/2020-09/25/c_139395872.htm

**SPRINGER NATURE**

# GPSR Compliance

*The European Union's (EU) General Product Safety Regulation (GPSR) is a set of rules that requires consumer products to be safe and our obligations to ensure this.*

*If you have any concerns about our products, you can contact us on ProductSafety@springernature.com*

In case Publisher is established outside the EU, the EU authorized representative is:

Springer Nature Customer Service Center GmbH
Europaplatz 3
69115 Heidelberg, Germany

The manufacturer's authorised representative in the EU is Springer Nature Customer Service Centre GmbH, Europaplatz 3, 69115 Heidelberg, Germany. If you have any concerns regarding our products, please contact ProductSafety@springernature.com

Printed and bound by CPI Group (UK) Ltd, Croydon, CR0 4YY
05/10/2026
02228122-0006